Essays in Social Anthropology

# Religion, morality and the person

Meyer Fortes (1906–1982) was one of the foremost anthropologists of this century, who for many years worked among the Tallensi of northern Ghana. Although he published seminally important monographs on Tallensi family and kinship and on political organization, his work on their religion has hitherto remained confined to disparate journals and edited volumes. This collection brings together for the first time in one place his major writings on religion.

The compilation is important both ethnographically, in terms of what it adds to the corpus of literature on a people who have been highly significant in the development of anthropology, and theoretically. Trained as a psychologist, Fortes was particularly concerned with the relationship between psychoanalysis and anthropology, and this volume both explores that relationship and presents his psychologically-oriented approach to the anthropology of religion. It also examines the moral implications, both personal and cultural, of religious action and belief in simple societies.

Although the material included in the volume is drawn mainly from his work on the Tallensi, Fortes is throughout concerned with the wider, comparative implications of the particular case for understanding religion in other societies, including our own. The collection will appeal to all readers interested in the anthropology and psychology of religion, as well as in religious studies generally.

# Essays in Social Anthropology

# Religion, morality and the person

## Essays on Tallensi religion

Meyer Fortes
*Late William Wyse Professor of Social Anthropology
in the University of Cambridge*

Edited and with an introduction by Jack Goody

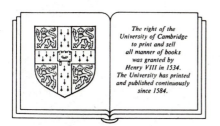

The right of the
University of Cambridge
to print and sell
all manner of books
was granted by
Henry VIII in 1534.
The University has printed
and published continuously
since 1584.

## Cambridge University Press

Cambridge

New York   New Rochelle   Melbourne   Sydney

Published by the Press Syndicate of the University of Cambridge
The Pitt Building, Trumpington Street, Cambridge CB2 1RP
32 East 57th Street, New York, NY 10022, USA
10 Stamford Road, Oakleigh, Melbourne 3166, Australia

First published 1987

Printed in Great Britain by
Redwood Burn Limited, Trowbridge, Wiltshire

*British Library cataloguing in publication data*
Fortes, Meyer
Religion, morality and the person :
essays on Tallensi religion. –
(Essays in social anthropology).
1. Tallensi (African people) – Religion
I. Title   II. Goody, Jack   III. Series
306'.6'0966/       BL 2480.T3

*Library of Congress cataloging in publication data*
Fortes, Meyer,
Religion, morality, and the person.
(Essays in social anthropology)
Bibliography:
1. Tallensi (African people) – Religion.
I. Goody, Jack.   II. Title.   III. Series.
BL2480.T3F67 1987       299'.683       87–9382

ISBN 0 521 33505 1 hardcovers
ISBN 0 521 33693 7 paperback

# Contents

# Figures

# Introduction

A book containing Meyer Fortes' work on the religion of the Tallensi of northern Ghana is of importance in the first place because it complements those on the political and domestic domains of Tallensi society which he published over thirty years ago (1945, 1949). The present volume, together both with the previous two and with other papers that have appeared over the years, make up one of the most important bodies of ethnographic work ever carried out by a single scholar on a particular people. As such it is comparable in scope to the studies undertaken by his British anthropological contempories, that is, Evans-Pritchard on the Nuer of the Southern Sudan, Firth on the Tikopia in the Pacific, and Gluckman and Richards on the Lozi and Bemba of Zambia respectively.

But while it is ethnographically important to collect together the corpus of work on a people who have become so well known in anthropological studies, not only of Africa but in a much wider comparative sense, to do so also makes a significant theoretical contribution. Fortes was trained as a psychologist as well as being interested in the relation between psychoanalysis and anthropology. This background was of great significance in all his work, but especially so in his study of ritual and religion.

Fortes always intended to write a book on the religion of the Tallensi to complement the two he had published on family and kinship and on political organization. Although he never wrote a major volume on the topic (except for *Oedipus and Job*, his Frazer lecture), he had in fact been thinking about it from the very beginning of his research, and his studies of kinship and politics were already impregnated with an interest in the religious aspects of these domains.

One of his first articles was entitled 'Ritual festivals and social cohesion in the hinterland of the Gold Coast' (*American Anthropologist* 38 (1936):590–604; reprinted Fortes 1970). It examined the way in which the interlocking cycles of Great Festivals knit together, in their content and in their performance, the groups that made up that ambiguously defined 'tribal' constellation known as the Tallensi. What he stresses is the role, in these societies without effective rulers, of the ritual festivals as forces not only for cohesion in a mechanical sense, but also as arenas for playing out political conflict and for assuring personal identification. His more general work on the Tallensi political system certainly pays more attention to the role of shrines such as the external *boghar* than it does to the wheelings and dealings of the struggle for secular power. And his important study of kinship and the family is noteworthy for the way in which he links parental relations with supernatural ones, men and women with the ancestors. That was the starting point of his original research proposal submitted to the International African Institute, influenced as it was by the psychology of Freud, Flugel, E. Miller and others, by the social anthropology of Malinowski, and by his experience of the interpretation of religion and the family in his own religion of birth, Judaism – although at this time he was ideologically an atheist or, at least, an agnostic. It was the starting point that led him to dwell on the subject of ancestor worship not only in his monographic studies but also in a number of general papers, especially in the Henry Myer's lecture for 1960, 'Pietas in ancestor worship', *Journal of the Royal Anthropological Institute* 91 (1961):166–91. This interest in the social psychology of family cults ran throughout his work. Family development involved relations with parents who had died as well as with those who were alive, and hence relations with the more extensive set of ancestors, those of the whole lineage or clan. Ancestor worship had been seen by a number of earlier workers in comparative sociology as the elementary form of the religious life, but it was also central to Freudian interests in anthropology, and this encouraged Fortes to explore the connections with the elementary forms of kinship. At the domestic level, at least, it is perhaps the most sensitive and sophisticated analysis yet made of a feature which, often in the more generalized form of the cult of the dead, is found so widely distributed in human societies.

The link between one's relations with parents and with ancestors, which was at the same time a link between kinship and religion as well as between anthropology and psychology, was the topic to which he returned later in his academic career when, in a more explicit way, he took up again the interest in psychoanalysis and psychology that had always remained an underlying theme in his writing and teaching during the intervening period. The context of this return to his past interests was the memorial lectures he delivered in honour of Emanuel Miller and of Ernest Jones in 1972 and 1973 to the Association for Child Psychology and Psychiatry, and the British Psychoanalytical Society respectively, and reprinted here as Chapters 9 and 8. In the early 1930s Fortes had worked in the East End of London under Miller, himself a pupil of the psychologist-anthropologist, W. H. R. Rivers, and the founder of *The British Journal of Delinquency*. Ernest Jones was, of course, the biographer of Freud, and the opponent of Malinowski on the subject of the universality of the Oedipus complex.

Fortes' contribution to the study of religion was made on a number of different planes. In his major books on the Tallensi he presents an analysis of the way religion and ritual enter in to both 'the web of kinship' (the domestic domain) and 'the dynamics of clanship' (the political domain), mainly ancestor worship in the first case and the twin cults of the Earth and the external *boghar* in the second. It was his superb command of the Tallensi language that enabled him to penetrate directly and profoundly into this difficult area of practice and belief, and then to link it to other aspects of the socio-cultural system. But his major contribution lies perhaps on a different plane altogether. Fortes not only side-stepped many of the discussions of religion and ritual that held the attention of his predecessors, but he was also little concerned with problems of the rationality of those beliefs and practices, even in the enlightened way these appeared in the works of his teacher, Malinowski, and his colleague, Evans-Pritchard. His approach was intellectualist neither in the sense of nineteenth-century writers nor yet of those currently interested in cognitive anthropology. Nor did it have much to do with the pragmatic concerns of Malinowski, or the logical and theocentric ones of Evans-Pritchard. Hence, for example, his lack of any continuing interest, brought out in Chapter 6 of this volume, on 'Totem and Taboo', in classificatory schemes or in what he spoke of as the totemic 'codes' of observer-centred analyses. In this important contribution he calls for an actor-centred approach to religion, a point that leads him directly to the question of morality and the person. Picking up from Durkheim, at the same time as going back to his own interest in Judaism (to which he so often refers in these essays) and to his earliest proposal for research in Africa, Fortes constantly stresses the moral aspects of religious behaviour. Hence too his constant recourse to the study of ancestor worship and his comparative neglect of healing and medicine cults; the latter not central for his understanding of the Tallensi.

Morality was a matter both of external rules and of internalized norms. It was the interaction that interested him. This is where his psychological interests provided so important a perspective on the sociological material. In his biographical account in the *Encyclopaedia of the Social Sciences*, Barnes remarked that all Fortes' work was based on principles that were basically psychological (the same comment, more critical in the latter case, was made by Fortes of his own teacher, Malinowski). In no domain was this as true as in that of religion. Morality was an intrinsic part of the person and of the concept of the person, *la personne morale*, in which the social and the psychological were inseparably fused.

In dealing with totems and taboos, he insists not upon their magical or logical aspects, nor upon their symbolic significance in some classificatory schema, but upon their moral (at times 'jural') meaning for the actors and for the society in which they live. One of the most significant statements in this regard is the sentence, 'Taboos are a medium for giving tangible substance to moral obligation.' It was this concern with the moral aspect of magical as well as of technical acts that led him to play down the Frazerian approach to magic and, in other contexts, even the material aspect of technology and property. It was this again that led him to stress the explicit effects of taboos and rituals on the actors, and the binding character of the moral obligations they imposed. His was essentially an actor-oriented structural-functionalism, based upon a deep understanding of the language and culture of the Tallensi. In the field he may have denied himself the camaraderie of the anthropologist-in-jeans; the solar topee was more in evidence, its use dictated not only by the habits of the compatriots to which he had to adjust, but also by current opinion about social roles as well as about medical precautions. Nevertheless his ability to participate, comprehend and analyse was as great as any social scientific observer has yet displayed working in a quite different culture from his own. This participation was essential for interpreting the significance of religion and ritual in the moral life of individuals and society.

I start this book with an article on divination since the search for a 'cause' of trouble and a prescription for getting back to normal is the key to much of the religious life of the area. Divination is the main way of discovering which supernatural agency should be addressed and what objects, gestures or prayers should be offered. The next chapter deals with modes of address to the supernatural, that is, prayer. This should perhaps logically have been followed by an account of offerings, that is, of sacrifice, and possibly of the altar or shrines where these offerings are made. Fortes in fact discusses sacrifice on a number of occasions in the course of his ethnographic work and his theoretical essays. He also chaired a symposium on the topic organized by the Royal Anthropological Institute in 1979, the proceedings of which he edited with M. F. C. Bourdillon (1980). His preface to this volume treats of sacrifice, but he also used the opportunity of a conference that brought together anthropologists and theologians to discuss their different approaches and, more specifically, his own, to the study of religion, and since it puts simply and clearly the issues raised in his writing on this topic it seemed most appropriate to include it an as end-piece to the present volume.

Sacrifice is directed to the principal elements in the supernatural universe. Information on these – the Earth, the ancestors, the medicine shrines, and the beings of the wild – is found in Fortes' main works on the Tallensi. Here I reprint a paper that discusses the relation of ancestors to the major ritual festivals, followed by a general paper on ancestor worship in Africa, which I include because it is the essential element for understanding not only Fortes' discussion of the person, but also his theoretical analyses of totemism, taboo and most of the other subjects treated in this book.

Chapter 5 discusses the role of ritual in relation to political office, both as a way of installing a chief and in maintaining his position once he is on the 'skin'. The following chapter deals with those two classic foci of anthropological debate, those of totem and taboo. The deliberate reference back to Freud heralds a general shift of emphasis in Fortes' work to the psychological aspects of the religious life, which dominate the remaining chapters. However, this move in no sense entailed a rejection of his sociological interests, but was rather a supplement to them. While he paid lip-service to the Durkheimian attempt to separate sociology from psychology, in practice one of the most significant features of his work was the way he managed to link these disciplines in a creative way, beginning with his important essay on 'Social and psychological aspects of education in Taleland' (_Africa_, 1938), continuing through his studies of kinship, family and marriage, and culminating in his work on religion and ritual, just as, in his earlier studies, the concern with morality had similarly provided a bridge between the two fields.

A complete collection of Fortes' work on religion would include his Frazer lecture on the concept of destiny entitled _Oedipus and Job in West African Religion_ (1959, C.U.P., reprinted 1983 with a comparative study by Robin Horton), as well as two earlier essays, that on the Great Festivals (1936) and that on 'Pietas in ancestor worship' (1961), both of which have been reprinted in the collection entitled _Time and Social Structure and other Essays_ (1970). Because of this previous reprinting, I have excluded them from this collection.

In presenting these essays in the form of a book, I have taken the liberty of slightly altering the titles of the originals in order to emphasise the links between them. Since it is a book on Tallensi religion and ritual, there was no need to repeat these words; in any case, Fortes always placed the societies with which he worked (the Tallensi and the Asante) in the forefront of every presentation.

The chapters originally appeared in the following publications, whose editors I thank for permission to reprint them. Chapter 1 was a contribution to a symposium of the Royal Society on 'Ritualisation in Man and Animals', entitled 'Religious premises and logical technique in the divinatory ritual' and appeared in the _Philosophical Transactions_ of that society, Series B 215, 1966, pp. 409–22.

The second chapter was called 'Tallensi prayer' and published in _Studies in Social Anthropology: Essays in Memory of E. E. Evans-Pritchard_, one of many festschrifts for his close colleague of L.S.E. and Oxford days, edited by J. H. M. Beattie and R. G. Lienhardt, Clarendon Press, Oxford, 1975.

Chapter 3, 'Tallensi ritual festivals and the ancestors', was given as the Marett Lecture for 1974 and was published in _Cambridge Anthropology_ 2 (1974): 3–31, with the help of the Marett Fund.

Chapter 4 appeared as 'Some reflections on ancestor worship in Africa' in the volume, *African Systems of Thought*, edited by himself and G. Dieterlen, 1965, Oxford University Press.

Chapter 5, originally 'Ritual and office in tribal society', was printed in a volume edited by Max Gluckman and called *Essays on the Ritual of Social Relations*, Manchester University Press, 1962.

Chapter 6 was the presidential address for 1966 to the Royal Anthropological Institute and was published in the Proceedings of that institute, 1966, pp. 5–22.

Chapter 7, 'Coping with destiny among the Tallensi', appeared in a symposium entitled *Fantasy and Symbol*, edited by R. H. Hook, Academic Press, 1979, pp. 65–94.

Chapter 8 was the Ernest Jones memorial lecture for 1973, delivered to the British Psychoanalytic Society and published in the *International Review of Psycho-Analysis* 4 (1977):127–52.

Chapter 9 was a lecture to the memory of Emanuel Miller delivered in 1972 to the Association for Child Psychology and Psychiatry and published in the *Journal of Child Psychology and Psychiatry*, 15 (1974):81–104.

Chapter 10, 'On the concept of the person among the Tallensi'. was a paper given at a seminar to the CNRS in Paris in 1971 and printed in the conference proceedings, *La Notion de personne en Afrique Noire*, pp. 238–319.

The end-piece was written as the preface to *Sacrifice* (1980, M. F. C. Bourdillon and M. Fortes, eds, Academic Press) based on the proceedings of a Conference on Sacrifice organized by the Royal Anthropological Institute in 1979 and entitled 'Anthropologists and theologians: common interests and divergent approaches', pp. x–xix.

Had he completed a volume of this kind, Meyer Fortes would have wanted to thank, as he did in the articles, the following sources for their support: the Nuffield Foundation, the Leverhulme Trust and the Wenner-Gren Foundation. On the personal level he would have acknowledged his collaboration with Germaine Dieterlen.

I myself also wish to thank the Wenner-Gren Foundation, and to add the names of Jean La Fontaine, Al Harris, Gilbert Lewis, Janet Reynolds, as well as that of Doris Fortes, who has contributed in many ways.

Jack Goody
*Cambridge*
*July, 1986*

# 1

## Divination: religious premisses and logical technique

Divination is a relatively clear-cut configuration of ritual action which embodies fundamental constituents of religious and magical systems and is easily accessible to repeated observation. It is a pivotal institution in very many of these systems the world over, and the diviner is a key functionary in the cult activities associated with them. This has been well known since antiquity. Greek and Roman omens and oracles, Hebrew prophecy and Oriental astrology are well-known examples. But I do not want to discuss divination in general. What I have in mind is to give some account of the configuration and technique of divination, as I have witnessed and participated in it among the Tallensi of Northern Ghana, in concrete illustration of the thesis I shall put forward.

To make my case, I must first indicate what I understand by the concept of ritual. Anthropologists are not all of one mind on this. In its colloquial sense the term has come to be widely used to include almost every kind of stylized or stereotyped verbal and motor behaviour that is habitual or customary in a given social environment. Journalists write of the 'ritual' of cricket, of Parliament, of the law, of taking a university degree. More commonly and narrowly, the word is associated with such things as the Christian communion service, coronations, funerals, etc., etc. Among anthropologists the current vogue is to emphasize the 'communication' function of ritual.

In a sense all these extensions are implicit in the most orthodox anthropological notions of ritual. Take the following definition from that highly respectable quarter, *Notes and queries in anthropology* (1951 edn., p. 175): 'Ritual, like etiquette, is a formal mode of behaviour recognized as correct, but unlike the latter it implies belief in the operation of supernatural agencies or forces.'

Note first, the juxtaposition and secondly, the antithesis here implied. To put it in Durkheimian language, ritual is a form of etiquette in the context of the sacred, etiquette is profane ritual. Interestingly enough, this is a way of looking at ritual which has affinities with the Confucian notion of 'li' as expounded in the famous book of etiquette and ritual the *I Li* (cf. Needham 1951, p. 14).

By this reasoning, if we emphasize their manifest form, the genuflection of the devout Catholic before the high altar is but a variant of the obeisance with which a commoner greets royalty. Both are customary gestures of respect.

By similar reasoning there are acts of ritual which can be subsumed under the same rubrics as communication in general, or language, drama, literature and art in particular, of epistemology, or – remember Frazer – even science, albeit only as a bastard offshoot of the latter. If, to give a trivial example, ritual is wholly subsumed within the category of 'communication', then the policeman on point duty is performing a very explicit and efficacious ritual. If ritual is only a kind of etiquette, then a dinner party is a ritual exercise. This of course ignores the fact which some might consider more important than his signals and that is the policeman's authority as representative of the law, the fact that his signal is a command. The relevance of this will appear presently.

It is a short step from this to the position that there is no such thing as ritual *per se*, no actions, utterances, ideas and beliefs that belong specifically to a domain we can identify by the term ritual, as opposed to everything else in social life that is non-ritual. Equally, of course, by this principle of classification, a great many other conventionally distinguished categories of customs and institutions would be abolished. Judged only by the cultural media employed, by the 'how' and not the 'what' they are doing, a judicial decision, a political speech, a dramatic monologue and a sermon are all merely specimens of linguistic usage. Jurisprudence, politics, drama and religion all dissolve into the general phenomenon of language. It is like saying that jails, churches and theatres are all buildings of the same class because all are built of bricks from the same kilns.

The facts of observation here come to the rescue. Actors and observers are equally positive that ritual and non-ritual configurations of behaviour, attitude and belief are distinguishable from one another even when they make use of the same media of expression. No practising Roman Catholic would accept that there is not a fundamental distinction of meaning between his genuflection in church and his bow to royalty. No orthodox Jew would accept circumcision by a surgeon as the equivalent of ritual circumcision, though the result is the same. In fact provision is made in Jewish religious law for ritualizing a surgical circumcision by the performance of a special rite.

How then is this distinction made? The traditional anthropological criterion implied in the word 'supernatural' points the way. It suggests that the distinguishing feature of ritual lies, not in the internal constitution of actions, utterances and beliefs, but in their external signification, in their relationship with the total cultural environment.

Let me illustrate what I mean by this. There is a well-known Anglican hymn which begins:

> There is a blessed home
> Beyond the land of woe.

Considered simply from within, as a linguistic communication, there is nothing to tell us that these words refer (metaphorically if you like) to a 'supernatural' realm. One can easily imagine an inmate of one of the ill-famed Japanese prisoner-of-war camps taking these words in a poetical (not religious) sense to remind him of his home in a corner of England. Placed in their ritual context – for the singing of hymns is a ritual performance in an Anglican religious service – these words have quite a different implication.

Yet 'supernatural' is an unfortunate term, in the light of modern field research, and such partially synonymous descriptions as 'irrational', 'superstitious', 'mystical', 'a-logical' and 'non-empirical' are just as misleading. The dichotomy implied between a 'natural' universe, subject to laws ascertainable by natural science, and a superimposed realm in which these laws do not operate is very much an artifact of literate cultures, our own and those of the Orient. The way the actor – the believer (at any rate in tribal societies of the kind we find in Africa) – sees his world is different. He sees it as made up of what one might call things patent and things hidden – or, to rehabilitate a much abused word, things occult – which present themselves in mixed sequences and combinations in a common reality.

The difference lies in the fact that the occult can only be known about indirectly by its effects, by its apparently arbitrary interventions in routine existence, whereas things patent can be known in the last resort by sensory experience. What is more, things patent fall into place, or are believed to do so, in conformity with the regularities of material, causal relations, as understood in a particular cultural community. This means that they are, ideally speaking, predictable, because they are susceptible of management by technical means. The occult powers, forces, agencies, relations and so on, hypostatized in ritual are not believed to behave in conformity with material-causal relations or to be predictable or amenable to technical operations. They respond only to ritual action. But conceptually distinguishable as they are both to actor and observer, the patent and the occult are mixed up in the objects and events of actuality. The occult is, by definition, only accessible to recognition and action through the patent, sometimes more so, sometimes less so.

Consider this from our point of view. Scientific explanation reinforces our confidence in our world-view and our knowledge of the universe. It never, I suggest, wholly eliminates the streak of superstition (shock or delight) with which even the most enlightened materialist reacts to the effects of what we call chance or luck in matters of such vital concern as life and death, health and sickness and so forth. In non-western civilization it is (among others) happenings which we would classify in terms of chance, luck and coincidence which are commonly taken to testify to the reality of occult forces and agencies of the kind which we translate by words like magic, witchcraft, ancestor spirits, nature spirits, etc.

My thesis is that ritual is distinguished from non-ritual by the fact that it is aimed at the occult. More exactly, I would define ritual as procedure for prehending the occult, that is first, for grasping what is, for a particular culture, occult in the events and incidents of people's lives, secondly, for binding what is so grasped by means of the ritual resources and beliefs available in that culture, and thirdly, for thus incorporating what is grasped and bound into the normal existence of individuals and groups. Thus regarded ritual is not synonymous with the whole of a religious or magical system. It is, so to speak, the executive arm of such systems. And in performing the task of prehending the occult it necessarily makes use of all the resources of society and culture, from the inborn capacities of the human organism at one end of the scale to logical thought, language, song, art and so forth at the other. But as I argued earlier, these serve only as the media of ritual. They are not distinctive of it.

To be efficacious, then, ritual must, first, get through to the occult (as in divination) and, secondly, accomplish what might seem to be, by definition, the impossible task of seizing hold of the occult.

This is where symbolism of the kind discussed by V. Turner (1966) becomes relevant. Symbolism has, ever since Tylor and Frazer, been regarded as the essence of ritual. But it is only since Freud that we have begun to understand the mechanisms of ritual symbolism. We see that ritual prehends the occult not by exposing it (as science does with the laws of nature, and the judicial process does with the motives of actors, cf. Gluckman 1955), but by disguising it and bringing it thus into the dimension of the patent.

The significance of this can be illustrated by a simple example. Among the Tallensi when a man's wife has a baby he sends a messenger to announce the birth to his parents-in-law. If the baby is a boy, the messenger arrives carrying a cockerel and a throwing stick of the kind men carry when they go hunting. If it is a girl, he brings a pullet and a calabash dish of the kind every woman uses in her kitchen. Passers-by, seeing the messenger on his way, call out, 'Whose wife has had a son (or daughter)?' The symbolism here is wholly patent and the occasion is not a ritual one. Contrast this with the following situation. Every Tallensi knows that if you see a man walking rapidly with a divining bag slung on one shoulder and a chicken in the hand he must be a diviner on his way home from a divination session at a funeral. And everyone knows also that it is a taboo for him to turn round and look back. He must go straight home to offer the chicken, which was his fee, to his divining shrine. The symbolism here relates to the notion that the diviner summoned his divining ancestors to attend at the divination session and that he must lead them straight back to their home on pain of disaster if he fails to comply. But finally to grasp the implications of this we must know that divining ancestors are peculiarly persecutory and unpredictable. This then is a ritual situation.

A great deal of ritual symbolism presents the occult as located in the natural environment – in trees and stones, in the heavens above and the earth below. This is deceptive. It is true that many people's theories of how nature works, what causes rain or drought, plant growth, or animal breeding, and so on, are couched in terms of gods and spirits, witchcraft and magic. Thus we find rituals which purport to be directed towards influencing or even coercing what we think of as physical and biological reality. But as Malinowski and others have shown, closely examined these rituals are in fact aimed at such ends as allaying the anxiety evoked by the unpredictability of many environmental forces or dramatizing (as Seligman called it) the conviction of man's power to influence nature by his moral conduct and intellectual skills. Thus much ritual directed towards the environment can better be regarded as a form of projection, to borrow a Freudian term, than as a substitute for technology.

In short, the occult that is the primary concern of ritual, inheres in the basic social relationships and the fundamental drives and dispositions of mankind without which social life could not go on. It is perhaps worth noting, in this connection, the evidence offered by psychopathology to the effect that many occurrences which we automatically attribute to luck, chance or accident, are in fact precipitated by hidden, that is unconscious, emotional factors. Though the man in the street is ignorant of this, and fortunately so for his own security of mind, he does feel that luck, chance and accident stand for the emergence into the routine of life of occult, unpredictable, ritually but not technically controllable forces. The relationship between his view and the psychopathologist's bears a close resemblance to that of the tribal believer and the anthropological observer.

To bring home my point, let us consider, for a moment, the 'passage' rites made famous by van Gennep's book *Les Rites de passage* (1908). It is not the physical mysteries of birth, marriage and death that cause them to be ritualized in all human societies, but the basic inscrutability and potential intractability of the social relationships and psychological dispositions represented in these events. Modern researches (Erikson 1966; Ambrose 1966) give us an inkling of the complexity of even such apparently elementary and spontaneously social relationships as those of mother and child. It is not surprising that there is some ritual in most human societies aimed at grasping, binding, and incorporating, into the overt customs and practices of life, the ambivalances of love and hate, dependence and self-assertion which underlie the relations of parents and children but cannot be understood in causal terms and dare not be admitted as motives of action. Likewise, rituals connected with death are aimed at repairing ruptured social relationships and at prehending the psychological mystery of mourning-grief and the sociological mystery presented by the fact that a person's physical extinction does not obliterate the impress of his life on his society. Material objects he created or was associated with outlive him, and what is more the living (especially his progeny) continue him, partly physically, but more mysteriously in their personalities and in their relationships with one another, as if he were in some sense still among them (cf. Goody 1962).

It would not, I think, be out of step with modern anthropological theory to say that most, if not all, religious and magical ritual is concerned with prehending the unconscious (in the psychoanalytical sense) forces of individual action and existence and their social equivalents, the irreducible factors in social relations (e.g. the mother–child nexus, at one end of the scale, the authority of society at the other). By bringing them, suitably disguised, or symbolized in tangible material objects and actions, into the open of social life, ritual binds them and makes them manageable.

This bringing out into the open of social life is important. It implies legitimacy, authorization by consensus. Ritual has two sides, like coin of the realm, a 'white' side and a 'black' side. Good, that is 'white' ritual, is ritual that has collective authorization. Bad, that is 'black' ritual, is secret and antisocial and is supported by collusion not consensus. Here I might just interpolate that anthropologists generally speak of 'ritual' rather than 'ritualization'. But there are appropriate usages of the verbal form. *Rites de passage* have already been instanced. In the same way if we consider the ritual of coronation from the point of view of its manifest subject matter, we describe it as the ritualization of eminent office, and we can describe food taboos as the ritualization of eating customs (cf. Fortes 1962a).

I return now to divination. In the most general terms, where divination is a central feature of a system of religion or magic, it is a ritual instrument by means of which choice is made, from among the total ritual resources of a community, of the right ritual measures for particular occasions and with regard to individual

*Figure 1.* Tallensi divination: a collection of code objects.

*Figures 2 a, b, c.* Tallensi divination: a divining session.
*Figure 2a.* First episode: the diviner summons his divining ancestors.

*Figure 2b.* Second episode: the diviner and consultor work out the diagnosis of the situation.

*Figure 2c.* Third episode: the consultor works over the diagnosis to confirm it.

circumstances. Customary ritual, unlike the behaviour patterns described as ritual by psychopathalogists, is standardized and universal in a given community. Much of it is as routine in incidence as is the normal run of social activities in the community. Meals come round regularly and so does grace before meals. But many ritualized happenings which are normal and regular within a community are unpredictable for the individual. Death, for instance, is a normal occurrence, but when it strikes a particular family it is experienced as a catastrophe. Luck, chance, accident, coincidence, and fate are some of the notions invoked to account for this. They may be ritualized. The Edo of Benin, for example, believe a person's luck to be associated with his head and a man makes a sacrifice to his head when he has a stroke of good fortune (Bradbury 1957).

In other cultures such a happening is taken to represent a particular and specific intervention of the occult forces recognized by the culture in the life of an individual or a group. The function of divination is to establish the particularity of this intervention, to connect particular persons and occasions with the omnipresent occult. As Evans-Pritchard (1937) showed in his classical study, every Azande knows that misfortune is due to the occult force of witchcraft but when misfortune strikes a particular person he needs to find out who it is that has bewitched him and for this he resorts to divination. Such connections have to be established also for prescriptive rituals that recur at regular times, for example, the annual sowing and harvest festivals common all over West Africa and elsewhere. The festivals recur in fixed form and at fixed times but the participants change from year to year as the result of deaths and births and the maturation of individuals, and divination is called for to allocate the standardized ritual duties and privileges.

I have spoken of divination as a ritual instrument. An apparatus of divination is often an essential part of the system, as among the Tallensi. But I have in mind more the fact that divination is often a specialized technique. The diviner may have to undergo training to become expert in it, or he may be selected for it by virtue of his talents or his psychological make-up. Not only this. A diviner must be properly accredited, often by a public initiation after evidence of his acceptance by the occult agencies.

The principle behind this is that the occult and the patent cannot, indeed must not, be known in the same way. If they were accessible to knowledge and experience in the same mode and by the same faculties the boundary between them would disappear. But that way lies chaos – or insanity. For though they are parts of a common reality they are complementary parts and must not be confounded. This indeed is the basic *raison d'êntre* for ritual.

This leads to another point. As divination is a technique, its practitioners will be judged by standards of proficiency similar to those that are applied to all technical operations. This predisposes towards a critical rather than credulous attitude on the part of the patrons. It is, moreover, not only a question of technical skill. The conceptual curtain between knowledge of the occult and knowledge of the patent must be kept in place. It is of the utmost importance therefore that purported manifestations of the occult must be verified by tests which eliminate the possibility of deception for ends which the frailty of human nature so easily tempts a person to seek. Hence divinatory verdicts are tested by posing the same questions in alternative forms, and by the well-tried method of seeking a second and a third independent opinion and by ordeals which use the logic of chance. Thus it is an essential aspect of divination that its revelations should be objectively verifiable as objectivity is understood in a given society. Objectivity implies public acquiescence. Divinatory verdicts must be seen and agreed to be right. Hence it is a common rule that legitimate ('white') divination must be public and formal. Secret divination is not accepted as decisive. At worst it will be suspected of being 'black', at best of being partisan and calculated to advance private interests. Provision is thus made on different lines to circumvent fraud and deception in divination. Diviners, however, are but human and known to be not infallible. Thus, there are always loopholes in a system of divination which enable the mistakes of its practitioners to be explained away and confidence in the system to be maintained.

This brings up another critical feature of divination. At some point in any system of knowledge or belief or orderly action we strike rock bottom; we have to invoke ultimate authority, be it intellectual or legal or moral. Even to say 'I saw it with my own eyes' in claim of truthfulness implies a claim to supporting authority, perhaps of expert knowledge or only of common human experience. One of the most important functions of divination lies in the authority it carries. A confirmed divinatory verdict is an authorization, a sanction emanating from the ultimate source of authority in matters that concern the occult, the occult agencies themselves, for the ritual action proposed.

Divination is an indispensable part of Tallensi religion.[1] To understand this it is necessary to know that their religion consists, essentially, of an elaborate system of ancestor worship. It so dominates their thought that the other occult agencies postulated by them, the mystically powerful Earth or the magically efficacious medicines, for instance, are all conceived of as being under the ultimate control of the ancestors.

An ancestor must of course be dead to be qualified for the service we call worship but he must also have left descendants. The dead without descendants vanish into oblivion. Tallensi do not think of their worshipped dead – the ancestors – as denizens of a supernatural world. They are in and of this world, accessible at all times by the right ritual in the shrines set up for them in their descendants' homes. Yet they are characteristically occult in being unpredictable and recalcitrant. They are enshrined and worshipped individually, by name, never anonymously, and they are thought of as eating and drinking in the homes of their descendants. Their presence is known from what are experienced as their importunities on their descendants, the signs of which are on the one hand – and most conspicuously – the illness, misfortune and death as well as minor accidents and frustrations which they inflict, and on the other – but less conspicuously – the births, the good health, success and long life for which they claim the credit. Divination is the path by which the concealed demands and the claimed benevolence of the ancestors are ascertained – the path connecting the patent and mundane with the occult. Every Tallensi will tell you at once that such and such a happening was indubitably brought about by the ancestors. What he cannot know is which of his multitude of ancestors is the actual agent in the particular case. This is what divination reveals to him; and divination also ensures – up to a point – that he will not neglect the just claims of any ancestors.[2]

Diviners are ordinary folk practising part-time, their main source of livelihood being farming, like everybody else's. But they are diviners by virtue of special qualifications. Only men can be diviners, since only men have the jural and ritual status to officiate in ritual. A man becomes a diviner by virtue of having in his possession a particular kind of ancestor shrine. But most mature men, though not diviners, have divining shrines and have undergone the public initiation which accompanies acquisition of such a shrine. A diviner accepts the role if he discovers by experiment that he has the ability for and interest in the work. A divining shrine is characteristically the ritual domicile of maternal ancestors. It is because maternal ancestors are vitally significant for everybody that most men acquire divining shrines. Most men also have the life experience that necessitates such a step. Maternal ancestors are, in this very patrilineal society, conceptualized as particularly persecutory. A man acquires the shrine after a long series of mishaps and misfortunes by accepting these ancestors and, as Tallensi put it, making a home for them in his home. Then they can be propitiated and if he has the skill they help him to divine and to prosper. The structural rationale lies in the fact that matrilateral connections spread in an endless web amongst the mutually independent patrilineal descent groups, and matrilateral ancestors are therefore deemed to have the ramifying ties which enable them, ideally, to be in contact with everybody's ancestors.

A divination session proceeds on the assumption that the ancestors of both client and the diviner are present or at least 'on call', and are controlling the search for a diagnosis of the client's problems.

Divination sessions are never secret. Public sessions are attended by people of many different clans. Private consultations can be listened to and even interrupted by callers or friends of either party. These take place in a room in the diviner's or the client's house. Furthermore, a diviner can be consulted by any skilled friend or kinsman on behalf of a client who is unskilled in the procedure. I should add that women cannot, of course, personally consult a diviner since they have the jural status of minors.

### The occasion

Normally a household head or lineage elder goes to consult a diviner when something is wrong, when there is a crisis of any sort, or when some special undertaking is ahead (e.g. if there is illness in the family, if a wife is pregnant and near delivery, when the farming season with its many hazards is in the offing, when the young men go off on a hunting or fishing trip where accidents are not uncommon).

If one asks a man why he goes to a diviner for a private consultation he will say that he goes because he is 'worried' or because he has 'something on his mind'. The underlying attitude comes out vividly in the course of a divination session. I have often heard a client exclaim, as the divining staff leapt hither and thither: 'My enemy, show me where is my enemy.' Tallensi explain that if you are troubled it is because you have incurred 'enmity' of some ancestor by a sin of omission or commission generally assumed to be unpremeditated. Your 'enemy' is that ancestor and once you know who he is and what he demands your anxiety is allayed. Such frank admission of the ambivalence of the relationship between the living and the ancestors is characteristic. It points neatly to the psychological sources of the demarcation line between the patent and the occult in Tallensi culture.

The invariable outcome of divination is a command to offer sacrifice to the ancestors or other occult agencies. Whether defined as propitiatory or piacular or thank-offerings, they are all of the same kind and may or may not be associated with other prescriptions such as food or work taboos. That this will be the outcome is known in advance. What is not known is which particular ancestors are the protagonists in the current crisis, what animals they demand in sacrifice, and what conduct or circumstances have occasioned these demands. If one suggests that surely an experienced elder must be able to make his own diagnosis of his situation, Tallensi say this is out of the question. Even a diviner cannot divine for himself. A man cannot be judge in his own cause. To attempt it would be not only to flout the authority of the ancestors but also to incur discredit among one's kinsfolk and friends.

Public divination is ritually obligatory on occasions of communal interest such as the eve of a festival, when a diviner is consulted in order to find out what sacrifices must be offered to ensure a propitious outcome. It is also obligatory for every death in order to ascertain the ancestral agency that caused it and to find out what ritual action must be taken in placation or expiation.

## Technique

I turn now to the actual technique of divination. I must emphasize that, granted the premisses of the Tallensi religious system, and considered purely in its internal structure, this technique is as logical, rational and consistent as any non-ritual technical process. First then the diviner's equipment. It consists of a gourd rattle, a stout staff about 3 feet long with a fork at one end and iron-tipped foot, and a skin bag – the *kologo* – filled with his *kpa'an*, as it is called. This is a miscellaneous collection of articles that looks exactly like a lot of odds and ends of rubbish when poured out in a heap in front of him. In fact these bits and pieces are standard *materia oraculosa*, if I might coin a barbarism for them, that is standard code symbols, as I will presently explain.

A divining session follows a set procedure. It is a dramatic dialogue in speech, gesture and expression with the use of a specialized but not esoteric vocabulary. There is no hint of mediumship or dissociation or any other abnormal psychological state in the diviner or his client. It is a strictly professional business. Though it is intensely serious, the diviner may, as has been mentioned before, stop in the midst of consultation to exchange greetings with callers or give an order to a member of his family.

Public and private divinations follow the same pattern. For private divination a client arrives at the diviner's house, and even if they are neighbours, kin or friends, asks formally and impersonally for a consultation. This is done by placing the fee he is offering in front of the diviner. A fee must be offered in advance, but it is not fixed and however minute it is, it must be accepted. The diviner sits on a board in his room with his bag in front of him and the client sits opposite him on the floor, cross-legged in a posture of respect. The diviner claps his hands on the bag and calls *sotto voce* on his ancestors to be present. He shakes his rattle rhythmically and chants, calling his divining ancestors, to come and sit – this is a technical expression – on their divining shrine. Presently he stops to pour out his bag. (The rattle and chant, although there is no mediumship, do produce a certain frame of mind, a rhythmic mood, but the diviner is never dissociated.)

Having poured out the bag and spread out the code-objects, the diviner puts two small flat stones (the striking stones) or pieces of iron in front of himself. He continues to rattle, head turned aside, and chant, calling on his ancestors to come and divine. Presently he picks up two other flat stones (the testing stones) spits on one side of each stone, grips them together, wet against wet and throws them violently on the ground, calling to his divining ancestors to come. This is the first use of the code and every adult male can interpret it. The stones can fall (1) both dry sides up: this means refusal, (2) both wet sides up: this means 'laughter', (3) one wet, one dry: this means acceptance. (I ignore irregular falls though all have a meaning.)

An actual case of public divination will elucidate. At the first throw the stones 'refused'. Everyone in the audience craned to look. It meant that the divining ancestor had not come (I am translating literally). The diviner cried out in annoyance, 'There is a quarrel here, there is anger here. Is it my divining ancestors who are angry and refuse to côme or the client's ancestors who are angry and obstructing? If the quarrel is on my side, let the stones refuse again.' He threw them again and they again 'refused'. So he knew that his divining ancestors were holding back. He cried out in apparent protest saying, 'One more trial to see if this is really the case.' He threw. The stones 'refused'. He leaned back and addressed his divining ancestors quite casually saying, 'I know what it is. It is because of the money I used to pay my son's bride price. When I got it and consulted about it, you, divining ancestors, declared that you wished the money to be used to buy a cow dedicated to you. But I gave in to pressure and spent it on my son's marriage. That is why you have a quarrel with me and now refuse to come.' The diviner sat back, chastened. Thereupon the consultor leaned forward and addressed the diviner. 'Diviner', he said, 'your divining ancestors are fully in the right. You have done wrong. But we beg them to exercise charity and to accept the divination, so that we can go on with the consultation which is what we brought you here for.' It was a plea for the diviner's ancestors not to let their private quarrel with him obstruct the professional task before them. Now the stones were thrown again and they fell in the acceptance pattern, and the whole audience – but not the diviner – clapped hands in thanks. There followed a second throw, also successful, and the seance could start. There must always be two successful throws – a throw and a check on the first throw – before a seance can start. (Why, incidentally, did the diviner not clap his hands in gratitude? Because the theory is that he is only the spokesman, the intermediary for the divining ancestors. The theory is that the client's ancestors and the diviner's ancestors are in communication and the former express their wishes through the latter.)

If the stones 'laugh' it means provisional acquiescence. It indicates that the ancestors will not go on to the main purpose of the session until some other issue has first been cleared out of the way. It may signify a promise of joyous laughter at good fortune on the part of the client; or it may mean a threat of jeering laughter by some ancestor if the client fails to settle a ritual debt already known to him.

In the seance, the diviner grasps the forked top of his stick in one hand, and with the other continues to rattle, chanting his invocation to his divining ancestors to be present and to search diligently. He sweeps the stick hither and thither, prods among the litter of objects in front of him, and, as he does this, sings in a rhetorical, staccato recitative, naming the objects and the gestures in the special language of divination – for the code includes both the objects and a variety of sign-gestures. This is the diviner's diagnosis of the situation. It is done with a flourish but impersonally. When he reaches the end, he raps on one of the two flat stones in front of him crying out, 'Thus it is.'

The consultor has sat quietly listening and watching perhaps for a minute or two, perhaps for 5 to 10 minutes – for the diagnostic probe can be complicated and devious. The consultor now grasps the foot of the divining staff. He holds it loosely and repeats the diviner's diagnosis. He recites the diagnosis item by item and as he does so the stick swings, stabs, picks out objects, points to his side, his abdomen, his mouth and so on. The diviner sometimes interpolates a phrase or a word to eke out the argument. It is very fast, intense, dramatic, elliptic and allusive.

The diviner's diagnosis is given in quite general terms. The items picked out come from the universe of ideas, beliefs, ritual objects and institutions, common and equally significant to everybody, that is to say, the common occult. The consultor transposes this general formula into the particulars of his own (or the client's) life history and ancestor shrines. And he checks each step in this secondary interpretation by a binary test on the two striking stones.

He puts questions as it were to the stick (often *sotto voce*): 'You mentioned a "mother", was it my own mother or my mother's mother?' – pointing to the left-hand stone for the first and the right-hand stone for the second alternative. A correct statement is vouched for by a bang of the stick on the appropriate stone, while incorrect statements or questions are ignored. The whole sequence will be repeated, elaborated, probed further, checked again by re-phrasing the questions, reversing alternatives, so that the stick must strike a different stone each time for the verdict to be consistently maintained. In the course of this working out, the consultor rehearses the sacrifices he is being commanded to give, runs over the prayers he will speak and sums up the verdict. The consultor then picks up the testing stones and speaking earnestly, addresses the ancestor whose wishes have just been revealed. He says, 'Mother (or Father, or whoever it may be), you say thus and thus and thus. If this is true, let the stones show acceptance, for I submit.' He hands the stones to the diviner who spits on them, holds them out to his divin-ing bag, invokes his divining ancestors to let the stones show accept-ance, and throws them down. If they 'refuse' or 'laugh' the impediment must be sought out and the original verdict returned to later. The consultation now goes on to the next episode in exactly the same way. There may be only three or four or as many as twenty or more such units, but finally the diviner says, 'That is all', and this will be tested by the stones.

This is the way the Tallensi describe the process. Since the consul-tor guides the stick all the time – or if he relinquishes hold for a moment at the diviner's instance, the diviner interpolates suggestions and interpretations – it is obvious that the choice of answers is being guided by the consultor himself. Yet Tallensi insist that this is not the case. They insist that neither the consultor nor the diviner knows what is going to be the outcome of the divination session. They insist that it is the ancestors who move the stick and put the words in their mouth and that the ordeal by the stones is infallible and beyond their own control. There are some very interesting problems of a psychological nature in this procedure but I can do no more here than mention them in passing. I must repeat though, that from the Tallensi point of view it is a thoroughly objective procedure.

At the end, the professional dialogue concluded, friendly greet-ings are exchanged for the first time between the diviner and the con-sultor. If it is a public occasion, his fee, often prescribed as in the case of a death (e.g. a small basket of grain, a chicken and some beer) will now be given to the diviner, who will be dismissed by a ritual leave-taking. Thus it is not till the formal task is finished that the personal relations of the parties are permitted to emerge.

## The code

Each of the material objects and the standardized gestures employed in divination has a fixed meaning attached to it by a simple rule of association or metaphorical extension which most men can interpret. Some sample code objects are:

(1) The astragalus bone of a sheep, goat or cow. This symbolizes a male progenitor and if a cow's bone, specifically a father. Pointed to in divination it generally indicates that a male ancestor is claiming attention or it may indicate that a living father's affairs are at stake.

(2) Head of a calabash ladle: a woman (e.g. a mother or wife). Implies that an ancestress is demanding attention or that a living woman's circumstances are at stake.

(3) Animal hoof of a sheep or goat, etc.: an animal of that species demanded in sacrifice, or of a past sacrifice.

(4) Fowl or guinea-fowl claw: a fowl or guinea-fowl to be sacrificed, or of a past sacrifice.

(5) Animal horn: a variety of ancestral shrine in which a medicine horn is important.

(6) The hollow husk of a wild fruit: a variety of ancestral shrine that has a pot among its appurtenances.

(7) A red rag: chiefship – an issue connected with a chief, perhaps an ancestor who was a chief or promises made at a time when a chiefship was sought. (Chiefs wear red caps as their distinctive insignia of office.)

(8) The stone of a wild fruit that is never eaten except at times of famine: famine, crops will fail unless a commanded sacrifice or ritual action is performed.

(9) A fragment of the shell of a water tortoise: cool water, 'coolness of heart' – that is contentment, peace of mind is promised if the commanded sacrifices and ritual actions are performed.

The number of code objects a diviner uses varies according to his taste and practice; twenty to thirty is normal.

Some sample code gestures are:

(1) Pointing to the abdomen: a child, *in utero* or already born.
(2) Pointing to the side: a collateral kinsman.
(3) Pointing to the hand: property, possession.
(4) Slitting the throat: death.

The following sequence shows how the code is used. The consultor puts questions as if to the stick, stating them in terms of alternatives, pointing to one flat stone for alternative (*a*) and the other for (*b*). The stick chooses by striking the appropriate stone or if the question is not to the point, by remaining suspended in the consultor's hand. A sequence might run: 'You point to a woman – is it a living or a dead one?' (If dead): 'Is it a mother or a wife?' (If mother): 'Is it my mother or somebody else's?' (If own mother): 'Is it my mother who bore me or a distant mother?' (If distant): 'Is it my mother's mother?'. (If no answer): 'Is it my mother's mother's mother?' (Answer affirmative): 'What then?'. Stick swings and points to sheep hoof. 'It is a question of a sheep.' (Answer affirmative): 'A sheep to be sacrificed or one already sacrificed?' (To be sacrificed): 'For what reason?' (Stick points to abdomen): 'Because of a child to be conceived or already conceived?' – and so on.

Tallensi divination, it can easily be seen, is from their point of view an objective technique, almost impersonal in its procedure. It follows from the premises of ancestor worship with its assumption of the co-existence, in a single scheme of reality, of the ancestors with the living and the corollary that communication by ritual procedure between the two sides is normal. But the technique itself conforms to the ordinary rules of logical induction and discourse within the framework of Tallensi culture. It is based on a conventional code, a kind of object and gesture dictionary of the ancestral cult and of the significant affairs of everyday life on which it impinges. It can very well be thought of as a special language. Taken in this sense it seems to me to illustrate rather well the analysis of ritual 'language' put forward by Leach (1966). The revelations are of a standard pattern and are arrived at by a formalized search conducted in collaboration and dialogue by the consultor and diviner; but they are not accepted unless they are confirmed by an action approximating, one might almost say, to a throw of dice in which the outcome is left to the quasi-objective influence of chance. The outcome is to provide a person with an authoritative and legitimate, though stereotyped policy for ritual action by which to grasp, bind and incorporate into his own life-course the threatening, harmful or hopeful incidents and experiences which have caused him to seek the aid of a diviner.

As a technique, Tallensi divination, like the Tallensi language, can be learnt and used by anybody who applies himself to the task. He does not have to accept the religious and ritual implications. Though I never became adept enough at it to carry through a whole consultation, I learnt enough to be able to demonstrate it. I took the role of a client often enough to see the game from that side, too, and the revelations offered to me were invariably couched in the idioms of Tallensi culture. I was advised to offer sacrifices to the local Earth shrines and to my ancestors and promised such delectable benefits as several wives and many sons if I would comply. But there are parallels in our culture to Tallensi divination and the beliefs and attitudes reflected in it. With most lay people in our society serious illness evokes anxiety no different from that which Tallensi experience in similar circumstances, and it has for us also an implication of threat from what is occult to us, namely, the mysterious forces of disease or of retribution for imprudent living. Likewise, for the layman, diagnosis of disease by the expert in medicine is quite comparable to Tallensi divination.

# 2

## Prayer

'There can be no doubt at all', says a famous authority on the subject,[1] 'that prayer is the heart and centre of all religion.' In Tallensi religion, as among the Nuer, prayer is normally associated with sacrifice or libation, and it is this complex as a whole that is the centre of their ritual system. Tallensi religious beliefs and ritual practices presuppose personality analogous to that of humans in all the significant agents and powers of their supernatural domain. The dead (*kpiinam*) participate in the existence of the living (*vopa*) as identified ancestors, not in collective anonymity; the Earth (*teŋ*), the complementary pole of their mystical and moral universe, participates in the affairs of mankind in the form of personified, named, and particular sacred localities or shrines (*tɔŋbana*). The religious system is pervaded by the personified representations of the ancestral dead and of the Earth. These draw all other agencies and objects and instrumentalities of ritual cult and action into their orbit. Medicines, for example, whether overtly magical or supposedly physical in action, are believed to be impotent without the concurrence of the ancestors and the Earth.

Given this system of beliefs and ideas, it is consistent for Tallensi ritual normally to include an interpersonal transaction between worshippers on one side and personalized mystical agencies on the other. Sacrifice and prayer are particularly apt media for such transactions and relations.[2] The Tallensi have terms for both. The verb for 'to sacrifice' is *ka'ab* and it embraces every kind of ritual offering or libation at a consecrated place or altar. It is commonly used in the expression *ka'ab ba'ar* which can best be translated as 'to sanctify' or 'to worship at' the consecrated place or shrine by prayer, libation, and blood sacrifice. The implication is that it is a ritual act directed at the altar to the supernatural recipient. The associated word *ka'* is what I am translating as 'prayer' but it is a verb and can more accurately be glossed 'to invoke' or 'call upon' mystical agencies. Both *ka'ab* and *ka'* are restricted in usage to their ritual context. One cannot in Talni 'sacrifice' oneself or one's time for a cause or address a prayer to a living person. One can however, plead with (*bɛlɔm*) or beg (*soχ*) living persons as well as mystical agencies.

I shall refer to sacrifice only indirectly since my theme is prayer among the Tallensi. And the first point of importance is that Tallensi prayers or invocations, from the simplest and shortest that occur in the setting of ordinary family life, to the long, elaborate, and rhetorical orations in the ceremonies of the Great Festivals, though stylistically distinct, are couched in the language of everyday discourse, easy to be understood.[3] They have no esoteric or liturgical language reserved for ritual occasions, as is to be expected in the absence of a church organization or a professional priesthood, or a written scripture in their religious system. Interestingly enough it is most conspicuously in the Talis cult of the External *Boghar* that hymn-like invocations occur, and this is clearly associated with its esoteric structural status as a prerogative of descent-restricted congregations of initiated males.[4] The ancestors and the mystical Presence of the *Boghar* are summoned by the chanted exhortation of the officiants accompanied by the rhythmic hand-clapping of the congregation. But the prayers which announce and explain the subsequent offerings, though ritually fixed, use the same colloquial language as do ordinary domestic prayers.

There are well-defined, customary procedures for libations and offerings but it is characteristic of the Tallensi that they are not sticklers for minutiae. It would be unthinkable for a sacrifice to be repeated because some detail in the ritual sequence was omitted through carelessness or ignorance, though the lapse would not escape criticism. Nevertheless, the patterns are fixed and are well known to responsible adults.

Prayers, analogously, have some fixed features of form.[5] They commonly begin with an invocation summoning the ancestors or other mystical agencies, and end with petitionary exhortations usually made up of stock phrases. There are routine sacrificial situations when prayer follows a stereotyped formula – as when the ancestral shrines are apprised, on the first sowing-day of the year, that the time for sowing has arrived and the customary pleas for propitious sowing and well-being are pronounced. But in most sacrificial situations, even those that pertain to the Great Festivals and therefore have a fixed location and calendrical incidence, there are distinctive incidental features related to the personal histories, circumstances, anxieties, and hopes of the officiants, to chance events such as abnormal drought or rain, to the public mood, and to communications from diviners. For, as Tallensi frequently insist, the future cannot be foreseen. One never knows when misfortune may strike or good luck supervene. This signifies that one cannot know from day to day or year to year what the ancestors and the other occult powers and agencies are demanding and expecting.[6] Hence it is normal for those responsible to consult diviners before making any offering, even if it is one that is regulated by routine or by calendrical fixture. Even if the offerings demanded by ancestors prove, empirically, to be the same – as does in fact happen – year after year in the same situation, they must on every occasion have the authorization of commands from the ancestors transmitted through the diviner. The norm is thus honoured and also adapted to the current circumstances of the donors. Tallensi, unlike Nuer,[7] never in the face of misfortune 'ponder how it may have come about' in order to trace the fault in themselves to which it must be due. Tallensi become anxious, assume that some responsible person has been at fault, and hasten to a diviner for a diagnosis that identifies both the offender and the offended mystical agencies and prescribes the piaculum. In keeping with this, the body of a prayer is apt to be a free and *ad hoc* construction reflecting the particular features of the occasion, though stock phrases will be used and stock sentiments and attitudes exhibited.

It was this aspect of Tallensi prayer that chiefly held my attention at the beginning of my field research in 1934. It was in the middle of the dry season and ritual activities were at their peak; and as they were commonly public, carried out in daylight with no particular reticence, it was easy for me to attend. At this stage, being still ignorant of the language, I was dependent on informants for the reproduction of the prayers I had heard and seen delivered; and they invariably gave me shortened, conventional formulas. 'He called his ancestors', they would say, 'to come and accept their goat and to permit peaceful sleep to be slept and livestock to breed and farming to prosper and women to be married and to have children...' It required no knowledge of the language to doubt the adequacy of this summary of a prayer that lasted fifteen minutes or more. Later, I learnt for myself that it was by no means easy to record (in those days before the advent of the tape-recorder), let alone reproduce, the whole flow of a prayer, full of personal allusions and eloquent exhortations such as normally accompany a sacrifice.

I must, however, explain why the flexibility and the apparent informality of prayer so early aroused my interest. Evans-Pritchard had just published his paper[8] contrasting the Trobriand insistence on strict adherence to the verbal formulas in magical spells and their monopolization by the rightful owners, with the verbal laxity and freedom and the indifference to ownership of Zande magic, with its emphasis on the material substances used in the ritual. The theoretical issues this raised were much discussed in our circle of postgraduate students. Was the essential point of difference merely that in one system magical power lay in the spoken spell whereas in the other the same power was embodied in material substances, or did it lie in the qualities and character attributed to the supernatural agencies mobilized? The evidence from African ethnography available at that time seemed to confirm Evans-Pritchard's analysis without, however, answering all the questions raised by it. This was the stimulus that directed my attention to the form of Tallensi prayers.

In describing Tallensi prayers as flexible or free or *ad hoc* or informal, that is, like Nuer prayers of 'no set form',[9] I do not mean to suggest that they are casual. To be sure the Tallensi do not have verbally fixed prayers like the Christian Lord's Prayer or the Hebrew *Shema*, or the Muslim *Shalaat*; nor do they have stipulated times of worship during the day, or week.[10] They do not offer a prayer on rising in the morning nor do they say grace at meals. Nor, however, do Tallensi ever utter prayers spontaneously. It would be inconceivable for a Tallensi in trouble to do as a Nuer does and 'pace up and down' in his homestead in the open uttering a supplication to the Earth or to his ancestors. As I have noted, his reaction would be immediately to have recourse to a diviner. Such pious ejaculations as *Naawun bɛme* – Heaven (God) is there (to protect and bless), *Naawun nna mari* – God will guard you, *banam ni yaanan bɛme* – our fathers and ancestors are there (to protect or bless), may be addressed to anybody at any time. But these no more count as prayers than does the corresponding curse *i na nye* – you will see. And, as I have already implied, there are no sacred words in Talni reserved for the proper ritual context and forbidden in mundane situations.

What regulates Tallensi prayers in their incidence, style, and general shape, is their normal association with sacrifice (*ka'abɔr*) and altars (*baghar*). The beings or powers to whom prayers are addressed are invoked to attend at a particular shrine or place of sacrifice and the invocation is aimed, as it were, at this visible and tangible material focus, and not launched towards heaven or into space. An audience is assumed to be present, and the postures and attitudes of the officiants and participants reflect this situation.

A diviner's shrine (*bakologo*) is one of many that are upright, standing four or five foot high. In sacrificing to it a man stands and speaks as if addressing another person face to face. Other ancestral altars, and Earth shrines, are on the ground or low down. In sacrificing to these a man squats, likewise addressing the recipient as if face to face on the same level. Sacrifice and prayer are offered thus in the idiom of mutually courteous everyday intercourse with elders. It is as if in salutation to an elder or chief that heads are bared and eyes lowered by the participants in solemn sacrificial ceremonies, and it is as a gesture of special respect that in certain sacrifices given during funerals the officiant washes his hands first (for 'you are offering food and drink to the dead'). A tone of intimacy and frankness runs through the supplication and confession. Tallensi may bow the head but they do not abase themselves either in prayer, or in the presence of living superiors by status.

I have said that spontaneous individual prayer is not a Tallensi practice. Perhaps the main reason for this is that freedom to offer sacrifice and prayer is not general. Women, being jural and ritual minors, are permitted to officiate in prayers and sacrifice only in special circumstances, and this applies also to youths and even to men of mature years whose 'fathers are still alive'.[11] Similarly, the right and duty of officiating in worship of the Earth shrines and of the founding ancestors of the lineage at the altars dedicated to them is regulated by age and office. There are also ritual restrictions on freedom to offer sacrifice and prayer. It is, for instance, ritually prohibited for the officiants, and all other participants, in a sacrifice at an Earth shrine or an External *Boghar* to wear a cloth upper garment; a man whose wife is pregnant or menstruating may not officiate in mortuary and funeral rituals; and there are many other ritual restrictions of this type.

Lest, however, the impression be conveyed that prayer is no more than a variant of ordinary respectful discourse, I must emphasize that it is clearly distinguished by its context of association with sacrifice and its focus in an altar, as well as by its style and contents; and an examination of some specimens will make this clear. We must bear in mind that there is no priesthood or scripture to ensure uniformity or conformity in prayer.

I begin with an example of a prayer as it was reported to me by an informant before I knew enough of the language to follow it myself. A minor headman had offered a chicken on the altar consecrated by his father's *Yin*.[12] According to my informant his prayer ran as follows:

> My father, you begot me, and then you died and you said that if I gain the headmanship I must give you [in sacrifice] a cow. I gained the headmanship and you said I must give you a cow. Today, I have been to thatch the white man's house and the District Commissioner has paid me. But people, some of them, have gone to Gambaga to report that I have withheld their money from them. If, when they return, no evil matter [i.e. prosecution by the District Commissioner] befalls me, I will buy a cow and offer it to you; but if, when they return I am put to shame, I will not give it to you.

This potted version of a long and repetitive prayer does scant justice to it. It does not convey the undertone of anxiety in the speaker's voice and leaves out all the details of his story, of his invocation, and of his expostulations. But it suffices to indicate what is the most striking feature of Tallensi prayer.

Prayer is a cathartic exercise. Let me explain what I mean by this. Prayer is the central element of a ritual act calculated to master what Tallensi represent to themselves, in the idioms of their customary beliefs and ideas, as a crisis or a threat of a crisis. To the observer the crisis might seem trivial and ephemeral or no more than a remote contingency, or even, in reality, non-existent. It is none the less experienced as a real and compelling one by the Tallensi themselves.

Prayer serves, then, as the main cathartic element of the ritual by making public and thus bringing into the open of social acceptability the state of affairs that is believed to lie behind the crisis. Now, in general all of this is known to the responsible participants, that is to say the lineage and family elders and the close relatives of the principals by whom or on whose behalf the offering is made. In many cases the relevant circumstances will also be known to a wider public. But revealing them in public in what amounts to a kind of confession, giving them explicit utterance in the ritually legitimizing situation of the sacrifice, gives the prayer its cathartic value. It enables the crisis to be grasped and interpreted and finally mastered. The fears and compunctions evoked by the crisis are openly expressed, the faults in question are admitted; and promises of the appropriate ritual services for restoring amity with the ancestors and other mystical powers are announced. On the other side, too, benefits received can be praised, triumphs flaunted, rights in relation to these powers asserted, and hopes of future benevolence declared. Piety is mobilized in action.

This explains why prayers always begin with an account of the reasons for the sacrifice, though it is well understood that they will be known to the main participants and, of course, by definition, to the mystical recipients. The past events that led to the demand for the offering, and the circumstances that compel submission to it, are rehearsed. The catharsis may be personal for the individual making the offering on his own behalf, or it may be vicarious when an offering is made on behalf of others. The prayer, however, is always a public and open utterance, directed as much at the company present as at the mystical powers addressed. Secret ritual activities are assumed to be associated with private medicines and charms that belong to the sphere of sorcery and magic and not to religion. It is a rule that legitimate religious activities must have witnesses entitled and obliged to share in them.

Though I am stressing the cathartic value of prayer it is, of course, the rite as a whole to which this pertains. The bustle of movement, argument, and cheerful conversation, when the sacrifice is shared in termination of the rite coming after the respectful silence during the prayer, is the best evidence of the relief experienced by the participants. But the prayer is the primary medium for the catharsis because it puts into words what the act of sacrifice can but symbolize. In particular, it affords expression to the ambivalence in the relations of the living with their ancestors and the other mystical powers which is of critical importance in Tallensi religion. The threat, in the prayer I have quoted, to withhold promised or commanded offering if a desired boon is not granted is a typical instance. Attempts at mutual coercion phrased in quasi-legalistic terms are characteristic of the relations of men with their ancestors. The public exposure of these relations in prayer is a way of trying to impose on the ancestors moral accountability to the living equal to the accountability of the latter to the former. Of course this never works. In the long run, death supervenes and this is interpreted as the victory of the ancestors or the Earth over the intractable living.

In the following prayer the catharsis is in part vicarious. To understand it one must bear in mind that a wife cannot offer prayer or libation on her own behalf; it must be done for her by her husband. One must also know that it is a sin for an infant to die in the arms of its mother. If this happens she must be ritually purified when she next gets pregnant or else the following infant will die in her arms when she first nurses it.

Daamoo's wife suffered this misfortune and when she was advanced in her next pregnancy the owner of the appropriate medicine was sent for to purify her. After spreading his paraphernalia in the courtyard, he took up the chicken provided for the offering and a dish of water. Handing the water to Daamoo he invited him to 'pour the customary libation'. Daamoo, squatting, spoke in a quiet conversational tone as follows:

> My father Y., I am calling you hither, do you call your father N. and let him call his father P. and when you have gathered, do you then call J. and O. and all other fathers and forefathers. This woman bore a child and it died in her arms. I have no mother of my own and not even a stepmother. Indeed, there was nobody at home then who could have taken the child and that is how it happened. Now it is said that when such a thing happens and when the woman conceives again it is customary to perform a certain sacrifice and it then finishes. I therefore sent for the people to come and perform the ritual. Accept this water for you to drink and now that this young woman has this pregnancy, do you permit her to have a safe delivery and may the baby take the breast satisfactorily so that well-being may come about.

Then he poured some water on the ground calling out, 'accept, accept, accept this water and drink'. This done, he turned aside and splashing some water on another spot spoke:

> O Zubiung Earth, I pray you, too, to accept this water, and you, all you departed Zubiung tendaanas, do you too accept this water so that you may support these medicine roots from before and from behind and permit this [mishap] to be like a light rain that passes quickly and not like a heavy downpour that goes on and on.

This prayer needs no gloss. However, it is revealing to put beside it the prayer spoken by the medicine owner. Taking this dish of water and addressing himself to the small bundle of magical material – the so-called 'roots' – he said, speaking in the same quiet conversational tone:

> My father A., I am calling you, do you call your father M., and he call his father T., and he call D. and O. I am calling upon you by reason of your having begotten me, for you have no concern with these roots. It is only that you may come and sit here and give support as I do what is to be done with these roots, so that it turns out to be light and passing rain and not a heavy and endless downpour. My mother, come and sit here by your roots and do you call my grandmother, your mother, and she call her mother and all of you assemble and sit by these your roots. You died and left this medicine to me. I, for my part, don't care to go about performing this ritual but it is you who said that it delivers people from trouble. That is why I am sitting here. An infant had remained in this woman's arms and that is why they have summoned me to come and perform this sacrifice. If you are really effective [as you claim], permit her to bear her child so that no sound [of pain] is heard, so that not even the mice hear a sound. Permit the child to be sitting in her lap so that they all realize that your roots do indeed exist [i.e. have magical power].

He then nicked the middle toe of the chicken's right foot, dripped some blood on the roots, and added 'here is your chicken, here are your money and your guinea corn too. Accept water and drink, accept your chicken, and permit everything to go well.'

These prayers are so typical of situations in which therapeutic or magical treatment takes place that they can be regarded as routine in form. It is noteworthy and characteristic of Tallensi religion that the power assumed to be inherent in medicine is inert until it is released and permitted to work by its original owners and transmitters. But they cannot be effective without the concurrent help of all the ancestors of all the principal participants. The patient's representative and the doctor have to solicit the help of their respective ancestors independently though it is in the same cause, for one cannot call upon ancestors other than one's own. The Earth, too, must be invoked to aid the cure.

It is essential that both the client and the doctor must make the circumstances which have led to the situation explicit in their prayers. The full significance of this would require a longer exegesis than is appropriate here. It is enough to note that it is not merely the words spoken that mobilize the mystical powers, but the words spoken by the person responsible for, and entitled to perform, the ritual. The medicine, its original owners, and the doctor's ancestors are not deemed to be present until the doctor himself invokes them; but they cannot succeed unless the patient's mystical guardians permit them to. And it is worth adding that it is always taken for granted that the ancestors, the Earth, the medicines, and so on must and will respond to the pleas. They will become spiritually present. It may turn out later that they have not given the help solicited – but this would be for reasons as yet unknown to the supplicants, not through absence from the occasion.

Note further that when both the patient's representative and the doctor thus invoke their respective ancestors they are also explaining the situation to others present. These are normally kinsfolk or persons otherwise entitled to be present, not random spectators, and the prayer enlists their participation in a very direct sense. It is a two-way catharsis – in relation to the ancestors and other mystical powers, and in relation to the living who have interests in and commitments to the principal parties. Prayer exculpates, on the one hand by relieving the worshipper's conscience, and on the other by affirming his moral standing in the community. What cannot be over-emphasized is that the crisis thus dealt with is real and urgent to the actors. Babies do die in the way they fear.

The communal orientation of prayer is most in evidence when the officiant acts in a representative rather than a personal capacity. Then sacrifice is often accompanied by what could as well be described as an allocution addressed to the congregation as a prayer, though its ostensible reference is to the ancestors and other mystical powers. The following is an example: Buntuya died, rich in years, in children, in grandchildren, and in possessions, having thus attained the fulfilment that every Tallensi aspires to. But at the mortuary divination it emerged that he had been slain by his own Destiny ancestors on account of a white bull he had promised and failed to sacrifice to them. It emerged also that if this bull was not offered before the obsequial ceremonies, there would be further deaths in the family. Thereupon Buntuya's sons procured a white bull and summoned kinsfolk and clansfolk, friends, and neighbours to attend. They came, a great throng, packing the inner courtyard in which the altar that was to receive the sacrifice stood. The bull was dragged to the altar and the dead man's oldest son, addressing the senior lineage elder, spoke as follows (I omit the repetitions and elaborations):

> Bulug, listen: Buntuya as a young man went to live at Biung. He farmed, he farmed immensely; he gained wives and more wives and children. But all the time he lamented saying that he was getting no returns for his work, that his Yin ancestors must be powerless else they would help him to farm profitably and get wives and children. But his Yin ancestors declared that he would farm and gain wealth and buy cows and be replete with wives and children and grandchildren. And they said that when he is thus satisfied he must give them a white bull, a spotless white bull. Buntuya promised, and he did indeed farm and get wealth and marry wives and abound with children and grandchildren and his Yin ancestors said let him give them a white bull, one that is spotless for they had prospered him and he again promised. Then he left Biung and returned to Tongo. Presently one of his wives conceived but became ill. He went to his Yin shrine and pleaded – permit this woman now lying in her room to get well, for if she were to die he himself would die and if she did not die he would with his own hands slaughter his bull for his Yin ancestors. But the woman died. So he said that he himself could not slaughter the bull for his Yin ancestors, it

would be for us to give it and send it after him. He did not kill
the bull and then he died and it emerged that his Yin ancestors
had come and slain him and were commanding us to procure
the bull to send after him. Thus indeed has it come to pass. Now
we have found the bull and we offer it to Buntuya. May he
accept his white bull at his Yin ancestors' shrine, to give to
them, and be gathered to his fathers, so that this house may
grow cool again and we be permitted to celebrate his funeral
propitiously and be granted peaceful sleep to be slept and wives
to accrue and children to be born.

This was no conversational piece. It was declaimed loudly and rhe-
torically, phrase by phrase, with mingled pride and piety, emphatic
repetitions, and evident feeling. The congregation sat or stood in
complete and attentive silence throughout its long-drawn-out
periods. Then Bulug responded in a similar but more sober and
solemn tone (again I abbreviate):

Buntuya's Yin ancestors [he said] had spoken fittingly. He had
indeed farmed and gained wealth and wives and children. Now
let him accept his bull and permit peaceful sleeping and grant
that those who do not yet have wives get wives this very month
and that children are born, so that this house may grow even
larger than it is now. May the guinea corn now sprouting ripen
properly and may we be permitted to slaughter this bull for him
without mishap and to perform his funeral rites propitiously.

This was the climax. One of the younger sons of the deceased, who
had been squatting on the flat surface of the altar all the time, now
poured a libation and slaughtered a chicken as a preliminary sacrifice and waited for the bull to be killed. He carried out these acts in
silence. The exchange of speeches between his older brother (for
whom he was deputizing) and Bulug here took the place of the more
usual form of prayer. Buntuya dead was thus reconciled with his
ancestors by the pious action of his sons, and the mystical security as
well as the moral standing of the family was thus re-established.

I have space for but a part of one more of the many dozens of
prayers I recorded. One of the most dramatic ritual events I have
ever witnessed was the acclamation of the most hallowed Earth and
*Boghar* shrines of all Taleland and the ancestors, in supplication of

well-being for the coming year, by the assembled Hill Talis tendaanas during the Golib festival. It took place just before dawn at
the site of their most sacred Earth shrine *ŋoo*. The dance, attended
by a vast concourse of perhaps 5,000 people, had gone on all night.
Then as the first glimmer of light appeared, the senior tendaana
cried out that it was time for the dance to stop. Within minutes complete silence descended and the multitude sat down on the ground.
Then the tendaanas spoke, each in turn, standing on the rocks which
are the altar of *ŋoo*, dimly visible, and seeming to tower above the
audience. They hurled their invocations towards the audience at the
top of their voices, with many dramatic pauses, with insistent repetition of the key phrases, and with many figurative variations. The
effect was that of a reverberating incantation; and the audience,
though well acquainted with this ceremony, sat as if spellbound in
complete silence.

I will not attempt to reproduce any of the invocations spoken,
even to the extent of the incomplete records I was able to make. But
their flavour can be indicated by some excerpts from the opening
allocution of the Wakyi tendaana. Turning first to the assembled
tendaanas he cried loudly, 'Speak for me – will you not speak for
me? Are we not all equal to one another? Does not each of us have
power over each and thus we abide together?' This was a gesture of
courtesy for he continued at once, addressing the audience at large:

> Pardon me then. Our fathers, our ancestors of yore used to send
> out the call [at this time] telling people that *ŋoo* was inviting
> them, strangers and all, to join in the ceremonies by day and by
> night. It is ordained that there shall be no quarrelling, that the
> people who congregate here shall not strike blows – these are
> forbidden on pain of fines and penalties.

The tendaana dwelt on this topic at some length as the danger of
fights breaking out between the dancing groups and among the spectators is ever present. Then he continued in a tone of high exul-
tation: 'Well then, I now call upon my father the Tendaana, to call
upon his father [and so on, in the usual manner enumerating a long
line of ancestors] for all to come and take their place here, for it is
*ŋoo* that calls them.' Then followed a long sequence of further invocations to ancestors of the other Hill Talis tendaanas and to all the

Earth shrines and External *Boghar* shrines of the Talis. Then his voice and manner changed. A personal, protesting note crept in as he continued, ostensibly addressing the ancestors and other mystic powers.

> Consider my coming here. How many years is it that I have been coming here [to this ceremony]? My coming up here, it is four years since I first came here and you permitted me to speak. I said long ago that I wanted a house [i.e. a family and many descendants].

Though he uses the first personal pronoun it is understood that he is speaking for the community as a whole.

> I want to live to see such a house. Have you given it to me? [He added further reproaches in the same vein and continued] I call upon you to take heed. First about farming, we beg for early millet and for guinea corn. We beg *ŋoo* to grant us a cow, to grant us a sheep, to grant us goats and chickens. It is *ŋoo* that must grant peaceful sleep, grant marriages and children to all of us [and so on with repetition and variations]. Next, rain, let there be one sufficient rain, one rain, [and so on with repetition] one rain, so that we need but one sowing for our early millet, so that orphans may have food, widows may have food, women and children may have food. Next, locusts. May they go down into holes. Let them not come to this land, let them go down into holes, go down into holes [with further elaborations]. Once more, I want to call upon you to take heed as I have called upon you in the past. Let the early millet be well rooted, let the guinea corn be well rooted [and so on]. We want wives and children, we want things of all kinds to be gathered together for us.

This allocution, as I have called it, needs little exegesis. Though addressed to the Earth and the ancestors it smacks of magical intention. It is as if its declamation at that ritually sanctified place and at that symbolically suggestive hour of dawn, in that taboo-marked period of the sowing-festival, expresses the deepest longings, hopes, and fears of the whole assembled multitude. They come from the whole of the Tallensi country and beyond, not only to dance but to receive, by their presence, and to take back with them, the blessings solicited in the prayers of the tendaanas. But in characteristic Tallensi fashion the appeals are couched in terms that appear to demand rather than to supplicate and they are addressed to the ancestors and the Earth, not to magical substances.

The other tendaanas now followed with their allocutions in turn, trying to outdo one another in eloquence, dramatic iteration, and indirect allusion to their relative superiority in the rank order of the tendaanas.

No libations or sacrifices accompanied this ceremony. They had, in fact, been made earlier at a ceremony in which only the tendaanas and their elders had participated. This gave added point to the prayers themselves. It brought home vividly to me what I have previously noted about the hopes and fears, wishes and aspirations voiced in them. They are not to be thought of as figures of speech or flourishes of rhetoric. They reflected what, for generations, had been the hard realities of their existence for the Tallensi. Erratic or insufficient rainfall at the right time of the year was a frequent occurrence and the result was often a failure of the crops which, even in the 1930s, spelled famine. Locusts came often enough at the height of the growing season to ruin the guinea corn and reduce people to starvation. Periods of drought and disease killed off livestock most years. And above all, sickness, food shortage, and lack of medical and hygienic knowledge conduced to a chronically high death-rate, especially among infants and the aged. The complex of divination, sacrifice, and prayer among the Tallensi cannot be properly understood without taking into account their experience of living under what had for generations been to them the shadow of perennial and inescapable uncertainty, unpredictability, and threat in the management of their personal and social life. They believed, as they recognized in their religious ideology, that these dangers came from external forces and agencies; and they were not wholly unjustified in this. Environmental conditions, added to lack of the necessary skills and knowledge and to the limitations of their political and social organization, gave some objective foundation to their beliefs. This has a direct bearing on the significance of divination, sacrifice, and prayer in their worship of their ancestors and the Earth. Given their system of religious thought, it is quite realistic for Tallensi to solicit the things they ask for in their prayers.

# 3

## Ritual festivals and the Ancestors[1]

I

A festival, the *Oxford English Dictionary* tells us, is 'a time of festive celebrations'. I am sure there is not now and never has been a human community which has utterly eschewed such celebrations. And nowhere, perhaps, are festivals so frequent and of such extremely varied types and complexions – whether movable or immovable – as in this country.

A recent guide book (Cooper 1961) enumerates over one hundred regularly recurring British festivals beginning with Crufts Dog Show in February and including all our musical and theatrical festivals, annual art exhibitions, test matches, and of course the boat race, and ending with a long list of what are called traditional festivals such as the State Opening of Parliament and Guy Fawkes Day. It is of interest that all of these so enumerated are secular celebrations. There is no reference for example to either Christmas or Easter, let alone the numerous Saints' days that are still listed in our University Diaries. But in contrast, Italy is credited with a veritable plethora of religious festivals. There is one or more of such festivals in every month of the year and both Easter and Christmas are among those listed and described. Harvest Festivals are not unknown in this country but are ignored in the guide book I have quoted. In Italy they are especially noted as times 'when there is singing of religious songs and it is considered blasphemous to sing love or humorous songs' – a prohibition of certain kinds of frivolity that would be appreciated in parts of Africa known to me. What is most striking about these Italian festivals, and indeed also among many other Continental festivals, is their commemorative character, looking back, often, to a divine miracle, hence the religious mould in which they are usually cast. And this I must say fits in much more closely with my notion of a festival than does Guy Fawkes, even though that too has a cheerful commemorative aspect. As a matter of fact, there was a time when it could be said that 'this anniversary, observed by a strict form of prayer and kept as a holiday at all public offices is a great day in the Church of England calendar'. I am quoting from an engaging compilation by one Horatio Smith, Esquire, entitled *Festivals, Games and Amusements, Ancient and Modern*, published in London 1831. Mr. Smith incidentally in a tone that might be echoed today, fulminates against the 'disgraceful scuffles and skirmishes' that often accompanied the celebration and denounces them as 'a sort of sanction for insulting, hating and ridiculing Catholics, a much more numerous class of Christians than themselves and inculcate therefore a feeling of bigotry and intolerance' (p. 156).

To be sure we do not have to go further than the portals of an Oxbridge College to find the ideal type of festival in the annual rites of commemorating its foundation. Is there not usually a chapel service, in which the Founder is piously commemorated and with him all later Benefactors, as a prelude to a feast that has quasi sacramental character despite its usual lightheartedness.

But my image of what a festival should be like was, I suspect, formed long before I had even heard of anthropology though I only became aware of this when I met with the Tallensi Great Festivals in the field. Implicitly rather than openly, the model to which I had found myself associating the African Festivals I have investigated is, I believe, the Jewish Passover. Interestingly enough, the aforesaid Horatio Smith begins his compilation with a long chapter on the festivals, games and amusements of the Ancient Jews, whom he praises for the 'festive', 'joyous' character of their religion in contrast to 'the notions of modern puritans and rigourists' (p. 17). As he rightly recognizes, anticipating more serious scholars such as Robertson Smith, all orthodox Jewish *holidays* have from time immemorial in fact been *holy days*. Passover typifies this rather better I think than any of the other dozen or so major festivals in the Jewish Religious calendar. It has moreover as I eventually discovered all the ingredients of the corresponding festivals of many traditional societies in Africa and elsewhere in the non-European world. It is seasonal; it dramatises what Malinowski would have called a mythic character – but which is believed by the orthodox to commemorate the true history of the miraculous deliverance of the founding ancestors by divine intervention; it prescribes special conduct and behaviour particularly with reference to food and drink, ordains ritual purity for domestic utensils and for the house, lays down a daily round that contrasts with that of the work-day round. In short it marks off an interlude in the normal passage of mundane toil – of, in Durkheim's terminology, profane interests – in the idiom of taboo. Lastly there is the feasting associated with the festival, though unlike most tribal festivals it does not include the dance.

There was one thing that used to puzzle me about the Passover and indeed about all the Jewish festivals. In contrast to Christmas Day and some other national festivals, they never fell on fixed dates. Sometimes they would seem to move backwards every year, a week or so at a time, sometimes forward. It was, again, years later that I realized that, like African festivals, they follow a lunar and seasonal calendar. This is not a minor point. In our Western world the calendar and the clock, impartial, objective, mechanical, external to us, fix our festivals, with some exceptions that are felt to be peculiar, and also provide the framework of structure for the passage of personal time. Among orthodox East European Jews, as of course much more so in traditional Africa, it is the festivals that structure personal time, in for instance fixing family anniversaries and shaping the working year, within the framework of each life and each family cycle. It is the festivals, also, which structure the cycle of time for the community as well. But, what is more important, it is the festivals which repeatedly confirm and sanctify the image the community holds of its origins, history and *raison d'être*.

Seasonal festivals in which the whole community participates, are common and frequent in all non-Western societies, perhaps more so than with us. There are of course many other kinds of festivals too, such as those associated with the initiation ceremonies of youths and maidens and the enthronement ceremonies of monarchs and other forms of installation into high political or religious office (Fortes 1966); and there is considerable overlap between the patterns of organization and the symbolic means employed in these ceremonies and those that pertain to seasonal festivals, since they draw on the same cultural resources. Anthropologists and other observers have given many accounts of many types of festivals: and the makers of theories have appealed constantly to these ceremonies.

One of Frazer's sources of inspiration was the account of the succession contest and installation of the Divine Kings of the Shilluk of the Southern Sudan; and Durkheim, it will be recollected, based his entire theory of the elementary forms of religious life on the analysis of the seasonal increase ceremonies of the Australian Aborigines so beloved of Marett.

Among anthropological accounts of seasonal festivals none has surpassed Firth's analysis of 'The Work of the Gods' in Tikopia (1941); and it is of particular interest to me, as an Africanist, to see how closely the organization and the patterns of ceremony, and of ritual activities and of festive celebrations of this Polynesian festival parallel those I observed among the Tallensi and the Ashanti. A key theme, which is the more surprising when the geographical and the large numerical, climatic and cultural differences between these communities is borne in mind, is the dramatization of the complex interweaving of patterns of differentiation with compensatory patterns of integration and interdependence in the organization of these ceremonies. Among the approximately twelve hundred Tikopia, as among the forty thousand odd Tallensi, there was, before Christianity and what is now called modernization became well established, an elaborate, one might almost say obsessional, scheme of cross-cutting internal segmentation and differentiation of the community by clanship, residence, political alignment, locality, and ritual status. This pattern of social organization, maintained by what looks like a scheme of regulated rivalry, seems almost ridiculous in the case of a small closed society like traditional Tikopia where everybody must be connected by marriage and kinship with one another. Comparison with the Tallensi, where it looks more appropriate as the basis of an extensive, politically acephalous society, makes us realize how fundamental internal differentiation by rules of group membership is to any ongoing society. And the seasonal festivals show this up by mobilizing the oppositions and rivalries in such a way as to display and evoke the sense of the inescapable interdependence of the different elements of the society on one another for the attainment of the common good of all. In 1935, I gave a preliminary account of the Tallensi Great Festivals in a paper presented to the Royal Anthropological Institute (Fortes 1935) stressing in particular this theme, that is to say of the festivals as dramatic portrayals of the moral and political interdependence of the constituent parts of the society, in obedience to powerful, generally accepted religious sanctions. Today I want to go back to this subject but from a slightly different angle, though this theme cannot altogether be left out of the picture.

The Tallensi Festivals, I might add, are by no means unusual for Africa in this respect. Seasonal and other calendrical festivals are particularly widespread in Western Africa. Most remarkable of all are the festivals that recur only once or twice in a normal life-time. An example is the *Sigui* festival of the Dogon of the Western Sudan, famous in the annals of anthropology for their elaborate cosmological and metaphysical systems of thought. The *Sigui* takes place once every sixty years thus marking out the passage of time in units of the single human life span, as this is conceptualized by the Dogon (Dieterlen 1971). Better known amongst Africanists is the Ashanti Odwira festival, first brought to the attention of the outside world in 1820 in Bodwich's narrative of his visit to Kumasi. A century later Rattray described the same festival again, showing how constant the main pattern was, and I have myself been present at a much modified but still magnificent contemporary version of it. It was timed to celebrate the main yam harvest (hence called the yam festival) at the beginning of the dry season, normally in September or October, but it was in fact a spectacular celebration of the King's political powers, wealth, and religious authority and responsibility for the nation as a whole. The huge concourse gathered from every corner of the nation, of all the chiefs, sub-chiefs and people, the libations and sacrifices, in former times including human victims, the rituals of purging the nation through the agency of its divinities and fetishes, of the evil accumulated during the previous year, the collective rejoicing over the harvest, the drumming, the dancing, the horn blowing, that recounted the legendary history of the mafia and the heroic exploits and sacrifices in war and peace of its leaders, all this added up to a massive demonstration of national solidarity, as well as a solemn commemoration of the nation's heroic dead and glorious history. It came as a climax to a year-long series of ritual festivals that are still celebrated locally in each chiefdom at intervals of twenty-one and forty-two days in all Akan speaking communities of Ghana and adjacent territories (Rattray 1929; Field 1937; Niangouran-Bouah 1964). Tallensi festivals are not as spectacular as Ashanti national festivals but the themes are essentially the same.

## II

We think of the year as beginning on 1 January and ending on 31 December and have come to regard this as a fact of nature, though it is well known to experts that this calendar was first fixed in 45 BC by Julius Caesar in order to replace the irregularities of the lunar year with the reliable and regular solar calendar. The connections between calendar dates, seasonal variations of a climatic kind, and other associated natural phenomena such as the changing length of night and day, are only of incidental interest to us as regards their bearing on the festivals we celebrate. The luni-solar calendar by which the incidence and sequence of Jewish festivals is regulated also has a fixed beginning and end, though these are associated by the layman with the festivals that mark them, more than with the sequence of the regular natural phenomena to which the year is in fact geared, and which, in the original home of these festivals determined their seasonal context.

The Tallensi, like other African peoples, do not think of the year as having fixed termini. Their concept *womr* is more adequately translated as 'a twelve month' than by our word year. They think of a year as made up of the two distinct seasons that govern the climate of their land, a dry season, *Uun*, and the following wet season, *Seug* or vice versa. And they think of these seasons as made up of lunar months, ideally six for each season, but, as their ritual leaders recognize, having to be augmented by an extra month in some years to keep them in line with the seasons. Significantly, the names of the months register the state of the rain and of the crops at that time.

The Tallensi live at the edge of the Sahel zone, which has recently been notorious for the long lasting drought and famine that has afflicted its inhabitants. Thus the Tallensi dry season, which lasts from about the beginning of October to about the end of March each year, is totally rainless at the height of the season. At the same time, the rainfall during the rainy season is by no means uniform or reliable from year to year. Its course is always watched with anxiety since the crops are wholly dependent on an adequate and properly spaced rainfall for successful growth and only in the best of years was it possible in the past to produce a substantial surplus above subsistence level. During the rainy season Tallensi are anxiously preoccupied with the weather and the state of the crops and next to this, with concern for health and general well being. Unduly erratic rainfall may threaten to turn the hunger month usually expected halfway through the rainy season into a time of famine, and excess rainfall is taken to forebode an abnormal run of disease and death. The festivals are explicitly concerned with these unpredictable potentialities of threat inherent in the climate and the environment. But they reflect also another aspect of the alternation of the seasons. For these are not merely climatical, ecological, and economic alternations. In accordance with the classical Durkheimian mode, they represent different, in some ways contrasting patterns of social life. The intensive farming activities of the wet season sink into the complete abeyance in the dry season, when hunting, fishing, building and repairing dwellings, travelling abroad for petty trade or for spells of cash-earning labour, take over. In the past it was generally expected that there would be less sickness in the dry season and consequently fewer deaths; and greater leisure and more food supplies made it possible to celebrate important funerals and carry out other time-consuming ritual activities.

## III

To make clear how the festivals are organized, it is necessary to describe briefly the social and political constitution of Tallensi society. The essential feature is that it consists of two major groups of clan, known respectively as the Namoos and Tallis. The former trace their origin to Mamprussi whence, their clan history relates, their founder came as a refugee and stranger to settle in the Tallensi country some fourteen or fifteen generations ago. Their clan heads have the title of chief, the most senior being the Chief of Tongo. The other group of clans claim to be the autochthonous inhabitants of the area, sprung from the earth itself. Their clan heads are the ritual custodians of the Earth in its non-material mystical aspects and with regard to its occult powers. Their title, Tendaana, which I have translated as Custodian of the Earth, distinguishes them sharply from the chiefs. The difference is expressed in contrasting ritual observances and taboos that are incumbent on chiefs and tendaanas respectively, and are symbolized in the contrast between a cloth tunic a chief normally wears and the antelope skins a tendaana must always wear. But it is an ultimate and sacred tenet of Tallensi religion, cosmology and political ideology, shared by all, that the well-being of the total society supposes and is inextricably bound up with mutually complementary statuses and the reciprocal social and religious relationships of chiefs and tendaanas. Theirs is a relationship usually compared to that of husband and wife. This is peculiarly appropriate because the two sets of clans are strictly differentiated from one another and amongst themselves by patrilineal descent according to which they are divided into a number of mutually exclusive patrilineal lineages that must however intermarry to conform to the laws of exogamy. An elaborate system of ancestor worship is followed in both sets of clans with the additional cosmological slant that the chiefly ancestors are supposed to have supernatural powers to influence the rain whereas the ancestors of the tendaana clans are bound up with the Earth shrines and sacred groves which govern the fertility of the material earth and have power over such earth creatures as locusts that might damage crops.

On the ground these clans are linked in a complex geographical as well as genealogical network which maps out both their jealously prized, totemically symbolized and juridically institutionalized differentiation one from another and their inescapable interconnection and interdependence by bonds of marriage, kinship and contiguity. The paradox here is that in former times Namoo clans and Tallis clans occasionally raided or went to war with one another since there was no paramount judicial machinery to settle disputes between them. But so tight-knit is the web of the interconnections between the different clans that mediators quickly appeared and peace was generally soon restored (Fortes 1940, 1945, 1949).

## IV

Within this framework of social organization the Tallensi see their festivals as a recurrent cycle of obligatory exchanges of complementary ritual benefactions supported by obligatory ritual collaboration within each of the groups making these exchanges. In religious terms they hope the exchanges and the collaboration mobilize the ancestors at one pole and the powers of the Earth at the other, as we shall see. The cycle depends, Tallensi assert, on the fact that each of the two groups is distinguished and identified by the time, the manner, and the purport of the festivals which are their exclusive prerogative, and they commonly declare the most distinctive manifestation of each group's festivals to be the dances associated with them. Namoo children of six or seven, aping their elders, will boast 'we Namoos dance the Gingaang; the Tallis have their Da'a, and Bogharaam and Golib'; and on the other side Tallis children proudly state the reverse. Nor are these dances thought of only in secular and aesthetic terms, for they were instituted by the ancestors and are a sacred trust.

Next to the dance, the feature that is most stressed in popular reference as distinguishing each festival from the other is a material relic pertaining to it. Characteristically, but not exclusively, these are different kinds of wooden drums and other sound-producing instruments. These relics are sacred and are claimed to have been magically procured by the founding ancestors. Ordinarily they are kept in a special place in a hut of the clan head which is set aside for the important clan shrines or, among the Tallis, in a sacred place out of doors. When the time comes the relics are brought out ceremonially, sometimes refurbished and offered libations of beer or water mixed with millet flour to accompany the invocations addressed to the ancestors or the Earth to open the festival. Other relics are similarly treated when they are brought out. It is interesting that the most famous of the drum relics are found in pairs one of which is said to be the original drum brought by the founding ancestors and therefore the truly sacred one, the other of later manufacture. The sacred drum, for instance in the case of both the Gingaang and the Golib festivals, is small and worn down, whereas the later drum is large and well preserved. It is this drum which is brought out to be played in the dance. The Gingaang drum is carried on a sling around the neck and is struck with a hooked stick. The Golib drums are differently shaped and are held between the legs to be struck.

As with the relics and the dances each clan or group of clans has its distinctive pattern of rites and ceremonies, though they are all made up of similar elements of prayer, libation, and offering. Lineages and clans that celebrate the same festival are assumed to be kin of one another, in a broad sense, by virtue of the rule that people who sacrifice together must be kin. This is often alluded to. At the time of my first visit to the Tallensi there was a long drawn out dis-

pute over a piece of farmland between the Golibdaana and the head
of a neighbouring Tallis clan. At one stage the Chief of Tongo, who
as I have said before was the most senior of the Namoo chiefs, and
who was related on his maternal side to both disputants, endeavoured to arbitrate. Pleading with them to come to an agreement, he
said, 'Your ancestors are different, these from those, but are you not
one stock, kin to one another, seeing that all of you join together to
celebrate Bogharaam and Golib?' At that time the Hill Tallis clans
were divided into bitter hostile factions by the dissensions provoked
by the then Golibdaana taking advantage of his great wealth and the
patronage his gifts had gained for him from the then paramount
ruler of the Mamprussi. Thirty years earlier, everyone agreed,
before the white man's peace was established, arrows would have
flown on the hill. I was bombarded from both sides with acrimoni-
ous accusations against the other and had to step warily to assert my
neutrality. But when the festivals came round the hostilities and
hatreds had to be suspended. The rites and sacrifices required the
collaboration of the lineage heads of both factions and these were all
solemnly performed in the customary way. The dances, likewise,
were thronged with contingents from all the clans, competing with
one another for the plaudits of the spectators in the traditional way.
Fears that some elders had that the young men of lineages belonging
to the opposing factions might be so excited and stirred up by the
dance as to come to blows, proved groundless. There is a strict
taboo on fighting and bloodshed during the Golib festival, the
penalty for a breach of which is a sacrifice of a cow to the Earth at
the dance ground. When I discussed this situation with the lineage
heads of the two factions they told me earnestly, though not without
some bitterness, that if they had not co-operated in these rites and
ceremonies according to custom, the ancestors who had instituted
the festivals, and the Earth which is the source of man's food and
security, and which provides the surface and the site for the dance,
would have been angry and this would have brought famine, sickness and death to all.

## V

As might be predicted on general and comparative grounds, the
major Tallensi festivals are timed to anticipate by a month the har-

vest of the main crop of late millet and guinea corn and to sanctify the anticipated first fruits in offerings to the ancestors and the Earth, on the one hand, and the onset of the rainy season as the prelude to the sowing of the key crop of early millet on the other and there is thus a proleptic orientation, one might say of hope rather than a response to fulfilment, in all of these festivals. But Tallensi also see the harvest festival as the celebration of a relief at the ending of the strenuous, taxing and often anxious, emotional economic and social demands of the rainy season. They see it as at the same time bringing in the dry season with its contrasting and, in good years – that is when the harvest has been plentiful – more agreeable pattern of social life. It is not only the season for the more elaborate domestic rituals and cere-monies, but also for visiting, for self display in the market places, and for courtship. It is significant that the Tallis combine *their* har-vest festival which takes place at the actual time of the late millet harvest with the initiation into the Boghar cult of the boys and young men whose turn it is that year. The timing of the initiation rites is not only, as some of the men aver, because the grain and the beer and the chickens and the leisure are all lacking in the rainy season but also because it is especially fitting at harvest time. The great taboo of the Boghar is that late millet may never be used in offerings to the collective ancestors assembled there. The harvest consecrated in the festival is that of the late millet. And the climax of the initiation ritual is the oath sworn by the initiands 'In the name of my father and his late millet,' never to divulge to a non-initiate what goes on in the rituals of the Boghar. The first fruits of late millet thus become the sanction and symbol of the initiate's new status. The pre-sowing festival, by the same token, celebrates the end of the social pattern of the dry season, dances it out so to speak, and gives expression to the hopes, wishes, and fears of the forthcoming rainy season.

It is consistent with the politico-ritual organization of Tallensi society that the rainy season is, in effect, terminated by the Gingaang festival of the chiefly clans, and is inaugurated again as the time of sowing approaches by the Golib festival of the tendaana clans of the Hills. Tallensi think of each festival as stretching over the month of days between one new moon and the next. It seems odd, though a little reflection will show that it is symbolically appro-priate, that these festivals are regarded as unlucky, *nefasti* in the

Roman sense. This is applied in a diffuse way to the harvest festivals, but in very precise terms to the sowing festival. The rule is that no activities may be undertaken that may lead to strife or contention. The explanation generally offered is that at these times, especially when the dances are in full swing, great numbers of people of many different clans and localities come together and it is easy then for friction to build up and develop into brawls or even bloodshed. There are many stories of fights that ended in bloodshed having taken place in the past at festival dances and indeed the 1937 sowing festival was preceded by the sacrifice of a cow at the supreme Earth shrine of the hills in payment, as the elders put it, of a blood debt to the Earth that was incurred in such a fight at a Golib dance many years ago. Thus the activities that proverbially create conflict are forbidden. These include marriage, the giving or receiving of any marriage payments and the celebration of final funerals, for two reasons, firstly because they are announced at night by the same high pitched cries of alarm that were traditionally used as warning signals in time of war, and secondly because funerals bring together men of different clans and communities traditionally carrying their arms to make a martial display in honour of the dead, and this sometimes ended in a fight between men of unrelated clans brought together by the accident of their common kinship of affinal connections with the deceased. During the harvest festival it was regarded as stupid and dangerous but not sinful to commit a breach of any of these rules; during the sowing festival they were spoken of as taboos, transgression of which was sacrilege requiring expiation by sacrifices to the Earth. Thus was affirmed the sovereignty of co-operation, mutual trust and charity, peace and good-will at this time when the benevolence of the supernatural powers which are believed to control the sources of human well-being and affliction is being solicited and besought. Thus was also dramatized the marginal character of these festivals, as times when normal mundane interests must be suspended.

The harvest, or end of rainy season, festivals take place in the lunar month which normally falls in the period covered by September and October. These festivals cannot start until the Baari Tendaana, whose home is on the northern border of the Tallensi country adjacent to the next tribal area of the Gorisi, gives the signal. It is his duty and privilege, in consultation with the senior

Tendaana most closely associated with the chief of Tongo, to keep track of the months and to decide which new moon marks the month for the beginning of the festivals. His announcement is awaited with impatience. During the weeks preceding it, it is a constant topic of conversation not only among elders but also among the women and children. Vehement differences of opinion are apt to arise in this connection. One afternoon in August 1936 I happened to be with the Chief of Tongo and some of his elders and conversation turned as it always does at this time to the forthcoming Gingaang festival. 'Those men of Baari' the chief remarked testily, 'they are just being obstructive, arguing among themselves. Some say the coming month is the festival month of Daakoom and some say no. But look at the guinea corn. It is just beginning to set grain and so surely it is the right time. We must have good rain now to bring the crops to maturity.' He added that he had sent an urgent message to the Baari Tendaana to find out why he had not 'poured the water' – as the libations to announce the New Moon are allusively called. He went on to explain the procedure to me as follows: 'The Baari Tendaana gets a message from the senior Tendaana of the Gorisi tribe next door to say that he has carried out his sacrifices. Then the Baari Tendaana consults with our senior Tendaana here, the Gbizug Tendaana and they agree what month it is. Then when they have carried out their rites, they come to tell me and the Baari Tendaana and I sit down together to perform our ties. Then we Namoos take it from them. When we have danced our Gingaang, the Tallis take it from us and perform their Bogharaam. Then the next tribe, the Namnam, take it and carry out their harvest ceremonies. Then we all look forward to the Golib festival. We can't start until the Baari people finish but again their prayers and sacrifices will be in vain if they don't come to see me and we do what we have to do together.' This statement neatly summarizes the obligatory steps in the sequence of the festivals, as one clan after another takes it up, and the inescapable interdependence of all the clans.

There was, incidentally, a practical as well as a ceremonial reason why the chief was impatient. He must brew beer of the new early millet crop to use in the libations and prayers to the founding ancestors with which he starts the festival. To find out what offerings the ancestors require of him, he must summon a diviner for consultation in the presence of all his elders; then there will be the animals, perhaps even a cow, to find for the required sacrifices; and all this takes at least a week.

## VI

The New Moon was seen a couple of days later and was welcomed with the loud yodelling that is customary at this time. But the Baari Tendaana remained obdurate. He called in to see me and declared firmly 'This is not the New Moon of Daakoom month. They [the chief and his elders] do not know the signs as I do. This is an empty month.' In effect therefore he had decreed an intercalary month which would bring the lunar calendar properly into line with the seasons and state of the crops, which he maintained, were nowhere near grown enough to be harvested, as is normal and proper, at the end of the Gingaang festival.

For the people at large the dancers and the songs or rather chants are the main interest of each festival. During the month or so preceding the festival season men, women, and children talk about the dances with excited anticipation and one finds them in the markets buying cloth for new loin cloths and materials for the new perineal belts the women will display in the dance. It is a time for jubilation they explain since as they put it 'we have lived to see another dance festival'. If the harvest looks promising a splendid turnout is expected for the dances; but in a bad year, it is said, people are weak and lack the spirit to come out in large numbers. Nevertheless the dance *must* take place since it is a ritual obligation.

I have myself taken part in these festivals four times, the last occasion being in 1963. And as it happened the harvests were good in all these years so that the dances were enthusiastically frequented. On the nights of the full moon sounds of the drums, the flutes and the falsetto chants rising above the thunder of stamping feet and of clanking ankle rattles could be heard from miles away. It should be borne in mind that each community, often each clan has its own dances. At the height of the season on a fine moonlight night, there will be Gingaang at Tongo, Yaung at Baari, and other dances going on at the same time in other settlements all over the country. There will be scores of spectators from neighbouring communities at each of the dance grounds. The dance steps and the chants of every clan are well known to people of other clans but no one who is not a

member of a clan by birth would take part in its dance. It is likewise
with the chants, all of which are cast in the same mould of topical
allusion. Sometimes it is to a recent scandal in a traditional opponent clan, sometimes to an item of general interest or concern.
Intermingled with these chants are the praise names of clan heads, of
other important people, or of the most admired young men in the
dance. Some years after I had left the country I learnt that I had been
the subject of the most popular of the Golib chants, the refrain of
which could be translated 'The white man who was here with us
came to pry out our secrets; where is he now and what will he do
with all he knows about us?' On another occasion the theme of one
of the chants was the sorry plight of the young men who could get no
wives because the chiefs were greedily snapping up all the young
women to add to their already huge harems. Yet another derided a
man who had come to visit his sick brother and had taken advantage
of his helplessness to seduce his young wife.

For the Chiefs, the Tendaanas and the elders, however, the significance of the festivals lies primarily in the ritual activities. They stress
the obligatory co-operation required for these rituals, their imperative necessity to ensure the well-being of the land and its people.
Most of all they stress the commemoration of the ancestors and the
homage offered to them in prayers and in sacrifices in order to enlist
their benevolence for the coming year. So for them everything that
pertains to or goes on during the festivals is stamped with the sanctity of its ancestral origins acknowledged in the taboos that mark it
out. The Namoo elders remind one that the dancing ground is
sacred, must never be cultivated and for this reason must never be
trodden upon with a leather-shod foot (a taboo broken only once in
a chief's reign when he is first installed). For the same reason no lineage elder will taste any food made of the newly harvested late
millet, guinea corn or ground beans until the ancestors have first
been offered them. At the height of the Gingaang season there is one
night when dead silence reigns and everyone stays indoors. Dishes of
food and water are set out in the courtyards of the houses, and fine
cloths or other garments are spread out beside them. This is the
night when the ancestors are believed to return to visit their descendants on a sort of tour of inspection and then to take over the dance
ground. The food, the water and the finery are all set out for their
enjoyment. In like fashion, among the Tallis the dances take place in

front of the ancestral homestead of each clan and the rites and ceremonies take place in the sacred groves where the ancestors dwell and
at earth shrines where they are supposed originally to have emerged.

Let me stop for a moment and say a word or two more about the
dances, though I fear I do not have the skill to do them justice. They
are predominantly male activities, mainly on the part of the younger
men and the boys, but the elders always come out from time to time
to show their paces. The dancers of the different communities and of
the different festivals are all quite distinctive in style. The Yaung
with its energetic slurred steps contrasts markedly with the shuffle
and foot stamping of the Gingaang and the measured tread of the
Golib. But all are accompanied by the drums and other musical
instruments pertaining to that particular dance and by the chants,
with a leader screeching the theme solo at the top of his voice and the
dancers coming in with a chorus. Women and girls may join in the
dances, at the side or in a line opposite the young men, but for the
most part they mill around as spectators, now and then shuffling up
to an admired dancer and hailing him with the loud ululating *kpele-
met* that is the customary congratulatory cry of a woman. Where, as
with the Gingaang, the dancers form a circle, women with infants in
arms are often to be found sprawling on the ground or standing
about at the centre.

As for the elders, if one presses them to account for the ritual activities they invariably invoke the ancestors and the powers of the
Earth. 'We must work together' they say, 'speak with a single voice,
else things will go wrong. Look at the Earth, if it were bereft of
people, would it not be empty and useless, and would people at large
without the earth to cultivate and to dwell upon be able to survive?
So it is with us.' They say likewise that there are many things to be
done in these ritual activities and that is why the duties must be
distributed amongst all the lineages that have to take part. I might
add this distribution and diffusion of ritual responsibilities and
privileges can be a great trial to the anthropologist. Many have been
the times when I have arrived at the sacred grove or ancestral shrine
chosen for a sacrifice with my hosts of lineage A only to have to wait
two or three hours in the blazing sun until the elders of lineages, V,
W and Z condescended to appear – this being an invariable gesture
to assert their rights and affirm the indispensability of all participants for the performance of the rite.

If all the lineages which are entitled and obliged to be present are not represented there the offerings will be rejected and the prayers will come to nought. Not only that. Tallensi perceive quite clearly that ritual collaboration in these circumstances is a binding force, a symbolical burial of hatchets, through which the participants commit themselves in principle to peaceful coexistence and mutual trust. So we find among the highlights of the harvest festivals the visit of the Baari Tendaana to the Chief of Tongo when the two together retire to a private corner of the chief's house to pour a libation of pure rain water – with its obvious magical implication – that has been collected by the Tendaana, and jointly pronounce blessings on the rain and invocations to the ancestors and the Earth to bring prosperity, peace and plenty to all. Reciprocally there is the solemn procession, following the path first marked out by the ancestors, of the men escorting the big Gingaang drum from Tongo to Baari to bring the chief's greetings and blessings to the people of Baari on the evening that they assemble for their most esoteric first fruit rites in their central sacred grove.

## VII

To illustrate better what I have been describing I want to take a quick look at one or two of the episodes that occur during the sowing festival, the Golib. Golib is the name of the dance, signifying the meandering circular movement of the dancers at the climax of the festival. It is also the name of the drums and the other sacred relics associated with the central Earth shrine at which the final ceremonies occur. The most important are the drums in the hereditary custody of the Golibdaana; but, characteristically, they can only be brought out for the rites dedicated to them at the proper time in the sequence and in the presence of the other lineage heads or their representatives who are responsible for the festival.

The Golib falls at the end of the dry season, in principle three months after the last of the first fruit festivals. It is the prerogative of the Hill Tallis, each of the fifteen lineages closely packed on top and around the hills having a distinct part to play and a specific ritual responsibility. But it can only start after the chief of Tongo has been apprised and the opening ceremonies are initiated and directed by the senior Tendaana associated with the chief. Thus the concatenation of all the festivals is properly maintained. One upshot of the intricate allocation of the ritual privileges and responsibilities among all the Tallis lineages is so closely to articulate them one with another that no one of them can claim to be supreme in all respects.

In the interval between the end of the first-fruit festivals and the Golib there are minor festivals every month. Most important of these is the Koot of the Tendaanas. It takes place around the end of January the main event being a search of the sacred groves and the areas around them for small animals such as cane rats. After the usual libations of beer and possibly the sacrifice of some chickens the high dry grass is ceremonially set alight. This is a signal for the general firing of the grass and stubble in the fields which always precedes preparations for the first sowing. Till then, firing the dry grass and stubble has been taboo. Explaining the ceremony to me, in 1937, the Gbizug Tendaana said 'We have been looking back to the rainy season and last year's harvest till now. From now on we are looking forward to Golib and the next rainy season and to the early millet crop. It is for the sake of this early millet crop that we do this.' At the end of the day the Tendaana called together all the people, the men, women and children, who had been 'doing the work' as they put it, all day. Then he addressed them in a form of a blessing as follows 'Now that I have finished this Koot ceremony, the early millet everywhere is what I am pleading for.' And as the crowd around him began to clap slowly and cry their thanks in the customary manner of expressing gratitude to superiors, he added 'You may rest assured you will all sleep well, there will be no headaches, no sickness of the stomach. You see this fire – it has driven all evil things away, driven away sickness and death. Go home now and be at peace and now you may chant the Golib songs and prepare for Golib.' 'Koot' he added turning to me, 'marks the half-way line, which divides the dry season into two.' And it is easy to understand the proleptic symbolism of the cleaning and firing of the fields in preparation for the sowing rains.


## VIII

In 1935 the new moon heralding the Golib festival appeared on 7 March when messages were sent from the senior Tendaana to the Chief of Tongo and to his brother Tendaanas. 'The Golib' the chief explained to me 'is a work for the sake of well-being, for the sake of crops, peaceful sleep and health. If I were not apprised before the Tallis start their rites, the country would not prosper. The dead would take offence. This is the way our ancestors did it and we have received it from them.'

A week later the lineage heads and Tendaanas of the Tallis started their beer making and on the 20th the inaugural rite of 'blowing the flutes' took place. Early that morning I received a message from the senior Tendaana saying the day had come. I found him waiting for me dressed up in all his splendid ceremonial antelope skin cloak, his string cap and leather bag without which a Tendaana will go nowhere. Tendaanas have a staff of office known as a *kinkar* which is made of the stalk of a special variety of guinea corn grown and used only by Tendaanas for libations and sacrifices. The senior Tendaana picked up his *kinkar* and taking his seat on what looked like a plain slab of stone in the floor of the inner courtyard, rapped on it thrice in slow succession. 'Yao', he called out 'my father Geribazaa call Tendaan Waaf and do you summon Kpon Kparik. When you have all arrived, go you and call hither all the sacred groves and Earth shrines, for the day has come and we are now going out to the blowing of the flutes. Do you all follow us from behind as we go there, and lead us from in front, so that all may be well. My father Geribazaa, hear me and let us go to our ritual.'

This finished we set off in single file, one of the Tendaana's sons carrying his *kinkar* and leading the way, another following with a large spherical calabash in a net bag and other members of the clan following behind. We were following a path said to have been first traced by the ancestors, and specially cleared for this occasion, to the neighbouring Tallis settlement some two miles away. The path wound past some Namoo homesteads and what struck me was the complete absence of anybody at the usual midday resting place under the shade tree. Namoos say it is a taboo for them to see the Tendaanas taking this path and they are very scrupulous in this observance as I had other occasions to check.

Soon we reached the homestead of the neighbouring Tendaana. Now came a long wait. One by one the other Tendaanas who were due to take part in this ritual arrived and presently we all trooped off to a nearby sacred grove. At the foot of a low mound in this grove lay a bundle of *viis*, the short flute-like whistles normally played for pleasure by cowherds. The local men led by their Tendaana each picked out a flute and blew a couple of blasts. These flutes are stored away by an elder charged with the responsibility from year to year and added to when necessary. They are only brought out for the Golib festival. Characteristically their origin is attributed to the founding ancestors of the clan and it is a ritual prescription that every male member of the clan, even an infant must, at every Golib festival, blow a few blasts on or at least touch one of the flutes. The same practice is followed by all the Tallis clans with their Golib relics. It is said to be a gesture to show belonging to the lineage. Next the visiting Tendaanas and their followers were invited to blow on or touch the whistles. Now came another long waiting period for all participants had not yet arrived.

It was an interesting interlude for me as I sat with the old Gbizug Tendaana. Reclining in the shade, he soliloquized as follows: 'This white man has come to us as a stranger in the same way as the ancestor Mosuor of the Namoos. When Mosuor arrived here our ancestors fled to the hills and when the first white man came here we also fled to the hills. Then Mosuor caught the Tendaana by a strategem and eventually they agreed to live in a friendship side by side. So the ancestors had accepted Mosuor and so must we accept this white man for surely he surpasses Mosuor.' I was intrigued and amused to be thus associated with the myth, or as they would insist the unique historical fact of the arrival of the Namoos among the autochthonous Tallis since it is the keystone of their whole politico-ritual structure. One of the scenes that marks the climax of the Gingaang festival is the ritual acting out of this myth by representatives of the two groups.

It was well past midday before all the eight Tendaanas who were due to take part had assembled. We returned to the mound of flutes and squatted in a circle as is customary in deference to sacred places.

Now the local Wakyi Tendaana spoke: 'Are we all here?', he said, and there was a murmur of assent. 'May I then make the offering?' Again there was a murmur of assent. The spherical calabash we had brought was pushed forward and some water poured from it into a shallow dish. The Tendaana struck the bundle of flutes lightly with both hands, took up the dish and called out 'Yao, my father Tendaana, arise and come and sit here by your Golib flutes. When you come do you call your father Sagbarug and let him call his father, Sorso, (then followed a long list of earlier ancestors to be sum-

moned) ... 'Well then', he continued, 'are you all here? Then call all
the Earth shrines and sacred groves [such a one and such a one and
such a one] for the day of our festival has arrived. Let them all come
and sit here; our sacred grove Kpal is calling them to be here where
the Golib flutes are.' (There followed a further long string of invocations calling upon the ancestors of all the Tallis clans, the sacred
groves and shrines from every part of the country to come and join
the assembly.) It was like a roll call shouted at the top of the voice,
dramatically and passionately, as if the speaker was addressing a
vast audience. Then, as if satisfied that all the ancestors of all the
Tallis clans and all the Earth shrines, sacred groves and relics were
present his voice changed to a pleading tone. 'Oh, Kpal, our sacred
grove,' he said, 'you must see to it that we have early millet, that we
have guinea corn, that we breed sheep and goats to give to you.
Look around. Are there any people here? Look around. Is there
anyone amongst us with a grey beard? Only children are here. Breed
up people for us, oh our fathers. Our ancestors met with nothing of
this kind; our people are at an end. Search out wives for us, search
out children to be born to us, permit the rain to fall propitiously so
that we may sow our early millet and women and children can have
ample food. Ancestors, Earth shrines, look at the sad state of affairs
we have here, join together all of you! Let crops grow, let marriages
take place, let children be born, let no evil befall.'

In parenthesis, let me add that the sombre background of childless
and dying people, hunger and penury so passionately pictured in
this prayer bears no relationship to the reality. It is the conventional
way of appealing to the ancestors in prayer containing almost a
veiled, ostensibly reluctant threat signifying: if you don't provide for
us and we all die out, who will care for you?, rather than an assumption that the ancestors do not know what the reality is.

To return to the Tendaana, he had finished and now he leaned forward pouring some water on the flutes. 'Accept this your water that
you may drink, here on your Golib flutes which we are about to take
up and blow. People have come here to dance, let there be no fighting! If there are quarrelsome people about, keep them at home. It is
up to you. Receive, accept your water here on your flutes.' He
sipped water himself and then handed the dish to a companion. It
was passed from hand to hand, everyone taking a sip. When it
reached the Gbizug Tendaana the old man shook his head, declining

the drink, whereupon his oldest son sitting by his side called out, 'You must drink, it is a taboo.'

'Choose your flutes', called out the local Tendaana. Everyone had been sitting in absolute silence listening intently to the invocation. Now all leapt to their feet and amid laughter and conversation distributed the flutes. They formed a circle and then began an animated piping and whistling in concert. 'Blow more loudly', cried out of the older Tendaanas 'we want the whole country to hear.'

The Golib festival had started. With this the local Tendaana marched off in the direction of a small clump of trees and all followed him. The congregation grouped itself around a small mound of stones, the Earth shrine, the Tendaanas on one side, the rest of us on the other leaving the path between us clear. This, as I learned subsequently, was for the ancestors to be able to enter and sit at the shrine. The leader looked round and cried out, 'Are you all here? All right then, let us do the ritual.' Whereupon he blew a loud blast on his flute, leaning forward as if to direct it to the shrine and the Earth. Immediately the congregation blew a similar blast in response. The action was repeated six times, by the leader with some solemnity, by the congregation half playfully. And this was the tone throughout the rest of the ceremony and indeed throughout the Golib festival, silent solemnity when the ancestors were being invoked being followed by cheerful laxity.

Following behind the local Tendaana the congregation stopped at a similar Earth shrine twenty-five yards or so away and repeated the ritual performance. Characteristically, an elder had commented that the correct procedure was to pipe only three times at each shrine. The leader thanked him adding that as it was the first time that he had had to take the lead he had confused this with another ritual. The number three, it should be added, is the ritual number symbolical of the male sex, hence all ritual that is concerned with males is carried out in units of three. Since all the ritual activities during the festivals are, like all other ritual activities connected with Tallensi ancestor worship, carried out by men only, and are directed towards patrilineal ancestors, it is appropriate for every rite to be performed thrice. But the lack of rigidity in Tallensi attitudes about ritual formalities is well illustrated in this episode.

For the next two hours the congregation was thus led to a dozen or more of such Earth shrines, one after the other, where the same procedure was repeated. What interested me particularly was that several of these Earth shrines were scattered amongst Namoo homesteads, in some cases only a few yards from the homestead gateway but nowhere was a single inhabitant of these homesteads to be seen out of doors.

It is a strict taboo for Namoos to see these rites or be seen, the senior Tendaana's son explained to me. Anyone who breaks it will have to bring an offering to the Earth in expiation. Let me add, again in parenthesis that Namoos do, as they say, chance to see these rites and do in fact know all about them. How could it be otherwise, seeing they are such close neighbours to the participants, very few of whom are, in fact, not related to them by some tie of kinship. But Namoos emphasize that those who thus sin, venial and minor as the sin is regarded to be, will always bring a small expiatory offering to the nearest Earth shrine. For one never knows whether or not one has committed an offence that will be resented by the occult powers. It is the location of these Earth shrines, by the way, that is cited as proof of the original possession of the land by the autochthonous Tendaana clans, and of their having allocated this area to the immigrant Namoos.

The circuit of apprising all of the Earth shrines and, as was explained to me, through them, also, all the other Earth shrines and ancestors of Tallis clans and indeed of the country as a whole, finished at a great boulder overgrown with bushes and scrub near the foot of the hills. This was the Earth shrine that would, like a herald, pass on the ritual task to the Hill Tallis who would be responsible for the subsequent episodes in the festival.

Here the flutes were all piled in a heap. One of the Tendaanas stepped forward with a calabash of water in his hand, pronounced a long invocation calling upon the ancestors and the Earth shrines in the same form and with the same requests and pleas as in the earlier opening rites.

# IX

We had all been squatting in the customary way during the invocation. As it ended an elder shouted out 'Come along now everybody, hoe the millet.' Thereupon first the Tendaanas, and following them the congregation at large, as they squatted there, began to go through the motions of pulling up weeds or wielding a hoe. Com-

plete silence reigned though smiles and even some laughter indicated
that this so palpably mimetic, magical, an activity was being taken
in a lighthearted spirit. This, let me add, is significant; for Tallensi
do not believe that such mimetic performances in ritual situations,
for all their apparently magical intentions, actually have productive
efficacy. Work, skill, and foresight, with the aid of the ancestors and
the Earth, are what produces crops. The miming rites are understood to express only people's hopes and wishes.

In a few minutes everybody trooped to a large flat rock where all
the Tendaanas sat down. Now a dance began at the edge of what
had become a crowd of a couple of hundred people. As they danced
they chanted at the top of their voice, 'The Tendaanas have seen the
moon and they have assembled here; the Tendaanas have arrived to
watch the dance.' The Tendaanas looked on benevolently as they
rested. A half hour or so passed and then the Tendaanas, pushing
their way through the crowd, all made for the homestead of the
founding ancestors at which we had first arrived in the morning.
They entered the homestead but soon emerged holding their *kinkar*
staffs aloft. They pushed into the crowd and all together broke into a
dance, leaping, stamping and gesticulating with their staffs.

They were inaugurating the Golib dance. It went on for a half-
hour or so by which time the elderly Tendaanas were obviously
exhausted. At this point, with much shouting and pushing, the
younger men cleared a large space in the centre of the crowd. Here
the Tendaanas assembled in a circle. 'Hoe your millet', shouted the
local Wakgi Tendaana; whereupon all the Tendaanas moved forward in what was to me the most extraordinary ritual of the day.
The leader intoned at the top of his voice, 'Hoe your millet, woo',
and the Tendaanas together with the crowd at large responded, so
that it reverberated in the hills, 'Wayoo, wayoo.' Chanting as before
the leader cried out 'Gbizug Tendaana, hoe your millet, woo', and
the crowd answered as before. One of the other Tendanaas took up
the chant 'Wakyi Tendaana, hoe your millet, woo', and again the
crowd answered and so it went on, each of the Tendaanas present,
and some absentees from distant parts, being thus called upon to
'hoe the millet'.

But this was not all. As the chant went on the Tendanaas marched
slowly forward with solemn dignified steps. Then they formed into a
circle and moving anti-clockwise slowly went through the motions

of hoeing the ground with their long staffs, the crowd surrounding them imitating with whatever stick or implement they could lay hands on. This went on for about half an hour. Then the Tendaanas threaded their way through the dancing crowd and entered the ancestral homestead. Spreading out they sprawled in the central courtyard, exhausted but cheerful, bantering one another about their various ages and commenting on the dance. 'Young men today', scornfully remarked the most wizened of these elderly men, 'haven't got the strength to dance the way we used to', and murmurs of assent came from the others. At that point five dishes of the cold gruel made of millet flour mixed with cold water that is commonly offered to guests was brought out and distributed amongst the Tendaanas. They drank their fill and then one by one rose to go home.

# X

My description of this opening ceremony of the Golib, detailed as it seems, does not, in fact, include all the minutiae. It is enough, however, to give an idea of the pattern of ritual activity that is typical of all the Golib ceremonies, and indeed, of those of the other festivals. The so-patent miming (may the shade of Sir James Frazer take note!) of the hoped for successful farming season is repeated at the climax of Golib in a dawn ceremony dedicated to the supreme Earth shrine of Hill Tallis. This is the last of the ritual activities carried out by these Hill-top clans. Their inconvenient (from my point of view) timing of them for the crack of dawn is explained by the notion – which we can easily see to be symbolically appropriate – that this is the most propitious time in the cycle of the day and night for occult powers of the ancestors and the Earth to be present. The pattern is the same: The relics are brought out, the lineage heads whose duty it is to come together gradually assemble, the Tendaana or other ritual officiant for a particular occasion pronounces an invocation exactly on the lines of the opening invocation that I have summarized. The themes are the same: give us propitious rain, good crops, wives, children, health and well-being. Crowds assemble and there is a great dance which lasts till the sun is high. The programme is repeated every other day for a week. Finally, the Tendaanas again followed by an enormous crowd of men, women and children assemble at the house of the Chief of Tongo. Libations are poured and the chief comes out to the multitude in all his finery to pronounce the blessing invoking his ancestors and ending with the wishfulfilling assurances that the rains would fall propitiously, crops would grow well, men, women and children would eat to satiety, and sickness and death would depart from the land. Up to that point, Namoos have been merely spectators at the dances and the Chief has played no part in the ritual activities. Now he receives acknowledgement as the holder of the pivotal office in the whole chain of ritual festivals, in relation to which the inescapable interdependence of the immigrant, secularly defined Namoos and the autochthonous ritually defined Tallis clans is most specifically focused.

It is worth recording that on the three occasions when I took part in the Golib ceremonies, rain fell within hours of their end and sufficiently within the next two weeks to permit of the sowing of the early millet. Naturally, the Chief and his elders on the one side, the Tendaanas on the other, all in private took the credit for this to themselves. But some of the credit also redounded to my presence and stood me in good stead in my later relationships with all the parties.

## XI

There is a question that will, I am sure occur to everybody, and that is as to what has happened to these festivals since I first saw and had the privilege of taking part in them forty years ago. In 1963, when my wife and I spent some time with the Tallensi, we found the Gingaang in full swing. The songs for the event were being enthusiastically rehearsed by a group of sixth form schoolboys home from their boarding schools for the holidays with the assistance of some young men also home for the holidays from their teacher training colleges and the local teachers, clerks, and, of course, the non-literate stay-at-homes. When we attended the dance one evening we were nearly turned away by some schoolboys because as they said we were wearing leather shoes which they said were tabooed at the dancing ground. I got around them rather meanly, I am afraid, by arguing that what were forbidden were the traditional leather *taghara*, sandals, not European shoes and with typical Tallensi practicality they withdrew their objections. The chants, the dance and the accompanying drumming and fluting were exactly like those of forty years ago and the spirit of the crowds and of the dancers was the same. The Chief and his elders described to me all the ritual steps that had already been taken and those that were planned and it was obvious that no changes had taken place in the general pattern.

I was assured that it is the same with all the other festivals. Indeed there were indignant protests when I hinted that with the spread of literacy, schooling and the encroachment of Christianity, modern economic and political changes – let alone the absence abroad of so many young men and women – the festivals would soon be abandoned. The old assertion that 'we will never give up the ways of our ancestors' came from all quarters, from the educated Tallensi clerks and teachers and the two Tallensi M.P.s as well as from the older, still non-literate traditionalist men and women. My wife and I had impressive proof of this when I went to see the old friend who had first enabled me, in 1935, to break through the resistance of the Hill Tallis and be initiated into their Boghar cult. It was just at the time of their Bogharaam festival. So, as is proper for every initiate I was invited to join in the festival and my wife and I attended all the rites of the Boghar like any other member of the cult. My wife had to undergo the initiation ritual in the capacity of a supplicant for the beneficence of the Boghar. As a matter of interest, when we were brought into the Boghar grove I was subjected to a severe cross examination as to why I had so long failed to discharge the debt of a cow I owed the Boghar which I had promised when I was originally initiated in 1935. 'You thought you could escape our ancestors', the presiding officiant scolded, 'but you see they have brought you back to pay your debt.' And pay up I had to.

Lastly, the Golib. In 1971 when I was back in Ghana I learnt that the festival was kept up in all its glory. But there had been an important change. It had become known all over Ghana, partly through the advertisements put out by the government tourist office and partly by reason of the large number of foreigners, whites and others now to be found all over Ghana, as a splendid traditional dance. So in 1970 a team of field officers had gone up from the University of Ghana Institute of African Studies to film and tape-record the festival. I was permitted to play through and listen to the tape recording of the final ceremony at the Hill Top Earth shrine and was deeply moved to hear almost the same invocation recited by a grandson of the officiant who had offered it in 1935 and 1937 and in almost the same words.

But there is another, to me less appealing aspect to the opening up

of these festivals to the general public which is now possible on
account of the excellent road system and the modern tourist-
oriented attitude of the national media and of governmental authorities. Every year now, I learnt, scores of 'foreigners', such as
educated Ghanaians of other tribes and communities who happen to
be working in the area as civil servants, professionals and so forth,
but also many Europeans and the ubiquitous Americans, travel up
to the Hills for the final dance. Films have been made, both by ama-
teurs and by professionals, tape recordings have been made, and so
forth. Indeed I know of one man in this country who happened to be
in Ghana on some mission who has a most remarkable collection of
colour photographs of all the sacred relics – nowadays readily displayed to visiting enquirers, doubtless for a consideration – and the
dances and other activities of the final days of the Golib. Needless to
say he has not the slightest idea as to what it is all about. He knows
that these are some kind of 'fetish' objects and that there are some
vigorous 'primitive' dances connected with them.

However, I have authoritative information that the more private,
traditionally esoteric rituals are still carried on in the traditional
way, sometimes with the ever-inquisitive Catholic missionaries present.

But will this go on for much longer? I suspect that there will be
some decisive changes, now that the privacy, the pride in the autonomy and the significance for the independent identity of each of the
participating lineages has been breached. The corresponding festivals in Southern Ghana continue. But their emphasis has changed.
Their ritual significance for the cycle of the seasons, the state of the
crops and the well-being of the community is now of secondary consideration, even though the libations and invocations continue to be
performed by the responsible chiefs and elders whether they be
Christian or not. They have been detached from their traditional
moorings, the religious and cosmological contexts of meaning, even
though the forms persist, and have become primarily demonstrations of local patriotism and communal self esteem, concerned
with the internal expression of solidarity as against other communities.

This is a trend which conforms to what has happened with similar
festivals in other parts of the world. Their religious meanings fade
out and the ritual activities and observances that are preserved turn
into more explicitly dramatic or rhetorical devices for singling out

and giving structure to the festivals in contrast to the mundane routines of normal daily life. In this way they serve to affirm the belonging-together, the solidarity and unity, of a community, be it only in a symbolic sense of making its members aware of their dependence on one another and of the need for some basis of mutual trust in their pursuit of common ends and values. Christmas and Easter take on this shape more and more. But a better instance is what has happened to such festivals as the Passover among Jews all over the world, not least in Israel. Non-religious and even anti-religious *kibbutzim* in Israel, as is well known, make a big thing of celebrating the Passover and other traditionally religious festivals; but they are turned into secular festivities for the display of patriotic pride and community identification. This trend towards emphasizing the communal and political as against the religious aspects of their festivals will, I suspect, come increasingly to the fore among the Tallensi, in step with the social and cultural changes that loom ahead.

And there is another feature of such seasonal festivals that seems to survive all changes. I refer to their commemorative signification. Here we meet with a propensity that, to my mind, lies at the very roots of human social organization. No society can hold together without a set of assumptions, crystallized in beliefs, myths, institutionalized practices and sanctions, that it has a past going back to knowable if not known founders, and these assumptions must, periodically, be asserted to be indisputably valid. At bottom this goes back, no doubt, to the fact that no individual in any society can feel himself and show himself to be a complete person if he cannot know and be known to have ancestry, at the very least to have had real, living parents. Seasonal festivals represent a special kind of elaboration of ways of making realizable this elemental fact of human nature as it fits into the matrix of a particular social system in its relations to its natural environment, its cultural equipment and its historical situation.[2]

# 4

## Ancestor worship in Africa

It has long been recognized that ancestor worship is a conspicuous feature of African religious systems (cf. Tylor 1971, II, p. 115; Smith 1950). Among the Tallensi of Ghana, as I have shown in previous publications, it so pervades their social life as to put them on a par with the Chinese and the Romans in this respect. To a greater or lesser degree this holds for all the peoples of Negro stock in Africa.

There is general agreement that, wherever it occurs, ancestor worship is rooted in domestic, kinship and descent relations, and institutions. It is described by some as an extension of these relations to the supernatural sphere, by others as a reflection of these relations, yet again as their ritual and symbolic expression.

Comparatively viewed, African ancestor worship has a markedly uniform structural framework. The congregation of worshippers invariably comprises either an exclusive common descent group, or such a group augmented by collateral cognates, who may be of restricted or specified filiative provenance or may come from an unrestricted range; or else the worshippers in a given situation may comprise only a domestic group, be it an elementary family or a family of an extended type.

In the paradigmatic case, congregations of the first kind represent ancestor worship in the structural context of the corporate lineage; and those of the second kind show us its family context. Here spouses, who are, of course, formally affines, not kin, participate by right of marriage and parenthood, not of descent or filiation, as do members of the first kind of congregation.

It may be thought that this paradigm does not apply to the worship of royal or chiefly ancestors. In fact we can see that it does if we look closely at the ethnographic details. The Swazi (cf. Kuper 1947, p. 192) illustrate this. It is the King who appeals to his ancestors on behalf of the nation, as any headman might do in the more limited descent group context. At the yearly sacrifice to the royal ancestors each animal 'is dedicated to a specific ancestor and may only be eaten by descendants in specific kinship categories' (ibid., p. 195). *Qua* cult, in the strict sense of the offering of ritual tendance and service, the worship of royal ancestors follows the pattern of family and lineage ancestor worship. Its national significance derives from the political rank of the worshipped ancestors not from their ancestral status.

It could be argued that the delimitation of the group of worshippers by rules of kinship, descent, and marriage is implicit in the very concept of ancestor worship. But it is in fact not just tautologously implied. For investigation has shown that a congregation does not offer ritual service or respect to all their common ancestors in every situation of worship. The ancestors acknowledged in a given situation are primarily only those who are exclusive to the worshipping group and therefore distinguish that group unequivocally from collateral and co-ordinate groups of a like sort, who have remoter ascendants in common with them, and worship jointly with them in situations of common concern. This is well exemplified in segmentary lineage systems with ancestor worship, where descent divisions of all orders are defined, as Freedman remarks for the Chinese, 'in terms of the cult of the ancestors'.

This is not the same as the purely mnemonic use and perpetuation of pedigrees and genealogies. They may serve simply as a calculus to distinguish persons and groups for jural purposes, such as the assignment of rights, duties and status, in relation to property, office and rank, or for ritual purposes, such as liability to death, birth or caste pollution, or for establishing titles to membership of a corporate group. This is not necessarily associated with a religious cult of ancestors. The Tiv (cf. Bohannan, L. and P. 1953) are a case in point, and this is true also of the Nuer (cf. Evans-Pritchard, E. E. 1956, p. 162). There is much more to ancestor worship than its utility as a means of mapping out and providing a charter for a genealogically ordered social structure.

Yet ancestor worship strictly defined presupposes geneonymy, that is the commemoration of ancestors by name. In the paradigmatic case (e.g. of the Tallensi) ancestors are worshipped by name and the names are perpetuated in the lineage genealogies and personal pedigrees in an accepted generation sequence. Moreover, these genealogies are equally essential for the correct constitution of congregations of worshippers, for the exact focusing of their ritual service, and for the organization of social relations in all domains of social structure.

An ancestor is a named, dead forbear who has living descendants of a designated genealogical class representing his continued structural relevance. In ancestor worship such an ancestor receives ritual service and tendance directed specially to him by the proper class of his descendants. Being identified by name means that he is invested with attributes distinctive of a kind of person.

I labour what might seem to be a trivial point because confusion has long prevailed in the literature through equating ancestor worship with cults of the dead. Yet Durkheim warned (1915, cf. English translation, 1932, p. 62) that 'by itself, death has no deifying virtue'; Radcliffe-Brown came close to seizing the point in noting that 'the belief in the world of spirits rests on the actual fact that a dead person continues to affect society' (1922, p. 304); and Gluckman, in following this up (1937), drew attention to differences between ancestral cults and religious concern with the dead. The distinguished and erudite authority on Chinese religion and philosophy, J. J. M. De Groot, was typical in his view that 'the worship of the dead in China is the worship of the ancestors' (1910, p. 60); and in African ethnography, to stick to our proper study, Junod's still unsurpassed description of a system of ancestor worship quite simply assumes that death is both the necessary and the sufficient condition for attaining 'deification' as an ancestor spirit (Junod 1927, ii, p. 424 ff.).

If ancestor worship is subsumed under the worship of the dead, then its meaning must be sought in customary beliefs and practices concerning death, the soul, ghost, spirits, and the after-life.

But the facts of ethnography and history show that ritual dealings with ghosts or spirits or shades, whose preterhuman character and existence is attributed to the transformation brought about by death and apparently recognized in funerary rites, are not the same as true ancestor cults. The ancient Greeks appear to have had elaborate cults concerned with beliefs about ghosts and shades, but no true ancestor cult (cf. Guthrie 1950). The two are found side by side, but well distinguished, in the religious system of the Chinese, as all our authorities point out (e.g. De Groot). Nuer sacrifices and prayers evidently express awe of ghosts of the dead but, as I have already noted, they do not have ancestor worship. And to turn to West Africa, my impression is that the Ga give ritual reverence to their dead forbears but do not have an ancestor cult in the precise sense in which I am employing this term (cf. Field 1937). Indeed we need look no further afield than our own civilization to see the difference. Catholics have a cult of saints as Tylor remarked (op. cit.) and say masses for named dead; Jews commemorate them by name in the course of the celebration of their New Year and their Day of Atonement, as well as on the anniversaries of particular deaths. Yet we do not consider either Catholics or Jews to be ancestor worshippers.

Following Tylor, those who regard the contents of the rites and beliefs and observances as the primary phenomena of ancestor worship necessarily seek to interpret it as a product of eschatological ideas and of doctrines about souls and spirits. Others follow Malinowski (1922, ch. III) and seek an explanation in the need for emotional reassurance against loss and against the dread of annihilation. I do not say that such considerations are irrelevant for a complete analysis of ancestor worship. I do not forget that it is a branch of religion and of moral philosophy, not to speak of its functions as a theory of causation. What I wish to bring out is that the structural matrix of ancestor worship which is my chief concern here, and the code of beliefs, values, and symbols used in the cult, are analytically distinguishable aspects. This is clear if we bear in mind that death is a necessary but not sufficient condition for the attainment of ancestorhood.

Every culture provides what Dr Field (op. cit. p. 93 ff.) has aptly called a 'dogma of human personality', that is to say an accepted formulation, be it pragmatical, mystical, or naturalistic, of the physical and psychical constitution of man. This establishes the conceptual premises and the symbolic images of the nature, causes, and consequences of death and of the relations between the living and the dead. It serves as the warrant for the lore and observances by means of which the experience of the individual's death as irrevocable is reconciled with acquiescence in the continuity of the living community. From a different angle, however, the dogma of personality is a representation of the social capacities and potentialities with which a person is endowed in virtue of his social roles and relationships. Doctrines of the soul and of after-life existence belong not only to religion but also to the apparatus of politico-jural and moral custom by means of which these capacities and potentialities are salvaged and ploughed back into the life of society after the individual's death. Tikopian ideas about the soul are, says Firth (1955), 'restatements of social structure at a symbolic level'. It is this structural framework that interests me here.

Thus ancestor worship, though it consists descriptively of ritual relations with dead forbears, is not co-terminous with the worship of the dead.

One indication of this, as Gluckman discerned (loc. cit.), is that full blown ancestor worship often goes with only the sketchiest lore about the mode of existence of the dead and a clear distinction, in belief and ritual, between them and worshipped ancestors. Pressed hard, Tallensi elders are quite ready to surmise that the departed must exist somewhere, in heaven or in the earth, and no doubt do so in ways that mirror life in this world. Mostly they say, how can we know? Some speculative elders point out that when a wife dies she is buried among her husband's kin and is invoked in her funeral rites to join his lineage ancestors, that is, her affines. Presumably, therefore, the dead live together in families as they did when alive. But a wife on her death is given two funerals, a primary funeral in her conjugal settlement where she is mourned by her husband and her children, as wife and mother, and a secondary one when she is 'taken back home' to her paternal lineage. There she is mourned as daughter and sister and is besought to 'reach' her own fathers and forefathers. Has she then, two 'souls', one which goes to join her husband's lineage ancestors and one which goes to join her natal lineage ancestors? No Tallensi would accept this argument. What is significant for them, as for the observer, is that cognizance is taken in the rituals that terminate her social existence in the flesh, of the two critical jural statuses a woman passes through in her life cycle. Again, vague suppositions that animals and libations offered to ancestors become their spirit flocks and herds and food and drink, can be elicited from thoughtful men. But this is not taken as serious doctrine and there is no hint of it in the complex and elaborate rituals, prayers and observances in which ancestor worship is daily put into action.

The picture is typical of African ancestor worshippers. The Thonga, according to Junod (pp. 347 ff. vol. 2) are just as vague about the after-life. If anything, they seem to distinguish more precisely between the ghostly dead without offspring, whose existence may be a nuisance to the living, and ancestors, who have descendants to bring them offerings and give them reverent service. The Dahomeans, whose religious institutions and ideology exhibit refinements not reached by the more matter-of-fact Tallensi and Thonga, distinguish precisely between the dead (*chio*) and the ancestors (*tovodu*), and have intricate ceremonies for 'deifying' their dead and so transforming them into ancestors ritually eligible to be worshipped (Herskovits, ch. XI. vol. I). With their subtle theory of the personality as made up of several souls inhabiting a body moulded out of a substance described as clay, the Dahomeans might be expected to have a rich eschatology and a vivid picture of the after-world. These elements of their religious system are certainly more elaborate than those of the Tallensi or Thonga but still meagre and amorphous by contrast with the ceremonies, rites, and social and political setting of their ancestral cults (Herskovits, vol. II, especially ch. XXXI). This is equally true of the Ashanti (cf. Busia 1954; Rattray 1927). Both religious systems have pantheons of gods and nature deities as well as ancestor cults. Yet by comparison, for example, with the Greeks or Hindus their mythologies of the 'spirit world' are thin and unimpressive. Worship in rituals of prayer and sacrifice, the observance of religious prescriptions in the form of taboo and injunction, and submission to such moral norms as the incest prohibition, may all be validated by reference to what we describe as spiritual beings, be they gods or ancestors or nature deities. But none of this, it is evident, necessitates a circumstantial cosmography of a 'spirit world'. Religious beliefs and practices can be carried on perfectly well without a doctrine or lore of the nature and mode of existence of the 'beings' to whom they are ostensibly directed.

In Christian civilization the popular notion of the soul appears to be that it is a detachable spiritual essence which leaves the body on death and then enters on a state of existence which must be accounted for. This is done by assuming a kind of law of the conservation of entities in a total universe made up of two complementary regimes, a regime of nature and a regime of deity. By this reckoning souls are indestructible essences that animate bodies and succeed them in the timeless realm of God, pending resurrection in a corporeal form. It is therefore logically necessary to account for their immortality by providing a picture of an after-life, as is done for us by our mythology and theology.

But we must not project our vulgar cosmology on to other cultures. The concepts of the psychical constituents of personality held by the Tallensi, the Ashanti, and the Dahomeans, for example, do not have the metaphysical implications of the Christian notion of the soul. They refer to activities, relationships, and experiences that are deemed to fall wholly within the regime of nature. So mortuary ceremonies, though couched in language and rites that appear to personify the dead, are in fact not directed towards consigning them to, and equipping them for spiritual existence in a supernatural realm, but towards discorporating them from the social structure. At the personal level this resolves the dislocation and assuages the grief of bereavement. But death and mortuary rites, though they must precede, do not confer ancestorhood. Specific rites are needed for that. The dead has first to be 'brought back home again', re-established in the family and lineage, by obsequial rites, and will even then not receive proper ritual service until he manifests himself in the life of his descendants and is enshrined (cf. Fortes 1949, p. 329).

When a particular deceased – and it is always a particular person – is thus reinstated as an ancestor it is, as I have argued, because he has living descendants of the right category. His reinstatement in this status establishes his continued relevance for his society, not as a ghost, but as a regulative focus for the social relations and activities that persist as the deposit, so to speak, of his life and career.

Can we identify the critical characteristics of ancestorhood more exactly? Ashanti doctrine is quite explicit on this issue. Only matrilineal forbears become ancestors who receive worship. So that constituent of the personality which is transmitted by the father and is symbolized in the *ntoro* cult and its derivative, the *sunsum*, is not imagined to survive in a supernatural realm after death. Rattray (1923, p. 53) says it is believed to remain behind to look after persons of the same *ntoro*. As to what constituent of the living person is transmuted into an ancestor, our authorities are vague and I myself never succeeded in getting a coherent account from my informants. An ancestral 'spirit' is not thought of as a kind of nebulous being or personified mystical presence but primarily as a name attached to a relic, the stool, standing for ritual validation of lineage ancestry and for mystical intervention in human affairs. In more concrete terms it is thought of as the counterpart, in the context of the lineage cult, of the matrilineal component of the living person.

As is well known (cf. Fortes 1950), an Ashanti father has a specially intimate personal relationship with his children during their infancy. He takes a direct responsibility for their upbringing which the mother's brother does not normally have. And the unique moral relationship thus engendered is recognized in the belief that the father's *sunsum* influences the well-being of his child before they have a common *ntoro*. It stands to reason that a father will live on in his children's memory much more vividly and affectionately after his death than will a mother's brother. But it is the latter and not the former who may have a stool dedicated to him and becomes the ancestor for purposes of worship. For, though sons honour their father's memory,[1] ancestor worship by sacrifice, libation, and prayer is a lineage cult; a cult, that is, of the basic politico-jural unit of Ashanti society, not of the domestic unit in which both parents count. In other words, ancestor worship belongs to the region of kinship and descent structure in which law, backed by the sanctions of the political order, regulates social relations and conduct, as opposed to the region of patri-filial relationships in which conduct is ruled by moral and spiritual considerations. In this sense, ancestor worship is an aspect of citizenship in the politico-jural domain, not of membership of domestic groups.

It is the same in other matrilineal systems, for example, that of the Nayar of S. India (cf. Gough 1958) and the Plateau Tonga (cf. Colson 1954). Ancestorhood is conferred on persons of the parental generation who have jural authority in living social relations, not on those who imprint their personalities on their offspring by virtue of their part in bringing them up. Indeed, the rule is more stringent than this. For among the Ashanti, as among the Nayar, ancestor-hood does not automatically supervene for everybody who has the status of a mother's brother. Normally it is only those members of a lineage who have been invested with authority, i.e. jurisdiction in the lineage, as lineage heads or as the holders of office in the external politico-jural domain, who become permanently enshrined in stools of worship. The rule applies, of course, equally in the patrilineal descent systems as was already discerned by Fustel de Coulanges, but with modifications. In a patrilineal system jural authority and parental responsibility are combined in the same persons. But it is only the authority component of the relationships between successive generations that is transformed into ancestorhood (cf. Fortes 1961).

Before we go further, let us see if the hypothesis is consistent with the converse of ancestorhood, that is, the status of the worshippers. In the paradigmatic cases worshippers stand in a filial or descent relationship to the ancestors they worship. This principle is of general application. It is rigorously observed among the Tallensi. Only a son can offer sacrifices to ancestors; and he can do so only if his relevant parent is dead, that is, if that parent has become an ancestor. Sacrifices to a pre-parental ancestor or ancestress can only be offered through a parent who has become an ancestor. Thus a man cannot offer sacrifices to his patrilineal ancestors of any generation whatsoever unless his own father is one of them. He has the right of ritual access, and the corresponding duties, directly to his own ancestor-father and calls upon other ancestors through him, just as he traces his descent through him. This is the normal rule for all acts and observances of ancestor worship. That is why a man cannot, for example, sacrifice directly to his deceased mother's brother, but must have the latter's son do so on his behalf, even if he and his mother's brother had close bonds of affection and trust during the latter's life.

The apparent exception proves the rule. This is the case where a chief, tendaana, or any other lineage head who has the custody of the lineage *boghar*, is entitled and bound to officiate in sacrifices to the founding ancestors. He does so then in his capacity as a *successor* to office (cf. the parallel case of the Swazi king previously referred to). But we must remember that a son, among the Tallensi as among other peoples with patrilineal descent, is a jural minor during his father's life, and becomes *sui iuris*, jurally autonomous within the limits of his lineage status, and in virtue of this capable of officiating in the ancestor cult, only when his father dies. In other words it is as a *successor* to his father's jural status that a son acquires the capacity to act independently in ritual. Hence the obsequial ceremonies which reinstate a deceased father as an ancestor in his family and lineage end by ritually releasing his eldest son from jural minority and ritual dependence and establish him as his father's heir. Jural autonomy is the prerequisite condition for entitlement to responsibility in religious matters, shown especially in the right to officiate in the ancestor cult; and this is achieved by a step analogous to succession to office. Roman law, with its characteristic sociological exactitude, understood and recognized this in the concept of the heir as the 'universal successor'. As Maine explains in his beautiful discussion of Testamentary Succession (Ch. VI), the 'prolongation of a man's legal existence in his heir or in a group of co-heirs' is exactly parallel to succession in a corporation. Thus in the instance we are discussing a man who accedes to an office vested in a lineage by right of succession has a status relation to his deceased predecessor analogous to that of a son who steps into his dead father's status in the domestic group.

*Mutatis mutandis*, the position is the same in matrilineal systems. Officiating in ancestor worship, as opposed to participating in group worship, is the prerogative of succession to the office or status of the class of ancestors to whom worship and offerings are given in a specific context of social structure and occasion. Reduced to its elementary core, among the Tallensi, the son has the right and duty to offer prayer and sacrifice directly to the father (and by extension, the father's forefathers) whom he replaces in the social structure – the lineage head, directly to the predecessors he has replaced as lineage head. This is an oversimplified formulation but it will help to sharpen the analysis. I have, for instance, left out the ramifications of matrilateral ancestor worship,[2] and the qualifications that should be made to take account of sibling relations, among the Tallensi, as well as considerations of the cult of 'royal' Stools in Ashanti. I refrain, also, from discussing the well-known fact that women, in such patrilineal systems as that of the Tallensi, have no right to officiate or even to take any autonomous action in the worship of either their own ancestors or those of their husbands, though they have as close personal relationships with parental kin as their brothers and husbands. The explanation long ago given by Fustel de Coulanges, to wit that women have no juridical independence, and therefore no religious status in their own right, holds for African patrilineal descent systems. Nor need I elaborate on the fact that accessory lineages of slave or stranger origin never acquire the right of direct access to the shrine of the founding ancestor of their host lineage.

All these data point to the same conclusion. Ancestor worship is a representation or extension of the authority component in the jural relations of successive generations; it is not a duplication, in a supernatural idiom, of the total complex of affective, educative, and supportive relationships manifested in child-rearing, or in marriage, or in any other form of association, however long-lasting and intimate, between kinsmen, neighbours, or friends. It is not the whole man, but only his jural status as the parent (or parental personage, in matrilineal systems) vested with authority and responsibility, that is transmuted into ancestorhood.[3] It devolves as an inescapable right and duty on the ancestor's filial successor to perform the service and duty of worship; and this is quite irrespective of what the personal relations of the ancestor and his custodian-worshipper might have been. Hence, not surprisingly, in such a developed system of ancestor worship as that of the Tallensi, the personality and character, the virtues or vices, success or failures, popularity or unpopularity, of a person during his lifetime make no difference to his attainment of ancestorhood. This was repeatedly brought home to me by Tallensi elders. A man may be a liar, or a wastrel, or an adulterer, a quarrelsome neighbour, or a negligent kinsman; he may be a mean and bad-tempered parent who has made his sons' life miserable; he may have been abroad for years and have contributed nothing to their upbringing. If he dies leaving a son, he becomes an ancestor of equal standing with any other ancestor. To put it in the believer's words, he acquires the power to intervene in the life and affairs of his descendants in exactly the same way as any other ancestor.

On the other hand, a man may be a paragon of virtue, as parent and as kinsman, respected as citizen and successful in his career, if he leaves no son he cannot become an ancestor; or, at best, among the Tallensi, if he has a daughter he may become a matrilateral ancestor, of secondary worth only, to her sons and their descendants. One of my friends, a man of a truly noble character, revered for his wisdom and benevolence, and one of his chief's most trusted councillors, was pointed out as being in danger of this grievous fate because he had no surviving sons; and daughters 'do not inherit'.[4]

From the opposite side, what holds for ancestors holds reciprocally for their descendants. It behoves a son to accept his parental forbears, in their character as ancestors, into his family and lineage, to tend their shrines, perform such ritual services for them, as making offerings and pouring libations when these are demanded, irrespective of his sympathies or aversions, and without regard to his character or achievements. It is the oldest living son who has the main responsibility for the ritual tendance and service of his parent ancestors. These duties begin with the obligation to attend to their burial and funeral rites and continue as the obligation and privilege of being the primary officiant in the ritual service rendered by all the members of the filial-sibling group. Now it makes no difference what sort of a person the eldest son may be. He may be a good-for-nothing, or a half-wit; he may have quarrelled with the dead parent and have left the parental home; he may be destitute, a notorious thief, what you will. The responsibility for initiating, supervising, and taking the leading part in the mortuary and funeral ritual for his parents is unavoidably his and so are the consequential, life-long duties of ancestor worship. He can refuse them only at the dire peril of disaster inflicted by the ancestors; he cannot be deprived of them, except at the dire peril of those who try to do so (Fortes 1949, 1959).

What must be particularly stressed is that ancestors behave in exactly the same ways, in the ways expected of them and permitted to them in the ancestral cult, quite irrespective of what their lifetime characters might have been. The ancestor who was a devoted father and conscientious provider for his family in his lifetime is divined to be the source of illness, misfortune, and disturbance in his descendants' lives in exactly the same way as is an ancestor who was a scoundrel and spendthrift. No other way of manifesting himself is open to him. All ancestor spirits exact ritual service, and propitiation in accordance with the same rules of unpredictable and more commonly persecutory rather than beneficent intervention in their descendants' lives.[5] From this it is evident that a lore or doctrine of an after-life in which rewards and punishments are meted out to the dead according to their moral deserts in life, concerns a different sector of religious thought and behaviour than does ancestor worship, as we find it among people like the Tallensi. And again the reciprocal conditions apply. The troubles and misfortunes attributed to the mystical intervention of ancestors are the same for descendants who are upright and scrupulous in their moral conduct and social relations as for descendants who are wicked and lax.

This is consistent with the principle that ancestors are deemed to be equally the source of misfortunes interpreted as retribution for failure in religious submission and service, whether this failure is witting or unwitting. The ancestors persecute in the etymological sense of persistently following and harrying their descendants; they do not punish for wickedness or reward for virtues, as these are defined by human standards (Fortes 1959). Thus homicide, among the Tallensi, must be ritually expiated whether or not it is deliberate or unintentional. This is done not because it is wicked to kill a man, but because it is sinful to pollute the Earth with human blood or to commit such an outrage against the supreme law of kinship amity.

Furthermore, there is an established order of precedence in this. As one might expect, it is the reciprocal of the order of precedence in worship. Ancestors can, ideally, only intervene in the life of descendants through the intermediation of the deceased parents of the right category through whom they are approached in worship. Naturally, too, the person who has, by right of succession, the right to officiate in their worship also bears the main burden of accountability to them. His faults of negligence are more apt to be invoked if things go wrong with any of his dependants than their own. Even adults who are jural minors (e.g. married younger brothers or sons of the head of a family) are only indirectly accountable to the ancestors when ill befalls them. In short, the persecuting ancestor is not a supernatural being capriciously punishing wrong-doing or rewarding virtue. He is rather to be thought of as an ultimate judge and mentor whose vigilance is directed towards restoring order and discipline in compliance with the norms of right and duty, amity and piety, whenever transgressions threaten or occur. When misfortune occurs and is interpreted as a punitive, or to be more exact, corrective intervention by the ancestors, they are believed to have acted rightfully, not wantonly. Moreover, they are subject to the moral constraint that emanates from faithful worship. Though one cannot be certain that one's offerings and tendance will gain their benevolence, one can rest assured that they will bind the ancestors to act justly (Fortes 1959).

There is clear logic in this. For in everyday experience authority is made patent more obviously in disciplinary actions than in indulgence. A parent shows his authority and asserts the rule of right when he gives commands and when he punishes disobedience, not when he is affectionate and protective. A chief's authority is similarly evinced when he exacts services or inflicts penalties for wrong doing. Such demonstrations of authority may be very infrequent, as is the case among the Tallensi, but if they are not known to be possible and legitimate, authority wilts. Benevolence and affection, hospitality and largesse, are necessary concomitants of authority but their function is only to make it tolerable.

Considered in relation to the social structure, therefore, ancestor worship, among such peoples as those we have been discussing, can be described as [*inter alia*] a body of religious beliefs and ritual practices, correlated with rules of conduct, which serves to entrench the principle of jural authority together with its corollary, legitimate right, and its reciprocal, designated accountability, as an indisputable and sacrosanct value-principle of the social system.[6] In these societies, jural authority implies not only control but responsibility and rests on mutuality of rights and duties. It is effective because he who holds authority is himself bound to superior authority and is both entitled and obliged to invoke this superior authority as the sanction of his status. He can fulfil his responsibilities with authority, if I might put the matter somewhat paradoxically, because the ultimate responsibility lies outside his control.

In these societies, the kind of authority and right here at issue is generated and exercised through social relations created by kinship and descent. Jural authority vests in a person by virtue of kinship status or of office that, in the last resort, depends upon descent. Ancestors symbolize the continuity of the social structure, and the proper allocation, at any given time, of the authority and right they held and transmitted. Ancestor worship puts the final source of jural authority and right, or to use the more inclusive term, jurisdiction, on a pedestal, so to speak, where it is inviolable and unchallengeable, and thus able to mobilize the consent of all who must comply with it.

In presenting this hypothesis, I lean, appropriately, on no less a guide than Maine. Discussing the unilateral limitation of agnation he declares that this ensues because 'the foundation of agnation is not the marriage of the Father and Mother, but the authority of the

Father' and, pursuing the topic further, he concludes: 'The Parental Powers proper are extinguishcd by the death of the Parent, but agnation is as it were a mould which retains their imprint after they have ceased to exist' (Maine op. cit., pp. 123–4). I have simply applied these dicta to the religious aspects of descent.

This leads me to a speculation which, I believe, deserves closer consideration. It seems to me that we have in all societies something like a general faculty, or factor, or jural authority or jurisdiction, *ius per se*. It pervades all social relations but is, of course, only recognized and experienced in particular contexts and situations, and in specific rules of conduct.

Lest this should be dismissed as another one of those 'bloodless abstractions' attributed to structuralist anthropology, I should like to draw attention to some parallels. One such parallel is the postulate of the Rule of Law in complex democratic societies. Thus Weldon (1946, p. 243) observes that 'the Rule of Law is invested with peculiar sanctity just because it is held that the law guarantees the inviolability of the individual...' More pertinent is Gluckman's discussion of the Lozi concept of the law as the quintessence of the *corpus juris* (1955). As he notes (p. 164) the word *mulao* is used by the Lozi 'to describe all the rules and the whole procedure by which their society is controlled: thus they say, "even the king is the slave of the law (*mulao*)"'. The concept *mulao*, he comments (p. 226), 'is a multiple concept covering all kinds of *ordered regularity and authoritative action*' (my italics). I am reminded of the Tale word *malung* which can be translated as 'ritually obligatory' but is often used to account for anything that is felt to be customarily obligatory. Again, there are the two terms *buurt*, right, and *yuko*, authority. Thus a chief awards *buurt* to the party in the right in a dispute that comes before him, and he does so in virtue of *yuko*; a lineage head is exercising *yuko* when he accepts the placation gift from a suitor for the hand of a daughter of the lineage; and the same term is used of anyone who is entitled to give orders to others. In Ashanti, the notion of the Stool as the sacred vehicle of the presence of the ancestors and both the source and the symbol of politico-ritual office, from the kingship down to the headship of a local lineage, embodies the same idea. Ashanti political and jural organization is permeated with the notion of the sanctity of ancestrally-ordained authority, as the institution of the oath graphically illustrates (cf. Rattray 1929, passim).

It is not too far-fetched, then, to suppose that some notion of a pervasive principle of authority, or as I have called it, jurisdiction, is apprehended, however loosely, in African societies. But what must be stressed is that its operation is experienced piecemeal, in particular situations, and that it is respected and complied with in relation to the particular persons, offices, or institutions in which it is vested for the time being. In these situations, jurisdiction is accepted by reference to sanctions deployed from the outside and to the symbols and usages that identify status and office; but it is also complied with by reason of habits, beliefs, and sentiments that are ingrained in the individual. In the domain of kinship and descent we are concerned with jurisdiction vested in parents and parental agencies and channelled through the social relations engendered by parenthood. But this jurisdiction, and the matrix of social relations in which it functions, outlasts the occasions on which it comes into play and, what is more, the persons engaged. Succession ensures that authority and right do not die with the bodily demise of men who have them. Descent ensures that the matrix of social relations remains more or less constant through the passage of generations. And the nuclear context of relationship for the incidence and experience of jurisdiction, as well as for its transmission, considered both structurally, at a given time, and genetically, over a stretch of time, is the relationship of successive generations. The condition of filial dependence, from infancy to adulthood, is the model of subordination to authority throughout the domain of kinship and descent. Hence the *experience* of filial dependence, as recognized and interpreted by the culture, provides the material for the code of symbolism and ritual by means of which reverence for authority can be regularly affirmed and enacted. For it is in this experience that the beliefs and sentiments of respect, reverence, and worship are inculcated.

The experience of filial dependence among the Tallensi is marked by ambivalence, as I have shown elsewhere (1949), and this is reflected in the images of the ancestors and the attributes given to them in Tale ancestor worship. Authority and right may be accepted as just; they cannot but be felt at times to be coercive and arbitrary. The avoidance and respect behaviour required of children towards their parents is well designed to deflect opposition to living authority when it is felt to be coercive. To counterbalance latent opposition and secure loyalty in spite of it, familiarity and affection are also evoked and allowed conventional expression. In their ancestor worship Tallensi make clear to themselves the fact that, though parents depart, the authority and jurisdiction they wielded – and which enabled them also to be protective and benevolent – still goes on. The symbolism and imagery used to this end purport to state that it is the parents themselves who survive in transmuted form and become accessible in the material objects dedicated to them. What in fact survives is the web of kinship and descent relationships generated by the parents and the filial experiences standardized in the norms, values, and beliefs inculcated by them. Ancestors are apt to be demanding, persecutory, and interfering for one reason because parents appear thus to their children when they are exercising authority over them, but also, in the wider sense, because this is a particularly effective way of representing the sovereignty of authority and right.

These reflections leave open some difficult questions. How does parental and lineage authority, as projected in ancestor worship, link up with political authority and its ritual symbolism and representation as in some forms of African kingship? Again, what is the nature of authority and what representation, if any, does it have in religious or ideological terms in genealogically based social systems like those of the Tiv and the Nuer which lack both ancestor worship and the equivalent of kingship? Is it that jurisdiction, in these societies, is so diffused and so collective as to rule out specific attribution and representation of authority?

In conclusion, I believe that the analysis I have put forward can usefully be extended to features of ancestor worship I have not dealt with. Take the crucial ritual institution of ancestor worship, the sacrifice. If we think of it as a mode of ritual reparation incumbent on every successor to authority, we can see that it may be connected with the hazards of succession. Succession means ousting a predecessor, even though it is lawful and inevitable. It is thus a reminder of the transience of authority and the dangers of arousing opposition to it. Tallensi point this out, saying, for example, that men who have the custody of ancestor shrines have a heavy responsibility because they are more exposed to the demands of the ancestors than are other people. Moreover, they arouse jealousy among their peers, and though this does not endanger their lives, it is irksome. So it is not only a safeguard for anyone in authority to show that he is himself the servant of higher authority, but it may be a reassurance to himself to be able to make the kind of reparation to his displaced predecessor which the beliefs and practices relating to sacrifice make possible. Here we touch on problems that call for psychological analysis, as indeed any comprehensive study of ancestor worship will be bound to do.

# 5

# Ritual and office

## Theoretical preliminaries

Few concepts in the vocabulary of sociology and social anthropology are so lavishly used as are 'role' and 'status'. Since they were first put into regular circulation by Linton[1] they have been the subject of discussion from many angles of theory,[2] some within but most, perhaps, beyond the customary range of social anthropology. It is as well, therefore, that I need say little about this literature. For I am not concerned with elucidating definitions. What I want to consider is how the kinds of attributes, capacities and relationships which we identify by means of such terms are generated, more particularly in a tribal society. I do not have to emphasize that this is a well-worn theme in anthropology. Some of our most illustrious forbears, presently to be mentioned, have explored it. And what I have to say is of value mainly as a reminder of how much still remains to be followed up in their theories and discoveries. I was tempted to take it up again in this lecture because it has been on my mind for some time.[3]

Colloquially speaking, terms like role and status help us to isolate and analyse the parts played by people in social life. They have status in domestic, local, political, religious, etc. groups, associations, classes; they exercise roles in economic, legal, ritual, military, conjugal, etc. relationships. And we use this terminology to show that what we are talking about is customary, or standard, or normal – institutionalized, if you will.

This is elementary. What is fundamental, however, is that roles and statuses must be legitimate in the society in which they occur;

84

that is to say, they must have moral and jural sanction. Parsons[4] showed this neatly by reference to the 'legitimacy' of sickness as against criminality in our own society. A person does not just step into a role or acquire a status as he might a garment. They are, as Nadel remarks,[5] allotted to, or rather conferred upon him by society.

But how, when, in what circumstances? Confronted with this question, an anthropologist immediately thinks of the roles and statuses which, in Linton's terminology, are achieved and which stand out as palpably conferred. Some appear to accrue to a person at successive stages of the normal life cycle and the basic achievement might well be considered to be staying the course from birth through childhood, adolescence, adulthood and so on.

This, essentially, is the theme of Van Gennep's famous study of *rites de passage*.[6] In setting up what we should not call his model of the standard and, to all intents, universal life cycle, Van Gennep demonstrated three significant theorems: first, that the critical stages, as he called them, of the life cycle, beginning with birth and going on to puberty, marriage, parenthood, and finally death, though tied to physiological events, are in fact socially defined;[7] secondly, that entry into and exit from these critical stages – or statuses – are always marked by ritual and ceremony, not only in primitive societies but equally in Christian civilization and in the civilizations of antiquity; thirdly, that these passage rites follow a more or less standard pattern. They begin with rites of separation, which remove the subject from the 'environment' or as we might say social field he is in, then come transition rites, while the subject is, so to speak, waiting on the threshold of the status or social field he is about to enter, and finally come rites of incorporation into the new status.

Van Gennep's model has become so entrenched in our thinking that it is seldom explicitly questioned; and rightly so, for it represents one of the major theoretical achievements of our science. Yet the most important questions are left in the air by him, though pregnant suggestions for dealing with them are thrown out in the course of his analysis. Thus the crucial question, why is ritual apparently indispensable in marking status change, is not pursued in detail. It is deemed to be accounted for, partly, by the hypothesis that progression from one state to the next is commonly a change from a

profane to a sacred environment or situation. But this proves to be a
Procrustean formula when, for example, initiation rites are in one
place summed up as 'rites of separation from the usual environment,
rites of incorporation into the sacred environment; a transitional
period; rites of separation from the local sacred environment; rites
of incorporation into the usual environment'.[8] In addition, there is
the implication that ritual is appropriate because it mimes or symbolizes the nature of the passage in each particular case. A simple
instance is the interpretation of 'rites which involve cutting something' ... the first haircut, the shaving of the head ...' – as rites of
separation, whereas naming and baptism are obvious rites of incorporation'. Other interpretations offered are more subtle; but
inspired as some of them are, they mostly remain at the level of
manifest meaning I have exemplified.[9] Again, Van Gennep makes
acute comparisons between passage rites marking status stages in
the life cycle and passage rites by which people are initiated and incorporated into secret societies, cult groups, age-groups, offices,
ranks and even the world of the dead. There is the brilliant observation that even where membership in a caste, class or cult group is
hereditary, 'the child is rarely considered a fully "complete"
member from birth ... he must be incorporated'; and he adds, casually, that in these ceremonies the 'politico-legal' and 'social' elements are more important than the magico-religious. All the same,
the point we would follow up is not considered. If we generalize the
model, attaining a status that is normal to the life cycle is equivalent
to admission to membership in a closed association and these are
equivalent to entering upon an office or rank, and to passing into the
society of the dead; and the critical step is the rite of incorporation.
If we ask, incorporation into what, the answer is clear: into a new
field of social structure, or conjuncture of social relations.

But why ritual? A clue lies in turning from the procedures of conferring it, to the recipient of status, role or office. The actor, docile
though he may be while undergoing the process of being incorporated, lives and acts the part once he possesses it. He appropriates his
part to himself, he knows it, he has a commitment to it. It is through
the acting of his part in accordance with the norms and sanctions
that legitimize it that he is incorporated in the social structure. This
has been recognized by theoretical writers like Parsons, Nadel and
others. What needs to be particularly pointed out is that there is a

dialectical connection between the actor and his part, the person and his roles or status or office. He is made to appropriate his part to himself because it is in a sense outside himself. This emerges, I think, from the ethnographic evidence presently to be adduced. I believe that this is where the clue to the need for ritual and ceremony in status-giving lies.

It is, of course, not a novel hypothesis. It follows from the analysis of what is meant by the concept of 'office' which I regard as the generic term embracing role and status as special cases. Its significance was first brought home to me, as, no doubt, to most of us, by Max Weber's classical exposition of the notion of 'calling' (or its equivalent in German, *Beruf*) in Protestant ethical and theological teaching.[10] As Parsons sums it up elsewhere,[11] it is 'the conception of an individual's "business in life" ... as a matter of moral obligation' which, as Weber emphasizes, derives its sanctions from the will of God. Weber's *Beruf* is equated with and translated appropriately by 'calling', 'occupation', 'profession', 'life-task' and 'office' in different parts of his work; but 'office' is, I consider, by its etymology, history and connotation the correct general term.

It is not within my competence, nor indeed is this the place, to go into the history of the notion of 'office' from its Roman origins until today.[12] Weber attributes its development, in the sense he gives to it, primarily to Martin Luther. It arose, as Dr Cargill Thompson shows in a forthcoming book,[13] from Luther's rigorous distinction between 'the spiritual, inner new man' and the 'carnal, external, old man'.

Thus the concept of office is not an artifice of modern sociological theory. In my view it is so essential to the management and comprehension of the social relations of persons and groups that it is present in all social systems, if only in an embryonic form. In Africa, for example, the distinction between the man himself and the office he occupies is as well understood as it is amongst us today and in earlier periods of European history. It is a common concept in African political constitutions, and is deeply ingrained in African legal institutions, moral values, and jural norms. I do not have to labour this point, since no one can be unfamiliar with its exposition and elucidation in Professor Gluckman's analysis of the judical process among the Barotse. At the outset of his book[14] he establishes the importance of separating the offices of the court-councillors from their holders, and as the argument proceeds we see how this fits in with the cardinal principle of Lozi jurisprudence, that courts 'deal with an individual person occupying specific positions in society' (p. 198); they are 'chiefly concerned with relationships of status' (p. 126).

Office, *par excellence*, is seen in chiefship and other forms of constituted political leadership, as well as in similarly established positions of authority in economic or religious or otherwise institutionalized activities. Ashanti chiefship exemplifies a way of recognizing the distinction I am discussing that is particularly apt for my purpose. The office is referred to by the term *akonnua*, commonly translated 'stool' in the same way as we use 'crown' and 'throne' to stand for Kingship. The culminating rite of the installation ceremony is the solemn seating of the chief-elect on the supreme ancestral stool of his chiefdom. From this moment he is obliged to observe a number of rigorous taboos and is regarded as 'invested with sanctity', as Rattray puts it.[15] Appearing then, before his people, he swears fidelity to them and is admonished by his senior councillors to remember, among other things, that he may never act without their advice, and must rule with justice and impartiality. It is impressed on him that he belongs to the whole chiefdom in his capacity as chief, and not to his lineage. The office is deemed to absorb the whole person during his tenure of it. Thus any treasure a chief takes with him when he is installed becomes part of the stool property, and any territory, persons or valuables he is instrumental in winning during his tenure of the stool accrue to the office.

As is well known, Ashanti constitutional law permits the councillors of a chiefdom who elect and install a chief to demand his abdication or to depose him if he offends against the laws and customs, fails in his duties, or commits sacrilege.[16] When this happens the chief is destooled by a ceremony that reverses the enstoolment rites. His sandals are removed so that he steps barefoot on the earth and his buttocks are bumped on the ground by the withdrawal of his stool from under him. Thus he transgresses two of the symbolic taboos of chiefship and is deemed to have degraded his sacred office. He is then banished, accompanied by only one wife and a servant. He is now a commoner member of his lineage again and is no longer treated with the reverential deference accorded to a chief. He can keep none of the properties or treasure or, nowadays, the money and clothes, which accrued to his office during his chiefship. In recent times this has been a source of grievance and litigation, for chiefs have been able to exploit their official authority and prestige to enrich themselves on the side, in the cocoa trade, by traffic in concessions and land rentals, by money-lending and so forth. Litigation has not infrequently taken place between a destooled chief and his former councillors and subjects over the disposal of such gains. Traditional constitutional law regards them as belonging to the Stool. But suits are brought on the basis of British laws of property and persons, and courts have sometimes ruled that a chief's capacity as a private citizen is not extinguished by his assumption of office. This entitles him to claim his private property and possessions irrespective of when they were gained.[17]

I have dwelt on this instance because it brings me back to a feature of office which Weber hardly considered and Van Gennep only partly investigated. I mean the part played by ceremony and ritual, not only in the conferment of office but also in its maintenance and exercise. And lest we should be inclined to think that this holds only for primitive society, I would draw attention to the perceptive and ingenious studies of various professions and occupations carried out over a period of years by Professor Everett Hughes and his collaborators.[18] 'Status', says Hughes (and I concur), 'is an elementary form of office', which he defines as a 'standardized group of duties and privileges devolving upon a person in certain well defined situations' – I would rather say, in customarily defined and sanctioned contexts of social relations. But what is most to the point in these studies is the observation that for the office represented in a profession like medicine or the law—and even in an occupation as low in our scale of class esteem as that of a janitor or dustman – to be fittingly exercised needs a 'mandate from society' given through its responsible organs and institutions. Thus it becomes 'licensed', or legitimate. It is this fact which determines how an office appears to its holder, how he apprehends the duties and privileges it entails, and how he fulfils them.

Here the ceremonial and ritual elements become specially relevant. Should we follow Van Gennep and say that the key lies in the phenomenon that office, status and roles are always conferred by *rites de passage* which move a person from a profane to a sacred set-

ting and state? This, as I have already implied, is much too facile. We
see this if we state the thesis in the more enlightening concepts developed by Robert Redfield in his notable analysis of the relationships
between the 'technical order' and the 'moral order' in civilization.[19]
What office, status or role is there which does not serve some instrumental or utilitarian – that is technical, end? And yet there is always
also this other dimension of duty and responsibility, enjoined, sanctioned, and above all symbolized in ceremonial or ritual forms (be it
no more than costume and etiquette) placing it in the moral order.
This is as obvious in the western professions described by Hughes as
in African tribal life. But being primarily concerned with and
interested in the latter, I will now turn to some of the evidence from
ethnography.

## Ethnographical observations

I remember the first time I saw a procession of mourners on their
way to a funeral among the Tallensi. They included both men and
women, dressed in gala clothes and carrying condolence gifts of
guinea corn and chickens. A drummer and a fiddler escorted them.
As they hove in sight, they were carrying on an animated conversation, laughing and joking. A bystander praised their admirable
turnout. This, he said, was the proper way to attend the funeral of
your father-in-law. All of a sudden the procession halted. Then, as it
began to move forward again, a heart-rending wail broke forth. It
came from the women. Tears were now streaming down their
cheeks; and, as their wailing swelled, the men joined in with a
melancholy dirge. In this way they arrived at the house of the
bereaved family. What was the meaning of this transformation of
mien and mood? Was it sincere or were the players simply putting
on an act for which they were cast in their capacity as the kinsfolk of
a son-in-law fulfilling a kinship obligation? I often discussed this
question with Tallensi. Invariably they insisted that the wailing and
the dirges expressed sincere grief. This, they insisted, is the customary mode of expressing condolence by a son-in-law's kin. How else
could the mourners have shown their grief? Are there not, they went
on, appropriate times, places and occasions for people to act in the
customary ways that show the world that one is a kinsman or an
affine or just a good friend? Mourners attending an in-law's funeral

do not give vent to grief in their own home settlements. The appropriate place is the bereaved clan settlement.

Here we see how occasions evoke, and thus confer roles, according to standard patterns. But this occurrence is fully intelligible only if we take into account the whole context of status relationships implicit in it. A man has unrestricted rights over his wife's reproductive capacity in virtue of the bride price he has paid to her father. But she never wholly forfeits her status as her father's daughter. This gives her residual claims on her father's protection and him a lien on her. If her marriage is unsuccessful she can, with her father's support, escape from it. A son-in-law is therefore in the perpetual debt of his father-in-law, being dependent on his goodwill, first for the original gift of his daughter, later for backing in maintaining the marriage. To mourn for his father-in-law is one of a number of customary demonstrations of respect he is obliged to make throughout his married life. If he inexcusably neglects these duties his wife's paternal kin may assert their rights and take her away. Jural right is here backed by moral justification. For people will say: how can a man be so callous towards his wife's feelings or so deficient in a sense of duty and propriety as wilfully to fail in his affinal obligations? The status of son-in-law carries with it not only rights and duties but also attitudes and sentiments, as shown, *inter alia*, by the appropriate mourning behaviour for an affine. We should note that a respectable son-in-law takes pride in this. It reaffirms the affinal relations created by his marriage and this is tantamount to advertising the rights he holds and making acknowledgement of the obligations incurred.

Let me state the conclusion prompted by this example in what might be thought to be somewhat far-fetched terms; but I think it will help to advance the discussion. Firstly, roles, even transient ones, are only evoked in persons who may legitimately exercise them — nay must, in certain circumstances, do so; and secondly, roles are performed not automatically, but in response to social controls that emanate from the relationships in which the roles emerge.[20] For what, in fact, is the capacity to take on a role other than the manifestation of engagement in social relations? If role is status in action then status is shorthand for everything that is required of a person or permitted to him in virtue of a specified field of social relations in which he is involved. This point, sometimes overlooked in theoretical discussions, is well made in the paper by Southall previously cited. So to establish precisely what the status of son-in-law implies we must specify that it belongs to the domestic domain of social structure.[21]

But status in this domain is less instructive for my purpose than its counterpart in the external domains of the political and the religious order. Let us therefore consider more fully what I have called office *par excellence*. To make my description clear I must remind you that the Tallensi have no indigenous political institutions of the type we associate with centralized government. Without courts of law, administration or over-riding authorities, the sovereignty of the exogamous, patrilineal local clan is kept in check partly by the complex web of kinship created by marriage but chiefly by an elaborate scheme of ritual interdependence. With a segmentary political system and with subsistence farming as their only source of livelihood, they have no framework of unity in the technical order of their culture. What political and moral cohesion they have arises from public ritual institutions.[22] And the pivotal institutions are focused in the two hereditary offices of the Chiefship, vested in one group of clans, and the Custodianship of the Earth, vested in another group, as I have described fully elsewhere.[23]

To summarize very briefly, the founding myth of the tribe tells how the chiefly clans entered the country as immigrants bringing the Chiefship with them, and came to live among the aboriginals who constituted the Earth-priest clans. A compact was then established which bound the two groups for ever to live in amity side by side. Neither group has any authority over the other, and indeed the Chiefs and Earth-priests have no powers comparable to what we would call political authority even in their own groups. But Chiefs and Earth-priests are bound to one another by complementary religious and mystical observances, ties and duties; for the two sets of offices are primarily religious, not technical, in Redfield's sense of these terms. The Tallensi believe that the common good of the whole tribe depends on the faithful ritual collaboration of Chiefs and Earth-priests, after the fashion, as they put it, of husband and wife. If this breaks down, famine, war, disease or some other catastrophe will descend on them. And an essential rule governing this complementary politico-religious relationship is that the two sets of offices are mutually exclusive. The clans eligible for one set are barred from

the other. In fact the distinctive attributes of each of the offices
derives from its complementary opposition to the other in the tribal
system. This is documented and demonstrated through the medium
of ritual observances. A Chief, and anyone who is eligible for the
office by clan descent, may wear cloth, ride a horse, and use
firearms. Earth-priests and their clansmen may not do any of these
things. They must wear animal skins, and may not ride a horse or
use a firearm on pain of mystical punishment by the Earth. A Chief
may not tread the bare earth unshod. Earth-priests may and do. A
Chief may not eat certain animals permitted to ordinary people and
to Earth-priests. And there are other ritual injunctions and prohibitions of these kinds binding on both. All these ritual rules are justi-
fied by appeal to the founding myth.

Let us note that it is not enough for the offices to exist and to have
what in present sociological parlance is often designated by the pon-
derous but indispensable word 'incumbents'. The holders must be
dressed for their parts, so to speak, and must show that they are
living their parts by observing a number of distinctive and often
onerous ritual restrictions which have no rational justification, let
alone utility, but only the sanction of myth and religious belief. This
of course is not confined to the Tallensi, or to the many other African peoples who have similar institutions.[24] It is characteristic of
office anywhere. Office needs must be distinguished, on the one
hand by outward and visible trappings, and on the other by
characteristic modes of conduct. Hughes (*op. cit.*) has pointed this
out. The evidence is all around us, in our police and bus conductors,
in the professions and the churches, in courts of law, universities,
banks, industry, business, wherever office occurs. But what is
brought home to us by a consideration of positions of rank and
authority in a tribal society like that of the Tallensi is that these
emblems and insignia are associated with distinctive norms of conduct and observance which symbolize jural capacities and responsibilities and bind those who hold an office to it by ritual sanctions.
And what I want to fix attention on is that this is the result of a social
act of investment by a deliberate and formal procedure.

I am, of course, referring to the well-known fact that a chief or
similar functionary in any African society is invariably installed in
office by a public ceremony. The Ashanti ceremony has already been

mentioned. Among the Tallensi, it is an elaborate and solemn ceremony which includes a number of esoteric rites. For both of the
politico-ritual offices it begins with rites which confer on the holder
the apparel and other insignia of his office. These are followed by
the more esoteric rites which can be understood as imposing on him
his taboos and other ritual observances. And their import is clear;
they confer a new social identity on the holder, symbolized by his
taking a new name. This was vividly impressed on me when I attended the installation of a senior Earth-priest. Almost overnight, an
ineffectual old man was turned into a dignified, self-confident, and
authoritative, if somewhat garrulous, leader.

Tallensi assert that if Chiefs and Earth-priests fail in their duties,
whether these appear to be secular or are clearly religious, they are
transgressing their taboos; and disasters will surely come upon the
whole country. Is it then simply superstitious fears that constrain
them to fulfil their tasks and obligations, as a superficial judgment
might suggest? To answer this question we must look more closely
at the relationship between an office-holder and his office. In the
first place, the office must be occupied. Tallensi give many instances
of how crops withered unaccountably and disease spread through
the country during the interregnum between the death of one Chief
or priest and the installation of his successor. I more than once heard
a Chief upbraid a group of difficult litigants by reminding them that
if he were to lay down his office in anger over their recalcitrance, the
rains would fail or other disasters immediately fall on the whole
country.[25] The office, as such, is otiose, or rather anomalous and
therefore dangerous to society, unless it is occupied.

Here we touch again on a point of principle mentioned briefly
before. An unoccupied politico-ritual office endangers the stability
of social life because law and order, personal security, and ultimately man's relations with nature, are jeopardized by the absence
of the king-pin of the social structure. Blackstone's maxim that 'the
King never dies' sums up the central issue. Offices of the type represented by chiefship and kingship may not lapse or be dissolved if
the society is to be maintained as it is: and it is they that constitute
corporations solely in their juridical aspect. The significant structural
index of this is the fact that they entail succession. To be sure the
duties and privileges of the office may be temporarily fulfilled
during its vacancy by some kinsman or representative of the

successor-apparent, or of the group that possesses it. But succession by due process, to borrow a phrase normally used with a rather different implication, must ensue, else there is discord, perhaps revolution. In fact the chaos of the interregnum, often accompanied by wars of succession, is, paradoxically accepted as inevitable in some societies.

This used to happen among the Tallensi and peoples related to them (e.g. the Mamprussi). Tallensi say that in the old days, when a major chief died the 'land fell to pieces' with famine and rapine and did not recover until a successor had been installed. Ashanti say that a vacant stool is repugnant to custom because there is nobody to take care of the ancestral stools and to offer libations and sacrifices to them. This is ominous for peace and social well-being. Indeed in some chiefdoms the danger of chaos during the interregnum after the death of a chief is magically averted by the seizure of the chiefly sacra by the hereditary controllers of the obsequies.[26] There is a curious parallelism between this practice and the rituals of rebellion described by Gluckman.[27] Among the Mossi the interregnum between the demise of a King and the selection and installation of his successor is stabilized by one of those neat devices that delight anthropologists. Immediately upon the death of a King his eldest daughter is dressed in his robe of office and, holding his staff, is seated on the royal skin to hold court daily until the funeral is over and one of her brothers is installed as the new ruler. Thus the office is kept warm, as it were, by a member of the royal lineage who is barred by her sex from the succession and from transmitting it to her sons but is qualified by descent to represent the lineage in safeguarding its title and the stability of the social order against the possibility of civil war over the succession.[28] The problem was dealt with as ingeniously in ancient Egypt. As Frankfort explains (*op. cit.*, Ch. VIII), the Egyptian solution was to appoint the heir-apparent co-regent with his father, the reigning king. He acceded to power immediately on his father's death but it was not until the conclusion of the coronation ritual that the danger of rebellion by pretenders was over.

It boots not to multiply the examples which abound in Africa. Wherever this type of office is found the death of a ruler is a major crisis. As J. D. and E. J. Krige put it, in writing of the Lovedu,[29] it 'dislocates the rhythm of nature, bringing drought and famine, the abrogation of law and order'. At best there is a state of public suspense and minor lawlessness, at worst the anarchy of a struggle for the succession by rival claimants. And order does not return until the office is revivified by legitimate reoccupation.

It is hardly to be wondered at that the installation of the successor so commonly includes elaborate ritual and ceremony, not only in order that he might be incontestably proclaimed but also in order that the bonds of office that bind the holder to those for whom he holds it may be irrefragably forged. Furthermore, the installation rites commonly devolve, as right and duty, on a special group of 'king-makers'. These are often, if not usually, hereditary councillors of the ruler, some at least being holders of priestly or religious office connected with sacred places or relics or shrines of the ruler's office, or else with his ritual obligations. And it is a cardinal rule that these electors must not themselves be eligible for the succession, nor may those who can succeed to the ruler's office hold an elector's office.[30] The Tallensi maxim 'Nobody installs himself' puts it succinctly. Lineage heads, whether Chiefs or Earth-priests, are installed by neighbouring lineage heads whose clans have the hereditary privilege of performing this task.[31] The electors are, in effect, the agents of the tribe and the custodians of the body of law and custom. It is in the name of the people, and of the sanctity of this body of law and custom, that they confer office on a ruler. This is dramatized in installation ceremonies.

But before I say more about these, I would like to draw attention to a corollary of the foregoing argument. I have used chiefship as the model of office *par excellence*. But it is, of course, only a preeminent instance of a type of office or status found also in other domains of social life. The defining structural criteria – that the office may not be left unoccupied, that it is, in consequence, perpetuated by succession, and that the holder, though chosen by virtue of prior title, must nevertheless be ritually invested with it by the agents of society – are also met by other institutions. The instances that come to mind are the 'positional succession' and 'perpetual kinship' practised by some Central African peoples.[32] But as a matter of fact, it is evident, in however rudimentary a form, wherever succession, as opposed to inheritance, is mandatory. Among the Tallensi a man's property passes by inheritance partly to his lineage brothers and partly to his sons. But his jural status as head of his family, wielding paternal authority, passes by succession to his oldest son, who is ritually invested with it in the concluding rites of his funeral.[33] It might be thought that there is an element of this in all status in a homogeneous and relatively stable society. But we can see that this is not so if we contrast the status of a son-in-law with which we began. This cannot be attained by succession, but only by marriage. Again, the status of initiated man or marriageable woman, which figures so prominently in the normal model of *rites de passage*, is not attainable by succession.

I must refrain from following this point further and return to installation ceremonies. Their resemblance to initiation rites was stressed by Van Gennep and their general pattern is known to all. One way of putting it would be to say that these rites extinguish an existing status, as defined for instance by kinship, and create a new status, as defined by political and ritual domains of action. And what I am concerned with is the ethnographic fact that this is accompanied by the imposition of distinctive imperatives of apparel, speech, conduct and observance.

Tallensi say that eminent office, be it no more than the headship of a lineage, brings advantages of prestige and authority, and even some economic gains. These make office sought after. Yet they never tire of pointing out that such offices also carry heavy responsibilities, on the one hand to the living, but more onerously to the ancestors whose place a chief or a lineage head now occupies. And the burdens of office are peculiarly symbolized, in their minds, by the taboos of office.

This is brought home to a newly elected chief or Earth-priest when he is installed. In the culminating rites he is secluded alone with the shrines of the lineage ancestors and the Earth, and it is believed that if he is not accepted by the ancestors he will not survive the ordeal.

The paramount duty of eminent office, Tallensi say, is to 'take care of' the country, that is, to maintain peace, and 'prosper' the people. This includes technical, jural and political tasks like arbitrating in disputes, representing the lineage and the clan in external affairs, and supervising communal undertakings. But secular authority and leadership are not enough or even fundamental. What matters most is the due performance of ritual obligations. That is why office holders have to be constantly vigilant in consulting diviners and bringing the right offerings to ancestors. In parenthesis, and bearing in mind what was earlier said about succession, it is worth adding that one of the major responsibilities of the head of a family or lineage is defined in similar terms with respect to his dependants in the domestic group.

But such private vigilance, left to the behests of conscience, is not, it seems, sufficient. Society, which confers office, demands that its proper exercise should be publicly accounted for. Tallensi recognize quite bluntly that this is necessary in part because men are fallible and prone to fall short of ideals. 'Who fears death', they say, 'until it is upon you?' But they also explain that accountability is part of the 'work' of office – that it is, in our language, a necessary feature of the tissue of rights and duties, authority and responsibility, which binds and incorporates office into society.

This accountability is ensured in a number of ways. In some societies it is built into the structure of political and ritual authority by being vested in countervailing office. This is the other side of 'king-makers' and electors. As hereditary councillors, or ritual functionaries, or custodians of sacred relics or myths or insignia that participate in the chiefship, they constitute a powerful disciplinary force to hold their ruler to his commitments, and friction between the parties is a not uncommon concomitant of the relationship. Indeed Dr Richards, in her latest summary of one of the more elaborate constitutional arrangements of this type found in Africa, that of the Bemba, implies that some degree of friction may be inevitable and even necessary for the *bakabilo* to be able to keep control over the paramount Chief.[34]

The Tallensi achieve a similar end, in the context of their more diffused political order, through the Cycle of the Great Festivals,[35] which lasts almost the whole dry season. The cycle begins with the celebration of the end of the rains, goes on to a sequence of harvest rites, and ends with ceremonies that foreshadow and hail the sowing season. But what is here relevant is that these ceremonies are the joint responsibility of all the politico-ritual lineage and clan heads of the country. They are so concatenated that every ceremony is either the necessary preliminary to another, or the essential conclusion of another; and each such leg of a sequence is the responsibility of a different office holder, acting in his capacity as the jural and ritual representative of his clan and lineage.

The prayers spoken in these ceremonies and the mimetic rituals employed have all the marks of the purely magical. In one rite, for example, the assembly of Earth-priests perambulates a sacred spot chanting invocations for good crops and solemnly miming the planting of grain. But the magic is really a secondary element. Such rites are bound to be about conspicuous common concerns, and crops are such a concern. There can be no general well-being without good crops in a precarious subsistence economy. But the magic cannot be mobilized without the support of the ancestors and the Earth; and this requires the ceremonial collaboration of all the officiants. Personal animosities may and do rage among them, for the clans of the Tallensi are jealously separatist and their heads compete for recognition. But they must collaborate or else they will anger the ancestors and the Earth, and so incur disaster for themselves as well as for the whole community.

The pattern of collaboration is easily seen. It consists in dramatizing salient episodes in the myths of the founding ancestors, and, what comes to the same thing, re-enacting key episodes in the installation ceremonies of the main officiants. So the ceremonial cycle confirms, annually, the occupation of each office and thus re-imposes on its holder his duties and capacities. This is quite explicit: the ceremonies are conducted in an idiom that highlights the ritual equality and indispensability of all the offices. All are equally essential. Each officiant can claim that his office and his ritual performances form the hub of the whole cycle and, consequently, the fount of tribal well-being.

Brief illustration must suffice. The cycle begins with a rite of terminating the rainy season on the day after the new moon of the first month of the dry season is seen. This rite is performed by the Bade Earth-priest, who sends messengers to inform neighbouring lineage heads when he has finished. Immediately, the senior Chief of the area ceremonially brings out his ancestral clan drum, which only leaves its sanctuary on such special occasions. The series is now set in motion and the other office-holders follow one after the other, each with his own rites and sacra. If there have been disputes between any of them, or their clans, the party which feels aggrieved will threaten to hold up everything until amends are made, and this sanction is always effective. The ceremonies cannot go on if there are unresolved quarrels between clans so they serve, incidentally, to reinforce peaceful relationships. In fact, there is an obligatory truce, phrased as a taboo on quarrelling in any form between clans and lineages, throughout the country during the cycle. As a consequence, marriages, which are the main sources of disputes and quarrels between clans, are prohibited during its culminating and most critical stages.

We can see how the Festival Cycle serves as a ritually enforced check on the due discharge of their duties by Chiefs and Earthpriests. But to understand why this works we must examine the ritual itself more closely. I have the space to describe only one of the simplest yet most solemn of the rites. It is, in effect, a dramatic recapitulation of the first arrival of the founding ancestor of the chiefly clans and his reception by the aboriginal Earth-priests. It takes place at night, at a sacred spot believed to be the site where these founding ancestors of the two groups first lived side by side in mutal amity. On this night no one, except those actually taking part in the ritual, is allowed out of doors. The senior Chief, as the living representative of his first ancestor, dressed in the full regalia of his office – his red hat, his rich tunic, his sandals, and his amulets – and carrying his staff of office, goes in silent procession, followed by the elders of the lineages of the clan, to the sacred site. There he and his entourage take their seats on the rock which is supposed to have been the traditional seat of the founding ancestor and his elders. Presently the senior Earth-priest arrives with his clan elders. He is also accoutred in the prescribed costume of his office, that is, antelope skins, a black string cap and official amulets, and he carries a guinea corn stalk of a variety which only Earth-priests may carry about. In the black silence, he and his followers take their seats on another rock, equally sanctified by the myth as the original seat of *their* founding ancestor.

The parties cannot see one another, for fire and light are strictly forbidden. Minutes pass in silence. Then the Earth-priest calls out, 'Speak'. An elder of the Chief, in tones of profound respect, announces that the Chief has come to greet the priest. Greetings are then gravely exchanged between the parties. A stranger would be bound to infer, from their manner and tone, that they had not set eyes on one another during the twelve months which have passed since they last met in this place – though, in fact, they live cheek by jowl and in daily contact. The priest asks if all the lineages of the chiefly clan are present, and if any of them is not represented he demands an explanation. This is important, since the ceremony is a reaffirmation of the original compact between the two clans, and its binding force is impaired if all branches of both clans do not partici-pate. At this point beer and flour for the libation are handed by the Chief's spokesman to the priest.

Now comes the most solemn moment. The priest begins his invo-cation. It is a lengthy, vivid, reverent and pious speech, addressed formally to the ancestors but in fact equally to the participants. The ancestors are adjured to attend and to receive the libation. They are exhorted to bless and prosper the people and the country so that he, the priest, and his colleague the chief, may have everlasting renown. But the principal theme of the speech is a recitation of the myth which, in Malinowski's words, constitutes the charter of the rite. At length the priest pours the libation and the dish is passed round for all those who are present to partake of it and so register their pledge of renewed amity. Parting salutations follow with mutual benedic-tions for good crops, good health for the people, and blessings on one another. Then the two parties file away in deep silence to their respective homes. When I had the privilege of attending this ceremony, which no stranger before or, I am sure, since, has seen, I came away filled with awe. But what is most significant about it is that it repeats one of the culminating rites performed by the Earth-priest at the installation of a new Chief. Thus it is not only a dramatization of the myth of the origin of the politico-ritual re-lations of the two clan groups; it is also a rite of renewal of the Chief's office.

The mesh of ritual collaboration, then, and the rites themselves, ensure that each office holder is accountable to his ancestors, to all his confrères, and through them to their clans. Furthermore, when each office holder is, in these ceremonies, reconfirmed in his office, he is graphically reminded that he holds it as a sacred trust granted to him on one side as the successor and perpetuator of the ancestors who founded the office and on the other as the representative of the clan in which the office is perpetually vested.

But let us return now to the taboos of office and ask again what their meaning is. Is it just a question of magical precautions inspired by insecurity and couched in terms of prelogical thought? Can they be explained by the theory of divine kingship according to which it is all a matter of a magical association between the vigour and fertility of the ruler and the well-being and fertility of his people?

Light is thrown on the problem if we consider what happens among the Tallensi when a man borrows land for farming. Normally, land is loaned for farming only to a person who is related by kinship to the owner.[36] In accordance with this practice, a friend of mine asked a distant maternal kinsman to lend him a plot of land for an unspecified term of years. It turned out to be part of the patrimonial estate of the lineage to which the man who farmed it belonged. So he had to have the consent of all his male lineage kin before agreeing to the loan.

From our point of view, of course, borrowing or leasing land for farming is a purely economic and legal transaction of a technical order. Not so for the Tallensi. Patrimonial property is defined as property held in trust by each generation for posterity. It must, therefore, be accounted for to the ancestors, and misuse of it incurs mystical penalties. This means that the ancestors must be informed whenever a change is made in the tenancy of such property, and they must be asked to bless the transaction. Hence the message advising the would-be borrower that consent had been given for the loan of the land to him also desired him to bring fowls and guinea fowls to the lender's home for the necessary sacrifices to the lenders' lineage ancestors.

The sacrifices were duly performed in the presence not only of the elders of the lender's lineage but also of senior members of the borrower's lineage, who were thus tacitly implicated as witnesses of the arrangement. Tallensi explain that it is precisely this ritual act which transfers the right to use the land to the borrower, while at the same time making it clear that it is only a loan and that will get no profit from using it unless he keeps in the good graces of the ancestors of the lender's lineage. They are, of course, also his own ancestors on his mother's side. This is important for a man has no ritual access to or claims upon ancestors who are outside his own genealogy.

But this was not the end of the formalities. Next day a meeting took place, on the land in question, between borrower and lender, each accompanied by senior and junior members of his lineage. Followed by the whole party, the lender first marched the borrower round the boundaries of the land. Rationally speaking this was superfluous, for they were known to all; but it is an essential feature of all such jural transactions among the Tallensi – as, indeed, in most African societies – that the subject-matter of any agreement shall be exhibited for all who are concerned to witness and approve; it must not be assumed to be known. This is a necessary safeguard in a culture which has no means of making written or other records.

The party now gathered in one corner of the land. Quite informally, the lender took up his hoe and cleared a small patch. As he finished, the two sons of the borrower took over and continued the hoeing for a short space. Having thus physically, as well as ceremonially and jurally, handed over the cultivation of the land to the borrower, the lender made a little speech: 'It is yours now to farm', he said. 'The blessings of the ancestors will be with you. May no illness or misfortune ever harm you while you farm this land. Only prosperity will come to you from it.'

And now followed an action which specially interested me. The lender took a small dish of flour which the borrower had brought, scooped up a handful of soil from where he had just hoed, and mixed it well with the flour. He then licked some of the mixture and handed the dish to the borrower, who followed suit. Characteristically for the Tallensi, the latter called his sons to do so too. But at this point one of his own elders intervened. 'No, no', he said, 'it is no affair of the boys or of anybody else. It is your affair only. You alone are responsible for the land and you alone are now bound by the taboos which anyone who starts a new farm has to observe.' The borrower nodded. He knew that he was now ritually prohibited from taking a new wife, attending funerals, hunting, and other common activities for a year from the time of the symbolical cutting of the first sod on his new farm. In addition, though a borrower never pays rent for land acquired in this manner, he is under a moral obligation to make a gift of grain grown on the land every year to the land-owner, who will use some of it to make a thanks-offering to his ancestors.

It would take me too far afield to spell out all the implications of this item, for every significant principle of Tale social structure and religious thought is encapsulated in it. What I want to draw attention to is only its relevance for my main theme. It shows us how religious ideas or rites are used to create a jural relationship between a person and property and so to place a technical fact within the moral order. And what is most striking is the parallel with the induction of an office holder into this office. For a would-be borrower of land is evidently turned into a tenant by a procedure of endowing him with a new element of ritual status in relation to the lineage and the ancestors of the landowner. This creates rights in the land, but also consequential obligations to the owners. Now these obligations are not enforceable by material sanctions. They are only morally binding. But the efficacy of the moral bond is assured in no uncertain terms. The tenant and the owner bind themselves to mutual accountability and trust by symbolically taking into themselves the land which is the link between them and their joint concern, in the rite of eating of the soil.[37] And this is further symbolized in the personal taboos which the tenant has to observe until he reaps his first harvest and so gets established in his status as occupier of the land. On the face of it these taboos have a magical intent, derived from Tale mystical notions. For Tallensi see a parallel between marrying a new wife and cultivating a new farm. Each requires a man's undivided attention. To mix them up is to risk conflicts of conscience and the anger of the ancestors; for one cannot serve them singlemindedly if one's mind is divided. Again, Tallensi believe that there is a dangerous antithesis between everything associated with death and everything associated with birth and new life, both among men and with crops and herds. But a little thought soon shows the true import of these taboos. It lies in their utility as a tangible embodiment of, and a daily discipline for, the moral obligations of tenancy.

The need for such a device is obvious if we consider how difficult it is to visualize and adhere to moral obligations in general or, for that matter, even in a particular context. Taboos are a medium for giving tangible substance to moral obligations. More than that, they are a means of keeping the feeling of moral obligation active all the time, so that whenever occasion arises to translate the duty into performance we are in a state of readiness for that. If an athlete does not keep fit by means of self-appropriated food, exercise and sleep taboos he will fail when it comes to the real test. And what is more, taboos refer to observable behaviour. So they serve as a means by which a person can account to himself, as well as to the world at large, for the conscientious discharge of his moral obligations.

It is easy to see how this analysis applies to politico-ritual functionaries. For them, too, their taboos symbolize to themselves and to the world at large their endowment by society with the parts they have to play – their licences, as Hughes puts it, to hold office. But more than that, they symbolize their appropriation of these parts, to return to the formula which I used earlier. Since adherence to them is in part a public act, the taboos also validate their incorporation into the social structure in their status as holders of office. Looking back on the brief account I have given of the religious context of their tasks, duties and social relations, we can see how their taboos have the same symbolical value in holding them to their moral commitment to their parts as do those of a borrower of land. It is not magic of the 'divine kingship' kind that imposes ritual forms on these offices. Their religious character is a way of investing with binding force the moral obligations to society, for its well-being and prosperity, which those who accept office must solicitously translate into actions.

It has long been understood that religious conceptions and ritual institutions fulfil critical integrative functions in primitive societies. Malinowski once spoke of them as 'the cement of the social fabric'. But what I have tried to examine is something more specific. If we look behind the networks and hierarchies of social relations to the persons whose conduct and activities make up the working of a social structure, we see that every part played in the stream of process is made up of diverse components. There are always economic components, in that goods and services of some kind or another are used up and produced, and there are invariably jural components, since roles are exercised as a matter of right and duty, subject to rules and sanctions of a juridical order. What I wish to stress is that there is also invariably a moral component. This represents the mutual commitment to his roles of person and society focused in status and office. Just as society expresses its commitment to the individual when it invests him with office, so he must feel committed to his roles, statuses and offices if he is to fulfil their requirements adequately. To paraphrase Redfield, I see religious prescriptions as serving to symbolize and focus this moral component.[38]

Does this analysis apply to every kind of status or is it limited to eminent office and to special categories of social and economic relations of the kind we would call contractual? A test case will come to the mind of every anthropologist. Among the Tallensi every person is ostensibly by right of birth a member of his patrilineal clan and lineage. From this irreducible fact of what Linton called 'ascribed' status flow numerous attributes of jural, economic and ritual status. They include eligibility for politico-ritual office, rights of inheritance and succession, the privileges and duties of cult allegiance and other elements of citizenship. The individual has no choice; he is bound by the chances of birth. Is there a parallel with office here?

Tale custom is conveniently explicit on this point.[39] A person has membership in his lineage by right of birth only if he is his father's legitimate child. Thus it is not the mere fact of birth but legitimate birth that is decisive; and legitimacy derives from the jural rights over his wife's reproductive powers conferred on a person's father in return for the bride price. It is because a man is invested with (licensed for) husbandhood that his children are able to be born into their 'ascribed' status. And, as might be expected, a religious hallmark is added. It is a strict rule that a child must be born under its father's roof. If a woman bears a child elsewhere than in her marital home, particularly in her father's place, it is a ritual pollution and a cleansing rite must be performed. Obviously this is an assertion, in the idiom of taboo, of the jural disjunction between a woman's status as daughter and her status as wife and mother, and the consequential differentiation of matrilateral filiation from patrilineal descent. But it is also an assertion of the father's right to incorporate his offspring in his lineage. Tallensi explain the custom by reference to the ancestor cult. A person must be born under the aegis of his patrilineal ancestors, since it is upon them that he will be dependent for the ordering of his life. Indeed a person is not incorporated into his natal lineage until his father has ascertained through a diviner which of his ancestors wishes to be his spirit guardian.

There is much more to be said on this subject, notably by adducing the contrast of the illegitimate child. But I think my point is clear. The fact of birth is only a necessary, not a sufficient, condition for kinship and descent status. There is a procedure for establishing this status as a relationship with society and the ancestors; and it is focused in ritual symbolism and observance. Analogous customs are found in other African societies. In Ashanti, for example, an infant is not deemed to be human until it has lived to the eighth day, when it is named and thus incorporated into its family and lineage.[40]

This is not the only way in which religious concepts and customs are utilized to mark status acquired by birth and thus to focus the moral commitments entailed by it. Tale totemic beliefs and avoidances, by reference to which separate clans and lineages are distinguished from one another, are obligatory by virtue of descent and kinship status. Like similar observances in other tribal societies, they have no obvious rational basis. What, for instance, can be the economic sense of a taboo on eating a fairly rare variety of grasshopper, or the utility of forbidding all first-born children from eating the domestic fowl? Their purpose is purely symbolical in the same way as are taboos that identify office. They are a constant reminder of the norms and commitments a person is bound to as a member of his lineage and clan. They stand for the inalienable bonds with the ancestors and with living kin.

The burden of my thesis is that societies distinguish between the individual and his offices, statuses or roles. It is because the individual is more than the offices or statuses or roles he may have, because he stands over against them, that ritual is needed in order to confer them upon him, or, alternatively, to deprive him of them. In this way office is entrusted to the holder in a binding manner, or again, conversely, legitimately stripped from him. Ritual presents office to the individual as the creation and possession of society or a part of society into which he is to be incorporated through the office. Ritual mobilizes incontrovertible authority behind the granting of office and status and thus guarantees its legitimacy and imposes accountability for its proper exercise.

This raises a complex problem. If there is such a dialectical relationship between individual and office, we must expect to find some degree of conceptual awareness, or at least of institutional recognition of the uniqueness, the individuality, as it were, of the individual in all societies. I believe this to be the case, paradoxical as it may seem. As I have shown elsewhere, the Tallensi, like other peoples of West Africa, give cultural recognition to this fact in their concept of Fate.[41] Religious concepts and values are used to assign individuality to the individual so that he may be able to take on diverse roles, statuses and offices in order to play his part in society.

Robert Redfield, whom I have quoted several times, speaking of early city-states remarks (*op. cit.*, p. 65) that religion becomes to them a 'way of making citizens'. Citizenship, surely, means the sum total of all the legitimate offices, statuses and roles a person can have in his society. In this sense Redfield's dictum sums up pithily the theme of my paper, and suggests what must be added to Van Gennep's model in order to explain why ritual is indispensable in *rites de passage.*

What I have in mind can be exemplified by reference to initiation ceremonies. In terms of Van Gennep's model they are the means of marking and organizing the transition from childhood to socially recognized adulthood. Restated in terms of the model I am proposing they are the means of divesting a person of his status as a child in the domestic domain and of investing him with the status of actual or potential citizen in the politico-jural domain.[42] Ordeals and mutilations are more than conspicuous ways of emphasizing entry into the new status. The right to exercise adult sexuality, that is sexuality in marriage for procreative purposes, as opposed to childish sexuality, is one of the distinctive prerogatives and responsibilities of citizenship. One purpose of initiation rites, and, for that matter, the main purpose of female initiation, is to confer this right and to do this in such a way that the commitments implied in its acquisition are accepted as a necessary moral and jural concomitant of citizenship. I believe that this reformulation assists in comprehending the need for ritual in such ceremonies.

### Postscript

This essay had gone to press when Professor Roman Jakobson drew my attention to Professor Ernst H. Kantorowicz's profound and erudite book, *The King's Two Bodies.* It is, in Dr Kantorowicz's own words, a history of 'corporational modes of thinking' concerning the connection between the king's 'Body natural' as a mortal man and his 'Body politic' as an immortal office, to re-phrase the celebrated formula in Plowden's 'Reports' of the mid sixteenth century. Dr Kantorowicz casts his net wider than did his illustrious predecessor, F. W. Maitland, and thus illuminates aspects of the problem that are of particular interest to an anthropologist. Dr Kantorowicz's elucidation of the notion that 'the king never dies' in mediaeval political theory and theological doctrine, notably in

England, is pregnant with matter for thought for an anthropologist concerned with the theme of my present essay. One cannot fail to be impressed by the acute understanding mediaeval jurists displayed of the sociological realities at issue in the question of succession to kingship.

My essay, limited as it is in its scope, would have been enriched in several places if I had had the stimulus of this book at the time I wrote it.

# 6

## Totem and taboo

I

This topic may appear orthodox to a degree at a time when our studies are reverberating with new words and new ideas. My excuse is that I did not choose it; it forced itself on me. Let me explain. In the heyday of functionalism, one of our preoccupations was to assert the autonomy of social anthropology as a discipline in its own right. When Malinowski proclaimed himself to be at heart an anti-quarian (1932: xxv) his tongue was not merely in his cheek but pro-truding provocatively in the direction of the searchers after pristine savagery. More soberly, as he put it in his posthumous manifesto for an independent science of culture, 'our minimum definition implies that the first task of each science is to recognise its legitimate subject matter' (1944: 14) By the same token Radcliffe-Brown went to special pains, in 1931, to dissociate the 'generalising science of cul-ture and society' from human biology, prehistoric archaeology and historical ethnology (1931). And it is, incidentally, very pertinent to my topic that, in order to illustrate the 'newer social anthropology', he outlined his functionalist theory of totemism. In the middle thirties the claim that 'anthropology deals with mankind as a whole' (Boas 1938: 1) was still authoritatively asserted by such eminences as Boas and Seligman. Nor must it be thought that this conception had support only from the diehards (cf. Beattie 1964). The case for 'an integrative framework for the study of human groups ...' was learnedly argued by one of my predecessors in this office, Professor Daryll Forde (1951).

And the ideal – some would say the chimera – of a 'unified science of man' continues to attract passionate advocacy (cf. Freeman 1960). But the trend of our times is against this.

Today, far from being denied that status, social anthropology has received both academic and public accreditation as a respectable social science. And this has brought an unexpected challenge. How, one is constantly asked, do you distinguish social anthropology from sociology proper (cf. Davis 1959; Murdock 1954)? Where do you draw the line, if not where the generation of Frazer and Tylor assumed it to be, in the dichotomy of savagery and civilization, primitive and progressive societies?[1]

I do not want to denigrate this issue. It has indeed a bread and butter side to it, as the Report of the Heyworth Committee (1965) reminds us. But it is of no use, when one is thus directly challenged, to refer to such admirable elucidations as Nadel's *Foundations* (1951) or the more recent reappraisal of the main problems by Gluckman and Devons (1964). And that is where I turn to totemism. I offer it, as Radcliffe-Brown did, as an example of a subject of enquiry that is distinctive of the data, the methods and the theories of social anthropology, and characteristic also of its historical development.

*Totemism* has, ever since McLennan put it on the scientific map, been a peculiarly anthropological subject in a way that, say, problems of kinship or law or politics or economics are not. It is the same with *taboo*. I have presumed to borrow the title of the epoch-making treatise with which Freud opened the gates of psychoanalysis to an alliance with anthropological research – why, will, I hope, become clear later. But no one can today discuss totemism without paying tribute to Lévi-Strauss; and my debt to his searching and already famous re-examination of the whole subject will be obvious (Lévi-Strauss 1962 *a* and *b*).

## II

'Totemism', said Radcliffe-Brown in 1929 (after having questioned its usefulness as a technical term) 'is not one thing, but is a general name given to a number of diverse institutions, which all have, or seem to have something in common' (Radcliffe-Browne 1952); and others, before that, had come to much the same conclusions, as Lévi-Strauss' survey reminds us. This has not deterred anyone from examining specimens of the syndrome so named; and I propose to follow suit. The important decision to take is in what frame of theory to examine our specimens. Banal as this precept may sound, it is prudent to emphasize it. Take, for instance, the trouble I have got into over 'filiation' and 'complementary filiation'. Everybody here is, I am sure, familiar with the forceful address with which Dr Leach launched the Malinowski lectures in 1961. Having disposed of Dr Richard's 'tautologies' and Radcliffe-Brown's 'taxonomic assumptions' (1961: 4) he dismisses my argument about complementary filiation as tautologous too; but there is a mollifying rider. 'I do not claim', adds Dr Leach, 'that Professor Fortes is mistaken, but I think he is misled by his prior suppositions.' And one moral drawn is that we must abandon comparison for generalization, and above all shun 'universal definitions and discriminations' such as, among others, 'Fortes's discrimination between filiation, affinity and descent'. And lest we underestimate the strength of Dr Leach's methodological puritanism, let me quote this passage too (1961: 17).

> The merit of putting a statement into algebraic form is that one letter of the alphabet is as good or as bad as any other. Put the same statement into concept language, with words like paternity and filiation stuck in the middle of it and God help you!

This is a formidable indictment, mitigated for me only by the fact that Dr Leach himself finds the word – I hesitate to say concept – of filiation useful in this paper and that in the following year (Leach 1962) he officially adopts the unfortunate term and concludes (in 'concept language'):

> This distinction (referring to his foregoing argument) is in fact made in the use which Cambridge anthropologists currently make of the terms 'descent' and 'filiation'. For us, 'descent' indicates a set of precisely designated relations; 'filiation' applies to relations in which option may be expressed.

As if these buffets from the left were not enough a homily from the *avant garde* right adds a further warning.

> Instead of typologies [concludes Dr Schneider in an otherwise admirable analysis] we need a series of relevant elements like descent, classification, exchange, residence, filiation, marriage,

and so on; these need to be rigorously defined as analytic categories and then combined and recombined into various combinations and permutations, in different sizes, shapes and constellations. The model of defined parts can be constructed with or without Lévi-Strauss's kind of intellectualist or Hegelian assumptions, or the kind of positivism which Fortes requires. I have dwelt somewhat longer on some of the positivist difficulties than on the intellectualist problems, but each has its share of problems. (Schneider 1964).

Problems indeed there are; but I must confess that I am bewildered by Dr Schneider's prescription, unless it be that he opts for geometry where Leach recommends algebra. What is clear, though, is that he wants us to do what Leach most objects to and that is produce some universal definitions and discriminations. But what have we positivists been doing all these years if not trying to establish rigorous criteria for distinguishing the very 'variables' Dr Schneider enumerates? The truth is that Dr Schneider is himself misled by the models. He believes, for example, that unilineal descent 'allocates a whole man to a group' (1964: 75) whereas in fact it does nothing of the kind: unilineal descent 'allocates' a person to a 'group' primarily in his politico–jural capacity.

Faced, therefore, with such contradictory methodol	ogial exhortations, I retreat to the straightforward empiricism of the old guard: *solvitur ambulando*, making the best use we can of any conceptual tools we can lay hands on.

## III

I shall waste no time on the historical and definitional problems of totemism. Lévi-Strauss has brought us up to date on both. Let it suffice that, in the societies I am concerned with, many observers have reported beliefs and practices in which relations of a special kind between persons and designated groups of persons, on the one hand, and natural species of animals and plants or artificial objects, on the other, are postulated; and, be it added, that some of these observers have been properly sceptical about the appropriateness of calling these associations totemism (cf. Delafosse 1912; 1920).

Indeed, nothing could have seemed more straightforward when I

first encountered totemistic[2] associations and observances amongst
the Tallensi. According to the literature, one could expect to find
patrilineal descent groups of a more or less uniform pattern
throughout the Voltaic region; these groups were likely to be exogamous and localized; each would have a totem animal or animals,
which its members were forbidden to kill or eat, more rarely, an artifact they were forbidden from handling in profane ways; and each
group would also have other distinctive observances of a ritual
character, notably, as Rattray (1932) emphasized, a clan-specific
oath. These observances would be accounted for by a myth of ancestral origins, but different descent groups might have the same forbidden animals or objects.[3]

French investigators, Delafosse[4] in particular (1912; 1920), had
established that so-called totemism, in this area, was not associated
with exogamy or with beliefs in descent from a clan-prohibited
animal or with other features assumed by Frazer, Durkheim, Van
Gennep and other scholars to be significantly correlated with totemism. All it amounted to, in this area, he maintained, was a special relationship between a clan, a part of a clan, a local community, or
even an individual, and an animal species or a particular animal, in
which avoidance of killing or eating or in other ways showing disre-
spect to the totem was enjoined.

The Tallensi seemed to fit this paradigm in all particulars. I found,
likewise, as Delafosse and Rattray had recorded, characteristic
animal avoidances and correlative observances associated with
sacred localities, pools, rivers, and thus only indirectly with descent
groups, by virtue of their residential propinquity or ritual responsibility for these places. Moreover similar observances could
devolve on individuals, regardless of their clanship, and others were
also bound up with what I called political-ritual offices (Fortes
1945).

When I looked for a theoretical framework into which to fit my
observations, the most promising seemed to be the neo-
Durkheimian analysis, as proposed by Radcliffe-Brown in 1929,
and elaborated in his papers on 'Taboo' (1939) and 'Religion and
Society' (1945) (reprinted 1952). Its crux, as Lévi-Strauss points out
(1962*a*: 83), lies in the argument that what are conventionally called
totemic institutions can only be understood as 'part of a much larger
class of phenomena which includes all sorts of ritual relations be-

tween man and natural species', representing the 'incorporation' of nature in the social order (cf. Radcliffe-Brown 1952: 96, 123–4, 127).

Lévi-Strauss (1962a: 84–9) regards this as a relatively crude theory by contrast with Radcliffe-Brown's 1951 revision. He argues that for Radcliffe-Brown, as for Malinowski, 'an animal only becomes totemic because it is first good to eat'. But Radcliffe-Brown makes it clear that it is the 'ritual attitude' to natural species and other objects or events which have important effects upon the well-being (material or spiritual) of a society, not this utilitarian value that he takes to be the nucleus of totemism (1952: 154); and this has implications to which I shall return.

Incidentally, it is worth mentioning why the 1951 theory created so little stir among British anthropologists. The fact is that the 'structural principle' which, to quote Radcliffe-Brown (1951) 'has here been spoken of by the term opposition . . . one which separates and also unites . . . and therefore gives us a rather special kind of social integration' – this principle which wins Lévi-Strauss' applause – was, by then a commonplace in British anthropology. And this was not without influence on Radcliffe-Brown, though the principle was in fact not new in his thought – or foreign to Malinowski's.[5]

## IV

Let me try to précis Radcliffe-Brown's theory in a connected, if cumbrous statement: totemism stands for a variety of institutions in which selected portions of nature serve as material objects by reference to which segments of a society express their respective unity and individuality, on the one hand, and their interdependence in a wider structure on the other, in terms of ritual attitudes, observances and myths. These have a moral value exhibited in the associated taboos and a symbolic significance reflecting the notion of the incorporation of nature in society, by the creative acts of primordial ancestors that are reaffirmed periodically in totemic ritual; and this is the basic premiss of the whole complex.

Lévi-Strauss (1962a: 89) contrasts the alleged 'functionalist' assumption that totemic natural species are primarily 'good to eat' with his interpretation of them as primarily 'good to think'. This is the gravamen of his criticism, if so generous and perceptive an appraisal can be so called, of such 'functionalist' description as Elkin's, Firth's and mine, of Australian, Tikopian and Tallensi totemism.

We should bear in mind that, though totemism is, under his ruthless scalpel, dissected down to a quasi-linguistic code, he too starts with the time-honoured problem of seeking to explain the association of social groups with natural species. He, too, posits a distinction between the 'system of nature' and the 'system of culture' or society. But contrary to Radcliffe-Brown, he describes them as mutually exclusive and opposed. The gap is bridged, as he phrases it, by different component systems of culture – at the 'infrastructural level' by technological and other forms of practice, at the 'super-structural level' by conceptual schemes and operations (1962b: 73).[6] It is only the second level that concerns him (1962b: 120); and in this frame of reference it is the 'distinctive function' of so called totemism, as an 'operator' that mediates between nature and culture to 'transcend their opposition', that he seeks to make intelligible. However we must not think of 'operators', 'mediation' and 'opposition' in instrumental terms. The relevant domain is that of ideas not action. 'The term totemism', he declares (1962a: 16), 'covers relations posed ideologically between two series, one *natural*, the other *cultural*'. 'Natural' categories are associated with 'cultural' groups and persons not because of their objective properties nor on account of mystical qualities that might be attributed to them, but because natural species are adapted for 'ideas and relations conceived by speculative thought on the basis of empirical observations'. The crucial feature is that they can be conceptually segregated from one another. They therefore provide a natural model for categorizing the differential spacing out, or sorting out of social groups. It is the differences that are decisive. 'Totemic institutions' we are told, 'invoke an homology not between social groups and natural species but between the differences which are manifested on the one hand at the level of the groups on the other at the level of the species'. This is a phenomenon in the domain of classification and it rests, like them on the universal logical principle of 'being always able to oppose the terms' (1962b: 100).

Thus the differences conceptualized between natural species 'provide the formal conditions for a significant message ... they are codes adapted to convey messages'; and being formal, they convey messages 'that are transposable with other codes and express in them, in their own systems, messages received through the channel of other codes'. An infinite variety of contents from different levels of the social reality can thus be coded, transmitted, converted and transposed in terms of one and the same formal code (1962*b*).

In contrast to Radcliffe-Brown, totemism does not for him belong to the domain of ritual beliefs and practices nor to that of moral relations between society and nature; it is as Leach explains (1965), 'just one specialised variety of a universal human activity, the classification of social phenomena by means of categories derived from the non-social human environment'.

The contrast is perhaps most explicit in Lévi-Strauss' solution of the question why totemic 'codes' are so often, as he puts it 'accompanied by rules of behaviour enjoining or prohibiting modes of conduct'. Food taboos and exogamy are those most commonly reported. It is, of course, now well established that they do not invariably occur together and that the correlation formerly believed to exist between totemism and exogamy is invalid. They are, in fact merely a particular case of large and complex ranges of rules that relate both individuals and social groups to artifacts, actions, natural phenomena and so on, as well as to animals and plants. Nor can the distinctions made between permitted and prohibited species be explained by either the physical or the mystically attributed properties intrinsic to them. Prohibiting certain species is, in effect, only one of a number of means of affirming their 'signification'. The rule of behaviour is 'an operator' in a logic which, 'being qualitative can work with the aid of conduct as well as with that of images' (1962*b*: 136); and rules that are formally identical but of inverse content can be used 'to say the same thing'. Thus, alimentary prohibitions and prescriptions appear to be theoretically equivalent means for 'signifying the signification' in a logical system of which consumable species constitute the elements, wholly or in part (1962b: 137). The fact that these prohibitions and prescriptions are taboos, that is moral and ritual injunctions, is apparently irrelevant. And it is important to realize that it is the 'global relationship' between the two series of differences – natural species on the one side, social groups on the other – not one-to-one correspondences or associations, that is regarded as distinctive of the totemic code. Thus the essence of totemism lies in the construction of the code, not its contents; hence the 'convertibility' of the messages it generates. An example is the parallel between an Australian section system and the Indian caste system adduced in Lévi-Strauss's Henry Myers Lecture (1963: and cf. 1962*b*: Ch. IV).

We can see why Lévi-Strauss hails Radcliffe-Brown's 1951 analysis of Australian moiety totemism with such enthusiasm. His apparent application of the principle of logical opposition to account for the pairing of bird and other animal species in the totemic representation of the moieties is fully in line with Lévi-Strauss's procedure.[8] For my part, I cannot see how it supersedes rather than supplements the 1929 theory. To be sure, it tells us that, *given* a moiety structure and *given* also the totemic ideology, the moieties will be represented by species that must be of one kind by one or more super-ordinate cultural definitions, and of two, contrastable kinds by one or some subordinate cultural definitions. This shows *how* the totemic ideology is implemented not *why* it utilizes animal species in general and these in particular. In answering this question, Radcliffe-Brown observes that eagle-hawk and crow are the two chief *meat eating* birds of Australia, that the aborigine *thinks of himself* as a meat eater and that eagle-hawk, a hunting bird, turns up to follow an aborigines' hunt whereas crow haunts camps to scavenge for meat. The connection, therefore, is not only on the level of postulated differences between the two series but on the level of observed correspondence between the habits and characteristics of the members of the two series. In fact, what Radcliffe-Brown is really concerned with is not the logical opposition of 'model' species but the representation of the structural opposition 'which separates and also unites' and thus produces 'a rather special kind of social integration' – opposition in the actual social relations of fighting, marriage, ritual activities and so forth.

This is the kind of opposition which, as I remarked earlier, had by that date been the subject of considerable ethnographical study in England, and it presupposes the empiricist view of social structure which Lévi-Strauss rejects.

Though it is to the 'how' of totemic codes that Lévi-Strauss mainly addresses his enquiries he also has an answer to the 'why' and 'what' questions. This is the reiterated hypothesis that differentiated social groups, e.g. exogamous groups, 'need an objective model to express their social diversity ... (and) ... the only possible objective model has to be sought in the natural diversity of biological species' since the only alternative 'objectively given model of concrete diversity', the cultural one 'made up by the social system of trades and occupations' is not available to them (1963: 9). Here in a nutshell, lies an implication that runs through the whole of Lévi-Strauss' analysis. It seems that the existence of social divisions is in some way the prior condition for the establishment of totemic codes. Take away social division by sections, exogamy, descent, etc., and the 'need' disappears.

One cannot fail to be reminded of Radcliffe-Brown's thesis (1929), that it is 'when the society becomes differentiated into segmentary groups such as clans' that the totemic relationship between groups and natural species arises. But whereas for Radcliffe-Brown the 'need' met by totemism is for a 'mechanism by which a system of social solidarities is established between man and nature' – both being part of a single 'moral order' – for Lévi-Strauss it is a 'need' of an intellectual order expressed in the propensity to classify. For Radcliffe-Brown the totemic objects belong to the *sacra* of society and serve as a necessary objective focus for the sentiments of attachment of persons to these groups; for Lévi-Strauss it is an inevitable objective gambit in a classifying code. All the same, to speak of 'need' here is to sail perilously close to the functionalist wind.

## V

Where then is the essential divergence between Lévi-Strauss' point of view and the functionalist view represented by Radcliffe-Brown? It hinges, to my mind, on the place accorded to the actor. Lévi-Strauss' position is that of the 'detached and external onlooker', as Jakobson puts it (1961) who 'attempts to break the code through a scrutiny of the messages'. The functionalist position is, as far as his techniques of investigation permit, that of the internal observer who – again I quote Jakobson – 'becomes adjusted to the native speaker and decodes the messages in their mother tongue'. His aim is to understand the 'messages' from the position of the actor in society – the giver and receiver of the messages.

From a functionalist point of view, the actor is at the centre of the enquiry;[9] and by the actor I mean the status-endowed person, sole or corporate (e.g. the proverbial unilineal descent group) exercising his (or its) socially bestowed roles and capacities, rights and duties within the matrix of social relations outside of which he (or it) has no existence. We are concerned with the actor as a social and moral person – the right-bearing, duty-serving identified person adumbrated in M. Mauss' famous Huxley lecture (1939); and the actor is not intelligible without reference to the ends of his action-patterns.

Looking prosaically behind the terminology in which Lévi-Strauss propounds his analysis I infer that the actor is irrelevant for him.[10] By his reductionist procedure everything that is particular in the actor's relations to his culture is distilled down to the universal stuff of the 'code'. It is like money, in terms of which the value of cultural items of every description can be uniformly 'coded' regardless of their 'contents'. By isolating the classifying, categorizing and communication functions of totemic institutions, Lévi-Strauss illuminates a fundamental aspect of the syndrome. But it is at the cost of neutralizing the actor. No wonder, then that we functionalists and Lévi-Strauss and his followers seem to be talking past one another. For we and they are looking at the configuration of actor, action, and cultural materials of action from opposite sides.[11] For us, language is verbal custom: for them, all custom is transposed language.

The first principle of an actor-oriented enquiry is that the actor must be properly specified. Unqualified hypostatization will not do, e.g. an Australian section or sub-section is not an internally undifferentiated corporate 'group'. It cannot and does not 'produce women' (Lévi-Strauss 1963).

This makes us realize what underlies the 'convertibility' and 'transformability' of messages from one cultural modality to another. It is the coalescence, or concatenation of actors, roles and statuses at the different levels. It is because the violinist combines in himself the two roles of score reader and performer that the transformation of the written into the auditory musical message can occur. Again, to return to Australia, a man in the status of an initiated senior takes an Eagle-hawk part in a totemic ceremony, in contra-distinction to a Crow man; then, at the level of a marriage transaction, this man takes the Eagle-hawk role of sister's son to the Crow moiety; and that is how the totemic 'message' is transposed to that level. Analogously, without a bilingual actor, translation from one language to another is impossible. In other words, the convertibility and transposibility attributed to the totemic codes in a message-centred frame of analysis reflect the structural consistencies elicited by actor-oriented analysis.

## VI

Functional analysis is actor-centred. This was the perspective from which my description of Tallensi totemism and Firth's of Tikopian totemism were undertaken. And the idea of 'structural opposition' then current amongst British anthropologists played an important part in it.

It was for use, however, as a principle not of logical thought, but of social structure that subsumed regularities expressed in customs and institutions but discernible in the actual familial, politico-jural, ritual and economic relations of persons and groups. One could not miss it among the Tallensi.[12]

In 1935, when I had the honour of addressing a meeting of this Institute for the first time, I gave an account of the Tallensi cycle of sowing and harvest festivals. I interpreted these as symbolical dramatizations of 'a political structure the essential principle of which is a polar opposition defined and emphasized by the most stringent ritual observances'. I showed that this polarity was exhibited through the medium of their ceremonial and ritual customs, but reflected their opposed political alignments in war and peace, as well as their moral obligations to collaborate in ritual for the common good, which united Namoos and Talis; and I described the 'bridging function' of the Gbizug Tendaana in maintaining an equilibrium over time between these two contraposed clan clusters (Fortes 1936).

The same theme was later elaborated in my analysis of clanship and kinship among the Tallensi (1945; 1949). There I showed how structural consolidation, segmentation and cleavage could be observed at all levels of the social system. I traced out their foundation in the kinship and descent system and their consolidation in polar politico-ritual offices and institutions. I examined the complementary structural ties of interdependence at the level of kinship and descent and at that of the common interests and values that periodically unite otherwise autonomous groups in obligatory political and ritual collaboration and cult.[13] And what became evident was that it was through the participation of the same structural elements, individually or corporately, in different combinations at all levels that an overall balance was maintained in the social system.

'Structural opposition' in this context of analysis isolates a general principle of arranging, identifying and constraining persons in social action, not a rule of logic. And to understand Tallensi totemistic observances and institutions we must appreciate the part they play in implementing this principle. To this end they do more than merely classify actors as individuals or corporate persons. To engage in any kind of social relations it is necessary that every actor be discriminated and identified from the outside. He – or the corporate group – must display his status or office. However, this is not enough. The actor must not only be identified. He (or they) must accept and appropriate, that is identify with, the statuses and roles, the rights, duties and capacities that are allocated to him in the social process (Fortes 1962a).

This dimension of the person, as actor in the homogeneous social systems of primitive societies, has been elucidated with profound insight by A. I. Hallowell (1955).[14] Insisting that a human society 'is not only a social order but a moral order', he adds to this Durkheimian postulate the thesis that 'the members of such an order are expected to assume moral responsibilities for their conduct'. And this, he contends, 'implies self-awareness' – that is realization of one's statuses and roles as belonging to oneself – or else the actor would be unable to 'appraise his own conduct in terms of traditional values and social sanctions'. This requires distinguishing between self and other, in the total 'behavioural environment' which embraces not only man and nature but the spatial and temporal frames of reference and the culturally postulated supernatural realm, which ensure the continuity of experience and relationship that underlies 'self-awareness'. Self-appraisal requires cultural devices for 'objectifying' the self as an 'object of value' that is, as an autonomous agent within roles, statuses and capacities exercised in the routine stream of social relations. And it implies the assumption that a person has 'volitional control' over his acts—in conformity with the norms and values of his society and culture.[15]

Person, then has two aspects relevant to my theme. On the one side is his public identification, externally, by and in his relations with other persons, sole or corporate. This is a question of how he is known and shows himself to be the person he is supposed to be. On the other side is his self-awareness – his conception or image of his identity in the social order. This is a question of his internal orientation, how he knows himself to be the person he is supposed to be.

We know that, regarded from the outside, a person can be seen as an 'assemblage of statuses'.[16] Furthermore these statuses are and must be differentiated from one another by structural location and by customary definition in all domains of social life, even where they appear to be fused together.[17]

Names, titles, kinship labels, costume, bodily markings, and to a striking degree, obligatory moral and ritual observances and distinctive jural rights and duties, are media that specify these differentiations. But they are not merely external indices; they allocate persons to their roles and statuses; and they objectify, for the actor, his representation to himself of his roles and statuses and his commitment to them. Totemistic institutions of the Tallensi type fall into this category of cultural devices.

For Lévi-Strauss all such discriminative customs equally 'signify the signification' and the key to this is the logic of opposition. The formula can certainly be applied to the Tallensi. There is a direct reflection in discriminative custom of the interrelations of persons and groups by complementary and polar ties and cleavages on all levels of social structure.[18] From the actor's point of view, however, differentiations thus 'signified' represent interests and loyalties, rights and duties, their convergence and their divergence in collaboration or in potential competition and conflict.[19]

The Tallensi are typical of the Voltaic peoples in that this principle of 'structural opposition' applies in all domains of their social life. And the ethnographic evidence is, to my mind, indisputable that its systematic exploitation in the social structure has its roots in the structure of the nuclear field of social reproduction (Fortes 1958) – the constellation of parents and children in which the complementarity of the sexes and the polarity of successive generations are the critical factors. Here – and not in the structure of the human brain – lies the actor's model for the structure of social groups and relationships at all levels, and it is the experience of the elementary social relations of filiation and siblingship in this context that is the basis of a person's conception of his social identity. The fact is that structural complementarity and polarity are not reducible to instances of mere logical opposition.

## VII

But let me return to the declarative and discriminative 'indices', as I formerly called them (1945: Ch. 9), and observances of the Tallensi. A glance at the ethnography shows that they do not all have the same kind of meaning to the actors. They are not equivalent even where, in message-centred language, they might be said to refer to the same things signified. Some have an external reference, others an internal one. Some can be read as manifest signs or indices, others have more abstruse symbolical implications. Some are plainly secular or profane, in the Durkheimian sense, others have ritual value.

Tallensi totemistic observances serve both to focus the actor's recognition and conception of his identity as a person in a given status and to declare his identification of himself in relation to and by others.

The distinction was not altogether overlooked in the description I gave of Tallensi totemism in 1945, but I did not then fully appreciate its importance. It is one of the main themes of Lienhardt's account of the totem-like clan divinities of Dinka religion. Much of what I have to say is confirmed by his analysis (Lienhardt 1961).

In 1945, following prevailing convention, I took totemism to refer to the special relations of a ritual character between defined social groups and species of animals. But as Lévi-Strauss emphasizes, these associations do not stand alone. They are part of a complex configuration of declarative and discriminative observances and beliefs. This includes the oath, the apparel ordained for the dead, mortuary and funeral customs and ritual festivals, as well as politico-ritual offices and the apparel and observances obligatorily associated with them. And this is not all. For example, in the vicinity of Baari one sees homesteads that are whitewashed side by side with others that are plastered red. Any child will tell you that the white homesteads belong to people of X lineage and the red ones to the Ys. Ask further and you discover that the Xs are an accessory lineage of Gorni origin; and that it is a taboo (*kyiher*) for them to whitewash their houses, accounted for by one of the stereotyped myths of an ancestral experience and commandment. A tendaana's homestead is always flat-roofed. This is a *kyiher*, a taboo of the Earth, binding on the office and the lineage. These are but two conspicuous examples of 'taboo' constraints on the construction of homesteads and their internal arrangements. And in no case is a rational or utilitarian reason given for the practice.

But it would be a mistake to think that the colour or roof style of a man's homestead has only the indicative value of identifying him as belonging to a particular lineage or holding a particular office. It is a crucial feature, from the actor's point of view, that it is ritually obligatory – a taboo, breach of which would be an offence against his ancestors and the Earth. A man's homestead is much more to him than a dwelling place. It is, as I have shown elsewhere (1949: Ch. 3), the material representation of the family and lineage nucleus in all its parts and relations, joining the ancestors with their progeny and objectifying the irreducible bonds of kinship and descent upon which the whole society is founded.[20] Here only may the procreative sexuality which is the source of lineage perpetuity, be licitly exercised (ibid. 123–4). The concept of the family-in-its-dewlling (*yir*) has profound emotional value; extended to the politico-jural domain it sums up the paradigm of lineage structure; in the ritual domain it stands for the perpetual presence of the ancestors. Thus it is packed with ritual implications and symbolic reference. The regulation of the sites, forms, external appearance and internal arrangements of homesteads by ritual injunction, is intelligible only if we bear this substratum of its meaning in mind.[21]

## VIII

The Tallensi distinguish precisely between declarative customs that are complied with for reasons of propriety – (*de nareme*) and those that are adhered to in deference to moral or ritual injunction. These comprise ritual custom (*malung*) and taboo custom (*kyiher*) though all ritual custom is regarded as to some degree infused with taboo. Fear of embarrassment is the sanction of the former. In the case of the latter it is the likelihood of mystical retribution.[22]

But much as they differ in significance, it is characteristic of all taboo customs that they are accepted as absolutely binding whether they seem to an observer reasonable or unreasonable, trivial or onerous and whether they are believed to have been instituted by ancestral fiat or merely to have existed from time immemorial. They are moral imperatives complied with in acts of individual observances or abstention or belief even when they are common to many persons, unlike for example the ceremonies of the Great Festivals, or the mortuary rites or sacrifices at ancestral shrines or Earth shrines, which are public and collective activities.

Depending on the gravity of the taboo, the automatic penalty of transgression may be no worse than an unpleasant dermatitis, but it may be as severe as a wasting disease or the extinction of one's descent line. The observance of a taboo signifies submission to an internal command which is beyond question.

All Tallensi totemistic observances and beliefs are *kyiha*, taboos. And they are absolutely binding for the whole of life from birth to death or, in the case of office, from the holder's installation, which is a kind of birth, to his death. They are binding on the whole person all the time. Exactly parallel is the totally binding force of the taboos declarative of the sanctity of localities and Earth shrines, quite as if they too were persons. Transgression is tantamount to repudiating one's identity, or one's identification with a locality or office of status. This is what I mean by describing it as an internal command and it accounts for the self-punishing form of sanction.

And this reminds us of one of the most important aspects of Tallensi totemistic taboos – indeed of taboos in general. They set apart persons, localities, offices, institutions. They insulate as well as communicate. From the actor's point of view they can often be described as ordained aversions. The emotional, often psychosomatic reaction to inadvertent breach shows this.[23]

What I am asserting, then – reasserting, if you like since it was the main point of my earlier analysis and is stressed in all the ethnographic literature on the Voltaic paople – is that the totemistic observances of the Tallensi are not intelligible from the actor's point of view without taking into account their taboo – that is their morally binding character. As I stated it in 1945, the emphasis 'is on the avoidance, on the act of conduct as such'. There are many aspects of Tallensi taboo custom that do not concern me here. What is relevant is that totemistic taboos ordain rules of conduct that are binding on the individual, in the first place because he is the person he is in the situation he is in. Compliance with them means that he identifies himself with, appropriates to himself, the capacities, the rights and obligations, the relationships and the commitments that devolve upon a normal person of his status in his situation. He has, it must be remembered, been cast in these roles or in roles preparatory to them since childhood. Being with him all the time taboos keep him aware of his enduring identity as a person in contraposition to other persons.

There is, however, a second factor of fundamental importance in these prescriptions. They are defined as obligations to the founding ancestors and to the Earth, not to the objects themselves. They represent acknowledgement of a particular form of dependence, as Radcliffe-Brown would, I suppose have argued, more precisely, perhaps, of bonds that amount to inescapable bondage.

## IX

This brings me to the contents of these observances. My earlier presentation emphasizes 'their correlation with structural ties and cleavages' (1945: 133 sqq.), as 'indices' of affinity and differentiation between Namoos and Talis, between and amongst lineages and clans, and as 'ways in which the corporate identity and the continuity of lineage and clan are expressed'. In developing this interpretation, I gave principal attention, as I have already noted, to the animal avoidances.

What I should now stress is the fact that the animal taboos are part of a larger configuration of totemistic custom and that within their internal context of social structure each of its components corresponds to a distinct and irreducible dimension of status for the normal person. Patrilineal descent is the crucial determinant of normal personhood. Without legitimate patrilineal descent or assimilation thereto by a fiction, a Tallensi is a politico-jural non-entity, a non-person devoid of the rights and duties of kinship and citizenship and consequently (which is more serious) of ritual status in relation to the ancestors.[24] The closest parallel with us would be a person without a recognized legal nationality. But the concept of patrilineal descent covers a number of factors. First and foremost is a person's recognized connection, by legitimate paternity and a known agnatic pedigree, with a unique founding ancestor, entailing binding politico-jural and ritual commitments. This is projected in the animal (or artifact) taboo. Secondly and consequentially is his membership of a contemporary body of co-agnates who constitute a person's lineage and clan and to whom he is bound by the norms of descent. This is represented by the oath, which symbolizes also the religious community to which he must belong by virtue of descent. His locality of domicile, binding him to moral norms recognized in the chthonic taboos may be significant. But what specifically characterizes the lineage is its unity as a corporate person presumed to have existed from time immemorial as an autonomous and perpetual politico-jural and ritual entity. Agnation means allocation to the socio-temporal continuum incorporated in the lineage. The ordained garb of the dead is the symbolic expression of this.

Individually observed though they are, patri-totemistic taboos are common to all lineage members. Complementary filiation creates connections that establish significant politico-jural and ritual capacities that differentiate individuals from their co-agnates. In testimony of this they will then observe the totemistic taboos of matrilateral lineages, for otherwise they could not partake of sacrifices offered to their matri-ancestors. It is relevant that uterine kin (*soog*) do not, on that account, have common totemistic observances. For unlike true agnation, or the crypto-agnation of lineage nephews and nieces (cf. Fortes 1945, Ch. 9; 1949, Ch. 11), this relationship is not in the politico-jural domain; it is not connected with ancestry that legitimates status; it does not fall under the ritual authority of the ancestors and the Earth. It is a peculiarly inter-individual relationship of amity, presumed to be of organic origin and activated by chance and choice, contributing nothing to status specification.

The important point is that agnation by legitimate paternity,[25] which assigns every person uniquely and irrevocably to a corporate politico-jural segment of society establishes the basic jural identity he must have to be able to act as a person in contraposition to other persons; and he has no choice about this. He cannot but accept his patrilineal assignment if he wishes to remain in and of his society. This means accepting as an obligation of conscience the commitments and capacities that pertain to each facet of agnatic status.

It might be supposed that the elaborate genealogical calculus of the Tallensi would suffice to identify all persons. But it has only external validity. It does not specify conduct or designate the rights, duties, capacities and commitments that constitute the actuality of being a person. Hence I argued in 1945 that the principles behind both genealogical assignment and the correlated norms are abstract and general. I claimed, then, that totemic taboos crystallize these abstract norms in concrete objects and precise rules of conduct which are the more effective because they are of no utilitarian or rational value (1945: 135). In this sense they can indeed be said to make 'thinkable' experience of social life that is not susceptible of exact conceptualization in Tallensi social philosophy. It is this un-equivocal form and concrete objectification of the moral imperative that enables the actor to apprehend the principles it stands for and appropriate them to himself – enables him, as I formerly put it (1945:68) to visualize his social identity and 'identify himself in thought and feeling with his clan and his ancestors'. And this is the aspect that is reflected in the contents of the taboos, whereas the rules of abstinence or of observance express the compulsion on the actor to accept their finality as edicts of the ancestors that affirm their authority and perpetuity. The correspondence between this aspect of totemistic taboo and the fact that descent is determined arbitrarily, as it seems, by the chance incidence of birth is patent. The moral and ideological stress is on the corporate identity of the descent group. And this is understandable, in the face of the internal cleavages, and the corresponding divergencies of interests, in the structure of lineage and clan due to the working of complementary filiation and segmentation by fraternal lines.

Thus what the taboo component reflects is the ineluctable binding force of agnatic relationship that cannot – dare not – be repudiated if one wishes to be a normal person.

## X

Fifteen years later Dr Lienhardt picked up the same theme in his splendid study of Dinka religion (1962). The Dinka, like the Nuer and other Nilotic peoples, appear to have a more complex system of religious beliefs and concepts than the Tallensi.[26] But among their divinities there is a group associated with the patrilineal clan system. Each clan has its own divinity (or divinities) which is accounted for by a belief that it was bestowed by the Supreme Divinity, for the clan's protection. And what Lienhardt calls the 'emblems' of these clan-divinities, are most commonly animal species, as well as grasses, trees, artifacts and other objects. Many of the natural species have no utilitarian value, and the selection of the emblems cannot be accounted for by their natural characteristics. 'They derive their importance,' Lienhardt writes 'from their associations with agnatic descent groups' (1961: 116). They are 'divinities of the father', having a direct and original connection through the father with all the paternal ancestors. The following passage sums up his conclusions in this regard:

> The clan-divinities are easily seen as representative of a particular limited field of Dinka experience, that of agnatic kinship, as we have pointed out. They reflect experience of the abiding descent-group structure of Dinka society. If Divinity represents among other things the situation of human beings as the children of a common father, the clan-divinities are the counterparts of the particular and distinct patrilineal descent-groups and reflect experience and knowledge of them and the value attached to them. By this I do not mean that they are merely the devices by which social groups, considered as entities, are represented, to focus loyalty and affection, on the familiar analogy with national flags or heraldic emblems. We have seen that the clan-divinities do not primarily face outwards, so to speak, from the clans to which they belong, providing a mark by which others may know them. The name of the clan is enough for that, and Dinka often know the names of clans other than their own without also knowing what their divinities are. The clan-divinities have their meaning in relation to the nature of clanship as members of their clans know it, as membership of agnatic descent-groups which transcend their individual members, and yet of which each individual membership is representative. They provide the clearest example of the structure of experience represented by the Powers. (1961: 165–6).

The resemblance between Dinka totemistic institutions and their more prosaic Tallensi counterparts needs no labouring. However, what interests me more is Lienhardt's interpretation of his data. I am not, I think, misreading it if I say that it is generally congruent with my analysis of Tallensi data.[27] In particular, I would like to draw attention to his repeated insistence on the inward-ordered significance of the clan divinities.[28]

Discussing Nuer totemistic beliefs Evans-Pritchard introduces a caveat that is relevant (1956: 134–5). He remarks that:

> It is rather the idea of crocodile than the saurian creatures themselves which stands for Spirit to a lineage. If a Nuer cannot see Spirit he likewise in some cases seldom, if ever, sees his totem; so that it is no longer a question of a material object symbolising an idea but of one idea symbolising another.[29]

All the same, the probability is that if a Nuer were actually to meet a saurian, he would recognize it and act with appropriate ritual respect towards it. The situation is the same for many orthodox Jews.

The point of importance, however, is that without some objective extra-personal reference it would be impossible for such an observance to be held in common by a number of people. Anyhow, Tallensi have no doubts about the real existence of the species and objects to which their totemistic observances are tied. Many are common enough to be frequently met with and tabooed, quite apart from the unquestioning trust everybody has in the authenticity of the stories of the origins of lineage taboos.[30]

However, Evans-Pritchard's comment reminds us that, for most Tallensi, their totemistic taboos are normally latent. Yet this does not make them nugatory. A person carries them about with him as he does the configuration of statuses with which they are bound up. They are psychological anchorage points. We may think of them (following Lienhardt) as 'images' or (as Hallowell does) as 'basic orientations' for the attachment of the 'awareness of his statuses in the social structure' (Hallowell) which, by focusing commitment to 'moral responsibility for his conduct' is a necessary condition for being a normal person.

It could however be argued that any symbol (e.g. a crest, a name) could fulfil this internal steering function. The selection of animal species (and elsewhere in the Voltaic area, some artifacts) is not accounted for thus.[31]

My incidental and, I admit, speculative hypothesis about the preponderance of 'teeth-baring' species among Tallensi totem animals has rightly been questioned by Lévi-Strauss and others. It is an

example of the dangers of observer-bias in interpreting cultural
data. But it draws attention to the main problem. Are these animal
species symbolical or merely declarative and indicative 'emblems' or
ideological counters in a classifying exercise?

## XI

To paint one's house red or white is a lineage-ordered taboo, which
reaffirms an ancestral vow for the house owner and is in this sense
symbolical, but in its external reference is purely significative. Permitted and prohibited categories of apparel (e.g. cloth *versus* skins)
tied to office or clanship are similar in that they have both external
significative reference and internal symbolical meaning. Even the
oath and the ritual garb of the dead have this quality. It is different with
the animal taboos. There are rarely public occasions for them to be
displayed to signify to others the identity of those who observe them.[32]

Lévi-Strauss argues, as we have seen, that it is the differences between animal species which provide the model by reference to which
differences between social groups can be conceptualized. Now animals figure in a great variety of Tallensi ritual customs and institutions, not only in their totemistic observances. In some cases the
relationship is between the individual and a particular animal. In the
case of totem animals and the sacred chthonic animals believed to
reincarnate deceased elders of the clan the connection is between a
lineage or clan and a species. On the other side, Tallensi hunt and
fish and have a considerable body of animal lore. But they do not
classify animals – or trees or grasses – in the way reported, for
example, of the Nuer or the Dogon, or by any other form of systematic taxonomy. They group animals broadly by habitat or
appearance: earth animals, water animals, tree animals, domestic
and wild animals, fish and birds, teeth bearers and horn bearers, for
example. And it is worth adding that particular artifacts, stones,
trees, and other material objects can like animals serve as the vehicle
of living ancestral presence. A tree may be such an ancestor's shrine,
or rather, metamorphosis. Its fruits may, then, not be eaten by his
descendants. Particular portions and items of the natural environment and the material culture are thus incorporated into the sphere
of a person's or lineage's moral and ritual commitments through the
ancestor cult and quasi-totemistic observances.[33]

Thus there is an extensive repertoire of knowledge about exploitation of, and potential ritual relations with animals, individually
and as species, domestic and wild, terrestrial, arboreal, and aquatic;
and it is only a small selection of the species known to the Tallensi
that figures among the 'totemic' objects.[34] If there is any principle of
classification or selection here at work it defies ascertainment; for as
I noted in my earlier account, these species do not constitute a single
type or class either to the Tallensi or objectively. The Tallensi themselves (like other Voltaic peoples and the Dinka) are not interested in
the question. The association of a clan or lineage with a species is for
them the result of a unique, accidental even quasi-miraculous, historical event.[35] And one consideration that certainly never occurs to
informants is that differences between totem species have any significance. Rather are the similarities stressed, as indications of some
sort of linkage.[36] Indeed, among the Hill Talis, where inter-lineage
differentiation is most elaborate – but is counter-balanced by
equally elaborate cross-cutting ties of locality, kinship, and ritual
collaboration – many totem animals are common to genealogically
distinct lineages, and this is accounted for by their quasi-kinship
association in *boghar* or *teng* congregations. This corresponds to
their claim that the Talis totems are linked to the ancestral External
Boghars, as is symbolically evidenced in the taboos of the Boghar by
which they swear their most solemn oath.

Again, in the case of the major cleavage between Namoos and
Talis, it is impossible to perceive, from an observer's standpoint, or
to infer from Tallensi cultural premises, a logical opposition or a
critical species difference between the fowl tabooed by Namoos
first-borns and the water tortoise and other Talis totem animals. A
distinction that strikes the observer, but is not recognized by the Tallensi themselves, is that the fowl is a household animal *par excellence*, intimately a part of the domestic life, whereas Talis totems are
predominantly 'earth' animals of extra-domestic provenance; and
one could make a case for the hypothesis that each is symbolically
apposite for the politico-ritual community to which it pertains.
Thus both the Talis themselves and their Namoo neighbours see a
connection between the chthonic character of Talis totem animals
and their status as Tendaana clans sprung from the Earth. The
Namoos *per contra* have no responsibility for guarding the sanctity
of the Earth. The respect they are obliged to show to the Earth

shrines of their place of domicile arises from the fact of residence. Their corporate unity is warranted solely by the dogma of their common patrilineal descent and is focused in the chiefship vested in their clan. One could argue that it is peculiarly apposite for the totemistic observances distinctive of Namoos to be fixed upon the crucial filio-parental relationship of agnation.

But this is hardly the kind of difference Lévi-Strauss seems to have in mind. In any case, though Namoos and Talis are in many important social and politico-ritual contexts of relations opposed *en bloc*, their constituent lineages are not thought of as falling into an ordered arrangement of differentiated units, corresponding to an homologous arrangement of differentiated totems.[37]

Tallensi, like Dinka, identify other persons and groups by lineage, clan, locality, office and politico-ritual responsibilities; not specifically by their totemistic observances. The emphasis is primarily on the internal meaning of the observance for the actor, not its external reference. The covenant that is its basis binds the descendants of the lineage founder by virtue of the internal unity and corporate continuity of the lineage that perpetuates him, not by reason of their differentiation from other lineages. It asserts their uniqueness of origin and thus documents their autonomy as a corporate person not their distinction from other like units. And the covenant remains perpetually efficacious because the animal species is as perpetual as the lineage. Species continuity by a succession of generations parallels lineage continuity and thus makes the species an ideal symbol for the continuity of a lineage. This is implicit in the totemic myths. The Earth has the same perpetuity and this is reflected in the species avoidances associated with it; and the key politico-ritual offices as a 'corporations sole' have something of this too. Furthermore, a species is uniform in the same way as all the members of a lineage together constitute one corporate person and are all equally members of it irrespective of age or sex or other individual characteristics. All depend collectively and severally on the same ancestors for their survival and well being.

## XII

Thus, one characteristic of animal species that makes them comparable with human descent groups is their reproductive continuity and uniformity. But this implies another characteristic that places them side by side with humans. They are alive; and Tallensi attribute to them the same sources of life – breath and soul – as to humans.[38] The relevance of this has been emphasized by Goody (1962) in his observations on totemism among the Voltaic LoDagaa. For it pre-supposes a notion of continuity between man and animal species, and this fits in with the assumption that animal species have a poten-tiality for quasi-human personality. The altruistic actions, such as might be expected of a kinsman, attributed to the totem animals in the myths, are evidence of this. So from another side is the ritual lustration of the slayer of certain big game animals as if he were a homicide. It supports the suggestion made in my earlier account, that it is the 'livingness' of animals that makes them apt symbols for the continued 'livingness' of ancestors and the Earth, as morally effi-cacious powers in the affairs of the ever-living lineage that incar-nates them.

But, as Goody infers, having life connotes also the possibility of death. Animals like men can die or be killed. They can, also, and in consequence – unlike men, but like plant kinds – be eaten. Further-more, artifacts can be subsumed in this category of evaluation, too, since they are also consumable in use and destructible. These are the properties upon which the critical rules of totemistic observances, the taboos on killing, eating and destroying are fixed, or in converse terms, the injunction to respect the object, as if it were human.

We must remember that it is an irremediable sin, believed to bring about the inevitable extinction of the sinner's whole agnatic progeny, to kill a clansman, or a kinsman, or a person with whom one has quasi-kinship bonds of ritual origin. Indeed it is morally pol-luting and mystically dangerous to shed any human blood upon the Earth, even when it is lawful in self-help or warfare. Killing, except for food or sacrifice, is felt to be a sin.

We have seen that killing certain game animals is construed as murder. It is more heinously so if the victim is a totem animal; for the totem animals are assimilated to a quasi-human status. In Vol-taic culture, this is equivalent to a quasi-kinship relationship – a sort of kinship symbiosis – with the lineages to which they appertain. It is the same *vis-à-vis* the sacred Earth which is the other pole of the moral universe for these peoples. For the Earth, we must remember, is, in its sacred aspect, envisaged as a kind of person, a living force, as Tallensi say, complementary to the collective ancestors.

The humanization of totem animals is quite explicit in the case of the local totemistic species like the crocodile and the python which elders of Earth custodian clans are believed to 'change into' or 'rise up as' after death, and the notion of such metempsychotic transformations is generally accepted. Chiefs for instance are believed sometimes to 'rise up' as lions. The belief is consistent with the theory of ancestral presence in animals, trees and artifacts dedicated to ancestors.[39] Like clan-tied totem animals, these may not be slain or eaten. But this is accounted for by the belief that they are the fathers and forefathers incarnate, who are, by definition, benevolent towards their human kin as long as they are not offended.[40] Here ever-living lineage ancestors, ever-living animal species perpetuating the ancestors spiritually, and the living Earth are patently fused.

What Hallowell says of Ojibwa attitudes applies also to the Tallensi. 'On the assumption', he writes, 'that animals have a body and soul like man, they are treated as if they had self-awareness and volition' (1955: 109). The Tallensi would add that they are capable of moral conduct. Hence a totem python or crocodile that wantonly kills people's livestock may be slain, though it must then be given burial as if it were human.[41]

It needs little imagination to understand how the prohibition on killing the benefactor animal (or on profaning its substitute, a benefactor artifact) which is quasi-human yet not human, cognate by origin yet not kin[42] capable of altruism but normally a-moral, can serve as a surrogate or neutral focus, as it were, for the ban on homicide which epitomizes the binding force of kinship. The important point is that killing, and its equivalent – profaning or breaking an artifact – is an individual act even if it is done in company with others.[43] It is interpreted by Tallensi as a wilful act, subject to the individual's moral control. To refrain from it postulates the 'self-awareness' Hallowell talks about; that is, the recognition of the jural and moral commitments entailed by one's relationships of kinship and descent and cult membership which, for the Tallensi, add up to one's status as a citizen in the total society. It crystallizes a configuration of inward-oriented norms acknowledging dependence on the ancestors and the Earth and given tangibility by the orientation towards the tabooed animal. This contrasts with the outward-oriented norms of incest and exogamy, both observance and breach of which require the concurrence of persons with other persons defined as jurally or morally forbidden or allowed. There is no such agreement between slayer and slain; it is a one way act.

And here the difference among – or rather the patent variety of – natural totem-species (and correspondingly artifact kinds) becomes significant. For though all persons, sole or corporate, must acknowledge their ancestry and status by abstaining from destroying some animal or object, their differentiation from one another by the same criteria of ancestry and status can be recognized by linking them severally to different species or objects. We know that there is no strict homology between the distribution of genealogically differentiated descent groups and kinship ties on the one hand, and the small and biased range of totemistic species on the other. This strengthens the inference that what we have is, in fact, a symbolical relationship between actor and object of observance in which the fact of the natural variations and resemblances among the species is exploited but no global pattern emerges.[44]

## XIII

However the taboo on eating[45] the totem animal is, I believe, the more fundamental one. This stands out in all the literature of the area. It is the way totemistic taboos are commonly phrased in other parts of Africa too. In the totem myths the ancestor's vow always binds himself and his descendants never to eat the benefactor-animal. The ban on killing it appears as a necessary corollary to this.

Arbitrarily prescribed or forbidden foods[46] are among the most explicit indicators of the structural relationships, statuses and situations of persons among all the Voltaic peoples. Commensality, whether or not enjoined, avows amity, whereas dismensality, eating separately, demonstrates cleavage and segregation.[47] Both are liable to be ritually or jurally obligatory.

Now eating has a number of important characteristics. It must be performed at regular and relatively frequent intervals, normally every day, to fulfil its function. More to the point, it is a socially licit yet peculiarly individual activity. Everybody must eat for himself. And closely connected with this is the cardinal fact that eating is subject to conscious, voluntary regulation, in a significantly different manner from other organic drives (such as excretion) and human capabilities (such as speech) which are also susceptible of voluntary control. Eating is a direct and one way relationship between the actor and a natural product. No other person is necessarily included, as in the sexual and in other social relationships, whether with real or with imaginary persons, like ancestors or gods. And yet it is inescapably relational, binding actor to environment, quite unlike the antithetical and no doubt organically comparable act of elimination. Eating takes materials that exist outside the organism and incorporates them, literally, into the body. It is a mechanism by which we are not merely made aware of external reality but take permitted parts of it into ourselves, paradoxically, by consumption, that is, a kind of destruction. It is, in short, the prototype of all incorporative – which means life-giving – activities, organically rooted and yet individually controllable and socially regulated. To eat is to appropriate beneficially; it is, prototypically, ritually clean in contrast to the prototypical uncleanness of excretion, sexual activity being, as it were intermediate in that it partakes of both, as many African verbal and customary usages testify (cf. n. 45). However, this is a theme I cannot follow up here.

A significant feature of eating is that it allows of a wide gamut of both qualitative and quantitative variation, between restriction (as in fasting) and indulgence (as in feasting), from the socially, aesthetically or ritually permitted to the forbidden. A scale is here available for the expression and symbolization of different social requirements and cultural norms. There is, moreover, a possibility of choice from a great diversity of natural products – including man himself. In this, natural properties and cultural evaluations are fused. Some consumable natural products are poisonous or otherwise noxious, and thus provide the basis for a division into the two opposed kinds of the naturally edible/potable and the non-edible non-potable. Cultural preferences and prescriptions reinforce this dichotomy with aesthetic, ritual, and other elaborations. Tallensi divide natural products along these lines, but unlike the Tikopia, who adapt this division to their form of totemism (Firth 1931), they do not. The totemically prohibited species are all assumed to be edible without explicit contrast with 'inedible' kinds, though some (e.g. grasshoppers, crickets, canaries) would not normally be eaten, except by young children.[48] It is the same in other Voltaic tribes. In any case, most of the prohibited species are not regular foods at all.[49]

The critical feature, clearly, is the moral rule itself, insignificant though it may be in realistic terms. One fact in particular emphasizes this. There is available a large variety of species which could be differentially permitted or prohibited. Thus the same moral rule could be laid upon everybody, but with reference to different species, to correspond (homologously) to structural differentiation by descent or status or locality, amongst and by the actors. To some extent this happens. But what is marked among the Voltaic peoples is that it is common for exactly the same species to be prohibited to groups differentiated by descent, or status, or locality, etc., and for segments of common descent groups to have superordinate common and subordinate divergent prohibited species.

To complete this analysis we should also take into account the significance of eating-and-drinking as the focus of individual self-differentiation in the process of psycho-social development. But let us rather stick to the point that eating is an autonomous, individual activity, which must be performed day in day out throughout the whole of life, yet is peculiarly susceptible of voluntary regulation, but unlike other necessary organic activities (such as elimination or sleep) can only be accomplished by incorporating permitted items from the external – ultimately non-human – environment. Thus eating is the locus of the indivisible interdependence of individual, society and environment; and food and drink (in which we should include all substances taken into the body by the mouth)[50] are exceptionally adapted to serve as the material vehicles of transactions and relationships of binding moral and ritual force. Nothing so concretely dramatizes acceptance – that is, incorporation in the self – be it of a proffered relationship, of a personal condition, or of a conferred role or status, as taking into one's body the item of food or drink chosen to objectify the occasion;[51] and sharing or abstaining from the same food, means uniting in common commitment. The intangible is thus made tangible – word is made flesh – and therefore assimilable and manageable.[52]

In short, eating lends itself uniquely to the imposition of rules. It is susceptible of regulation both by external sanctions and by the internal sanctions of moral scruple. Totemistic eating taboos belong to the latter category. Distinctive clothing can be laid aside in situations where the implicit contrapositions and public testimony that give them significance are irrelevant.[53] If a man whose dwelling declares his lineage membership is away from it, his connection with it will be undetectable. Mortuary rites are collective and public indices of status and descent group differentiation. Oaths, likewise, have public declarative meaning. In all of these cases the framework of structural oppositions amongst the different politico-ritual segments of society is effectively present.

The taboos forbidding the eating and killing of totem animals are different. They are, as I have previously remarked, a part of the individual himself, carried about with him day in day out, as his statuses in society are carried about with him. But whereas the taboo on killing the animal ranks as a remote contingency in his moral economy, the prohibition on eating it serves as a daily reminder to himself of his identity in relation to other persons and to society at large. It focusses his conception of himself as a person in the vital activity which is not only intrinsically tied to a specific objective referent but which also plays a unique part in mediating his identification with other persons and the object-world. Likewise it invests that conception of his identity with awareness of its moral and affective implications. To eat or not to eat is optional for him. To maintain the intention never to eat such and such an animal in obedience to an ancestral vow is to acknowledge to himself the source of his identity – namely, his indebtedness for his existence as a person to his agnatic ancestry. It fixes in his mind his dependence on his ancestors, anchors the obligations that permeate all his social relations by reason of the irreducible fact of his lineage membership. It is a significant feature of the total configuration that ego's tabooed animal is good to eat – that is, pure – but *not for him*.[54] His taboos set him apart, in unity with his co-agnates, from persons of other lineages and clans in the total scheme of group relationships with which he and they are identified. But it is of the same form and social efficacy as those in which every other person in his society must be placed. If this were not so there could be no social relations between him and persons of different descent or status.

In sum then, the primordial ancestor's renunciation of killing and eating the totem animal is an act of gratitude. Animals, as we have seen, are contrasted with humans not, primarily, as things to kill (men can be killed) but as things to eat. However, the totem animal behaved in a peculiarly human way in displaying the kind of amity that is ideally due from a kinsman. What the supposed vow implements is redefinition of the animal, for the beneficiary, as no longer a thing to eat. This removes it, for him, from the animal-thing order and assimilates it to the human order as a moral being the primary connotation of which is 'kinsman'. This is not an intellectual reclassification but a moral realignment. A person's moral commitment to the taboo signifies the perpetual commemoration of the ancestral vow which extended fellow-feeling, brotherhood, kinship amity – call it what you will – to the totem creature. It is a daily affirmation, ordered to a specific configuration of action and material object, of the unique and miraculous beginning of the corporate person perpetuated in and through him by physical descent as well as jural axiom. Herein lies the reminder of the corporate unity and identity of the lineage which binds him as the ultimate condition of his existence as a person.

## XIV

Taboo is the form commonly taken by the totemistic rules, and not only in Africa but in other parts of the world too. Taboo may be thought of as authoritative commandment that is internalized. It is arguable, I think, that supreme authority, especially in matters of morality, ideology and ritual conduct, is more effectively shown in rules that prohibit and enjoin than in rules that merely permit and countenance, and what is more, in commandments of an arbitrary kind for which no rational or utilitarian grounds can be given to the actor. This holds, I believe, even more emphatically for conduct adopted to demonstrate identity. The promise, from however omnipotent a source, that one's days will be long in the land if one obeys certain moral rules is far less convincing than the dogmatic edict that one will become unclean and abominable, perhaps liable to die, if one breaks a food taboo, as in Leviticus. In our cosmological myth of Adam and Eve, God's power and authority over his creation are epitomized in the taboo he imposes, quite arbitrarily, on the fruit of one tree, and the penalty he is able to enforce. It is much to the point that the taboo is on eating and thus incorporating the vehicle of the knowledge which, in Biblical language, signifies the awareness and powers of adult sexuality, the root of good and evil.

Here also lies a theme that goes beyond my present subject matter.

In thus emphasizing the central importance of the taboo on eating the totem animal, and its surrogate, the taboo on destroying a totem artifact, I have obviously picked up a thread of theory that runs back through Radcliffe-Brown and Malinowski, to Frazer and Robertson Smith, Durkheim and Freud. Wide of the mark as some of their hypotheses now seem, I owe something to each in trying to understand the totemistic system of the Voltaic peoples. I cited Radcliffe-Brown at the outset. As regards Freud, the inspiration such studies as mine owe to his famous work goes back not of course to his fantastic reconstruction of the supposed prehistory of the Oedipus complex. Nor are the direct (though guarded) parallels he drew between totemic taboos and obsessional neuroses now acceptable.[55] But the direction of enquiry he adumbrated is highly pertinent (cf. Freud 1925).

The view he espoused was that totemism could not be understood without reference to its taboo components. These, he showed, could not be explained by their ostensible instrumental use. They represent tendencies generated in the actor by cultural pressures conflicting with organic or personal urges. Thus the crux of the problem of taboo is the 'nature and emergence of conscience'. And conscience is renunciation of impulses on no other grounds than awareness of its own behests. Taboo is a command of conscience (1925: 85). Freud went on to argue (1925: Ch. 3), on the analogy of the case of 'Little Hans', that the animal species upon which totemic taboos are projected are 'father surrogates', to which ambivalent attitudes towards the real father are deflected in obedience to the behests of conscience. I follow him only so far as to see in Tallensi totem animals a symbolic representation of paternity perpetuated in the lineage, conscientious identification with which is crystallized in the taboo. At the same time there is no denying that these taboos stand for unquestioning submission to ancestral, that is, magnified paternal, authority which, as the ancestral cult shows is very ambivalently regarded (Fortes 1957). There is a pregnant remark of Malinowski's which has a bearing on this. Discussing the Trobriand concept of *bomala,* taboo, he says (1932: 388–9):

> This noun takes the pronominal suffixes of nearest possession
> ... which signifies that a man's taboo, the things which he

must not eat or touch or do, is linguistically bound up with his person; parts of his body, his kindred, and such personal qualities as his mind (*nanala*), his will (*magila*) and his inside (*lopoula*). Thus *bomala*, those things from which a man must keep away, is an integral part of his personality, something which enters into his moral make-up.

I have confined myself to the Tallensi and their Voltaic neighbours. But, as I have several times indicated, their totemistic customs and beliefs have many parallels in other parts of Africa.[56] It cannot be doubted that there is surely nothing in these customs or beliefs that would seem odd or 'primitive' to such adherents of scriptural religions as an orthodox Jew or Brahmin or Moslem. For such a one, the roots of identity lie in his membership of the community of his co-religionists; and his apprehension of his identity is focused on arbitrary food taboos, believed to be divinely ordained, and symbolizing, to him, his rights by descent, and his consequential moral commitments, to being a Jew or a Brahmin or a Moslem. As with the Tallensi, obligatory avoidance of animals that are intrinsically 'good to eat', and are permitted food to others, sets Jews, Brahmins, and Moslems apart from them, in a relationship of 'structural opposition' though one that is more comprehensive and exclusive, than is found in the Tallensi lineage system. The converse, that is, sacramental commensality in which amity among co-religionists, and their merging into one in submission to divine ordinance, is periodically reaffirmed, also – one might argue necessarily – occurs in these groups too.

Herein lie the germs of a wider problem than the one I have attempted to look at, one in which the dialogue between message-oriented theory and actor-centred theory might well be further developed. It is the problem of how the structural oppositions, as seen by functionalists, that are expressed in the segregative, internal valencies of totemistic institutions are interlocked with and counterpoised by structural opposition in another, external domain of social relations. It is the problem for instance of what caste-taboos mean to a caste-member, *vis-à-vis* his fellow members on the one side and other castes on the other.

So we come back to the question of whether so-called totemism is to be explained by the hypothesis that natural species are 'good to think' or by the hypothesis that they are 'good to eat'. The answer, for societies bound to their natural environment in the way the Tallensi are, seems to be both — but not, as I understand it, in Lévi-Strauss' sense of the former. It can be said that natural species, in particular animals, lend themselves peculiarly and appositely to the representation in thought, the symbolization, of the critical features of kinship connection as it is conceived by the actors. One could say that animals, generically, provide a model for 'picturing' the perpetuity of descent, and consequently, as species, provide a conceptual sorting scheme to mark the differentiation of social groups distinguished and connected by descent and equivalent structural criteria. But this is only one side of the syndrome. The other more fundamental side is the fact of observance. Totemistic observances identify the actors to themselves and to the world at large; and this is mediated by the binding rules of abstinence or performance which we conventionally label taboos. Animals, I suggest, are peculiarly suited to objectify these moral imperatives because they are 'good to forbid'. They lend themselves specially to this form of moral constraint because, being alive, they are 'good to kill' and, above all 'good to eat'. If they did not have these properties, the prohibitions fixed upon them would be nonsensical, as Freud demonstrated. And having these properties makes taboos fixed on them transferable to any objects that can be destroyed or incorporated — even to utterances. Let us remember that the basic and original reference of the word 'code' (Latin *codex*) is to a digest of legal and moral rules, not to a set of conventional signs for transmitting messages. Thus regarded, there is a totemistic tinge even in the (often personified) flags and state emblems of modern nations, especially the new ones.

# 7

## Coping with destiny

A belief in a principle usually glossed as Fate or Destiny, parallel in many particulars to analogous notions in the religions of classical antiquity and in such extant scriptural systems as Calvinistic Christianity, Islam, Buddhism and Hinduism, is a prominent feature of many West African religious systems. At the level of doctrine it postulates a supernatural or mystical determinacy in human affairs such that the whole course – or at least significant parts – of each individual's life is set, if not minutely pre-ordained, by pre-natal allocation, prescription or commitment. Whether it is beneficent or maleficent in the way it works out, at this level it is conceptualized as inescapable, irrevocable, and unknowable until it manifests itself. But there is another level, the level of practice, where dogma is translated into ritual action directed towards coping with the vicissitudes of daily life. And here we meet with a paradox, whether or not there are formulated doctrines or no more than the loosely phrased metaphysical or cosmological premises that can be inferred from the practices of non-scriptural traditional religious systems.

Fate, which is in theory irresistible and irrevocable, is in practice taken to be controllable. This applies particularly, as one might expect, in the face of what presents as injurious or evil Destiny. And the prophylactic or defensive measures that may be resorted to are as customary and as sanctioned, as much part of the accepted complex of metaphysical and ritual beliefs and practices, as the notion of Fate itself. It is thus recognized that it is not in the nature of man to submit blindly to what purports to be mystically inevitable. Our Western science and medicine, our politics, cosmologies and moral or religious systems, testify even more imperiously to this than do

145

the attempts of Hindus, Buddhists or West Africans to control by ritual means what they designate as Destiny. Amongst us the most uncompromising hereditarians are at one with the most convinced environmentalists in promoting medical, social and economic pro- grammes of action to overcome the genetic defects or to develop the genetic assets they claim to demonstrate.

The contradiction between theory and practice, doctrine and action, I am talking about is conspicuously – I would almost say intrinsically – embedded in the complex of beliefs and practices re- lating to the notion of Destiny throughout West Africa. Twenty years ago, analysing the Tallensi variant of this complex, I described how Destiny is supposed to manifest itself for ill as well as for good in people's lives (Fortes 1959). I cited examples of the kinds of cir- cumstances that were apt to be diagnosed as manifestations of a maleficent or 'bad' Predestiny, and referred briefly to the ritual pro- cedures that are available for attempts to expunge it.

It is these procedures that I want to examine more closely in this essay. For they not only exemplify rejection of the irrevocability of Fate; they also exemplify fundamental Tallensi ritual concepts and patterns of action. What is undertaken is ostensibly to constrain Fate by specific ritual means. But this depends inseparably on setting in train a complex series of social arrangements that mobilize the jural and moral and economic participation of responsible and con- cerned kinsfolk and lineage relatives, affines and neighbours. This is simply a reflection of the fact that a Tallensi is a person strictly and solely by virtue of the status he or she is endowed with by kinship, descent, marriage and residence. The creature of flesh and bone and blood, equipped with capacities to think and feel, with its organic needs and appetites and its vulnerability to failure, disease, and death, is of significance to himself as well as to others only as he is encapsulated in his identity as a person (cf. Ch. 10). It is in relation to his career and fulfilment as a person that his Destiny impinges on his life; but it is a career that is inextricably embedded in the matrix of his social relationships. In a very real sense every individual's Destiny is part and parcel of the Destiny of his family and lineage.

The case of Sinkawol's (of Tenzugu-Kpata'ar) wife Soorbon is typical. When Soorbon's second baby died soon after its birth like her first, and to add to her distress she became crippled with an ulcerated leg, the young woman's despondency could not be assuaged. Though she could not bring herself to speak to him of her grief, Sinkawol was well aware of it and indeed felt with her. It would have been unbecoming for her to complain directly to her husband or her in-laws. But she could and did talk to Naghabil, her husband's classificatory 'son' (and therefore hers, too, though he was older than both) who was also a 'sister's son' of her natal lineage and who had therefore served as the customary intermediary (*poghasama*, the marriage witness) for her marriage. Naghabil, as was his duty, then relayed her pleas to his 'fathers' – that is, to her husband (Sinkawol) and his 'fathers'.

> He told us [Sinkawol explained] that she was saying that we don't care for her. If we did we would take steps to fix [literally, to build, *me*] her Destiny [*Yin*]. See how she has given birth to one child after another, beautiful babies, and then her bad Predestiny comes and slays them, yet we are doing nothing to fix her Destiny. She had heard that her father has obtained the goat he must provide for his part of the ritual and it is only we who are holding back.

Thus reproached, Sinkawol's 'fathers' – his proxy father Teezeen (actually his deceased father's brother) and the head of the family, Nyaangzum (his deceased father's father's brother) – gave leave for the process to be taken in hand. He himself, being still jurally and therefore ritually dependent on them, could not initiate any action in any ritual or jural matter concerning himself. This, it was explained to me, is his father's responsibility. Indeed, and this is a fact of importance, it is on the jurally defined fathers of the couple that the duty to decide about and organize the ritual falls.

Teezeen set aside the malted guinea corn for the beer that would be needed and sent Sinkawol off to market to buy the goat, the fowls, the guinea-fowls and the 'things' (*laghat*) their side had been commanded by diviners to provide for the ritual performance. And at the same time they sent a message to inform Soorbon's father at Sii of their decision.

This was the prelude to the ritual procedure of 'building' or fixing Soorbon's 'bad Destiny' (*Yinbeog*) which I recorded in March 1937. Some months earlier I had attended a similar ceremony for Mansami, a young man from a Namoo lineage (Sinkawol's lineage is Hill Talis)[1] and I recorded several informants' accounts of the procedure

– the first in July 1934 when I had no proper understanding of the Destiny syndrome. So I had plenty of evidence that the pattern is, as Tallensi claim, a standard one throughout the area.

I have in my earlier publication (Fortes 1959, pp. 38–9) referred to the ritual of ridding a person of a bad Predestiny as 'exorcism' but this is, strictly speaking, a misnomer. The *Oxford English Dictionary* defines 'exorcism' as 'The action of exorcising or expelling an evil spirit by adjuration, etc.', echoing, one suspects, the gospel stories of Christ driving out devils and unclean spirits and the long tradition of similar practices in Christendom right down to modern times. As a method of healing or of relieving suffering, exorcism has a place in many non-Western religious systems, both scriptural, as among some devotees of Buddhism,[2] and non-scriptural, as in the many African societies in which some form of spirit possession is regarded as the cause of illness and other afflictions and exorcism is resorted to as a prelude to initiation as a diviner or as a member of a cult group.[3]

But the very notion of spirit or demonic possession, or mediumship in any form, is totally alien to the prosaic Tallensi concept of human nature. It arouses scepticism and repugnance. Tallensi who have seen Ga or Akan priests and priestesses in such states are apt to scoff at them as imposters. It is unthinkable, for them, that the dead can return among the living by taking possession of a living person's body, and they have no nature divinities. The malevolent powers they attribute to certain kinds of rocks and trees are not thought of as spiritual but rather as magical animation (cf. Fortes and Mayer 1966).

Specifically as regards Predestiny, there is no question of its being thought of as invading or possessing (as among the Ga and other African peoples dealt with in Beattie and Middleton 1969) or (as for instance in the Hausa Bori Cult) as being mounted upon and driving its bearer (cf. Besmer 1977) and therefore requiring expulsion for the sufferer's health to be restored. Fate, Destiny, Predestiny, beneficent or maleficent, under whichever aspect it emerges in a particular case, is associated with the head,[4] which is the seat of good luck (*zug-song*) or bad luck (*zug-beog*), as if, knowledgeable informants say, it were perching or hovering (*yaghal*) on, over, or beside, that is outside, the head. This, of course, is a metaphorical way of referring to it as 'hanging over' him or her in the same way as, say, a debt hangs over or follows a debtor. More exactly, Destiny is thought of as a component of a person's personhood. It is supposed to be chosen by himself or herself pre-natally (while he was still 'with Heaven above') and therefore to be already effective from his birth. Destiny distinguishes and indeed creates him as an individual encapsulated in his social being but endowed with a personal variant of the normal career pattern for someone of his status, as individual as his physical appearance and personality yet, equally, like every other man or woman in his society. Even animals, both domestic and wild, I have heard it said, surely have each their Destiny, not only as distinguishing a cow from a sheep or goat, or an antelope from a crocodile or leopard, but also as determining what happens to an individual cow or sheep, antelope or crocodile, in its lifetime – in other words, as distinctive of its nature and species.

The essential point is that Destiny is conceived of as accruing and adhering to the individual from the outside, as it were, like his shadow (though this is not explicitly stated by the Tallensi), not as being inside his head or body – as are, for instance, thought (*puteen*) or anger (*suhkpeleg*) or sickness (*toog*) – and yet Destiny is chosen by the individual though it must be awaited to manifest itself, as I have outlined in my analysis of 1959.

Given these ideas, it is consistent that Tallensi define the ritual of ridding a patient of a bad Predestiny as a ritual of 'sweeping away', divesting the patient of his or her lot and casting it out to make way for its reversal.

More precisely, to make the sweeping away possible the abstract and intangible Predestiny must be recognized and then captured, so to speak, and materially fixed so that it can be ritually handled; and this is the essence of the ritual of 'building' it. A good Destiny also has to be recognized and 'built', but in this case it is embodied in a permanent shrine at which sacrifices and offerings are made by its beneficiary, always a male, since females do not have the jural autonomy to officiate directly in religious rituals.

This is not exorcism in the strict sense. Nor, incidentally, would it be appropriate to speak of 'purging' an evil Predestiny, as is done, for instance, in the Zulu treatment of affliction by inducing vomiting of the 'bad' internal stuff engendered by strife among kinsfolk by means of 'black' medicines to make way for 'good' internal stuff which restores amity, as is exhibited in vomiting induced by 'white'

medicine (cf. Ngubane 1977). This type of internally located soma-
tic representation of infringement and restoration of moral status is
as alien to Tallensi conceptions of human nature as is its antithesis,
the notion of spirit possession.

And there is one further and crucial point. The religious system of
the Tallensi is dominated by their ancestor cult; and, as they have no
specialist priests, the ritual activities and obligations of their
ancestor cult are primarily family and lineage responsibilities. In
their world view the ultimate power in the affairs of men, for good
and for ill, for life and for death, and the ultimate sanctions of morality, rest with the ancestors. Thus, in the last resort, even Destiny
falls under their jurisdiction; and this is the key to the possibility of
bringing under ritual control and reversing the workings of an evil
Predestiny.

Let us now go back to Sinkawol's wife, and let me begin with the
explanation given by the head of Sinkawol's family, his proxy
grandfather, Nyaangzum.

> Destiny is an old story among us, hence there is a known and
> customary way of dealing with it. When the young woman's
> first infant died, there was the customary divination to find the
> cause. They learnt from the diviner that it was her *Yin* [her
> Destiny] which had killed the child. Before her birth she had
> declared that she did not want children. They were instructed
> to *veel* the *Yin*,

*Veel* is a reduced, placatory, almost token version of the 'building'
ritual, retaining only the most indicative elements. It serves as acknowledgement of the power of the 'bad' Destiny which, previously
concealed or dormant, had betrayed itself by causing the child's
death and had made itself known in the divination. To accept, to
submit, is the first and obligatory step in any procedure for coming
to terms with any occult power or agency, be it ancestors, Earth or
Destiny. Where *veel* mainly differs from the full ritual (Nyaangzum
and others explained) is in the omission of the major sacrifices. It is
of interest that a similar *veel* ritual is carried out as the first stage of
setting up a divining shrine. Sometimes this is sufficient. The malign
Destiny is mollified, 'cools down' or relents (*maageremi*), and the
woman bears children who survive. In Soorbon's case the *veel* procedure failed. When her second baby died and she was laid up with

an ulcerated leg divination revealed that her Destiny was still hostile and the decision was taken to 'build' this evil Destiny.

To help follow the procedure, I list here the principals and the responsible parties.

1. The afflicted woman, Soorbon, and her husband, Sinkawol – the patients.
2. The marriage witness of this couple (or his representative), who must be a member by birth (a 'son') of the husband's patrilineage and a 'sister's son' to the wife's lineage (Naghabil).
3. The father and the lineage elders of the afflicted woman's lineage, as the responsible agents of her patrilineage.
4. The proxy father, Teezeen, and the family head, Nyaangzum, of her husband's family and other elders and members of his patrilineage, as the responsible agents of his patrilineage.
5. The womenfolk of the husband's home.
6. Women of the wife's natal home.

As I have already noted, the decision to proceed with the ritual was taken by Sinkawol's 'father', Teezeen, with the concurrence of the head of the house, Nyaangzum, but only after consultation with diviners. Such decisions, though in fact arrived at for practical reasons, are phrased as acquiescence in diagnosis and prescription revealed by diviners as emanating from the ancestors. This is taken to imply a successful outcome if conscientiously followed. No important ritual activity is ever undertaken without such authorization by divination. Yet it is both characteristic and significant that in Tallensi ritual practice the whole sequence is standard. Ask any elder what would be the likely diagnosis in a case like that of Sinkawol's wife and he will say it is probably due to a bad Predestiny; and he will go on to describe the appropriate ritual procedures which, though customary, will be formally prescribed in divination and thus relieve the principals of ultimate responsibility for the event. This fits the general character of Tallensi ancestor worship as a system of beliefs and practices concerned with what I have called externalized representation of conscience. This also reflects the essentially realistic Tallensi attitudes about human affairs. It is well understood and accepted that human affairs are always unpredictable. In terms of their religious beliefs this becomes an understanding that ancestors are not bound by the prayers and offerings they exact. They remain unpredictable, and therefore inferences about promises revealed by diviners are grounds of hope but never of certainty.

It is worth stopping for a moment to consider what types of affliction are apt to be attributed to an evil Predestiny. Tallensi do not regard these afflictions as forms of sickness. A wife who is childless as a result of successive miscarriages or successive child deaths or sterility is an almost certain candidate. The bad *Yin* is said to kill her children or to spoil her fertility. So is a mature man who has been unsuccessful in finding a wife and settling down to a stable family life (as was the case with Mansami), or who has failed, after several marriages, to keep a wife. In such cases the bad *Yin* is said to drive away the wife. These are the commonest and the stereotypical victims generally quoted as examples. Their plight is understandable. They have failed to achieve normal adulthood as reproductive members of their families and lineages. An anomalous failure or accident (for example, a youth climbing a tree to rob a beehive and falling to his death) or a lingering illness may be attributed to the victim's evil Predestiny. I have a record of a case in which a daughter's evil Predestiny was divined to endanger her mother's life if they remained together in the same house. Diviners prescribed that the child should be sent away to live with her mother's brother – rather conveniently, since there is always tension between the three families of her paternal family, her stepfather's and her mother's brothers, for possession of the child – and, similarly, I have a record of a case in which the death of an infant brother was attributed to the evil Predestiny of his immediately preceding brother – again perhaps consistent with the customary expectation that successive siblings of the same sex will be by nature rivalrous and mutually hostile, though loyal to each other in relation to outsiders.

This does not exhaust all the possibilities but it serves to indicate the general pattern. An evil Predestiny is apt to be diagnosed to account for a condition or a mode of conduct that, from the Tallensi point of view, runs unnaturally counter to the customary norms of personal development, social and familial relationships, and productive and reproductive efficacy. It is, in other words, apt to be diagnosed where the victim or those who have rightful control over him could logically be held to be, at bottom, himself or herself, responsible for his or her condition or conduct. In objective terms, it seems that a bad Predestiny is apt to be adduced in cases where there is a difficult or impossible moral dilemma to be resolved. Soorbon's husband could not, for example, repudiate her, though she was failing him in his most ardent hopes and wishes. Indeed, the standard formula, as Nyaangzum put it, is that the bearer of the evil Predestiny did himself or herself repudiate these norms – but pre-natally, before he or she became human by birth, and he or she is therefore exonerated in his or her human capacity – a formula which can be interpreted as shifting what would have been the guilt of deliberate choice to the plane of unconscious choice appositely displaced to work as if from the outside, diachronically as having originated pre-natally, synchronically as becoming conscious only at the time of its revelation.

Better to appreciate what is distinctive of the Tallensi Predestiny complex, let us look very briefly at some contrasting African schemes of belief. Among the Ashanti the plight of Sinkawol's wife would undoubtedly be attributed to the maleficent witchcraft of one of her closest maternal kinsfolk, her mother or a sister or a brother, as the cases cited by Field (1960) amply demonstrate. To redress the injury the accused must make public confession of her or his secret maleficence and do penance as prescribed by the priest of the witch-finding cult. Among the Ndembu her affliction would be attributed to a variety of occult powers, above all to the shades of the woman's female matrilineal forebears, who are deemed to be punishing her for neglect or some wrongdoing, and the cure consists of an extremely elaborate ritual of purification and magical restoration of the fertility of the woman and her husband (Turner 1969). Among the Zulu, lineage sorcery would be blamed and treatment with protective medicines would be prescribed (Ngubane 1977). And lastly, among the non-Muslim Hausa the trouble might be attributed to some form of spirit attack, and treatment is by initiation into a cult group through spirit possession (Last 1976).

These few examples must suffice to bring out the point I wish to emphasize here. It is that, by contrast, Soorbon did not perceive herself as being persecuted and betrayed, nor did she blame herself for her plight, nor is there any implication of pollution in her circumstances; and this is how her husband and other members of her conjugal and, for that matter, her natal family looked at the situation – and it would be the same with anyone else who is found to be encumbered with a bad Predestiny. Being outside her, so to speak, to sweep it away is the appropriate treatment.

To return to the sweeping away ritual, the beer having been brewed at Soorbon's conjugal home and the other standard items prescribed by the diviners having been obtained, the first episode followed. Escorted by an elder, Bogharaam, and the marriage witness, Naghabil, of her husband's lineage, she was sent off to her father's home at Sii, about three miles away, with the beer, millet flour, fowls and guinea-fowls that would be required for the sacrifices there. I was not present, but received a very full account of the proceedings from Bogharaam. Soorbon's father sacrificed one fowl to his long-dead father and another to his own divining ancestors, who were Soorbon's guardian ancestors. 'He told them', Bogharaam said, 'that she had no child and pleaded that they might permit her to conceive. He said that her Destiny was being blamed but they, the ancestors, were her guardians and must deal with this Destiny that was dogging her.' After these domestic sacrifices, all went up to the house of the clan head. There, all the elders of Sii being assembled, the clan head offered a fowl and guinea-fowl provided by the visitors on the altar of the collective clan ancestors, the External Boghar,[5] with similar pleas for the woman to conceive, and sent them away with blessings promising that the ritual would be successful and that Soorbon would soon conceive.

That evening I asked Sinkawol what account he had received of his wife's visit to her paternal home. 'Oh', he said, 'they told me that all the fowls sacrificed had "received".' This is the literal translation of the Talni term, *ba deeya*. It refers to the posture of a sacrificial fowl – and it is always and only the domestic fowl which is thus used – when it expires. If it dies on its back, wings outstretched, this is a propitious sign indicating that the offering has been accepted, and thus augurs a successful outcome of the ritual. If it dies lying on its breast or on its side, this signifies rejection by the ancestors or other occult agencies to whom the offering was made. The usual interpretation, then, is that this is due to some fault of omission or commission on the part of the supplicants which must be put right before the ancestors can be expected to respond benevolently. Tallensi insist that the way the chicken expires is not under human control.[6] How could the presence and responsiveness of the perceptually inaccessible occult agencies be verified, or their benevolence ascertained other than by some such test which the Tallensi consider objective? At the same time, Tallensi well understand that there can never be a complete guarantee of success in matters of ritual since human affairs are, at bottom, unpredictable. As for details of the ritual at Soorbon's paternal home, Sinkawol was totally uninterested. The fowls had 'received' and that was all that mattered; and this is a typical attitude in such circumstances.

It is significant that the ritual 'building' process begins at the Destiny patient's father's house. Why thus, I asked the elders. Surely it was obvious, they replied. Was it not her father who begot her? It was as her father's daughter in the care of his ancestors and in fulfilment of his Destiny that she came into the world. Her Destiny, to which she was already committed before her birth, came down trailing along with her father's Destiny. It was as her father's daughter that she grew to womanhood and was endowed with fecundity. It was as her father's daughter that she acquired her basic social identity; and it was her father who gave her in marriage and thus transferred to her husband the sole right over her sexuality and procreative capacity. To be sure, the 'building' ritual concerns her *performance* as wife and mother, not daughter, but it is the *capacity* for this that is at stake and to protect it the ritual must go back to its origins. Thus it becomes her father's responsibility to put things right. But it is important to add that this is a responsibility he has by reason of his jural status as father. There is no implication of his having to repair a conscious failure which he might have been able to avoid originally. He does not consider himself, nor is he considered to be, guilty through sins of commission or omission. Indeed, he is not even exclusively and solely responsible. The task is shared with his lineage elders and the ancestral help that is sought is that of the collective clan ancestors at their Boghar shrine. This, too, is a reflection of the premiss that a person is a person primarily by virtue of his or her lineage membership. He is responsible but, let me emphasize again, there is no question of guilt in this. The formula is that his daughter chose her own pre-natal Destiny, that is, when she was still 'with Heaven above' – a state of affairs for which Tallensi have only an oblique explanation. They say that it has to do with the fact that sexual intercourse does not invariably lead to conception but only when Heaven above in some mysterious way permits it.

The father's role is that of the duty-bound benevolent intercessor commending his offspring to his, and therefore her, ancestors.

In accordance with custom, her father had checked with diviners and was told to provide a white chicken, a white goat, white millet flour, and a white cowrie shell for the main ritual task. This took place, appropriately, at Soorbon's conjugal home or, as Tallensi would put it, her husband's home, where she was as wife and mother suffering the malice of her Destiny. It took place on the day after her propitious visit to her paternal home. It had naturally to be carried out jointly by the two parties with a stake in her well-being and fertility, her father and his lineage kin on the one side and her husband's father and his lineage kin on the other.

Preparations began in the morning, desultorily, as is usual among the Tallensi on such occasions. By mid-afternoon a group of Kpata'ar men, elders and others, were all assembled in front of the gateway of Teezeen's homestead impatiently awaiting the contingent from Sii. It was nearly sunset when they arrived, led by Kurug, an elder to whom her father had delegated the task of performing the ritual. They brought with them the goat, the chickens, and the other items prescribed as the Sii contribution to the rituals and, what was much more important, the *boghakyee*, the portable shrine of the clan ancestors which, Tallensi say, draws the ancestors themselves along to the scene of the ritual.

This is not the place to recount the whole course of the proceedings over the seven hours through which the ritual activities were spread. As is characteristic of occasions of this sort among the Tallensi, the proceedings began and were interspersed with arguments about differences of customary practice between the two parties and the episodes of ritual concentration alternated with a hubbub of general conversation and movement. I must limit myself to the critical ritual activities.

Let me first note, however, that these activities are always conducted by men – the only woman directly included is the patient, who is passive throughout. Partly this is because officiating in a ritual is a male prerogative and responsibility associated with men's status of jural majority which women can never attain. When women carry out a ritual activity it is always under the direction of men. But in this case what is also represented is the circumstance that the responsible parties are the two sets of 'fathers'. Appropriately, therefore, the proceedings take place in the male space out of doors and in the family head's *zong* room which houses the shrines of his earliest ancestors. This room is separated from the living quarters, which are ruled over by the wives and mothers, where the children are licitly produced and where everyday food is properly cooked. This is also symbolically appropriate, in that the bad Predestiny is dealt with outside to make way for admitting the good Destiny into the homestead, as we shall see.

The proceedings opened with a sacrifice in the *zong* room, symbolically, therefore, in the presence of the Kpata'ar ancestors, who would thus be both made aware of the occasion and enlisted on the side of the Sii group's efforts. A very short account of this episode, which took nearly an hour, is all I have space for, but it will suffice to show up the critical elements that recur throughout the ritual sequence. Kurug crawled in and placed the *boghakyee* on the floor and was followed by a dozen or so elders, some from each side. The patients were summoned and seated in a corner, legs stretched out and heads lowered in the customary posture of humility required of supplicants. Squatting over the *boghakyee*, Kurug sprinkled on it some millet flour from a calabash handed to him and, holding up a small dish of beer, called out, 'Speak up now. Speak up and tell her it has come about.'

'What do you mean "speak up"?' protested Nyaangzum, the senior Kpata'ar elder. 'It's the woman's Destiny you have come here to build and what is there to talk about?' – emphasizing, that is, that the circumstances were fully known to everybody present. But Kurug insisted. It was necessary for the ritual to be properly performed. Thereupon the Kpata'ar elder who had the previous day represented Teezeen and the lineage at Sii spoke up, addressing himself to the spokesman of the other side. It was a long, elaborate and rhetorical speech, as is usual on such occasions, studded with vivid figures of speech, fervent exhortations, and reiterated pleas. He told how 'We of Kpata'ar' had sought the girl in marriage; how she had, as was hoped, borne children, which had died; how diviners had revealed that the cause was her evil Destiny. He concluded:

> That is why we informed you and asked you to come over, so that we could share our trouble. We prepared all the things we need for the ritual and now we ask you to do what is necessary

so that the woman's Destiny may become cool and she may conceive a child, so that farms may be farmed and livestock bred and well-being abound.

'Thank you', said the Sii spokesman, and turning to Kurug he went on: 'Kurug, listen. This is their story. We and these people of Tenzugu, we have had much to do with one another. Doesn't our kinship connect us? We went and married our wife and she bore us this child and she grew' – and he described how she had been given in marriage to the Kpata'ar people. 'Men marry', he continued, 'in order to have children.' He dwelt on how her children had died and how diviners had declared that 'when she was still with Heaven, she had spoken in an ugly way saying she did not want children, or a husband, or good farming, or livestock breeding', and concluded that 'having been told all this, we have come to put things right and build this Destiny – here is this Destiny's red chicken, his beer, all his things, may he permit this chicken to be accepted and may he let the woman conceive.'

These are the bare bones of a long, declamatory, much embroidered exhortation, listened to attentively and silently by all those present. It struck me then that this recapitulation of the history, circumstances, ritual prescriptions and hopeful expectations of the occasion, fully known as the details were to all present, had the effect of a formal presentation to Kurug of the equivalent of a material document. A similar procedure is followed in court cases. The responsible officiant cannot carry out his task if such a formal and public statement, concurred in by all participants, is not presented. This ensures that, as Tallensi put it, 'we are all of one mind' and, what is more, that the ancestors of all participants are apprised and at hand.

Responding to this, Kurug clapped his hands over the *boghakyee* and, speaking in a loud and commanding tone and with many rhetorical flourishes and exhortations, addressed himself to the *boghakyee* as follows (again I summarize drastically):

It is Tongnaab[7] that I here take hold of, great brother of Bem, of Zubagah, and of all of us – Ancestor Tongnaab, hearken to me. We married a wife, took her home, and there she bore a child, an only child, and the child grew up, became a woman, and then this son of Teezeen came and begged for her – and we,

would we deny him? Are we two not one stock? Well then, the
woman bears a child and it dies, bears again and it dies. So they
went to diviners, and diviners declared [and his voice rose as if
in dismay] that it was her Destiny, that she had said she wants
no child, that her husband would not farm his farming, breed
his livestock, that she would have no child, that she spoke thus
when she was above with Heaven before she came down here.

And he went on to recount how they had first *veel* this Destiny, but
to no avail, and that the diviners had then commanded them to
'build it', prescribing the animals and other items required. He continued urgently:

> Tongnaab, Ancestor, here stands your goat, here is your beer
> and your chicken, grant that this Destiny may depart to the
> distant low land and disappear in the wilderness. It is Soorbon's
> Destiny which we are going to sweep away, so that off-spring
> may come and farms be farmed and livestock be reared.
> Tongnaab, you are master of everything, you can calm
> everything that is disturbed. Grant that these two may be at
> ease, that children may be born, farms farmed, livestock reared
> and restful sleep slept. Grant that a houseful of people may be
> built and that their names may be praised.

And so he continued repeating in different locutions the insistent
call that it was Soorbon's evil Destiny they were sweeping away, the
ugly Destiny which she had assumed when she was still with Heaven
above, and reiterating his pleas that it might be made to vanish and
childbearing be restored 'so that', he ended emphatically, 'we may
know that you really exist'.

He poured some beer on the shrine calling out, 'Here is your beer.
Accept it and may it prompt you to accept your chicken too.' And
then, holding up the chicken, he added, 'Here, take your red cockerel, grant that it is accepted at once and permit us to rejoice.' He
slaughtered the cockerel, dripped some some blood on the
*boghakyee* and still invoking, threw it to the floor. It fluttered and
died on its breast, 'refused'. A moment's consternation was followed by a hubbub of comment and a call for another cockerel. This
was quickly produced and, invoking as before and ending urgently,
'Tongnaab, Ancestor, accept this your chicken, accept it', he offered
it and threw it down. It fluttered and died on its back, propitiously.

'Good, good', shouted Kurug laughing, amid a burst of approval from those around.

Though I have omitted many details and have severely compressed the invocations, their significance is clear. The threefold repetition of the same, fully familiar story and the same urgent appeal might seem supererogatory to an obsessional degree. But this does not, in fact, signify an intention or hope of persuading the occult agencies invoked by the sheer weight of redundant repetition. The case is presented from different points of view by the two parties. The Kpata'ar spokesman addresses the Sii elders, soliciting the intercession and help which they alone are qualified and obliged to give and the theme is the concern of the husband's lineage that the woman should be set free to fulfil the primary purpose of marriage, which is the production of children. Note that, far from blaming her, the spokesman implies sympathy with her plight. The Sii elders, first through their spokesman and then directly through the officiating elder, Kurug, address their ancestors. The way their spokesman restates the Kpata'ar story amounts to accepting accountability (but not culpability) – incurred, to be sure, in good faith and unintentionally – for the crisis. The stress all through is on the woman's tribulations being due to her own pre-natal vow, even though it was not a conscious and deliberate repudiation of the normal humanity which she now yearns for. She is not a sinner deserving retribution but rather a sufferer, almost unjustly so, pleading for relief. And the implication is that her father, and consequently the ancestors, have some responsibility for her plight since they must be concerned for the well-being of their descendants and have the superhuman power and authority to annul the pre-natal vow. Note also the repeated emphasis on the animals and 'things' demanded by the Destiny and the ancestors through the diviners as having been conscientiously provided. These are offered not as a bribe but as earnest of the trust in the goodwill and powers of the ancestors and of submission to their authority.

The Sii ancestors thus having been enlisted, as their acceptance of the sacrificed cockerel signified, the company moved outside to the gateway for what is regarded as the crucial ritual phase. They sat down on two sides of a small heap of wet puddled mud. After some preliminaries, Kurug put the *boghakyee* down beside the heap next to a hoe blade and instructed the 'sister's son' of Sii, the Kpata'ar marriage witness, Naghabil, to prepare four mud balls. Naghabil quickly rolled out four largish mud balls and laid them in a row beside the hoe blade. 'Bring the things', called Kurug, squatting down and Sinkawol, squatting behind him, held out a handful of wriggling, grey grubs and the dried carcase of a white egret.[8] Kurug pressed one of the grubs into each mud ball and put the egret carcase down beside them. A youth came over with a handful of earth which he said was the 'mousehole dust' he had been sent to fetch. Kurug sprinkled this over the mud balls, and told the patients to go and stand in the gateway, where they wedged themselves in uncomfortably. Then he called to the marriage witness, 'Tell your "fathers", the Kpata'ar people, to speak out.' 'What do you mean?' exclaimed Nyaangzum, protesting again that they had been through it all. But the Sii elders insisted it had to be so. Sighing, Nyaangzum addressed himself to the marriage witness and launched out on his speech, speaking as if it was all completely new to the company. No details were spared. The whole story of the woman's privation was repeated in the customary declamatory manner, ending with a rehearsal of the diviners' verdicts and of the call to her natal lineage – 'so that we could be of one mind and they might sweep away the woman's evil Destiny, so that I might get some good farming and livestock and a child and build up my house'. Naghabil thanked him and addressing the Sii people, said, 'My uncles, you have heard, have you not?' A Sii elder repeated this to Kurug. 'Indeed', came the answer and Kurug drew a handful of ebony leaves out of the *boghakyee*, picked up one of the mud balls with the hoe blade and placed it on the leaves in his hand and walked slowly to where the patients were standing impassively in the gateway a few yards away.

Silence fell suddenly on the seated gathering and all eyes were fixed on the scene at the gateway. Raising the ball of wet mud and the ebony leaves towards the patients, Kurug addressed them in a loud, singsong voice, every phrase of his incantation being very distinctly enunciated – and being immediately repeated by the patients in the same singsong tone, but in so low a voice as to be almost inaudible.

'Yin Yoo! Yin Yoo! Yin Yoo!' called Kurug, summoning the Destiny as one would a distant person, each phrase being repeated by the patients.

We have heard that Soorbon when she came into the world
talked crazily, coming hither from high up Heaven, saying that
she is going thence, but she will never clasp a child in her arms –
she does not want any children – indeed she will have nothing
to do with a man – for him to farm so that they may have food
to eat – he will not have a farm – he will not rear livestock –
never will he acquire livestock – nor ever will he go out to hunt,
no, never go hunting – and we have gone round to diviners,
consulting them, and the diviners revealed that Soorbon had
declared that she does not wish for a child – she does not wish for a
husband – she does not want a mother – she does not want a father
– that is what the diviners revealed – it was her bad Destiny
– they picked out Sabeg [to be the ritual officiant] and Sabeg
deputed me – to come here, to cast it out – here is its beer – here stands
its goat – a white goat – here is its chicken – and all its things are
here – so it is that we have come here purposely to sweep it away.

At this point he lifted the mud ball and the leaves higher and made
a sweeping gesture thrice[9] down the woman's abdomen and repeated this with her husband. Then he held up the mud ball and the
leaves to the mouth of each and commanded, 'Spit!' Each spat once
on the mud ball and Kurug walked around to the back of the homestead and threw the mud ball away. He returned, took up the second
mud ball in the same way as before and repeated the earlier procedure, though with some curtailment of the exhortation. 'Yin Yoo,
Yin Yoo, Yin Yoo', he began, and repeated the invocation he had
made previously. Again he 'swept' the patients, made them spit on
the mud ball and went off to throw it away (cf. Fig. 3).

A third time he repeated the whole procedure, though now with a
much shortened exhortation – his voice sounding quite tired. When
he stopped to pick up the fourth ball, a Sii elder leaned forward and
pushed a (white) cowrie shell into it. Kurug took a fresh supply of
leaves out of the *boghakyee* bag (the first lot had been thrown away
with the last mud ball) and at the same time picked up the egret carcase. With the leaves and the dead bird in one hand and the hoe
blade on which he was carrying the mud ball in the other, he again
took up his position facing the patients.

*Figure 3*. Sweeping away Mansami's evil Destiny (cf. reference to Mansami, p. 152 above). The officiant 'sweeps' the patient and his 'wife' with the leaves of the *gaa* tree as he calls on the evil Destiny to descend. In this case, the patient being a man, the ritual took place during the daytime and I was therefore able to obtain some photographs, which was, of course, impossible in Soorbon's night-time treatment. Note that in this case the patient sits humbly on the ground outside the homestead side by side with the little girl who takes the role of the wife Mansami has failed to win. Note the white goat and the white chicken in the background.

He repeated the invocation, again much shortened, and as the patients repeated each phrase after him he waved the leaves and the dead bird in front of them. At the end he called in a louder voice, 'Be it a white Destiny [*Yinpeeleg*] let it descend hither, or be it a red Destiny [*Yinziug*] let it descend hither, or be it a black Destiny [*Yinsableg*] let it descend hither' – the patients still repeating after him. Then he 'swept down' the patients from head to foot with the leaves and the egret, held the mud ball out to them with the command to spit, and then said 'take hold'. Each placed a hand on the bunch of leaves and the dead bird he was holding and together they walked back to where the mud balls had first been placed and put the mud ball Kurug was carrying and the leaves and the dead bird down on the ground.

*Figure 4*. Sweeping away Mansami's evil Destiny. The rite of 'sweeping' the patients with the white chicken. The bird is presented wings spread out for the 'wife' to spit under the wing.

This done, the patients returned to the gateway. 'Where is the chicken?' Krug asked, and he was handed the white fowl with which he went up to the patients again. With the fowl he 'swept' them down as before and then, opening out first one wing and then the other, told them, in turn, to spit under the wing (Fig. 4). He was just turning away when the Kpata'ar marriage witness called out, 'You haven't cried out Red Destiny come down, White Destiny come down, Black Destiny come down.' 'Oh, I forgot', said Kurug and, turning back to face the patients, he held the chicken up towards the sky and called out, in a quavering voice, 'Red Destiny come down, Black Destiny come down, White Destiny come down.' He then returned to where the mud ball and the leaves and the egret had been placed. Squatting down, he put down beside the heap the *boghakyee* which he had been carrying slung over his shoulder all the time, and asked for the beer, against a background of conversation which was the more striking in contrast to the silence that had prevailed throughout the rites at the gateway.

Again there was an argument about procedure, the Sii elders insisting that the Kpata'ar elders should invoke their ancestors to stand by, the latter protesting that it was not their responsibility since it was the duty of the woman's paternal kin to perform the ritual. However, characteristically, they nevertheless yielded and Nyaangzum as head of Sinkawol's own branch of the lineage complied, followed by the heads of the two other branches.

Kurug meanwhile went on with his task. The beer for which he had called was brought to him in a large earthenware dish. It was not in fact real beer, but token or symbolic beer made of malted grain he had brought from Sii, coarsely ground and steeped in hot water by the women of the household. Kurug emptied this on to the heap made up of mud, ebony leaves and the dead bird, significantly without a prayer – as if to say this is not real beer or a real ancestral shrine, on which properly brewed beer accompanied with prayer would have to be poured, but only a symbolic, a make-believe shrine, built in order to bring down the evil Destiny to a manipulable material embodiment and due to be thrown away as no ancestral shrine can be.

Kurug then asked for the chicken to be handed to him again. Now the Sii spokesman addressed him, transmitting to him, as in the *zong* rite, the Kpata'ar story, in the same rhetorical style and in almost the same words as before. Squatting by the *boghakyee*, Kurug took a handful of millet flour from a small calabash dish and scattered it over the 'shrine'. Addressing the shrine in the same declamatory, almost demanding, tone as before, he began, 'It is Tongnaab that I am taking hold of', and then came the Sii story of Soorbon's beginnings and of the crisis. Again the diviners' revelations – 'Did they', he exclaimed, 'perhaps offend a [dead] father? Or perhaps a more distant ancestor? But the father said he has no hand in it – the ancestors said they have no hand in it – it came out instead that it was the Destiny she had.' The diviners' prescription that they should take the ancestral shrine, Tongnaab, to Kpata'ar to sweep away the Destiny and the conscientious provision of the various animals and 'things' demanded were eloquently enumerated. Ancestor Tongnaab was invoked to put things right and to drive away the evil Destiny. 'Tongnaab', he ended, 'if you really exist grant that this Destiny may relent, that it may depart to the wasteland, that it may depart to the wild bush, grant that the woman may bear a child, that farming prosper, that livestock increase, and that the house be built up.' He poured some beer on the *boghakyee* and then, holding up the chicken, called out, 'Take your chicken, here is your chicken, a pure white one.' He slaughtered it, dripped some blood over the *boghakyee*, and threw it down, crying out, 'Accept your chicken, arise and accept your chicken.'

It was refused. There was a moment of silent dismay followed by an outburst of loud and anxious discussion. Had some preliminary ritual requirements been omitted? Another chicken was called for. Holding it up, Nyaangzum appealed for a clear sign of where the fault lay. There was a call for Teezeen in his capacity as custodian of the External Boghar and Earth shrines of Kpata'ar to appeal to them, which he did, pouring a libation of beer on the ground. Then the Sii spokesman invoked Tongnaab to intercede with whichever ancestor or other occult power on their side might be the impediment, promising to made amends later, and as Kurug slaughtered the chicken, Nyaangzum cried out, 'If the Destiny has indeed come down may he permit the fowl to be accepted and we will tomorrow make amends for any fault on our side.' Kurug dropped the chicken on the ground. It leapt in the air and landed on its back, to the loudly voiced relief of all at this sign that the Destiny had 'descended' to accept its 'things'.

Now a couple of Kpata'ar youths slaughtered the white goat brought by the Sii people and took some of the blood in a dish for Kurug to drip on the *boghakyee* and the mud 'shrine', after which Kurug called for a large calabash full of flour mixed with beer to be handed to him. The patients sat down, legs outstretched, beside the mock 'shrine'. Kurug took a mouthful of the liquid and, stooping, squirted it out four times on the *boghakyee* and the shrine, then made the woman first and Sinkawol second repeat this action. They went back to sit at the gateway and Kurug, after scraping some consecrated dry red mud, which he took from the *boghakyee*, into the liquid, carried the dish to the patients and made them each take a sip. More beer was added and they were offered a good drink and allowed to scoop out and eat some of the flour. This was the first food and drink they had had all day as they had been obliged to fast from dawn. The ritual was over for the time being and the visitors were invited into the homestead to partake of the lavish hospitality that had been prepared for them.

The concluding episode took place around midnight. I did not see it but had a full report from Sinkawol and others. Porridge had been cooked outside at the gateway and marked as of ritual significance by the use of an ebony stick to stir it instead of the normal stirring stick owned by women. Sinkawol told me:

> When they finished cooking the porridge, they pulled the ebony-wood stirring stick out and scooped some porridge into a calabash dish. They scraped off the porridge stuck to the stirring stick and gave it to the officiant [Kurug] who plastered it on to the 'Yin' shrine to seal it up, and gave some to me and my wife to eat. The officiant then put the ebony stick on the shrine and slung the *boghakyee* [which had been brought out for the rite] over his shoulder and escorted me and my wife into the house as far as the outer courtyard. This means bringing into the house the good Destiny. The woman's Destiny had been harsh and they threw off that Destiny and took the good Destiny to bring it into our home so that my wife may bear a child which will live. And then one of our sister's sons gathered up the shrine – the mud ball and all the things as well as the stirring stick – that's the evil Destiny – and went off some distance and threw it all away. When the officiant sealed up the 'Yin' shrine he pronounced the same invocation as before, calling upon it to accept [the offering] so that the Destiny could be pacified and the evil Destiny depart utterly and so that farms may be farmed and livestock be reared and the woman may bear children and a house be built. He pours some beer on the shrine and then seals with the porridge.

The visiting Sii elders did not leave for home until the moon rose at about 2 a.m., nearly ten hours after their arrival. They had been royally regaled – as Nyaangzum commented next day: 'If we had not treated them so well they would have gone home and scoffed at us and some would have said that we are poverty stricken, and others that we are only mean.'

The next day I asked Sinkawol how he and his wife had felt at the time of the ritual and after. He described how he had been anxious all through, especially after the white fowl had 'refused', and what a relief it was when the next chicken, brought in specifically to test whether or not the Destiny had 'come down', was accepted. And he added that when it was all over, he and his wife were extremely happy – *ti poor peeya pam*, he said, which literally translated means 'our bellies were extremely whitened [with joy]'. Now all would be well, he thought, and they would soon have a child.

Much significant detail had to be omitted in the foregoing account of the 'sweeping away' ritual. But what I have recorded invites some exegetical comment. Let me begin then by noting again the quasi-externality attributed to Soorbon's evil Predestiny. It is defined as being external to her conscious, socially embedded self: developmentally as having been chosen in a pre-existent state and contemporaneously in respect to her current existence. The invocations that accompany the sacrifices and libations repeatedly emphasize this.

Let me risk an interpretation. Soorbon's plight is perceived by others and experienced by herself as an unnatural commitment in which she is trapped. For no woman voluntarily repudiates motherhood, the most ardently desired and indeed lived for crown of life for her: and no normal person voluntarily repudiates parents and siblings, husband or wife or the normal sources of a family's livelihood, its farming and its livestock rearing and other male productive pursuits. Yet there it is. Why should a woman's so much desired children die one after the other? It would be unthinkable by Tallensi norms for her husband or any of his kin or her own kin to wish it. Perhaps, in some obscure and incomprehensible way, she herself brought it to pass. She could never know this directly let alone admit it; nor is it possible, given Tallensi family ideals and moral norms, for her to be accused of this. It comes out into the open, as Tallensi put it, as an incontestable revelation of the ancestors transmitted through the authoritative medium of divination. And it is the more acceptable because it is transposed by customary, hence socially legitimate, evaluation into an external compulsion, exonerating the sufferer from any implication of guilt.

Would it be too far fetched to think of the evil Predestiny as a projected representation of perhaps feared and self-recriminatory impulses? I will not venture to suggest more than this. For if one tries to discuss her problems with a woman like Soorbon, one elicits a confession of grief and despondency, but also a statement of the conventional evaluation in terms of Predestiny. At all events it is evident that the attribution of externality to the evil Destiny amounts to defining it as detachable and therefore susceptible to being 'swept away'.

Speculative as this interpretation is, it does, I think, throw light on the ritual process. It is worth recalling that the patient is not thrown back on herself, or her husband, to overcome the oppression of which she is the victim. For, as I pointed out earlier, she exists as a social and moral person only in virtue of her relationships with kins-folk conferred by marriage. Her tribulations are theirs too and her struggle is absorbed into their response to her plight. It is significant that the treatment consists in mobilizing paternal duty and benevol-ence (the good father accepting accountability, if not responsibility, for her condition) and exercising their rightful claims on the good-will of ritually transposed fathers and forefathers on behalf of their 'daughter'. The cure consists in restoring the hope and self-esteem with which she entered into marriage.

What of the procedures in contradistinction to the actors? Invok-ing and enlisting the mystical intervention of the ancestors at the outset reflects the general principle that all human affairs are under their ultimate jurisdiction. I have remarked earlier on the length, the rhetorical elaboration and especially the apparently redundant re-iteration of all the information relating to the patient's plight and of the pleas for redress for her. As I noted earlier, the main reason for the exchanges preceding them and for the form of these prayers is to ensure full participation and mutual accountability of all present to one another and to the ancestors.

I have described Tallensi prayer as a cathartic exercise and this aspect is prominent also in the way the invocations to the ancestors are offered in the present context. What cannot be over-emphasized is that the ancestors are believed, one might almost say are felt, to be mystically present. The rhetoric and repetitions convey an insistence on being heard and understood, and a concern to ensure that no rele-vant information is left out. The liturgies of scriptural religions follow the same lines for they, too, are addressed to occult powers and agencies whose response to prayer cannot be directly known. So the 'red' cockerel – red here standing for any mixtures of brown or orange or similarly coloured plumage – is offered not as a sacrifice to persuade the ancestors but as a vehicle of appeal to test their responsiveness.

The offering of a red cockerel is standard procedure in this epi-sode of the ritual though it was represented as having been com-manded by diviners. Tallensi sacrificial animals fall into three large colour clusters: the white (which includes all light colours), the red (which covers another broad range of red-tinted colours), and the black (which includes all dark colours, for example, green and dark blue). A red chicken is a common sacrifice to occult agencies invoked to repel or crush a mystical source of enmity such as is implied in the case of an evil Destiny – red being the colour of anger.

Colour symbolism enters also into the ritual directed at the Destiny itself. Expert informants assured me that an evil Predestiny has been known to demand a 'red' or a 'black' chicken or goat for the sweeping away ritual, but in the two cases I witnessed and in others I was told about the demand proved invariably to be for a white goat and a white fowl. White stands for light, calmness, coolness, benignity, for what is propitious in general. In the present case the ritual of ridding the patient of her malign Destiny is, as it were, suffused with whiteness and the Destiny itself is tempted with white offerings to come down to take its 'things' and go. Furthermore, the participants, and in particular the patients, having fasted all day and so having symbolically cleared themselves of their preoccupations,[10] eat and especially drink of the white offerings: the beer and white flour sanctified by having been used in libation; the ritually marked porridge; and portions of the flesh of the sacrificed chickens and of the goat. This communion aspect is much emphasized as an essential act in the appropriation by the patient and her husband of the good Destiny that is assumed to take the place of the expelled evil Destiny.

As regards the most dramatic episode, when the evil Predestiny is actually swept away, the symbolism is almost self-evident. Again the excess, the overdetermination of the magical effectors, is noteworthy. Words, though indispensable, are evidently not enough. Consider the Destiny's 'things'. Nyaangzum gave me the conventional explanation which I also received from other elders on this and on other occasions. All the 'things' he said were 'revealed' by divination. What do they mean? The mousehole dust was demanded by the Destiny, he explained, because 'there are always mice in a woman's sleeping room and when a woman gives birth there the mice flee and get away'. I asked if perhaps the idea was to hide away the evil Destiny in a mousehole, but he rejected this. 'What!' he exclaimed, 'drive out an evil Destiny and let it come back into the sleeping room?' No, the point, as I understood it, was that the mousehole dust signifies an empty mousehole and consequently the flight of the mice which would herald the hoped-for birth of a child. As for the white egret, Nyaangzum continued, 'these birds disappear completely when the rainy season (which is the propitious season for a Destiny-building ritual) comes. We don't see even a single one then and we don't know where they go to – perhaps to your distant land!' Swallows are sometimes demanded, he added, though they don't disappear completely, and sometimes other birds that are very rare in the rainy season.

This item, then, images the Destiny as being carried off, as the invocations phrase it, to such far away places as the remotest wilderness. The magical intention is clear from the use of a dead egret. Indeed, I was assured, if it was impossible to obtain a whole bird, a wing or even a single feather would suffice. Similarly, the invocations explain the 'earth dog' (*tengn-baa*). This small grey grub, Nyaangzum explained, 'burrows into the earth' and has to be dug out. The Destiny is summoned, by the implied authority of the ancestors vouchsafed through the *boghakyee*, to descend into the mud balls of the mock shrine like the 'earth dogs' that are 'burrowed' into it – in order, as the cowrie shell expresses it, to engender the coolness of a mind at peace.

Next the ebony tree leaves and stirring stick. The ebony (*gaa*) tree is believed to be a dangerous or evil tree, liable to be magically animated and then to injure or even kill people. This is well known but I was never able to elicit a reasoned explanation from even the best informed of my friends and it would lead me too far afield, in the present context, to explore further the beliefs about 'good' and 'bad' trees and the properties that might give rise to such ideas. In the 'sweeping away' ritual the leaves are taken to be imbued with the power of the *boghakyee*. In this situation it is 'bad' power since it aims at driving out the 'bad' Destiny, like driving out like. In contrast, the red clay which is also taken from the *boghakyee* and crushed to be added to the beer given to the patient and her husband, is the vehicle – quite literally internalized, to replace the expelled evil. Ebony leaves and the consecrated red clay are used in similar ways in the rituals of initiating Talis youths into the Boghar cult.

The 'sweeping' which is accompanied by the summons to the Destiny to descend and take its 'things' is self-explanatory. What the imagery comes to is that the Destiny shall descend and adhere to the patient and her husband so that it can be swept off them into the mock shrine made up of the balls of mud. It thus becomes manipulable in a concrete way and can be literally carried away from the homestead and thrown away. I was unable to obtain an explanation of the spitting rites. A similar action is required of initiants into the Boghar cult in a rite which pledges them to absolute secrecy on pain of death for betrayal. But a possible interpretation suggests itself from a consideration of the significance of the mouth as the organ of speech.

The Tallensi do not have a belief in the 'evil eye'. The equivalent for them is the 'evil mouth'. Envious or threatening words and curses, especially if spoken by kinship seniors, can injure or even kill and, conversely, spoken blessings can do good. It will be recollected that an evil Predestiny arises because the sufferer spoke 'crazily' or in an 'ugly way' pre-natally. It is as if the patient turned her 'evil mouth' against herself. The spitting and squirting rites would appear then as gestures of renouncing the pre-natal evil mouth, giving it back, as it were, to the Destiny. This is most evident with the sacrifice of the white fowl. It is offered to the Destiny, through the ancestors, with pleas for the Destiny to come and take its 'things' and depart. But what is critical is that it should be accepted; and if it is refused additional birds will be offered until the sign of acceptance is vouchsafed. For this is taken to show that the Destiny has descended to take its 'things' and depart. It is in short a 'scape-fowl'. The goat has similar attributes but it is offered primarily as a gift, as if to recompense the Destiny for descending to take its 'things' and departing. The distribution of the meat is typical and is explicitly regarded as demonstrating the amity felt by the participants for one another and their common concern for the ritual to succeed.

I asked some of the elders why the patient's Destiny was being summoned as if from a great distance and in the sky, seeing that the Destiny is also spoken of as if it were close to, hovering over, her. Laughing at what they regarded as my *naïveté*, they answered: 'We can't see Destiny. We think it comes from Heaven. But how do we know where it really is? That is why we call upon it to come from wherever it may be.' Not knowing what it looks like accounts also for the invocation by colours. The implication is not that it might be white or red or black. These colour terms are used metaphorically to imply all conceivable modes of existence the Destiny may have; and the emphasis is on the Destiny's externality in relation to the patient.

At the end, the last section of the Destiny's mock shrine is 'sealed' with the porridge and offered to the Destiny as if it were customary hospitality to a guest. It is finally carried away by a 'sister's son' who throws it away, preferably in an uncultivated area some distance from the homestead. He calls out 'Yin Yoo, Yin Yoo, Yin Yoo, come and receive your things and take them all away. Go down into a river with them, not into a pool; hide them in a hole in a rock, not in a tree hole.' When he returns he is rewarded with a dish of porridge and some of the goat meat. On the earlier occasion, when I took part in the ritual of sweeping away Mansami's evil Predestiny, it turned out that there was no 'sister's son', even in the widest classificatory sense, among the participants. Thereupon a boy was sent off to the neighbouring clan area about a mile away to explain the situation and request the help of a young man who was known to be a 'sister's son' of Mansami's lineage. In about half an hour he arrived, duly performed the ritual service requested of him, took a token mouthful of the dish of porridge placed before him and excused himself. 'This is the custom', explained the head of Mansami's lineage.

> Have we not besought the Destiny to depart from us and leave us and once you have said so would you thereafter again touch it with a hand? No. We flatter and ingratiate ourselves with the Destiny, so that he might have pity on us and let us rest, so we give him the things he wants and cook this food for him to take all and go quickly to his own place.

The point, he elaborated, was that the whole lineage is implicated in this action on behalf of one of its members and having been decontaminated, as it were, by the ritual, it would be tantamount to bringing back the evil Destiny if they were to be in contact again with the shrine and the 'things' that now contain it. As with the marriage witness, a 'sister's son' is by matri-kinship on the patient's side and therefore to be trusted to care for his well-being, but by patri-descent excluded from participating in the corporate responsibility for him and therefore, as a quasi-outsider, immune to the evil Destiny.

What, it may well be asked, would have been the expectations and hopes left with Sinkawol and his wife – and their kin on both sides – by the apparently successful removal of her evil Predestiny? I have already mentioned Sinkawol's relief and expectations. His wife too spoke of her relief and hopes, as did the lineage elders. But the Tallensi have far too pragmatic a philosophy of life to expect certainty in the fulfilment of such hopes, even though they are engendered by successful ritual action. The hazards of daily existence remain, reflecting, as they would put it, constant possibilities of intervention in their lives by ancestors and other occult agencies. It has been known, Teezeen once remarked to me, for an evil Predestiny to return as if from a tactical retreat. Tallensi religious beliefs and ritual practices, paradoxical as it may seem to us, serve them effectively as a means of coming to terms with the realities of individual and social life.

# 8

## Custom and conscience

Kehren wir zum Über-ich zurück! *Freud*

### Perspective: of custom

Anthropologists are constantly asked to explain what their subject is specifically about.[1] Following the tradition that goes back to Tylor and Frazer, I take the view that the core of our studies is the fact, the phenomenon, of custom. I find it useful to think of this as a target concept, pointing to what we must aim to understand and explain in anthropological theory, rather than as a fixed conceptual category. To make it clearer I draw attention to the etymologically cognate word 'costume' which, like 'custom', is ultimately also derived from the Latin *consuetudo* and does not necessarily mean only attire. Nakedness, remarks Flugel (1930) in his delightful and not yet superseded book on *The Psychology of Clothes*, can in primitive society be a sign of social status just as at the other extreme special forms of clothing can be of rank and office (pp. 56–7); and this holds equally of course for our own society.

Here the customary use of body decoration as a form of costume, so to speak, halfway between nudity at one end of the scale and head to foot clothing at the other, is enlightening. In the south-eastern Nuba area of the Republic of Sudan, there are still tribal groups amongst whom men normally go completely naked, not even wearing a penis sheath such as is customary in parts of New Guinea, and girls are likewise nude until they become pregnant for the first time. But there is one item of apparel that is obligatory for all, and that is a belt around the waist. 'To be without this belt is to be naked and shameful' writes Faris (1972, p. 30). Such customs with their moral overtones are familiar to us from many parts of the world. Thus among the Tallensi, in the 1930s, it would have been immodest for a young woman to wear a perineal belt to cover her nakedness before her first pregnancy whereas among the neighbouring Mamprussi, exactly the opposite rule prevailed. Where the south-eastern Nuba stands out is in their elaborate forms of decoration which may cover the body from head to foot and are obligatory from infancy. The scarring, oiling and painting of the body, which can be painful, varies in accordance with the age and status of each person, and special patterns are associated with particular social, ceremonial and ritual occasions. In other parts of the world, facial and bodily scarification and tattooing serve the same ends. Among the Nuba it is obvious that anyone who knows the decorative code can tell a great deal about persons and occasions from its manifest use; and conversely anyone who is ignorant of the code will be at a loss as to how to conduct himself and as to what to make of the conduct and actions of others; and, again, the parallels with our own clothing customs and habits are obvious.

Connecting custom and costume brings out an important point. Customs signify in ways analogous to those of costume. Customs like costumes can be changed and transported across time and space, within and between communities; they dress up and make manifest states of individual existence, stages of individual biological development, personal and social circumstances, status, rank, office. Speech, posture, gesture, all manner of activities, individual or collective lend themselves to consideration from this point of view. Thus custom falls into place between the biological individual, naked 'behind his face', as somebody once put it, and the outside world of people, places, objects and events which he has to make sense of and, in particular, relate to in order to live successfully. Custom is sometimes subsumed under the more general notion of communication, but this is only one of its aspects. There can be no communication without relationship and custom can only be properly understood as the instrument of relationship, the bridge of interaction.

What is important from the anthropological point of view is that different customs in different places can be seen to mark similar or identical situations and vice versa descriptively similar customs may mark different situations. Nudity on the London stage has not the same purpose, at least on the surface, as in the Nuba Hills. In the latter case it is a sign of strict confirmity to general social norms, in the former, presumably, of privileged protest against conformity.

This brings me to the aspect of custom that particularly interests me here: custom regulates conduct. There is felt to be a contradiction between what is customary and what is perceived to be utterly idiosyncratic. Costume, again, is an example. 'The whole relatively "fixed" ... system of [a man's] clothing is ... an outward and visible sign of the strictness of his adherence to the social [*sc.* moral] code' (Flugel 1972, p. 113). Language, which Malinowski once called 'vocal custom,' provides similar examples. Correct grammar and syntax are learnt and obeyed as if they are morally binding and extreme eccentricity in their use is taken as a sign of deviance, perhaps even of madness.[2] Sin, crime, madness, ignorance, unmannerliness are some of the labels common in all human societies to designate deviation from customary norms and standards.

Custom therefore implies consensus, collective authorization and compulsion. Yet to be of service to the individual custom, as the example of language shows well, must be at his fingertips, assimilated, appropriated, internalized. Custom transcends the individual but without custom he cannot be human.

A problem is thus posed which has been of perennial concern and not only to anthropologists. A comment which shows up elegantly what underlies this problem is due to that arch-connoisseur of the foibles of mankind, Michael, Lord of Montaigne. Writing 400 years ago in his essay 'Of Custom and How a Received Law Should not Easily be Changed' (Montaigne 1580) he notes that many foreign customs seem bizarre, foolish or even repulsive to the educated Europeans of his day. But then he asks how it comes about that custom 'gradually establisheth the foot of her authority in us' even to the point of 'forcing' [i.e. distorting] 'the rules of Nature'. And he answers thus:

> The lawes of conscience which we say to proceed from Nature rise and proceed of Custom; every man holding in special regard and inward veneration, the opinions approved and customs received about him cannot without remorse leave them nor without applause apply himself to them. When those

of Crete would in former ages curse any man they besought the
gods to engage him in some bad custom, but the chiefest effect
of her power is to seize upon us, and so entangle us, that it shall
hardly lie in us to free ourselves from her holdfast and come
into our wits again, to discourse and reason of her ordinances;
verily because we suck them in with the milk of our birth and
for as much as the world's visage presents itself in that estate
unto our first view it seemeth we are born with a condition to
follow that course.

Here surely lie the ingredients of an answer, as to why the customs
of a community, no matter how bizarre or onerous or even repulsive
they might seem to the alien observer, are generally adhered to and
why their transgression is felt to be disturbing.

Montaigne's prescient 'because we suck them in with the milk of
our birth' accords well with the discoveries of modern science. I am
reminded of Erikson's (1950) description of the 'oral zone' as the
newborn's 'first general mode of approach, namely to "incorporate"' and his conclusion that 'the oral stage ... forms the springs of
the basic *sense of trust and the basic sense of evil* which remains the
source of primal hope throughout life' (pp. 67, 75). I am also reminded of one of Freud's early observations on the subject of taboo
which, to adapt a saying of Victor Turner's, may well be regarded as
'quintessential custom'. Freud (1913, p. 67) notes: 'Taboo conscience is probably the earliest form in which the phenomenon of
conscience is met with'; and he goes on to point out that linguistically, 'conscience' and 'consciousness' overlap, especially in what
we describe as 'consciousness of guilt' – a line of thought echoed
later in Malinowski's masterly *Crime and Custom in Savage Society*
(1926) and one to which I will return.

Anthropologists will recognize that what I am here designating by
the term 'custom', corresponds to what is usually described by the
more comprehensive concept of 'culture' (cf. Kroeber and Kluckhohn 1952). What I have in mind, in this usage, is to emphasize the
authority and constraint with which, as Montaigne observed,
custom is invested. And interestingly enough, the same idea emerges
in the celebrated Blackstonian formula, that a custom to be acknowledged must have existed from a 'time whereof the memory of
man runneth not to the contrary' and must be public and obligatory

(cf. Allen 1972). Belief in its antiquity, often buttressed by claims of divine or ancestral origin is the commonest ground for accepting the legitimacy and binding force of custom.

## The challenge of psychoanalysis

If, as is now generally agreed, it was Freud's (1913) *Totem and Taboo* that first drew attention effectively to the insights psychoanalytical theory might offer for the elucidation of anthropological problems, it was the advocacy of Ernest Jones that really brought home to anthropologists its revolutionary importance. This began with a confrontation that became famous in the annals of British anthropology. In 1924 – two years, to be noted, after the simultaneous publication of Malinowski's (1922) *Argonauts of the Western Pacific* and Radcliffe-Brown's (1922) *The Andaman Islanders*, the two books which launched modern functionalist anthropology – he gave a lecture entitled 'Psychoanalysis and Anthropology' (Jones 1924) at a meeting of the Royal Anthropological Institute. It proved a heated and by no means wholly sympathetic discussion. But it also excited the interest in the application of psychoanalysis to anthropological problems that led up, later, to his controversy with Malinowski. Though this was, as Jones declared, 'the first time that the doctrines of psychoanalysis had been propounded before an anthropological audience', a number of anthropologists in this country, and abroad, had already been making use of psychoanalytical theory.[3] And though it was the first, it was by no means the last of Ernest Jones' incursions into the field of anthropological studies. Deploying his formidable command of the anthropological literature he repeatedly challenged anthropologists to confront the universally human in custom and social organization.

Speaking of his anthropological contemporaries in this lecture, Jones comments that, in contrast to their predecessors, 'they have made considerable contributions to what may be called the humanization of primitive man'. What he means is that they were revealing 'primitive' man to be moved by the same kind of motives and to be preoccupied with the same basic concerns about food and shelter, birth and death and procreation, the body and the mind, as we ourselves are. This was a break with the nineteenth-century stereotype of the 'savage' as of interest primarily because he represented early

' stages through which the 'civilized' races of mankind have passed (cf. for example, Frazer 1910, vol. 2, pp. 94–5).

This break, however, only became definite with the publication in 1922 of the first functionalist ethnographies by Malinowski and Radcliffe-Brown to which I have just alluded. Both speak of 'savages' in these and later publications. But this was with the deliberate intention of drawing out the common humanity of all mankind. Differences of manifest custom, they argued, may seem to contradict this claim but its validity is clear when we look beneath the surface; for the same laws of mental and social life apply to all human societies. As Malinowski (1922, p. 517) put it: 'our final goal is to enrich and deepen our own world's visions, to understand our own nature...'

Malinowski and Radcliffe-Brown were, of course, not unique in thus emphasizing the common humanity of 'savage and 'civilized'. In the United States for example, Kroeber, Lowie and above all Edward Sapir, all expressed similar views; and Durkheim and his heirs, notably, Marcel Mauss, habitually proclaimed the comparability of all human societies.

But Malinowski showed more directly than any of his contemporaries how this orientation reflected the crucial experience of field research and, in turn, determined the course of field research in the new mode. He thus put the *actor, the user of custom and social relationships*, into the centre of the picture. This meant viewing custom in the contexts of motive and intention, right and duty, the demands of conformity and the propensities towards evasion to which Malinowski (1926) gave such prominence in that early and challenging work *Crime and Custom in Savage Society*. And what I want particularly to stress here is the influence of psychoanalytic theory on this development, as Malinowski himself abundantly testified in *Sex and Repression in Savage Society* (1927) and later (cf. Fortes 1957).

But as an influential paper by Sapir (1932) reveals, ambivalence if not suspicion was the prevailing attitude to psychoanalysis among anthropologists at that time. What is significant here is the critical distinction between 'actor-centred' and 'message-centred' study of custom and social organization (Chapter 6); for it is only from an actor-centred point of view that we can appreciate the relevance of psychoanalytical theory to the data of social anthropology. Essentially actor-centred, functionalism gave primacy to the pragmatic and instrumental value of custom for individuals and groups. And that is why Malinowski, stimulated by the psychoanalytical concepts of repression and ambivalence emphasized the significance of looking behind the façade of customary behaviour to identify 'real' motive and purpose. Thus, in *The Sexual Life of Savages* (1932), discussing alleged transgressions of the incest taboo, he contends that there is a serious 'discrepancy' between native statements of ideal morality and the observed facts. Custom is manifest, conscious, public, of social origin, pragmatic and adaptive, but under the surface of conformity there is always the possibility of rebellion and evasion due to private passions or desires. From this stem conflicts of duty and self-interest, of law and crime, of morality and sin.

## The Malinowski–Jones controversy

But this implies that custom does reflect, if only through a glass darkly, intrapsychical processes and dispositions as well as external constraints. Custom gives evidence of incestuous lust as a reality and not only in myth, points to conflicts of love and hate, of rivalry and solidarity, in all spheres of social organization beneath the surface peace and harmony.

Whether or not this image of human nature corresponds to reality, is a question outside my scope here. For Malinowski it followed directly from psychoanalysis, which, he said, 'has forced upon us the consideration of the unofficial and unacknowledged sides of human life' (1927, p. vii). This emerged in the course of his famous controversy with Ernest Jones, which not only marked the climax of his psychoanalytically orientated period, but also had a profound influence on later developments in the relations between psychoanalysis and anthropology. *Sex and Repression in Savage Society* documents the controversy in detail.

Let me remind you briefly of what it was about. Malinowski's investigations among the Trobrianders led him to propose to substitute for the Freudian Oedipus complex what he called a 'nuclear family complex' traced to the organization of the matrilineal family and not to the unconscious forces of infantile love and hate of the father with its roots in repressed sexual desire for the mother. His 'nuclear complex' is conceived of as a social and cultural product harnessing and directing the instinctive and emotional dispositions provided by nature. Jones, in contrast, considered the split between lawful avuncular authority and affectionate paternal care, as described by Malinowski for the Trobrianders, to be elaborate defence institutions. Their purported ignorance of physiological paternity, he argued, permits escape from the guilt of infantile sexuality. And the deflection on to the maternal uncle of the less amiable qualities of the father image, protects father and son from mutual hostility. In short, the customary norms, beliefs and practices described by Malinowski, are to be regarded, according to Jones, as expressions or even actual creations of unconscious affect, fantasy and defence mechanisms (Jones 1924).

This controversy aroused widespread interest, not only among anthropologists, psychologists and psychoanalysts, but also among the lay public. It was and indeed still is interpreted to have been about the question of the universality of the Oedipus complex. But this is in fact only one side of the main argument, as has been incisively shown by Anne Parsons (1964). As she suggests, it is possible to reconcile the views of Jones and Malinowski in the light of current theory about object relations and about parental roles in the socialization process, and thus to confront the deeper theoretical issues raised in the controversy. Before I turn to this, let me note that field studies for the post 30 years or so of the social and personal relations of parental and filial generations in matrilineal family systems in many parts of the world tend to support a Jonesian rather than a Malinowskian interpretation of the situation. For example, Gough's (1955) researches among the matrilineal Nayars of South India argue plausibly for a 'normal' (if well disguised) Oedipus complex, centred on the parents, in early infancy and my own observations among the matrilineal Ashanti of Ghana broadly support her thesis.

Where Malinowski went wrong, we can now see, was in misinterpreting the Trobriand father's role in the socialization of his children, and in his consequent misunderstanding of the kind of moral authority and responsibility vested in the father (cf. Fortes 1957; Robinson 1962). But a basic theoretical issue was raised in this controversy, relating to the question of verification. The question is, how can it be indisputably shown that manifest custom is a product of, or is generated by, or even corresponds directly to mental mechanisms of the kind revealed by psychoanalysis?

How do we bridge the gap between the level of observation open to the ethnographer and the level of observation and theory at which psychoanalysis operates? Is it valid (as Leach 1958, has questioned) to reduce the variations and diversities among the social and cultural facts revealed by anthropological research to the operation of a limited number of allegedly universal intrapsychical dispositions and mechanisms, the very existence of which must be taken on trust by anthropologists? In short, what if any causal or functional connections can be demonstrated to hold between the data accessible to anthropological observation and the data – let alone the theory – of psychoanalysis.[4]

It is worth adding that the same problems have arisen in regard to other branches of psychological theory. The fallacies of jumping from the so-called precausal thinking processes of West European children described by Piaget (1925, 1928) to the animistic magical beliefs attributed to primitive peoples, was stringently exposed by Susan Isaacs and others (cf. Hallowell 1954, pp. 26–8). Since then there has been a huge increase in cross-cultural psychological research, particularly in the field of cognition (see the excellent summary of these studies by Lloyd 1972); but the main conclusion to be drawn from them is that the mind of man works in essentially the same way in all human society, differences being due to the contexts of the social relations and to the cultural material at the individual's disposal.[5]

## The Durkheimian reaction

Confronted thus with what appeared to be an unbridgeable gap between psychoanalytical theory and anthropological observation, British anthropologists of the generation following Malinowski, turned towards a Durkheimian framework of method which seemed more rigorous and objective. From this point of view the facts of custom and social organization constitute a relatively autonomous field of social life which must be understood in its own terms. 'Social facts' must be explained by reference to other 'social facts' of the same manifest level. It was a point of view particularly congenial to the interest in the rigorous analysis of kinship systems, political systems and social organization that was developing under the leadership of Radcliffe-Brown (cf. Fortes 1953, 1955b); and largely on account of the limits accepted for it, it proved to be a powerful

instrument of research, as Gluckman and Devons (1964) ably demonstrate.

It is worth stopping for a moment to consider what anthropologists generally regard as the classical example of this neo-
Durkheimian orientation, Evans-Pritchard's (1937) famous
monograph on *Witchcraft, Oracles and Magic Among the Azande.*
It is the more significant because, around the same time, Kluckhohn
(1941) was investigating Navaho witchcraft explicitly applying psychoanalytical theory, which Evans-Pritchard was as explicitly avoiding.

What Evans-Pritchard showed was that a people's witchcraft and
magical beliefs and practices fit together consistently and, for the
actors, rationally, given the premises from which they start. He
showed that these beliefs and practices constitute a closed system of
pseudo-casual mystical explanations of misfortune serving also as
moral sanctions for regulating the conduct of individuals. The irrationality of the beliefs from the observer's *external* point of view
has no bearing on the actor's *internal* point of view. And his great
discovery was the distinction between what he called *witchcraft*, believed to be an involuntary (i.e. unconscious), hereditary, intrapsychical constituent of the personality that is revealed only and *ipso
facto* when it has supposedly struck down a victim and, by contrast,
what he called *sorcery*, defined as the intentional (i.e. conscious) and
deliberate manipulation of magically injurious materials and spells
to afflict people. The victims, or others on their behalf, might attribute the same motives of malice and envy to both, but their character and mode of action are fundamentally different. This distinction
has been the basis of a vast amount of research on witchcraft and
sorcery, not only in preliterate societies but recently also by his-
torians of our own society (cf. Marwick 1965; Macfarlane 1970;
Douglas 1970). Certainly Evans-Pritchard does consider how these
beliefs and practices serve to sidetrack the attribution of what we
would describe as guilt and responsibility, but he sticks strictly to
the manifest level, taking Zande statements of motives at their face
value and refraining from speculating about underlying psychological mechanisms.

### Positive influence of the Malinowski–Jones debate

On the negative side therefore one result of the Jones–Malinowski controversy was to discourage anthropologists from having any dealings with psychoanalysis. But there was also a positive side to the debate. In spite of the admitted difficulties of bridging the conceptual and theoretical gap between manifest custom and the intrapsychical dispositions and mechanisms postulated by pscho-analysis, some anthropologists continued to look to psycholanalytical theory for sources of insight if not for explanatory paradigms. There was not only the general Malinowskian injunction to look behind the façade of the conventional in order to discover 'real' motives and purposes, but there was the more important implication of the hypothesis that forms of family structure regulate and mediate the manifestations in overt custom and social organization of the dispositions and mechanisms identified by psychoanalysis. Not only did this suggest a way of bridging the theoretical gap, but what is of more importance, it fitted in with the new advances in studies of social structure. So, for instance, in the post-war structural studies among peoples with matrilineal family systems (admirably reviewed in Schneider and Gough 1961; cf. Fortes 1969, Ch. XI) we are given an inside view of the relations of parental and filial generations, of kinsfolk and of spouses, that expand our understanding of these systems far beyond the lines drawn by Malinowski. We learn that when fathers are indulgent and protective this is a mitigating counterpart to the authoritarian surveillance they are required to exercise over the moral and sexual development of their children, especially of the daughters. We learn of the conflicts and tensions that arise through the hidden competition between and within successive generations of men for control over the economically and politically critical reproductive capacities of sisters, wives and daughters; and we learn, likewise, of the ambivalent sexual, aggressive and homicidal fantasies that are thus generated and projected in the beliefs about witchcraft and sorcery that are invariably directed towards the closest kinsfolk. We are also shown how the internal organization and development of family relations are regulated by the wider structure of kinship, neighbourhood and tribal institutions. We are beginning to understand the interlinked socialization processes through which the demands and constraints of society, crystallized in patterns of custom and forms of social organization, are transmitted to the individual, on the one hand, and how on the other the adaptation of the individual to the social order is mediated by the family structure (cf. P. Mayer 1969).

How does this image of the human situation square with psycho-analytical theory? Let us see what Ernest Jones has to say about this. I quote from the fragment of his autobiography, which was published after his death (Jones 1959):

> It is a tenet of psycho-analysis that man is throughout a social creature . . . By this is meant that his mind develops entirely out of interaction between him and other human beings, and that an individual not so built up is unthinkable . . . An analysis of the mind will show that it was built up as I have just indicated: from social relationships (p. 153).

More specifically I would like to suggest that this view can be link-ed to that part of psychoanalytical theory which Freud (1933) called 'the anatomy of the mental personality'. More than 20 years ago Talcott Parsons (1952) suggested that there is an overlap between Durkheim's concept of collective representations and Freud's con-cept of the supergo. Durkheim, says Parsons, described collective representations as emanating from the total society and as charac-terized by the moral constraints they exert on the members of the society. He suggests that this corresponds, at the social level, to Freud's concept of the superego, the internalized representative of parental authority, as that is in part shaped and moulded by the social structure and the cultural norms and values of the society. Malinowski, hostile as he was to Durkheimian notions of collective consciousness, would nevertheless, I think, have accepted Parsons' model, in principle. I think he would have agreed that it provides a model of the possible processes by which the public and collectively sanctioned norms of custom accessible to anthropological obser-vation are incorporated in a binding form into the attitudes, motives and behaviour patterns of the individual.

Be this as it may, it can plausibly be claimed that this model corre-sponds to later developments in anthropological theory and re-search. The central role of filio-parental relationships in social structure and in the transmission and maintenance of customary norms and values was well appreciated by anthropologists of the perfunctionalist period, as their descriptive ethnographies (as e.g. Junod 1927; Spencer and Gillen 1914) clearly show. But what was

not realized before the confrontation with psychoanalysis dramatized in the Malinowski–Jones debate, was the crucial importance
of the element of parental authority in the structure of these relationships. In one way or another, explicitly or implicitly, recognition of
this fact henceforth becomes a standard feature of anthropological
studies of kinship and family systems. This is evidenced, in particular, by the attention paid to intergenerational and intra-familial
conflicts and hostilities though straightforward recourse to
psychoanalytical explanations was eschewed (cf. Fortes 1949;
Turner 1957; Nadel 1947, pp. 1–109). Many traditional problems
fell into a new theoretical perspective in the light of structural analysis of intra-familial and other conflict situations along these lines.
The study of the witchcraft syndrome to which I earlier alluded is an
excellent case in point. The restricted ideological interpretation put
forward by Evans-Pritchard is now placed within a framework of
motivational dispositions that are intelligible only on the basis of
psychological hypotheses however neatly disguised in sociological
language (cf. Marwick 1965; Douglas 1970 *passim*; LeVine 1973,
pp. 265–7).

Looking back, one might conclude that this development ran directly counter to the prevailing paradigm, with its focus on lateral
analysis restricted to the manifest level. But in truth it emerged from
within this paradigm. When, as with Malinowski, the facts of field
observation forced some of us to ask not only *how* a body of custom
operates and hangs together in a given structural setting but also
*why* particular norms, beliefs, practices and values occur within that
setting, recourse to psychological and psychoanalytical insights
became indispensable. And there was plenty to draw upon in the
psychologically and psychoanalytically inspired field research and
theory that was forging ahead side by side with structural studies,
notably in the United States. (I must refrain from discussing these
developments here and content myself with drawing attention to
LeVine's 1973, authoritative review of the field.)

But why did these important and often seminal developments continue to be regarded with suspicion by the general body of professional anthropologists in Britain and America? The main reason,
I believe, was (and remains) the distrust of any form of reduction
that is characteristic of anthropologists. The difficulty, which I mentioned earlier, of demonstrating just how the universal psychical dis-

positions and mechanisms postulated by psychoanalysis are transformed into the manifest phenomena of culture and social organization in all their variety and diversity was (and remains for many) to all intents insuperable.[6] A breakthrough could only come with field work in which it was shown that better sense could be made of certain data of observation by drawing on psychoanalytical theory than by lateral analysis.

A good example is the interpretation Gluckman (1954) offered, 20 years ago, of the Swazi first fruit ceremonies. Overtly, the ceremonies purport to renew and reconsecrate the King's magical powers and potency. What Gluckman argues is that the ceremonies in fact represent a symbolic ordeal which resolves the ambivalence inherent in the relations between the King and his subjects and so confirms the sanctity and authority of his office.

I am not here concerned with the validity of Gluckman's thesis, which has in fact been questioned by some authorities (Wilson 1959). I cite his study as an example of frank recourse to a psychoanalytical concept in order to bring out, in a body of custom, motives that are not explicitly admitted. Victor Turner similarly draws extensively on psychoanalytical theory in his studies of the symbolism of Ndembu ritual practices. For instance, he interprets a ritual treatment of barrenness in a woman, which is attributed to the persecution of ancestral shades, as a procedure for symbolically revealing the alleged persecution to be in fact a projection of unacknowledged parts of her own personality (Turner 1969, pp. 31–7). Goody (1962) does likewise, in his application of the Freudian theory of the mourning process to the analysis of LoDagaa mortuary and funeral ritual. And Melford Spiro, in a series of notable studies of non-western religious systems, has shown how particular configurations of beliefs and ritual practices serve the actors as customarily legitimate defensive actions to cope with the experience of conflict or threat or socially maladapted impulse of unconscious origins (e.g. his analysis of Burmese witchcraft accusations as the projection of hostility and aggression in a society the official religion of which is a variety of Buddhism: Spiro 1969).

As a last example, I want to mention Freeman's (1968) masterly study of the Semang cult of the 'Thunder God'. Why, he asks, is the anger of this deity and of his wife, which is believed to be expressed in the violent and often destructive tropical thunderstorms, supposed to be especially aroused by incest and other sexual sins? Why, again, does the mockery of certain animals or injury to a leech which might on the surface appear to be of relatively trivial import, also arouse the anger of the Thunder God? He then shows how these beliefs become readily intelligible if the Thunder God and his spouse are seen as projections of parental figures, the 'father god' representing the 'threatening and terrifying aggressive super-ego figure'. Freeman offers his interpretation in contrast to an interpretation put forward by Needham, according to whom the Semang beliefs embody 'natural symbols' arising out of primordial affective human reactions to impressive natural phenomena. It is enough to state the contrast for the greater explanatory power of Freeman's hypothesis to be perceived.

And the divergence here illustrated continues. Take, for instance, the point of view of Monica Wilson, whose researches on Nyakyusa religion and witchcraft are unrivalled for their ethnographic detail and sensitivity. Representations of oral themes and of beliefs about blood and faeces, coitus, birth, death and incest abound in Nyakyusa ritual and religion; and Wilson is well aware of psychoanalytical implications of her observations. Nevertheless she insists that her task as an anthropologist is to 'lay bare the symbolic pattern of the Nyakyusa' without reference to the 'Western tradition' to which she ascribes psychoanalysis (Wilson 1957, p. 7). Her objection is that no native informant can provide the kind of associations or commentaries that directly confirm psychoanalytical interpretations. She does not consider the possibility that these ritual practices and beliefs form a defensive apparatus for the management of potentially dangerous unconscious motives and preoccupations.

A more contemporary example is to be found in Tambiah's (1970) brilliant and learned study of Thai village Buddhism. A model of anthropological method, it sticks firmly to the manifest level of cognitive symbolism, broadly along the lines laid down in the linguo-structuralist theory of Lévi-Strauss. Consider, for instance, his account of the entry of a man into monkhood, usually after an earlier period of novicehood. At the village level monkhood is generally a temporary commitment, followed by a return to permanent lay life. Restating the descriptive data in anthropological language he concludes: 'If ordination of monkhood is in religious terms a rite of initiation, in social terms it is distinctly a rite of pass-

age for young men before they marry and set up their own house-
holds' (p. 101). 'Why then', he continues, 'do youths and young men
lead a monastic life as a phase of their lives?' The answer is that this
confers merit on their parents. The ordination of a monk is usually
sponsored by his parents, and becoming a monk is, Tambiah notes,
an expression of 'filial piety' (pp. 102–3). Entering a monastery signifies obligatory withdrawal from lay life. And this means above all
the 'renunciation' (p. 104) or 'suppression' (p. 144) 'of male virility
or sexuality and similar attributes of sexual life'. This is dramatized
in the ordination ceremonies, which include a head-shaving ritual
interpreted by Tambiah as 'symbolic renunciation of sexuality',
thus marking the passage of the ordinand from the lay state to the
'opposed state' of monkhood. Other features of the ritual of ordination are interpreted in the same way, and 'the ritual as a whole',
says Tambiah, 'states a reciprocal relation between, on the one hand
parents and kin and laymen (in general), and, on the other, the
monk; it also emphasises the essential features of a monk's life that
distinguished it from a layman's' (p. 108).

What then is the nature of this symbiotic reciprocity of relationship (p. 143) between monks and laymen? The monks cook no food
for themselves – their food is provided by the villagers as a special
merit-making act and is brought to them by unmarried girls who
'can do so without danger because the monk has suppressed himself
sexually and is asexual' (p. 144). Other services to satisfy his needs
(e.g. clothing) are similarly rendered by the lay public; and here
comes an important point. These practical lay activities are regarded
as polluting entered into, Tambiah argues, so that 'the religious
specialist can be freed to pursue purity from the world's contamina-
tions'. Thus the 'opposition' of monks and laymen is an opposition
also of purity and pollution, the critical feature of which is the opposition between non-productive ritually obligatory celibacy and asce-
ticism, on the one hand, and the productive and procreative lay
activities without which the monks themselves could not exist (pp.
148–9).

It seems to me that this account of monkhood in a Thai village
community takes us no further than the manifest descriptive level –
simply restating in anthropological language what the eye sees and
what informants tell the enquirer; but psychoanalytically considered these data raise more complex theoretical issues. Why, one

might ask, should adolescent boys be willing to renounce their aggression and sexuality in order to confer religious merit on their parents? To answer this question let us assume that the ordination rites represent a symbolical, ritually legitimated working out of repressed rivalry and mutual hostility of fathers and sons. Could it be then that the ritual Tambiah interprets as the renunciation of sexuality is better understood as expressing filial submission to symbolic castration as preparation for symbolically regressing to the seclusion of infantile innocence and dependence on parents in the monastery, and by this sacrifice winning the merit later to re-enter safely the 'polluting' life of normal, that is of sexually and economically active adulthood? Is it wildly speculative to interpret the 'filial piety' paraded in the institution of monkhood as a customarily legitimate device for converting repressed filial hostility into socially respectable humility? And it is of interest to learn, in this connection, that the coffin bearers in the cremation ceremonies for a dead man were his sons and a son in law, and that 'they are exposed to the danger that the dead man's *phii* [a kind of spiritual double] may take hold of them or harm them' (p. 182). Again would not the descriptive opposition between purity and pollution make analytical sense and raise important questions for direct observation, if it is thought of as a phase of infantile sexual innocence and oral dependence on the mother defensively enforced by ambivalent parents, metaphorically speaking a 'back to the womb' phase, in contrast to the parent rejecting stage of sexually active, married adulthood?

Granted that this is all speculation, I would nevertheless argue that such an approach opens up questions and suggests hypotheses that do not emerge in the strictly descriptive ethnographic narrative – especially if it is constructed in terms of the intellectualist approach to the study of ritual that is now favoured by many anthropologists (cf. the criticism by Horton 1968).[7]

## The evidence of fieldwork: the ancestors

Let me restate the aim of this enquiry. It is to understand why custom binds and how it serves the actors in the management of their social existence. It will be evident from the preceding discussion that I do not think this aim can be achieved, even to the limited degree which the nature and quality of our data permit, without the help of psychoanalysis. I want to explain now how I reached this conviction not *a priori* but in response to the facts of observation in the field. The crux of this lesson was that the binding force of custom among the Tallensi depends, in the final analysis, on their ancestor cult, and that the key to this lies in their family and kinship system.

I started my field work among the Tallensi of Northern Ghana in January 1934, at the height of the dry season, a time when funeral ceremonies are of almost daily occurrence. I was thus immediately faced with the problem of understanding Tallensi beliefs and practices relating to sickness and death – 'the painful riddle', as Freud remarks 'for which no remedy at all has yet been found or will probably ever be'. This is doubtless why death, and sickness which is its common precursor, are universally regarded as the greatest of afflictions.

Tallensi, however, like most tribal and oriental peoples, do not consider physical death as such to be the ultimate misfortune. Everybody knows that death is inevitable and unpredictable, for, as the Tallensi say, death does not announce his coming by banging on a drum. For them the ultimate calamity is to die childless, more particularly, sonless. Like the very different people of Benin, famous for the bronze and ivory sculptures which record their elaborate state system and kingship cult, they say, as Bradbury (1965) puts it, that 'to die childless, is the most dreaded fate', for then there is no one to bury you well. It signifies annihilation and none of the most desired and striven-for material or social rewards of life make up for this.

But I did not realize what lies behind this anxiety until the Tallensi ancestor cult became intelligible to me; and this I owed to clues from psychoanalytical theory. I want to make a point of this because I came into social anthropology after a training in experimental psychology and some experience of clinical psychology under the tutelage of Emanuel Miller (cf. Fortes 1974). I had indeed some grounding in psychoanalytical theory from J. C. Flugel and C. G. Seligman. But partly as a result of my own experience with intelligence tests and partly under the influence of the prevailing anthropological paradigm, I started my field work in a spirit of scepticism about psychological explanations of custom and social organization. It was the facts of observation, of trying to make sense of the customary religious ideas and beliefs and practices of the Tallensi that compelled me to change my approach.

## Death and the ancestors

So why do Tallensi dread a childless death? It is connected, in the first place with their notion of the person (cf. Fortes 1973). A person (as distinct from his or her personality) in Tallensi thought is a complex socio-psychological entity. Rudimentary components are the body, the life and the soul, which emerge at birth. To these must be added identity, which is rooted in ancestry, and achievements which are ruled by Destiny. And as these accrue through the life cycle, so personhood grows and develops. But personhood is not regarded as complete and fulfilled until ancestorhood is assured and for this one must have surviving children, at least a son to install one as an ancestor. To die childless, therefore, not only condemns one to oblivion, it negates the entire personhood that might have been achieved during a lifetime. To have and to rear children is therefore the highest aim of life.

The structural foundation for the achievement of full personhood by the individual in economic and social, no less than in conceptual and religious terms — lies, consequently, in the concatenation of successive generations; and this is governed by the ancestors. They have the ultimate control over the whole course of one's life. Successful parenthood is due to their beneficence; and childless death to their enmity. Their omnipotence is most decisively displayed in their power over life and death. For the ancestors have the sole prerogative of ensuring life and of inflicting normal death. It is a rule of law and of religion that a person cannot just die (like an animal). Ancestors must declare themselves to have brought it about. If you are not killed, as Tallensi put it, by ancestors, you were never a genuine person. This is not a causal theory; the immediate and material causes of death are recognized to be sickness or accident or old age or an arrow or a blow. Ancestors kill as judges do who sentence a man to death, and the judicial parallel is apt; for Tallensi ancestors are essentially projections of the jural authority vested in parents (cf. Fortes 1965) reflecting the combination of discipline and devotion exercised in their tasks of inculcating traditional norms and values and of incorporating offspring into lineage and clan continuity. Ancestors are arbitrators, not wanton executioners. Besides the ancestors, there is the complementary mystical power lodged in the Earth (cf. Fortes 1945). However, though Earth can punish sins against its own sanctity, it cannot kill without ancestral consent. The rules relating to death are absolute. My records of deaths run into double figures, and in not a single case was a normal death attributed to any other source than ancestral edict. So also were the lesser evils of sickness and other misfortunes such as crop failure or accident or a wife's miscarriage.

Similar beliefs are found all over the world. As Simone de Beauvoir says, 'there is no such thing as a natural death' – that is for humans and universally. Tallensi do not accept death as merely a natural event. Like the rest of mankind, they have a theory to account for it. This is a necessary step in the ritual provision for tolerating its occurrence, which is often also a phase of the jural action that is, as in all societies, a prerequisite for any life to be properly terminated.[8]

It is distinctive of the Tallensi that the ancestors who control their lives are named and identified, are ritually accessible at specified locations, and inflict misfortune on or adjudge to death only their actual descendants. They cannot, for example, as in some other tribes, trouble collateral kin. Accountability to the ancestors is personal, either by the responsible individual or by the corporate lineage as a jural person.[9]

## The ancestors in daily life

The Tallensi terms I am translating by the English word 'ancestors' should more exactly be rendered as 'fathers' and 'forefathers'; and though it is always clear from the context of speech and of ritual that the reference is to the dead and not the living, the terminology indicates how close they feel to their ancestors. They are constantly reminded that their ancestors play a part in their daily life, for recognition of ancestry dominates all social relations. A person's social and juridical identity is irrevocably fixed by his membership by birth of his father's lineage and his connection with other lineages through his mother. This determines where he lives and gets his living, and what his life chances are. But, more directly, the ancestors are felt to be close because they are not relegated to an extra-human world of the dead. Their graves and the shrines dedicated to them are beside and inside the homesteads of their descendants, objectifying their accessibility to and perpetual presence among their descendants. So, though dead and gone, the ancestors yet have their place in the world of the living, invisible but effective, and accessible through the special medium of religious ritual.

Here we meet with a paradox. Ancestors need descendants to perform the ritual services that confer, and maintain them in the state of, ancestorhood. Why then do they mostly make their powers felt by persecuting and even slaying their descendants? Ancestors cause trouble, as Tallensi see it, in order to assert the claims to the offerings (which Tallensi say are their food and drink) and the submission they are entitled to. But they act thus under provocation, in requital Tallensi believe, for beneficence that has been ignored or to punish ritual or moral wrongdoing such as flouting kinship norms. But this takes the form of retribution for neglect, or for breach of promises, of offerings and services demanded. Hence ancestral demands and harassment are not considered to be unjust, let alone malicious; indeed they always take predictable customary forms, though they are experienced as affecting individuals.

It is consistent with these relations with their ancestors that Tallensi do not go about in perpetual dread of them. Ancestors are supposed to be always watchful; and they are apprised of all significant family or clan events. But they are seriously attended to only when they signal their intervention in the affairs of men through occasions of good fortune or of unforeseen coincidences, or above all through a warning misfortune. Diviners must then be consulted to ascertain what they are demanding in order to ensure a propitious outcome. But, characteristically, men procrastinate in meeting these demands until a crisis of illness or death forces compliance, though even in the face of death Tallensi realism comes to the fore. I have known a dying man, protesting that nothing could save him, refuse therefore to order the sacrifice which the diviners had declared would save his life. The debt, as it is called, devolved on his heirs in accordance with the rule that 'debts never die' and this was accepted as proper. Ancient debts to ancestors are often revealed at funeral divinations as the causes of death.

The notion of debt in this context is not fortuitous. Tallensi have words that can be translated as 'to suffer' and 'to endure pain'. But they interpret illness and death as afflictions imposed on the sufferers not as states incurred by them, as a Christian might, in retribution for sin. Tallensi religion has no theodicy, that is, a theory to 'justify the ways of God to man' in spite of apparently undeserved suffering and of unaccountable evil. Afflictions are, in the last resort, just, and the appropriate response is the customary piacular sacrifice which is a debt until it is given.

To sum up then, ancestors and descendants belong to the same moral universe, linked together in complementary opposition that is bridged by ritual action, predominantly in the form of animal sacrifice. As Tallensi see it, the ancestors and the powers they have are part of objective reality, tied down to earth, as it were, in their graves and shrines. For us, of course, all this is imaginary; and, what is more, on a superficial view not compatible with their realistic temperament. For the Tallensi are a prosaic, down to earth, densely populous tribe of subsistence farmers working a none-too-fertile soil in a difficult climate. Their interests are concentrated on this world. They desire long life, children, food, livestock and good crops. They have no inhibitions or prudishness, either in speech or in behaviour, about sex (when they regard as naturally given for procreation), or about nudity or menstruation or excretion, or other bodily processes. They are not afraid of or disgusted by dead bodies even when, having been kept for three days in tropical heat, they are bursting with putrefaction at the time of burial. Witchcraft and sorcery are remotely peripheral in their world view; possession and trance which they know about, through hearsay, they scorn as preposterous and spurious, since in their philosophy the ancestral dead and the other occult powers they recognize are not cast out of human society but are contained within it and therefore need no human vehicles to return.

Tallensi like things to be out in the open, tangible in the garb of known custom, even when private in origin, and above all having material representation. Thus it is easy to see, in the field, that their religious beliefs and ritual have a restorative function. When things go well they confirm confidence. When misfortunes strike, though one cannot avoid anxiety or grief, one is spared conscious moral guilt since they are deemed to emanate ultimately from just and omnipotent ancestors. Since, moreover, there is customary provision for making reparation by service and sacrifice, confidence and hope revive. Tallensi often experience fear and suffering in relation to the external dangers they cannot escape. Even nowadays famine threatens in a bad year and individuals succumb to penury, accident or disease. Yet Tallensi do not ordinarily appear apprehensive or insecure. The first hint of trouble sends a family head to a diviner and what never ceased to amaze me was the relief with which ancestral rebukes and demands conveyed by diviners were received. 'You have learnt who your [ancestral or other occult] enemy is', Tallensi explain, 'and so you are at peace.'

Curiously, then, considering their inescapable dependence on one another, it seems that descendants and ancestors are engaged in a continual struggle (like parents and children in reverse as we shall see), the living trying by means of service, sacrifice and prayer, to ensure the beneficence of the ancestors, who in turn continually assert omnipotent claims on the living. It was observations of this sort that led me, in the field, to speculate about Tallensi ancestors being comparable to externalized representations of conscience rather than of the terrors or the envious hostility commonly supposed to lie behind 'primitive' religion.

## The sources of ancestral worship

Given, then, its regulative power, what is the source of Tallensi ancestor worship? As we have seen, the way to achieve ancestorhood is through successful natural parenthood. Nothing else counts; men and women of impeccable worth may die childless and may therefore never become ancestors, whereas people of bad character succeed by leaving many children. It all depends on how propitious one's ancestors are; and they do not go by ordinary standards of human worth. This is the keynote; in the last resort it is they who decide. But how are the transactions between ancestors and descendants implemented? Only men have the right of direct access to ancestors, therefore a man depends upon rearing a son in order to achieve ancestorhood. Sons (and daughters too) are, however, conversely dependent on parents. They must be legitimately fathered and mothered to have jural and ritual status as normal persons; they are, of course, also dependent on parents for their upbringing and for all the resources they need for carrying on their lives. But a man is not jurally autonomous, that is, master of himself, until his father dies. Only then can he deal directly with his ancestors, both paternal and maternal for it is only through a parent, living or dead, that anyone has access to or is affected by his ancestors. Paradoxically then, having a son a man must in the end relinquish his life, and with it his paternal power, in order to attain ancestorhood; and conversely a son must wait for the death of his father in order to succeed him and thus attain the jural and ritual emancipation that gives him paternal power and a chain to ancestorhood in his turn. Women are never wholly emancipated from male control but marrying out and achieving motherhood frees daughters from parental control.

## Intergenerational conflict, its resolution

Now Tallensi, in common with most people of the world, regard parenthood as established once and for all with the birth of the first child (Chapter 4). The ideal is for a first-born son to be the successor who will establish his father as an ancestor; any other son is substitute for him. Thus the whole weight of the relations of interdependence between successive generations falls ideally upon father and first-born son, and as Tallensi also stress the equality of the parents in procreation, parallel rules apply to mother and first-born daughter. Tallensi describe these relationships as a mixture of lifelong mutual attachment and antagonism, the mirror image, as it strikes the observer, of the struggle between ancestors and descendants and Tallensi think of these relationships as intrinsic to the very nature of intergenerational relationships.

Very briefly, for I have dealt fully with this subject elsewhere (Fortes 1949, 1959, 1974) from about the age of six a first-born son is barred by stringent avoidance rules from direct or symbolical contact with his father. Thus he may not eat with his father or use any of his belongings. A man often says, as if in jest, that this son is waiting for him to die so as to take his place.

These taboos are most punctiliously observed. They are explained by the doctrine that the Destinies of fathers and first sons are for ever at enmity. As the son's Destiny fosters his advance to adulthood so the father's powers decline.

Now a person's Destiny is ruled by the ancestors who reveal themselves as its guardian (cf. Fortes 1959). The individual exercises no choice, the initiative lies with the ancestors. Thus, though fathers and first sons apparently experience and often even express their presumed antagonism, they do not feel responsible for it, for it is imposed on them from the outside by the Fate that made them ineluctably father and son, at the mercy of their ancestors.

This is Tallensi dogma. From the observer's point of view, it is the controlled ambivalence in the relations of father and first son, mother and first daughter, that arouses attention. Is it far-fetched to see in this an oedipal conflict between consecutive generations of the same sex, symbolically focused on the first-born? Significantly, the mutual trust and affection that are essential for successful child rearing are identified with younger children, thus, as it were, splitting up the intergenerational ambivalence. Does not attributing the latent antagonism between father and first-born son to their Destinies suggest that the taboos make sure that the temptation to destroy each other is kept in check?

To speak of this situation in terms of an oedipal conflict takes us back to the problem of how to justify such a deduction from the observation of custom. For me, the justification lies in the insight thus afforded to connections between different items of custom that would not otherwise emerge. Take the rule that first-born son may not wear his father's clothes or use his tools. The Tallensi explanation is that their 'body dirt' must not mix; if this happened one would die. Brothers by contrast may borrow each other's clothes and tools. 'Body dirt' refers to sweat, bodily odour and other such exudations. It is, in Tallensi thought, uniquely representative for the individual himself and is particularly associated with adult sexuality. Does not the taboo make better sense if we suppose the antagonism between father and son, mother and daughter to have a sexual undercurrent though this is not overtly admitted? Does the three-year post-partum sexual abstinence of parents, which Tallensi adhere to not for religious or magical reasons but to ensure the survival of the infant, perhaps point to suppressed rivalry between father and child for the mother (cf. Fortes 1949). In Chapter 7 I suggest that the notion of a lifelong struggle between father's Destiny and son's Destiny invites interpretation as a symbolical acknowledgement of a conflict of potencies. The relationship of consecutive generations originates in procreative sex, which is licit mixing of dirts; to mix across the generations offends against this norm.

The incest rules fit this interpretation. Sexual relations with own or classificatorily near sister or daughter are stupid and disgraceful, not sinful. Incest with one's own mother is unthinkable; by contrast sexual relations with a mother's co-wife, even symbolic allusion to the possibility by sitting on her sleeping mat, is irreparably sinful. The son may never thenceforth sacrifice to his father. Thus cut off from his ancestors, he is doomed to the annihilation of a childless death. Perhaps fantasies of destroying each other do underlie the overt attitudes of parent and first born which symbolically focus the confrontation between the generations.

It is to be noted that these avoidance customs are not enforced by external economic or legal sanctions, nor are they adhered to out of obvious self-interest; they are inculcated by parents from earliest childhood so that an internal control is established supported by beliefs that the ancestors would be outraged by transgression. The reward which Tallensi quite consciously appreciate, is that the hostilities which, if they broke open, would destroy both parties and their society are contained by these avoidances.

But containment is not enough, there must be resolution of the struggle. This comes with the death of the father when the first-born son or his substitute performs the funeral rites for this father. These terminate the father's mortal existence, when he is besought with many offerings to join his ancestors; and his ancestorhood is then established by the ritual of bringing him back into his own home in his new status and condition.

It is a crucial feature of the Tallensi type ancestor worship that the dead are first extruded from the living community as extinct humans, and are then brought back again into the family, redomesticated ritually, as ancestors. This reincorporation follows the investiture of the son with the hitherto forbidden vehicles of the father's soul, dirt and social status, that is, his clothes, his property and his office, in a typical ritual of status reversal (cf. Fortes 1949, Ch. 8). The son becomes father in the context of the living, henceforth permitted but also *obliged* to give ritual service to and through the father to ancestors. His newly acquired paternal authority among the living depends on the very fact that he is now subject to and representative of the mystical authority of his father; or to put it the other way round, he now becomes accountable to the overriding moral and ritual authority of the ancestors. As to the father's reinstatement in his family in his new capacity as an ancestral figure, it is not implausible to think of the supra-mundane power and authority with which he is now endowed, as a compensation for dying to give way to his son.

And now his son will care for him as the son, when a child, was cared for by him. I say this because to an outsider, the demands attributed to an ancestor sometimes smack of childish intransigence. For the son as successor, henceforth privileged, yet inescapably obliged, to render ritual services to the ancestors, the offerings he makes to them through his father are in part reparation for having ousted him. Tallensi sacrifice is not a form of gift; the accompanying prayers give the impression, sometimes, that an offering is a payment of a tribute or a fine to expiate wrongdoing, or of a bribe to win benevolence, or even, of a challenge to ancestral omnipotence. There is a struggle between the worshippers trying to control the ancestors and the omnipotence of the latter. And one can see how having the ancestors in the family is a necessity for the worshippers, helping to assure them of being directly under the protection of the ancestors, but enabling them to believe also, that they exercise some control over them. It is a striking thing that, whereas genuine expressions of grief are common at the death of a parent, spouse or child and during funeral ceremonies, overt signs or expressions of guilt are noticeably lacking. This is understandable, since all deaths are ultimately attributed to the ancestors. In contrast, and again understandably, Tallensi are very prone to anxiety; and it is easy to see how divination and sacrifice assuage this.

## The ancestors as internalized parents

What I have tried to make clear in the foregoing account, brief as it is, of the connection between Tallensi ancestor worship and filio–parental relations, is the key significance of the ritual reincorporation within the family and lineage of the ancestral dead. If we bear in mind the Tallensi concept of the lineage as an ideally perpetual jural person, embracing both the living and the dead predecessors (cf. Fortes 1945) and if we realize, as I shall presently make clear, what a closed and internally integrated unit the domestic family is under its head, a suggestive parallel comes to mind. Do we not have here a process of internalizing a lost parent and then externalizing or projecting this in his morally coercive aspect almost literally on to the shrines and paraphernalia of the ancestor cult, with the family and lineage, instead of the individual, as the incorporating entity?

This psychoanalytical parallel strengthens the interpretation I have previously proposed of the ancestors as externalized representations or projections of conscience, endowed with omnipotent powers of surveillance over the life history of individuals and families. It is important to recollect that individuals and groups are accountable to known and named ancestors, not to the anonymous dead for their ritual and moral conduct. Conversely every individual is subject to the surveillance of particular named ancestors exclusively concerned with him. The way this works is that each dimension of personhood distinguished in Tallensi thought comes under the aegis of identified ancestors. Every person has from birth a paternal identity and a maternal identity. He has his life and he has his Destiny; he acquires rights and duties, as well as bodily and mental skills in the course of his lifetime; and each of these components of his personal make-up is subject to the oversight of a particular group of ancestors. He owes obedience and service to one group of ancestors for the preservation of his life, to another group of ancestors for watching over his Destiny and so on for the other dimensions of his personhood. And, be it remembered, all these ancestors are located outside himself, symbolically objectified in their shrines.

It might seem strange, therefore, that Tallensi conduct their lives as if they were quite free of outside control, acting in normal ways in moral and social issues as well as in practical affairs. Sickness is treated, farms are skilfully cultivated, livestock carefully tended. It is only the ultimate responsibility or credit, not the management of routine existence, that is thrown upon the ancestors. A man must have a propitious Destiny to succeed in life; but he must exert himself to get a livelihood, to find a wife, to keep well, to care for his children. Ancestor worship is a moral regulator in the way of individuals and families, not a source of power over the order of nature.

## Why ancestors are punitive

The most difficult problem presented by Tallensi ancestor worship is how to account for the predominantly judicial, punitive and demanding character attributed to ancestors, granted that beneficence is also conceded to them, though more as a response to faithful service than as a normal character trait. At one time (Fortes 1949, Ch. 8) I speculated that this could be explained as a projection of fantasies of omnipotent and aggressive parents, provoked by the inevitable frustrations infants must suffer at the hands of even the most tender and loving parents. Later, arguing from the sociological end, I gave precedence to the principle of the jural authority vested in parenthood and exercised in the name of the ancestors and the lineage. I suggested that acts of apparently arbitrary punishment are more distinctive of authority than acts of beneficence. The point is that it is not the whole parent, tempering his or her disciplinary actions with love and care, but only the authority-wielding side of the parent that is, after his death, translated into ancestorhood (cf. Fortes 1965).

Alternative hypotheses have been put forward to account for the punitive character commonly attributed to ancestors, in ancestor worshipping societies. What we are confronted with is the observation, for which there is now voluminous ethnographic evidence, that the ambivalent tensions between parental and filial generations to which psychoanalysis first drew attention are universal features of human social life. Whether they are generated in the socialization process or are sucked in with the mother's milk as Montaigne opined and as perhaps some modern theorists would, metaphorically speaking, agree, must be left to experts to decide. The interesting anthropological observation is that customary modes of dealing with them are to be found everywhere. In some societies custom permits open expression to intergenerational conflict and rivalry, in others the harmony that should prevail is stressed either in denial or in dismissal of the underlying antagonisms. Many factors, ranging from demographic variables and material possessions at one end of the scale to cosmologies and mythologies at the other end, and of course, the rules of family organization, kinship and descent, all play a part. What is striking, however, is how often such customarily defined filio–parental relations are implicated in the religious system, including our own of course, as Freud long ago demonstrated.

Ancestor worship is the example, *par excellence*. This is what

gives the problem of the punitive character so often attributed to
ancestors wider theoretical importance. It is clear that my emphasis
on the elevation to ancestorhood of the authority component in the
exercise of parenthood, assumes the intergenerational struggle to be
intrinsic to the relations of parents and children and not to be an artifact of social or customary conditioning. I think of it as the converse
of the notion of the ancestor cult, as an externalized representation
of the conscience. Thus I see custom and social organization as
mobilizing or providing outlet for what is in effect an in-built human
propensity. Others, however, think differently and define the
character of ancestor worship in a particular society by social and
cultural determinants. Goody (1962) argues that the struggle between consecutive generations is centred on the allocation and transmission of rights to productive property. In societies where law and
custom designates a man's son or sister's son as his rightful heir, the
holder of property at a given time jealously guards his rights in it
and, on the other side, the prospective heir impatiently awaits the
death of the holder so that he can inherit. Starting from the same
proposition, Freedman (1967) suggests that the conflict can be
sidetracked by conceding victory in advance to the filial generation.
Contrasting the benign and aloof Chinese ancestors with the punitive character attributed to African ancestors, Freedman notes that
in China mature sons are not seen as a threat to the father's status. It
is customary for the father to distribute his powers and possessions
among all his sons during his lifetime and no one son replaces him.
Misfortune is blamed on to impersonal non-human agencies. At the
other extreme, among the Bagisu of Uganda for instance (cf. LaFontaine 1967), the conflict can erupt into parricide when ambitious
adult sons are thwarted by fathers and fail in their duty of arranging
for their sons' initiation. This is superficially remarkable, since the
initiation ceremonies culminate in a ritual of brutal and sadistic circumcision which is closer to a real than a symbolic castration. In this
society initiated sons compete fiercely with fathers for economic and
political power. But what seems crucial is the powers fathers appear
to have over the adult sexuality of their sons and daughters. Bagisu
ancestors appear to have a mixture of punitive and protective
characteristics of the usual African pattern. But Bagisu also have beliefs in witchcraft and sorcery to explain evil happenings such as
death and other misfortunes, though these malign powers cannot

operate without the consent of the ancestors. Among the Bagisu, then, it would appear, the struggle between the generations is bitter and open and centres round competition for political power and authority as well as for sexual potency. To cite a last example, the Lugbara of Uganda, as Middleton (1960) shows, come somewhere between the Bagisu extreme and the moderation of the Tallensi and LoDagaa in dealing with the conflict of the generations. Lugbara ancestors have a vindictive character that appears to reflect the openly expressed envy and greed for power both of elders who invoke ancestors to injure rivals or dependants, and of sons who resort to similar ritual aggression to get rid of fathers, and here too the ancestor cult overlaps with beliefs in witchcraft and sorcery.

These few examples must suffice to indicate the range of the customary manifestations of the conflict between successive generations that are permitted to emerge in ancestor worship. It is a conflict which, as I have already indicated, I believe to be intrinsic to the human reproductive sequence. In non-western societies it is absorbed into diverse ritual practices and interpreted in terms of diverse religious and metaphysical doctrines. This does not mean that these always take the form of an ancestor cult. It is only that here I am limiting myself to a consideration of ancestor worship and the feature that stands out most conspicuously in all varieties of ancestor worship – even among the Chinese as some recent research suggests, *pace* Freedman – (cf. Ahern 1973) is their punitive character. As regards the Tallensi, I think it can plausibly be argued that the persecutory and punitive authority ascribed to the ancestors is essential for their cult to serve as a customary defence against and resolution of the potentially disruptive life crises and conflicts of right and of will that beset their way of life. It is arguable that only such demanding and persecuting ancestor figures could satisfactorily account for, and reconcile sufferers to misfortune by enabling them to expiate wrongdoing; that only such qualities could acceptably explain arbitrary differences in the incidence of luck; that only apprehension of ancestral retribution could keep people from sin and sacrilege. But these considerations do not explain why this formidable institution of moral censorship should take the form of an ancestor cult rather than of any other system of religious or magical belief.

I have already indicated that I relate this to the way that the succession of generations is experienced and managed among the Tallensi. Let us look more closely at its focus in the family system.

## The Tallensi family system

We are dealing with a society that can be compared to a honeycomb. We can think of it as made up of groups of cylindrical family cells that are clustered together into larger cylindrical units of the same form which are fixed on the ground side by side with other such large units. The family cell is the dwelling of a small group of close male patrikin, ideally a man and his sons, he being the head, together with their wives and children other than married daughters. The encircling wall of the homestead marks off an inner, domestic world in which the production and consumption of food and other necessities is centred and to which licit procreative sex and the rearing of children is strictly confined. The family's livestock, grain supplies, material possession, and ritual accessories, such as the shrines of its immediate ancestors, are kept within this dwelling.

In this sphere wives and mothers take precedence of other members. Outside the homestead is the world in which political, jural, and economic affairs and the ritual responsibilities vested in lineages and clans and the Earth priests are dealt with. This is the men's sphere.

Tallensi culture is marked by the propensity to conserve and contain. The good is identified with what is conserved and contained, evil with what must be cast out of the family and the community. Thus catastrophic deaths, e.g. those due to smallpox or suicide or drowning, are defined as 'bad' and the victims are perfunctorily buried without proper funeral rites outside the community and never redomesticated. Those who die normal deaths are buried beside the homestead and, as we know, reinstated within it as ancestors. Household refuse and other waste products of everyday life are likewise accumulated beside the homestead, and as the lengthy lineage predigrees show (cf. Fortes 1945) whatever of the past is still relevant to social life at a given time is piously preserved.

What is next most striking about the Tallensi family system is the highly regulated constraints that are built into it. These are based on the exact differentiation and specification of each class of role and of status in the system. The constraints begin at birth for a Tallensi must be born in his or her paternal home, under the protection of his paternal ancestors, thus literally into his lineage. Birth elsewhere is magically dangerous and sacrilegious. Thus he begins life in his father's power, indebted to him for the one credential, which he can never in his life reject, without which he would never become a full normal person.

It is significant that each wife has her own quarters in the homestead, reserved for herself and for her children, and her husband must come to her there. Husband and wife have distinct but complementary spheres of economic activity and of social and moral responsibility. They also keep their separate social identities as members of their respective clans throughout life. What they share is above all exclusive procreative sexual relations and parenthood, and they must co-operate to maintain the family. Thus from a filial point of view, and in the child's experience, father and mother represent precisely differentiated, complementary and mutually dependent spheres of life. Through their father children are united in common membership of lineage and clan, symbolized in common clan taboos and in dependence on common ancestors. This is the source of jural status carrying rights and duties that link one to society at large. Mothers, in contrast, split up patrilineal siblings linking each group of maternals to their mother's kin and ancestors and thus differentiating them from their paternal siblings. So closely identified are a mother and her children that they are deemed to be of one spiritual substance, united not by right and duty but by spontaneous generosity and love. Mother's brother is therefore the classically affectionate gift-giving uncle devoid of authority but free to protect. Father wields authority and discipline by unquestionable status right. He will, in anger, chastise a disobedient child; but he is also responsible for his children to society at large and must be sufficiently affectionate and protective to fulfil his socializing tasks and bind his children to himself by trust as well as duty. Mother, in contrast, gives nurture, comfort and above all food, freely out of love. She may scold, she will not chastise a child. She is obeyed not out of duty, as with father, but out of love, and in return submits to unlimited demands. The attachment of men and women to their querulous old mothers is touching to see. For both parents, it must be emphasized, children are a source of pride and fulfilment.

Across this division runs the generation sequence clearly marked by custom. In contrast to the cleavage between parents and children, siblings are on equal and familiar terms, though rivalry is acknowledged particularly between consecutive children of the same mother. Deference and respect for their conjugal privacy, amounting to a mild avoidance associated with the incest taboo is proper in relation to parents. But with parents' parents one has a joking relationship, which reconciles respect for the paternal grandfather's authority with the affectionate trust in the relationship of alternate generations that is found in most human societies, and serves as a foil to the deferential obedience due to the father. Father's mother is the acme of indulgence, for unlike mother she never has to forbid or scold and feels no responsibility for a child's conduct. And in the background are the ancestors made very real when sacrifices and libations are offered on their shrine. Far from being excluded, children are particularly drawn into these ritual activities.

In this constellation each person has a clearly defined social and personal identity, specific to his status in the family by sex, generation and filiation, and firmly anchored through his kinship and descent ties to society at large. Roles are never confused, the moral and affective attributes, as well as the economic and jural responsibilities customarily allotted to each being clear cut and distinct, correlated to specific rules and patterns of behaviour. Quarrels occur but there is normally an atmosphere of benign and consistent mutual trust in such a family. The ordered structure and the necessary dependence of the members of the family on one another entail such attitudes for the family to be able to hold together and fulfil its reproductive task.

In due course, as the family cycle develops (cf. Fortes 1958) the differentiation of sibling groups by paternity and by maternal connection take effect and married cousins go their separate ways to start up new families. Characteristically, this is precipitated by some unwonted trouble which turns out to signal a demand from a deceased father for his sons to set up a separate homestead where he can receive ritual service as the mystical head of his own family. But fission does not break up; it only expands the family. The lineage framework determines this. A new family becomes a new cell in the cluster, inescapably bound to all the other cells by their lineage connections. Here lies the ultimate constraint, in political and jural terms, on each person's and each family's mode of existence. There is no way of being a Tallensi without lineage membership. The lineage, of course, is the secular embodiment of the ancestors and it is in the name and under the rule of the ancestors, in their mystical aspect, that lineage authority is exercised.

Growing up in this family system, a Tallensi is able to achieve a stable and integral identity compounded of clearly differentiated but complementary moral and affective elements of basic trust and love derived from the mother through 'the milk of his birth' on the one hand, and on the other, as firm a sense of right and duty pragmatically orientated to the realities of the natural environment, the economic needs and the social and political relations, derived from the father. This identity, be it noted, is, in a sense, thrust upon the individual by the structure and the norms of the family system in which he is inescapably enmeshed for the whole of his life. The experience of constraint from the outside, mediated originally by parents to their children, is deeply ingrained among the Tallensi. Its source is felt to be society at large, which to the Tallensi means lineage and clan and therefore ultimately the ancestors, and acquiesence is comfortable and easy as long as one accepts filial status of perpetual dependence on outside powers. The ancestor cult provides for this, the more so since, though external to the actor, it is yet contained within the secure boundaries of family and kin.

But there is another side to the configuration. Take the question of identity. To the external constraint of family and lineage, there corresponds another type of constraint, equally arbitrary as experienced, the constraint of Fate. How it works out for the individual is neither predictable nor controllable. Then, as regards filial dependence, there is the tempering conviction, however much it may be suppressed and kept in check, of the inevitability of filial succession. Sons are a living threat to fathers, whom they must eventually replace, fathers a constant impediment to sons until they die and become ancestors and as we have seen the situation is parallel, though in a lower key, for women and their daughters. This is the fundamental link for the whole network of the Tallensi social system. It must be defended and preserved against all threats from outside or from within, and it is the latter, the hostilities and rivalries inevitably engendered in the relationships of successive generations that are potentially most dangerous. But constrained as they are by the family system and the attachment to it which they have internalized they cannot escape from the situation. They must live with it or else the continuity of the lineage and of the society cannot be maintained.

For this, fathers must not be tempted by fear of sons to use their power and authority to get rid of the son. Sons, likewise, must not be tempted by feelings of suspicion or hostility to rebel. Rather must fathers be made to feel it to be right and incumbent to cherish sons, and sons, for their part, must feel it right and incumbent to respect, obey and trust fathers. In other words, their reciprocally induced ambivalence must be kept in check and turned round to support the values accepted in the community. The ancestor cult is the apparatus provided by custom to achieve these ends. There is the post-mortem immortality it offers fathers in compensation for making way for sons. But what is most important is their investment with omnipotent punitive powers. It is as if father's will and power to destroy, as it could, if permitted, be experienced by himself, but also as it must appear to son's imagination, is shunted on the ancestors. In more general terms, bearing in mind how real the ancestors are to the Tallensi, how they are conceptually and morally incorporated in the family and lineage, we can understand them representing not just the father, but parenthood as an all-pervasive institution that is the focus of moral control in the whole society. I say parenthood, for though I have for simplicity's sake spoken only of fathers and sons, maternal ancestors are just as persecutory in their particular idiom as are paternal ones (cf. Fortes 1949; McKnight 1967). However the significant point is the punitive omnipotence personified in the ancestors who, as we have seen, indeed have the final control, in Tallensi thought, over the life and the death of each person.

I see no difficulty in regarding the ancestor cult as a customary provision, in effect a conceptual and symbolically specified dramatic cast for representing, as if split off, the coercive and potentially destructive part of parenthood. This, I suggest, leaves intact for living relationship the caring aspect that is indispensable for the socialization process. The judicial quality of ancestral demands fall into place in this picture; for the ancestors are felt to be forever watchful, ready to seize on any action that can be interpreted as transgressing the moral order.

In short, it seems to me that it is not too farfetched to compare the

Tallensi image of their ancestors to the internalized parent figure of the classical Freudian superego. But the Tallensi ancestors are externalized, projected into the public realm of custom, yet being still within the family and lineage and therefore susceptible to appeasement. Reconciliation with them, through the communion of sacrifice and libation, brings reassurance and defence in the troubles and crises of ordinary life that culminate in the finality of death. An analogy with the way good parents comfort small children in distress immediately suggests itself.

Let me make it clear that I am not proposing an historical or aetiological explanation of Tallensi ancestor worship. My concern is to show how this body of religious custom is implemented in the life of the community. I see it as a critical component of the total institution of parenthood in Tallensi society. I do not mean by this that it is to be thought of as simply an extension or as a reflexion, at the level of religious belief and cult, of the family structure. I see it more as an extrapolation or transposition to the domain of open custom, in conceptual and symbolical format, of propensities generated in the filio–parental relations that would, if permitted expression in the actualities of these relations, destroy the whole family structure. Customary expression, which legitimizes and offers symbolical as opposed to pragmatic outlets in action, convert these dangerous propensities into moral obligations. These are felt to be binding by reason of their ascription to the irresistible demands of the ancestors. The mechanism of this conversion and the forces which insure individual and collective compliance with the norms thus established, are to my mind only satisfactorily accounted for by psychoanalytical theory, more particularly the theory of the superego. And let me add that, in describing the Tallensi ancestor cult as, metaphorically speaking, an externalized superego, I am in the company of much more sophisticated ethnoanalysts. For this, broadly speaking, is the way Ortigues and Ortigues (1966) represent the part played by ancestor worship in the psychical economy of the Wolof of Senegal.

## Witchcraft – why absent?

The observations of the Ortigues brings to mind one thing about Tallensi religion that puzzled me in the field. Why do they, unlike some other African peoples, with or without ancestor cults, relegate their version of the notion of witchcraft to a marginal and relatively dormant symbolical role in their theory of human nature and of causality? Tallensi recognize the existence of evil. They experience and give vent to envy, greed, hate and malice. Old men have medicines that are supposed to be able to injure and kill an enemy, though their use is so wrapped in obscurity, and so morally deprecated, that no accusations are ever made against individuals. Catastrophic death as I have noted, is rejected by the ancestors and customarily defined as evil. But even such a death cannot be attributed to witchcraft or sorcery — that is to say to the unconscious or to the deliberate aggression of other humans. It is interesting in this connection, as my wife, Dr Doris Mayer (cf. Fortes and Mayer 1969) discovered, that Tallensi psychotics say the voices they hear are kind and comforting and not, as is reported for example of the Ashanti (cf. Field 1960) threatening. Not evil thoughts or evil feelings conscious or unconscious, but evil deeds are what matters; these, Tallensi believe, sooner or later rebound on the heads of their perpetrators by reason of ancestral anger. In short, every aspect of human conduct, bad as well as good, comes under the all-embracing jurisdiction of the ancestors, just as all the activities and products of human existence, the good (such as food and children) and the bad (such as corpses and excrement) are kept within or close by the family. And I attribute this denial of magical power to destructive human impulses to the integrity of individual identity owing to the incorporation by the individual of the family structure.

I became particularly aware of this in the ritual system of the Tallensi, when I met with fully-fledged witchcraft beliefs during my field work in Ashanti (cf. Fortes 1969, Ch. 11).[10] These are customary beliefs, not psychopathological symptoms, though they lend themselves to the self-accusations and paranoid delusions reported in the previously cited work of the late M. J. Field. A person accused of witchcraft was hauled before the priests of a witch-finding cult, subjected to ordeals and if found guilty forced to confess. Full public confession, extracted by persistent threats, followed by treatment with native medicine and penance, purged the culprit and restored him or her to normal life.

Accusations of witchcraft occurred in response to misfortunes, particularly to accidents, sickness, childlessness and death. The anxiety, bordering on terror, and the conviction of malicious persecution expressed by the accusers in such cases were unmistakable; so was the credulity of all concerned including the accused and the audience amongst whom there were usually a number of literates and Christians.

Ashanti notions of witchcraft conform to the pattern now well established for most of Africa (cf. Marwick 1965; Mair 1969). The alleged witch is unaware of his or her evil propensities until accused and convicted. A witch then confesses to all the unnatural, immoral, sacrilegious and perverse habits that negate ordinary humanity, and characterize witchcraft – killing a child or a sibling for a feast of the witches' coven, flying by night to consume the soul or the womb or the potency of victims, committing incest, consorting with animal and other evil familiars, and so on. Such fantasies of sexual aggression and perversion, of soul cannibalism and of the gross immorality that signifies their repudiation of normal humanity, are common in African witchcraft beliefs. They are quite alien to Tallensi ways of thought.

The Ashanti have a matrilineal family and clan system. Now witchcraft everywhere in Africa is believed to operate only among people closely bound to one another by the obligatory moral and legal bonds of kinship or marriage, neighbourhood or occupation. Thus Ashanti witches are invariably found among close matrilineal kin, mothers and uncles and siblings and first cousins. These are the nucleus of the family and are the descent group defined as 'one blood and flesh'. They grow up together often under the same roof, and remain for life bound to one another by law and morality in obligatory mutual amity and solidarity. Sexual relations between maternal kin is incest and is both a crime and a sin that pollutes the community; and correspondingly, the witchcraft which can only destroy within the close-knit, mother-centred group is hereditary in the mother's line. By contrast witchcraft can never be used against spouses, or against paternal kin with whom Ashanti believe one has only spiritual, not blood, ties and relationships which are morally and affectively, not legally binding.

Unlike the Tallensi, the Ashanti were traditionally organized in a complex national state based on military power and great riches in material goods, gold and food resources. They live in well demarcated villages and towns that are political units made up of diverse groups of mutually independent clans. Kinship and matrilineal descent are important primarily in determining political and legal rights in a community. The Ashanti have a complex religious system and cosmology centred on divinities and nature deities, priests who practise spirit mediumship, a prolific mythology, and an elaborate theory of the human personality, but no domestic cult of ancestors. Only matrilineal forebears who held high office are commemorated in sacrifices and libations by their successors. Recently deceased parents are believed to be shades vaguely present and capable of causing trouble to offspring but usually supposed to be well disposed. Witchcraft beliefs seem incongruous in such a society until one realizes that they operate only in the framework of close matrilineal kinship like a self-destructive, self-hating power as Field's case records show.

A striking thing about Ashanti, in contrast to Tallensi, is their personal sensitivity and vulnerability. To call a person a fool in Ashanti is not only felt as a mortal insult but is in fact actionable in a court of law. A mild scolding evokes not the protest it would arouse from a Tallensi but brooding distress.

Periphrasis and prudery in public are as characteristic of Ashanti attitudes to bodily processes as their absence is amongst Tallensi. They are preoccupied with questions of purity and pollution; toilet training begins very early; parents, particularly fathers, tend to be authoritarian; significantly, the latrines, garbage dumps, cult houses, cemeteries, and formerly menstrual huts are in the bush, at the boundary of a village or town-quarter where, for Ashanti, the anti-human world of witchcraft and other mystical evil forces begin.[11] Thus is concretely symbolized the extrusion from the community of everything that is bad or dirty or mystically dangerous or polluting, including the dead, the very opposite of what happens among the Tallensi.

Here field observations become relevant. Ashanti impress one by the very high degree of autonomy shown by the individual quite early in life. Women are to all intents the equals of men. But with this goes a sense of insecurity, a vulnerable self-image and a divided sense of identity. Ashanti behave as if they had to have eyes and ears on all sides to feel safe. They readily suspect malice in others.

My guess is that the roots of this lie in the family and descent group organization. Whereas among the Tallensi the individual is supported and given a firm anchorage by the complementary balance of legal father-right and normally spontaneous mother love in the enclosed family and localized lineage, among the Ashanti the individual is apt to feel pulled two ways, through the opposition between matrilineal uncle-right and the supposedly spontaneous (because without legal sanction) affection and care of the father. This corresponds to their theory that the individual is made up of flesh derived from his mother and spiritual essence derived from his father. In 50 to 60 per cent of families in Ashanti, husband and wife do not share a home; each lives with his or her close matrilineal kin, and young children move backwards and forwards for meals or for sleeping room between the parents. At adolescence, children who have grown up in the care of their parents are apt to change residence, boys to live with their mother's brother, girls to join a husband for a short time. Every man is continually faced with choices between his legal obligations to his maternal kin, in particular his nephews and nieces, and his feelings of personal affection and responsibility for his own children and wife. Every woman is pulled in two ways between her obligations to her matrikin and her conjugal attachment to her husband and children. No wonder divorce is the rule rather than the exception in marital histories. It is a family system very reminiscent of that of the Trobrianders as described by Malinowski and it presents similar problems.

However witchcraft beliefs may have originated in Ashanti, it seems to me that they are consistent with their customary ideas about the make-up of a person, about things bad or dirty, about purity and pollution. Everything bad must be anxiously cast out, not as among the Tallensi kept within the benign domestic environment. As to why Ashanti so readily accept and use witchcraft beliefs, this perhaps is to be referred to their insecure sense of identity due to the conflicting patterns of authority, responsibility and nurturance with which the individual grows up. Matrilineal ties are extemely close and yet the security which a person should find amongst his closest maternal kin, who are supposedly bound to him by the full force of law, of morality, and of mutual interests, can be deceptive since all of them may be suspected of being secretly more committed to conjugal and parental loyalties that undermine their matrilineal obligations. Continual watchfulness in defence of one's own interests and identity is essential. If in Ashanti basic trust is sucked in with the milk of birth, opposed rather than complementary parental roles supervene in the socialization process and lead to a split self image.

This comparison makes it reasonable to suggest why there is no scope for beliefs in witchcraft and sorcery in the Tallensi religious theory of final causality. The basic trust they develop survives to adulthood and is enshrined in custom, whereas among the Ahanti it looks more like basic mistrust that is engendered and enshrined in custom. Tallensi can consistently off-load ultimate responsibility on to their parent-surrogates who serve as externalized foci of conscience, whereas Ashanti have to carry the responsibility for their conduct about with them all the time. Characteristically, Ashanti have taboos, such as the incest taboo, breach of which is treated as sacrilegious crime, dangerous to the whole community and therefore punishable by the chief and his council sitting as a court of law, the sacrilege being attributed to individual wickedness. Corresponding wrongdoing among the Tallensi is an issue between the individual, his kin, and the ancestors. Ashanti have a concept *ti-boa*, literally 'head creature', which can quite accurately be translated by our word 'conscience' and which they locate in the head; the nearest Tallensi equivalent is *pu-teem*, literally, 'stomach thinking', which has an affective rather than, as with the Ashanti, intellectual implication. Here, I suspect, lie the germs of a much wider comparative investigation of the nature and sources of witchcraft and sorcery beliefs from the point of view of current ideas about 'object relations'. But this is beyond my competence. All I have tried to do is to show how insight or hypothesis derived from psychoanalytic theory may reveal significance and show up connections in the conventional anthropological data of custom and social organization that would not otherwise emerge. And I have, as far as possible, avoided use of technical psychoanalytical language or recourse to the technical literature of psychoanalysis. One reason for this is that I lack the competence. But more deliberately, it is because of the aims I have had in mind. It is when their data are interpreted in the technical language and concepts of psychoanalysis that the resistance of anthropologists is most apt to be aroused. What I have tried to show is that critical questions and fundamental answers that would not otherwise emerge, present themselves at the level of custom and social organization in the light of psychoanalytic theory. On the other side, I should like to think that I may have reminded psychoanalysts of the continued relevance of the data of the anthropological study of custom and social organization to the development of their discipline.

As I said at the outset, the distinctive task of social anthropology is to understand and to seek explanations of the nature and significance of custom in human social life. Custom is kept going by the vigilance of conscience; and it is because the natural history of conscience is more fundamentally explored by psychoanalysis than by any other scientific discipline, that anthropologists must give attention to its discoveries and theories. What I have tried to do, in the present study, is to apply the model developed by psychoanalysis, of the genesis and modes of action of conscience in the individual, to a body of customary religious beliefs and ritual practices that regulate social and personal life among an African tribal people I have worked with. I have been led thus to offer interpretations of variables of conflict and rivalry, and their resolution, in the relations of parents and offspring, as these are channelled by the family structure, that conventional anthropological methods do not take into account. And the stimulus to this approach came to me originally from re-examining the debate between Malinowski and Ernest Jones in the light of my own field experience, and continuing from there to seek what psychoanalysis could further teach me. Today, 50 years after Ernest Jones's famous address to the Royal Anthropological Institute, the collaboration to which he there pointed the way is fairly launched. Psychoanalytical anthropology is a flourishing branch of anthropological scholarship and research, notably in the United States. But it is a technically and professionally specialized branch. What is perhaps more important is to note how psychoanalytical points of view are being assimilated into the mainstream of anthropological theory and method in the elucidation of specifically anthropological field and library data. It is in this context, I believe, that the cross-fertilization which Ernest Jones and such of his anthropological contemporaries as Seligman sought to promote, will be most fruitful.

# 9

## The first born

All that openeth the womb is mine (*Exodus 13:12*)

I was recommended to Emanuel Miller by Morris Ginsberg, my
then academic mentor, and thus became attached, early in 1928 to
the East London Child Guidance Clinic which had just been set up
under the auspices of the Jewish Health Organization.[1] We had a
suite of bare rooms in the Jews' Free School in Bell Lane, White-
chapel. I was supposed to be the educational psychologist. To tell
the truth, I had but the vaguest notion of how to conduct an intelligence or aptitude test, let alone how to assess a youngster's personality traits. However, the necessary technical proficiency was not
difficult to acquire. What I got from Emanuel Miller was much more
important.

The research I was engaged upon was in a field that was already
then, in 1928–30, fiercely controversial. I was attempting to devise a
non-verbal, culture-free test of intelligence for inter-racial use. In
pursuit of this I was immersed in the minutiae and monotony of
assembling the primitive test material that was later so brilliantly
developed by Raven for his progressive Matrices test
(cf. Fortes 1932). Miller helped to open up to me the more exciting
intellectual prospects that eventually tempted me away into
anthropology.

But let me get back to my subject. In describing it as a subject that
would have appealed to Miller, I have in mind, in particular, the
interests and points of view reflected in his book, *The Generations:
A Study of the Cycle of Parents and Children* (1938). Our work at
the Clinic brought us up constantly against problems of the family

background and the social environment of our patients. As Hindley relates (1970), Miller was never content with a purely practical or even strictly psychiatric approach to these problems. He had to set them in a broader biological, philosophical and historical perspective. His concern, as Dr Edward Glover observed (1971), was with the human situation in the round, not merely with the particular clinical or social problem. His book shows this. Its basic theoretical orientation is psychoanalytical. But, interestingly enough, it starts with an examination of the anthropological evidence for the universality of some form of family organization, based on parenthood, in all human societies.

As Miller presents it, the psycho-social development of the individual is seen to be integrally bound up with a three-generation cycle. It begins with the complete dependence of the infant on its mother, moves on to childhood, when the father comes significantly into the picture, then through adolescence with its undercurrents of intergenerational tensions associated with the strains of sexual and moral maturation. Next, comes marriage and then parenthood, often bringing new stresses in its wake, and finally the completion of the cycle when the initial generations become grandparents and revert to the dependence of old age.

I daresay this model of the family cycle was 'in the air', so to speak, in the mid-thirties. Be that as it may, I arrived at a very similar model of what I later described as the 'developmental cycle' in the study I began of family structure in tribal society in 1934 (cf. Fortes 1949, 1958); and the stimulus for this came from my experience in the clinic.

What the model implies is in a way self-evident. The crucial feature is the conjunction of successive generations in the relationship of parents and their children, and this it is obvious, comes into existence, uniquely, once and for all, with the birth of the first child. Multiplying offspring produces the sibling group and thus makes a parent, perhaps, more of a parent in a quantitative sense; but it only builds on, it does not generate the condition and status of parenthood. This is the essence of my subject tonight.

## II

But before I develop it, I must say a little more about the background. My interest in the first born was originally aroused by experience with our Clinic patients. To what extent I was also influenced by the fact that I am myself the first born of a large sibling group and thus acquainted at first hand with the tribulations of that status, I will not endeavour to decide! What I do know is that the attention paid in the Clinic to familial factors in patients' problems was the stimulus for an inquiry I undertook in 1931. Some years earlier Goring had reported an excess of first and second born children in an adult prison population. Karl Pearson used this in support of his own odd theory of the congenital inferiority of first borns (cf. Fortes 1933). My study, comparing a group of Clinic patients with a sample of juvenile delinquents and a control group of school children, revealed a similar excess of first children among both the delinquents and the Clinic patients.

There was already, at that time, a considerable literature, going back, indeed, to Francis Galton (cf. Sutton-Smith and Rosenberg 1970) on the relationship between birth order and various psychological and social capacities and disabilities and its general drift was to confirm the apparent excess of first borns at either end of the scales of both achievement and of deviancy. A vast amount of research has been devoted to this subject since then, and Miller kept track of it for some time. In a definitive review of the whole field (1944), he showed that the evidence for a critical association of birth order with personality variables or with the incidence of deviancy or deliquency was as yet inconclusive. I shall return to some of these matters later.

Here I only want to note that studies at this level are not really concerned with the feature of the family cycle that interests me, namely the status of parenthood, as it is uniquely achieved with the advent of the first born. Their concern is, primarily, with the effect of ordinal position in the sibling group. The accent is on the filial generation, with parenthood as the dependent variable.

I did not grasp the full import of this distinction until my next encounter with the syndrome of the first born. Its effect was memorable. It made me realize what a central place the status of the first born holds in human social organization, being often invested with religious, as well as legal, moral and political meaning, from ancient times until today. Above all, it led me to see in a new light the conclusions of modern psychology and psycho-analysis to which Miller gave such prominence, about the relationships of parents and children and of sibling and sibling.

## III

This encounter occurred in the course of my anthropological field research among the Tallensi of Northern Ghana in 1934–7. At that time they were still far removed from modern influences and were following their traditional ways of life in all aspects; literacy and modern social and political developments are now rapidly changing their social life. But it is noteworthy that their family system still retains its traditional form.

I have described many aspects of Tallensi social life and culture in a number of publications (cf. Fortes 1945, 1949, 1959). But a short outline of their family system will be useful here. Long settled subsistence farmers, still at the simple technological stage of the hand-hoe, the adze and the bow and arrow, they are organized in exogamous patrilineal lineages and clans. Distinctive totemic observances and an elaborate cult of their particular ancestors mark clans and lineages off from one another. The domestic unit is a polygynous joint family of two, three, or occasionally four successive generations (depending upon the stage reached in the developmental cycle) of males, their in-married wives and young children. At its head is the oldest man who would be grandfather or father to the other males in the family, some of whom might in actuality be sons or grandsons of a near collateral kinsman of his, that is, a brother or a cousin. The family head has, first of all, legal authority over all its members; secondly, he exercises oversight in the economic affairs of the family; thirdly, and most important of all, he is the custodian of the family's ancestor shrines, responsible on behalf of all his dependants for the sacrifices that have to be made when required. These ancestors are spoken of as if they are tangibly present in the homesteads of the descendants, 'sitting at their shrines' as Tallensi say. But what is most characteristic of them is that they are believed to be more apt to show their supernatural power over their descendants by causing troubles and misfortunes, than by acts of benevolence. They are the final arbiters in all matters of life and death among their descendants. To them is attributed both the credit for things going well, and also the ultimate causation of misfortunes,

especially sickness and death. They must therefore be regularly pla-
cated with libations and with sacrifices.

> The significant feature here is that the ancestors are only
> accessible through the parents. Only males may offer sacrifices
> to ancestors. But a man does not have the full right so to
> officiate until his father dies. This gives him juridical majority,
> makes him *sui iuris* as lawyers put it, and this is the
> indispensable qualification for the ritual capacity to officiate in
> sacrifices to his ancestors.
>
> Reciprocally and logically, ancestors cannot intervene in the
> life of a descendant except through the latter's parent, living or
> dead. Living, a parent, especially a father, has binding
> authority over and responsibility for offspring; dead, parents
> become the first in the line, and by that token the most
> powerful, of the ancestors, the unavoidable mediators and
> arbitrators between the living and the ancestors. The Tallensi
> rationalisation is 'if a man's father had not begotten him or his
> mother borne him his ancestors would have no one from whom
> they could receive offerings and service.'

Tallensi consider the crowning glory, indeed the only worthwhile
object of life, to be assurance of leaving descendants, ideally in the
male line, to perpetuate the memory and above all to fulfil the ritual
tasks of ancestor worship. To have lived successfully one must die
with the hope of achieving ancestorhood and that is possible only if
one leaves male descendants. That is why, Tallensi say, one desires
sons but longs for grandsons. As in many tribal societies, and consistently with this point of view, the restraint that is customary between parents and children is counterbalanced by a classical joking
relationship between grandparents and grandchildren.

## IV

The status of the first born, female as well as male, is crucial in this
family system. It is dramatized in a series of eloquent customary
practices and beliefs.

> First borns are designated by a special term. From the age of
> about five or six a first born son may not eat out of the same

dish as his father, whereas his younger siblings commonly do. Tallensi say that if a father and his first born son eat out of the same dish the son might accidentally scratch the father's hand, and this would cause the death of one of them. The same accident, with a younger son, is not dangerous. I have protested to Tallensi friends that these beliefs are patently illogical. They answer that this may appear to be the case, but it is a taboo laid down by their ancestors and is not to be trifled with. It is part of a whole configuration of prohibitions and injunctions. Any first born will rattle them off. Said Badiwona, aged about six: 'I share my mother's dish of food. I never eat with my father. If I did I might die of a wasting disease. It's because I'm his first born. We first born sons may not eat chicken, we may not look into our father's granary, we may not wear his cap or his tunic or carry his quiver or use his bow.' Always, there is the implicit contrast with younger siblings and the certainty that breach of these taboos would lead to some vaguely apprehended disaster. I never came across or heard of a case of deliberate flouting of any of these rules. The 'moral regulator' (to quote Miller) inculcated from earliest childhood and backed by the whole system of social arrangements and of religious beliefs, works irresistibly.

It is important to add (see Fortes 1949, p. 223) that similar taboos are binding on first born daughters in relation to their mothers.

These obligatory avoidances come to a climax at the parent's death. The terminal obsequies must be initiated by the eldest, by right the first born son. They end in a dramatic rite, by which the deceased is finally translated into ancestorhood. His human status as father and husband, family head and holder of office, owner of fields and custodian of ancestor shrines is dissolved and redistributed among his heirs and successors as Goody (1962) describes in his book about a closely related Ghanaian tribe.

A man's designated successor, in his family roles, is his eldest son. If he is a first born – and not, I must stress, merely the eldest surviving son – he, accompanied by his first born sister, undergoes a distinctive ritual. It is this that specifically terminates the obsequies. After a libation to the dead, a senior elder takes up a cloth tunic and a cap that had belonged to the deceased. He turns them inside out and puts them on the son, with the left hand sleeve of the tunic hanging loose. He and the first borns now lead all the children of the deceased, as a sibling group, in a rite of mourning the loss of their father. Next the elder solemnly leads the two first borns into the central courtyard of the house up to the deceased's granary, the thatch lid of which has been removed. Standing on the step the elder beckons to the son to come up beside him; and then, holding the deceased's bow, the symbol of manhood, in his left hand, he places his right hand on the son's neck and gently pushes his head forward as if forcing him to look into the granary. Thrice is this silently repeated and then the first born daughter goes through the same procedure. Finally the son, discarding his reversed tunic and cap, leads the assembled crowd in a mock war dance, amidst laughter and joking, and with beer passing around to heighten the mood of relief and conviviality.[2]

I witnessed and discussed with friends this finale to an elderly man's funeral many times – and likewise for elderly women, for whom the corresponding ritual is carried out by the first-born daughter with the mother's main storage pot appropriately in place of the granary. Note well that if there is no surviving first-born son or daughter, a surviving eldest son or daughter does not perform this ritual sequence. If, however, the first born son or daughter is alive but unable (e.g. by reason of illness) to take part in the rites, a proxy must take his or her place. First-bornness, as the ideal replacement for the parent, must, so to speak, be enacted, if such a successor is available.

It is not without significance that these ritual activities are carried out in a matter of fact manner, with only ceremonial display of emotion. The participants deny that they are anxious, though they admit that the rituals are awesome and that they feel sad, especially when the mournful dirges are sung. Of course, grief, anger, resignation, all the emotions normally associated with bereavement, are as strongly felt by Tallensi as by all peoples. But it seems that the ritual performances, by their overt and customary dramatization of feelings and fantasies usually kept in check, do drain the emotional pain out of the situation.

## V

To understand this avoidance syndrome, we must realize that Tallensi accept, and openly admit, that hostility and rivalry are normal and inevitable in the relations of parents and their children. The critical feature is that this is focused on the first born. Not surprisingly, there is an undercurrent of apprehension as to what might happen if the avoidance rules were flouted. A comment made in 1963 by an educated and sophisticated young politician is to the point. He was a first born and he admitted that the traditional taboos were not rational by modern standards. But it would be disrespectful to his father, he said, to flout them. In particular, he declared with an embarrassed laugh, he had never dared to look into his father's granary, adding 'I would be afraid. I might see snakes there.' Overtly Tallensi think of snakes either as being potentially dangerous or as being totemic creatures of the earth which may not be killed; deeper symbolic meanings which we might suspect in my friend's comment, would not be apparent to them. In reality, of course, snakes would be most unlikely to get into a granary.

Thirty years earlier, speaking of the granary-showing rite, an elder remarked to me, 'You may not believe it, but that young man, grown up as he is, has never before even peeped into his father's granary. Henceforth it is no longer taboo for him. It is his now; he is the owner.' This shows neatly how Tallensi regard this rite. They think of a man's granary as an extension of his personality, embodying his status as family head. A man's soul, they say, is tied to his granary, whereas his bodily existence imbues his clothes and distinctive implements and weapons (cf. Fortes 1949, p. 57).

Given these beliefs, the symbolism of the reversed-clothing and granary showing rites is so patent as to need no gloss. They are seen as installing the son in his father's place, as if he were taking over his father soul and body, as well as in the legal sense. Their relative positions are now reversed, the son being clothed with tangible and real paternal power and authority, the father, transposed to ancestorhood, being now dependent on the son for commemoration, offerings and service. When the first borns are permitted, or rather symbolically compelled to look and see what was previously tabooed to their sight, it is, of course, a purely fictitious secret that is revealed to them, for no one over the age of six is ignorant of what is normally to be seen in a granary. As in many initiation rituals in tribal societies the rite does not reveal the unknown; it sanctions the open exercise of knowledge and capacities that were previously unauthorized. It is the taboo that is lifted, not a secret that is revealed. And the symbolical meaning of the right to look, ostensibly thrust on the first borns though it is their due, is not difficult to understand. Like us, Tallensi regard the eye as the organ *par excellence* for gaining true knowledge. So there is no question here of acquiring ownership of the granary in an economic sense. If this were the issue the daughter would be excluded as daughters cannot gain property rights in any of their father's possessions. Furthermore, in the corresponding ritual for a deceased mother, the climax is when the daughter is for the first time made to look into her mother's storage pot, which is then sealed.

Some likely interpretations suggest themselves, but they would not, of course, occur to Tallensi. They do not for example see any of the allusions to sexual and procreative replacement that one suspects are implicit in these rituals.[3] The essence, to them, is what they signify in terms of heirship and succession. It is worth adding that Tallensi are singularly frank and uninhibited. They are devoid of prudery about sex and coitus, do not seclude menstruant or confined women, and withdraw only so far as to avoid offence to others to meet excretory needs.

> To return to the first born's taboos the most onerous but also the most revealing take effect when the son reaches adolescence. Thereafter father and son must never meet face to face in the entrance to the homestead. The underlying attitude was typically expressed once by one of my friends. Pointing to his small son he said, half mockingly, 'See that boy. He is my first born. Small as he is, he is only waiting for me to die so that he can take my place.' This shows that the avoidances enjoined on first borns are not considered wholly to extinguish the antagonism supposed to exist between them and their like-sex parents.

It follows that when a first born son reaches the maturity to marry and become a father in his turn he must have separate quarters. An eldest surviving son is, of course, free to stay with his father. Tallensi cite this taboo as the key to the whole syndrome. They say, as I have explained elsewhere (1959), that it is due to a clash of their Destinies and Souls. With increasing years, as his powers wane, the father's Destiny is supposed to weaken gradually, whereas the son's Destiny waxes ever stronger at the expense of the father's. These beliefs give added point to the concluding rites of the funeral which so patently symbolize the reversal of filio–parental status and relationships. It cannot be too greatly stressed that the replacement of father by son takes place, not by usurpation but lawfully, with the consent and participation of the whole community.

What these funeral rites quite explicitly dramatize is the ambivalence intrinsic to the relations of successive generations and their origin and focus in the first born. Janus-like the son faces two ways. As prototypical offspring he incarnates the conflict between (on the one hand) filial dependence on, and affection for his devoted parents and (on the other) the latent hostility in his rights to succeed. We have seen how the taboos contain this. As brother, and head of the sibling group he is himself the target of ambivalent attitudes of deference to his seniority, mixed with competitive claims of sibling equality and familiarity. Sibling rivalry is regarded as normal, though focused particularly on successively born siblings who are assumed to hate each other. (And what goes for the son also goes for the first daughter in relation to her mother, with modifications.)

The crux is that legitimate parenthood with all its incidents is as indispensable for the offspring as these are for realizing the life goals of the parents. It is only through legitimate parents that everyone acquires the legal status and religious identity, as a member of his family and clan, without which he cannot be a normal person.

Consistently with these rules, children grow up in their paternal home under the care of their own or proxy parents (Fortes 1949) and under the spiritual surveillance of their dead ancestors. This mutual interdependence, in which deference to parental authority is coloured with the knowledge that offspring will and must inevitably replace parents, underlies the ambivalence of inter-generational relationships. These are matters of daily experience; the ritual observances make them supportable.

## VI

We can see why paramount importance is attached to first *parentage*.

Whatever may happen thereafter, it marks the irreversible transition to *parenthood* and the prospect of personal autonomy and, perhaps, immortality. But the transition becomes manifest in the bearing, rather than the begetting, of a child, and this is signalized in a rite that bestows motherhood when it is achieved, once and for all, by a first pregnancy. It is performed by a co-wife of the girl's mother who girds her with a new perineal belt and admonishes her never again to be seen without this covering. Until then she would, by traditional custom, have gone about nude.[4] A woman's first pregnancy was thus publicly proclaimed as the proud transition from maidenhood to matronhood. Even if she miscarries, or her first born dies in very early infancy, or she never bears again, she is a matron for life.

Among the Tallensi, as in most societies, marriage is the proper and, indeed, necessary qualification for legitimate parenthood. Without marriage,[5] a man acquires no rights of fatherhood over his children. But marriage can be annulled by lawful divorce in most societies. Parenthood, like birth itself and death, cannot be annulled, once the first birth, or its equivalent, publicly recognized first pregnancy, has taken place. Leaving aside the symbolism of the belt-binding rite, I want to emphasize that it is not a magical rite purporting to guard against the possible dangers of a first pregnancy.[6] The husband's ancestor spirits are supposed to take care of this. It is quite explicitly intended to confer matronhood and it is also a declaration of the husband's legitimate fatherhood of the expected child. An interesting detail is its performance by a proxy for the mother. It reflects a notion of competition for limited reproductive resources between successive generations of the same sex. Her mother is the source of a woman's fertility: but Tallensi say it is repugnant, possibly forbidden, for a woman to continue to bear children when her eldest daughter becomes a child-bearer. The parallel with the notion of the clash of father's and first son's Destinies is obvious. It would, one imagines, be too fraught with jealousy for a mother herself to come and bestow matronhood on her first born daughter.

So much for the initial step in parenthood. Its outcome, however, hangs in the balance until the last stage when it is, ideally, this same first born who, replacing his father, becomes responsible for serving and tending him in his spiritual state of ancestorhood as if, one might almost say, in reparation for having replaced him with the assistance of death. Tallensi ancestor worship resolves the ambivalence in the relations of living parents and children by transposing the parents after death to the supernatural realm and there investing them with apparently arbitrary powers of life and death over the offspring, who owe them service but nevertheless enjoy the autonomy denied to them in the parents' lifetime (Fortes 1970, chap. 7). Comparably, Goody writes of the LoDagaa, those not too distant cultural cousins of the Tallensi, that 'parenthood is the first prerequisite for having an ancestor shrine carved to one's name' (Goody 1962, p. 225).

## VII

The Tallensi are neither unique nor eccentric in thus singling out first birth. Customary rules and observances that make explicit its pivotal significance in the developmental cycle of the family and in the life-history of the individual are common, possibly universal among non-western peoples. I have not examined all the available ethnographic sources; but the selection of data I have considered, drawn both from the literature and from personal communications to me, is conclusive.

The syndrome of the first born occurs among nomadic or transhuman pastoralists (like the Fulani and the Nuer) as well as among sedentary agriculturalists (like the Tallensi and the Mossi); in societies with patrilineal family systems (such as those already mentioned) as well as among those with matrilineal or with bilateral systems (like the Ashanti and the Gonja); in societies of small scale and limited populations, such as we find in New Guinea and Polynesia, as well as in societies with a large population and elaborate social and political organization, like the Ashanti, the Mossi, the Hausa, the Zulu; in traditionally literate, culturally complex, economically and politically sophisticated societies like India and China, no less than among the simpler non-literate peoples of the world.

I argue that there are beliefs and practices in our own society that are attributed to individual experience but reflect the same underlying forces in family relationships as are made explicit in such customary beliefs and observances as those of the Tallensi and other tribal peoples; and in this connection I want to draw attention to the Biblical prescriptions and narratives in which the essentials of the syndrome are presented with particular clarity.

I cannot set out the evidence in detail here,[7] but I must ask you to accept that the Tallensi case provides an excellent paradigm for the analysis of the syndrome. It exhibits the most characteristic components of the syndrome, all or some of which appear in differently accentuated combinations in other societies. Let me review them:

1. Parenthood is desired and required in all tribal and oriental societies. In part this is for legal and social reason (to provide heirs, to mark status and prestige). But behind this lie notions that parenthood is proof of the attainment of social maturity, which implies full male potency and female fecundity. What is, however, equally implied is that it offers assurance of some sort of personal immortality which in tribal society is explicitly aspired to. The stories of the Hebrew Patriarchs in Genesis and Exodus vividly portray these attitudes.

2. Marriage, or more exactly, legitimate cohabitation, is commonly regarded as the normal and necessary prerequisite for legitimate parenthood especially for the father. In many societies marriage is considered to exist primarily for the sake of parenthood, or as it is sometimes put, for the founding of a family. Hence a marriage is not deemed to be established until the birth of the first child, e.g. among the patrilineal Nuer (Evans-Pritchard 1951, pp. 72–4, 99), among the patrilineal Fulani (Stenning 1958; Dupire 1970, pp. 190–2); among the matrilineal Siuai (Oliver 1955, p. 186); and among numerous other peoples.

3. The first birth, whether surviving or not, or even the first publicly recognized pregnancy, creates parenthood, once and for all. In many societies both patrilineal and matrilineal, the ideal is for this first born to be a son (as among the ancient Hebrews, the Nuer, the Ashanti, the Hindu and the Chinese, not to speak of the British aristocracy in the nineteenth century). In some, as among the Tallensi, first-born son and first-born daughter are bracketed together.

4. This implies that the first born – in Biblical language 'the opener of the womb' (Exodus, 13. 12), an expression also common in tribal cultures (e.g. Bemba, A. I. Richards, personal communication; Maori, Koskinnen, *passim*) – is strictly distinguished in law and custom from eldest surviving. This is the case with the Tallensi,

the Mossi (Skinner 1961) the Gonja (Goody 1973, Ch. 8); the Nuer (Evans-Pritchard 1951, p. 139) and many other African peoples. The Biblical prescriptions repeatedly emphasize the distinction (Exodus, 34. 19); upon which there are also extensive Talmudical commentaries (e.g. the Mishnah, Bekhoroth, 8.1–10); and it is recognized in Polynesia (Koskinnen, *passim*; Firth 1967, p. 59) and in New Guinea (G. A. Lewis, personal communication) as well as in Hindu (Prabhu, p. 246; Carstairs 1957, p. 222) and Chinese (Waley 1938; Freedman 1970) thought.

5. The distinction is made explicit and the first born is thus set apart in almost every aspect of social organization, firstly as creator of parenthood, secondly as founder of the filial generation, thirdly as head of the sibling group thus constituted. In the domain of law and politics, he may be the designated heir, by primogeniture, as among Tallensi, Mossi, Tikopia, Hindu, Chinese and other patrilineal peoples of antiquity as well as of today. In ancient Hebrew law, a first born who is also surviving eldest was entitled to a double portion of the paternal estate (Mishnah, *loc. cit.*; Neufeld 1944, pp. 262–3). An extreme example in which the political rules are buttressed by beliefs about the 'inherent sanctity' of the first born (Mead 1930 p. 118; Firth 1967, Ch. 2; Koskinnen, *passim*) is the Polynesian ideal for chiefs to be first born of a line of first borns. Similarly, among the ancient Hebrews, the first born son was ritually singled out by the law that he belonged to God and had to be redeemed (Exodus 13. 12; 22. 29); and this religious prescription still prevails among the orthodox Jews. Among the Nilotic Dinka first sons are similarly picked out by their special relationship to the father's totems and divinities (Lienhardt 1961, p. 197).

The unique status accorded to the first born is widely shown in the etiquette of address, as among the Zulu, who give them the honorific titles of 'prince' and 'princess' (H. Sibisi, personal communication) and in the *ariki* title given to them in Polynesia (Koskinnen, *passim*). Another indication is the belief that there is an inherent incompatibility between first birth and twinship. Thus in Ashanti, first borns are tabooed from contact with the rituals for the protection of twins. And again, in the Bible, twins are portrayed as bitter rivals for the status of first born (cf. Esau and Jacob, Genesis 27; Perez and Zerah, Genesis 38.27–9).

First born and last born (the 'opener of the womb' and the 'closer

of the womb' as Bemba say) are often contrasted, first born as rightful heir of the parent and founder of the sibling group being kept at a
distance, last born, who, because he has no rights to succeed and
because he marks the end of the parent's procreative career by completing the sibling group, being shown more overt affection. Dinka
couple them together as the lucky ones in contrast to middle siblings
who are defined as unlucky (Lienhardt, *loc. cit.*). The LoDagaa bury
brothers and their wives in one grave until the last brother of the sibling group dies, when the grave is sealed forever (Goody 1962, p.
146).[8]

6. The first born – ideally a son even among matrilineal peoples –
is always ardently desired in proof of the achievement of full maturity by the parents. In some cultures (e.g. Hindu, cf. Prabhu, p. 246),
the procreation of the first born is defined as a moral and religious
duty. He must be cherished to survive as it is he, ideally, who confers
immortality on the parent, most explicitly in the form of ancestor
worship and commemoration as amongst many African peoples, as
well as in India, Polynesia and China. It is the more noteworthy,
therefore, that first borns are, at the same time, commonly identified
as the focus of rivalry and hostility between the generation of children and their parents. Such rivalry and hostility is believed to be
normal and inevitable in the relations of parents and children in
many tribal and oriental societies. Focusing it on the first born
generates powerful ambivalence in their relations with their parents.
On the one hand as I have said, they must be cherished and on the
other they are apt to be resented since they will inevitably and of
right at the end oust and replace the parents. They incarnate both
the longed for achievement of parenthood and the inescapable
threat to the inevitable extinction of, parental authority and autonomy. The ambivalence thus focused on the first born finds symbolic
expression in various forms of ritually enjoined and socially sanctioned avoidances which serve as a defence against the possibility of
the intergenerational antagonism erupting into parenticide or filicide. Most extreme are customary avoidances, either during the
infancy of first borns or even throughout their life, in which fearful
and hostile rejection by the parents seems to be acted out (e.g.
Hausa, see M. F. Smith, pp. 188–9; Fulani, see Dupire, pp. 190–2;
Songhay-Zarma, Jeanne Bisilliat, personal communication). Less
extreme is the ritual avoidance by commoners of Polynesian first
born chiefs on the grounds of their sacred status (see Koskinnen,

*passim*; Firth 1962, Ch. 6) and the Tallensi pattern, which permits life-long coresidence of parents and first children but keeps them apart by ritually sanctioned avoidances. Most explicit are the customs of separating the generations by fostering first borns with relatives in early childhood (Gonja, Mossi, Nuer – see E. N. Goody, *loc. cit.*; Skinner 1961; Evans-Pritchard 1951, p. 139) or by residential segregation (Ndembu, see Turner 1957, p. 238; Nyakyusa, see Wilson 1951) or by assignment to distinct age sets as among the Nilo-Hamites (see Peristiany 1951, pp. 188–302). The principle is the same. First born and parent of the same sex must be kept apart, symbolically by taboo and injunction or by physical separation which admits the existence of hostility or rivalry between them.

7. To account for the antagonism between successive generations, magical and religious beliefs and concepts regarding the nature of the person and his development are commonly adduced. The ideals of a successful life include, over and above parenthood, longevity, health, prosperity, numerous progeny, high office, and political and ritual authority. Such success is attributed to forces that are not consciously controllable. Plain luck, destiny, ancestral protection, divine blessing, and hereditary qualities and capacities of a mystical nature are among such forces specified in tribal and oriental religions. These forces are often identified as different manifestations of a general quality which I think can best be described as 'mystical potency' and which is associated with reproductive vigour and fecundity. The Tallensi belief that a first born son's good fortune in growth and development to adulthood conflicts with the father's Soul and Destiny and thus depletes his vigour and success, has parallels elsewhere (e.g. Gonja, E. N. Goody, *loc. cit.*). In other words, the first born's growth brings him continually closer to rightfully ousting and replacing the parent; and this is interpreted as a progressive drain on the parent's vitality and mystical potency. This is phrased in concrete psycho-physical terms in the Hindu belief that a man's vitality depends on his store of semen. Sexual intercourse depletes this store and is therefore, at least ideally, to be indulged in only for procreation. Making it obligatory for the first born to ensure the perpetuation of the father's status and the regular performance of the religious duties of commemoration of the ancestors, assuages the guilt about later children, who are the fruits of mere lust (see Carstairs 1957, pp. 83–4; Erikson 1970, p. 120). Turning to Polynesia, we can suspect similar beliefs to lie behind the

reluctance of chiefs to hand over, as they must, to their successors-designate (i.e. first borns) the most important items of esoteric knowledge and of mystical power vested in the office, until they are near death (Firth 1936, pp. 173, 360; Koskinnen, *passim*). African parallels for both the Hindu and the Polynesian beliefs abound.

For women, the same notion emerges in the belief that daughters' and mothers' fecundity conflict. Gonja (E. N. Goody, Ch. 8) like Tallensi (Fortes 1949) consider a first daughter's first pregnancy to be the signal for the mother to stop child-bearing.

I must refrain from multiplying examples and will only say that there is wide spread among tribal and oriental peoples some form of belief which amounts to an assumption that there is underlying and essential to parenthood a fund, but only a strictly limited fund, of male vitality and female fecundity, which is partly physical but largely metaphysical (hence my term 'mystical potency'), which must be transmitted to the filial generation to ensure the proper continuity of the family and thus of society but which can only be transmitted at the cost of the parental generation. There is no alternative for parents but to sacrifice themselves for their children and focusing this obligatorily on the first born may (as I have suggested) be seen as a defence against the resentment likely to be evoked.

The sample of ethnological data I have thus cursorily reviewed suggests the following conclusion. The advent of parenthood is experienced or at least customarily defined among many peoples as a life-stage fraught with conflict. On the one hand there is the fulfilment and the promise of immortality it signifies; on the other the threat to the parent's vitality and potency it foreshadows. Thus on the one hand parenthood evokes the protective and tender impulses that will ensure the growth and survival of the offspring, but on the other it is prone also to stir up impulses of hostility and resentment, against its very creator. Parents have power over offspring, and not only because of their generation status; for it is authorized by society. But they also by the same token have responsibility for their offspring's proper socialization. Their task is to exercise power without hostility, responsibility without misplaced partiality. We can see how useful it is for the underlying conflicts of impulse and obligation to be regulated from the outside, as it were, by irresistible custom, in submission to divine edict or mystical taboo. In the Hebrew case, for example, belonging by his birth to God frees the first born from suspicion of inborn rivalry with his father. Redeeming him – like paying bride price for a wife – gives the father legal and religious rights over him with a symbolically contractual rather than moral and affective basis, both in relation to his real owner, God, and in relation to the son himself.[9]

There can be no rivalry in such an ostensibly artificial relationship; for inter-generational rivalry goes with birth-right.

Similarly the Polynesian *ariki* has no option but to pass on the mystical potency of which he is the chance and fated bearer. Any tendency to resent his eventual displacement by his son is likely to be thrust aside since it is due to the gods. The Tallensi analogue is the expected reparation of becoming a worshipped ancestor.

## VIII

An anthropological investigation is often like throwing a stone into a pond: the eddies spread in all directions and it becomes difficult to set limits to it.

What I have tried to do is to build up a composite picture, a paradigm of the critical features of *customary* – as opposed to *idiosyncratic* – recognition of the significance of first birth in tribal societies.

Why this accent on the customary? One answer was given a long time ago by Montaigne. In his essay 'Of Custom' he says (in Florio's translation) – 'I am of opinion that no fantasy so mad can fall into human imagination, that meets not with the example of some public custom.' The implication is that what may appear as idiosyncratic or even bizarre individual responses (e.g. to the first birth) in one culture will be embodied in public and normal custom in some other culture. What appears, in our culture for instance, as the affective or emotional responses of individuals, whether of conscious or of unconscious origin, comes out in manifest custom in other cultural contexts.

This takes me back to my starting point; and though my present concern is with a different aspect of the position of the first born from what it was in 1930, a brief look at the current research relating to my earlier interest is not out of place. There is now a veritable Himalaya of research material on the kind of question I then sought an answer to. Fortunately, however, the essential topics are concisely and wittily reviewed in an American book entitled *The Sibling* (by Brian Sutton-Smith and B. G. Rosenberg 1970).

This book covers all types of statistical, psychological and social enquiry, takes account of every conceivable economic, social and personality variable that has hitherto been investigated. The authors begin by confirming that members of a sibling group, especially the younger ones, are, in fact, influenced by the sex and age of their siblings. This applies particularly to first borns who are said to show 'higher power tactics' to their next siblings whom they often, thus, provoke to aggression.

More specifically, they conclude that many enquiries, biographical, anecdotal, observational and experimental, ever since Francis Galton first asserted it, confirm the 'intellectual primogeniture' of first borns, that is to say, their preponderance among eminent scientists, scholars, men of letters, and in college populations. It is suggested that this springs from a need to achieve, fostered by their special relationships with their parents. An interesting byproduct is the observation that middle children seem most handicapped – a conclusion that corresponds to some of our ethnological observations, as for instance among the Dinka.

> Next come studies of parents' relations with first borns, as opposed to later children. These show that 'the first born continues throughout childhood to be the subject of special expectations on the part of the parents and to have a special relationship with them' (p. 100). First children are represented as being more serious, conscientious and adult-orientated, by contrast with the placid and easy-going second children, probably, it is suggested, because they model themselves more directly than later children on parents, whom they perceive to have the power in an hierarchically ordered family system. First borns seek authority and hierarchy in social situations and are apt to be critical and hostile in the interest of group norms and consensus. Later children appear to be more egalitarian, though sex differences as well as ordinal position are significant.

Anyone acquainted with the field will recognize how inadequately this arbitrary selection represents current research on this subject. It will suffice, however, to indicate the kind of questions the authors are concerned with, and this is typical. British investigations follow the same pattern. James Douglas, for example (1964, chap. XI) reports, amongst other findings, that first borns in families of two or three do better than expected from measured ability and later borns worse in secondary school selection examinations, and it is last not first borns who are frequently reported as bed-wetters and otherwise disturbed children.

> Or take a study much more directly reminiscent of the investigations Miller and I undertook. Starting from a finding that first born (*sic*) working class males were 'much more successful in individual activity than intermediates, who proved most successful in group activity', the authors (Lees and Newson, 1954), examined a County authority's records of juvenile delinquency with this in mind. They conclude that 'eldest' are more likely to be individual delinquents, whereas 'intermediates' drift into groups and 'youngest' from good homes are least liable to become delinquents. In explanation they adduce typical common attitudes said to be developed in working class families by all boys in particular ordinal positions – e.g. first borns develop a preference for activity as individuals, intermediates for groups, and youngest for either. Supplementary hypotheses assert that 'similar experiences tend to produce similar personality configurations'. Thus among working class males, 'eldests' (*sic*) learn they are first born, feel bigger and stronger than, and superior to following siblings, and in a position from which they cannot be displaced. Thus 'unconsciously they learn to face up, as individuals . . . without the aid of sibs, to the adult world . . .'. They are the 'trail blazer, the initiator, the mediator between adult and child's worlds, held to be most responsible, if only because they are the eldest'. Intermediates, displaced by younger siblings, 'cannot however find compensation in the knowledge that they are superior to all their siblings'. They are neither held to be responsible like the eldest nor privileged like the youngest, and they tend to be squeezed out.

Similar studies relating to psychosis and neurosis are now so numerous as to constitute almost a sub-discipline with psychiatry; and perhaps all I need say is that the findings seem to me to be far from conclusive.[10] The pattern is broadly the same. The investigations, exemplary in respect of their statistical validation, concentrate on ordinal position in the sibling group. Now as I implied earlier, research of this type does not bear directly on the problems raised by my anthropological paradigm. But its general drift is clear. It leaves us in no doubt that first borns are marked out in various ways; and the explanation offered is, generally, by reference to child-rearing practices, for example, the extra anxiety and solicitude, and the special demands therefore made on them by one or both parents.[11] These characteristics are, of course, not ascribed to customary norms; they are regarded as the statistically preponderant outcome of individual habits and decisions.

Anyone who cares to ask among friends and acquaintances will find that there is, certainly in middle class circles in this country, a well defined stereotype of the first born in contrast to second and later children. It is put forward as the fruit of personal experience, though it may well have been influenced by (and perhaps have influenced in turn) current psychological and sociological research and theory on this subject. First borns are said to be self-assertive, ambitious and demanding as well as over-conscientious and conformist. Their preponderance amongst university students and eminent people is often remarked upon and attributed to their distinctive personality. In addition to the excessive solicitude and anxiety of inexperienced parents, the shock of 'dethronement' (in Alfred Adler's vivid terminology) from the centre of parental care and attention by the next sibling, is usually cited, the contrast with the casual treatment of subsequent children by experienced parents being specially stressed.[12]

I think we can conclude that the setting apart of the first born reflects experiences deeply rooted in the relations of parents and children in every society. But where research is singularly meagre is in regard to the question, suggested by the anthropological paradigm, as to whether parenthood is desired and sought after and what it signifies in cultural contexts that do not appear to attach religious, legal or economic importance to having offspring.

Where there is a family estate or title, for which it is necessary and estimable to make sure of heirs, the incentive is obvious. Nineteenth century novelists such as Jane Austen and Trollope, playing on the theme of the entailed estate, richly illustrate this. But we do not know if the first born is considered to suffice to satisfy such aspirations. Current discussions on the desirability of limiting families to two children – the first to achieve parenthood, the second to round off a minimally sufficient sibling group and thus establish the family, as the informant I quoted earlier put it – suggest that the desire for parenthood is as powerful in western as in tribal societies and that fulfilment of it is sought regardless of economic considerations or the warnings of population experts. A small enquiry carried out in Cambridge by Mrs E. Morgan and myself strengthens this view.

Better confirmation is afforded by a recent study by Busfield (1973). She points out that there are now, in our society, no demographic or other external pressures, such as a high infant mortality or a lack of means for controlling fertility, which might influence people's choices about parenthood. It is easy nowadays to separate sex from conception. Yet parenthood remains almost universal. Is this an anachronism? Following anthropological theory she argues that there is a fundamental connection between marriage and parenthood. One reason is the stigma still attaching to illegitimacy. But her main conclusion is that childbearing is assumed to be a proper and desirable concomitant of maturity and marriage. Hence childless married women are liable to be either criticized or pitied. Children are desired, first, for the emotional satisfaction expected from them, but also for the 'immortality', the possibility of passing on to offspring and keeping alive, part of one's self by heredity not education, thus ensured. There is even evidence that grandparenthood is desired. There is also, it appears, some preference on the part of fathers [13] for a boy as a first child. My own enquiries are consistent with this picture.

However, the most eloquent testimony I have come across is the following from Bertrand Russell's *Autobiography* (vol. II, 1968, p. 150). It is a man's point of view, frequently met with, indicating that men do not consider themselves to be fully mature until they are fathers. It is not only women, in our society, who think of children as completing their personal development; and this has nothing to do with property or prestige.

> Ever since the day, in the summer of 1894, when I walked with Alys on Richmond Green after hearing the medical verdict, I had tried to suppress my desire for children. It had, however,

grown continually stronger until it had become almost
insupportable. When my first child was born, in November
1921, I felt an immense release of pent-up emotion, and during
the next ten years my main purposes were parental. Parental
feeling, as I have experienced it, is very complex. There is, first
and foremost, sheer animal affection, and delight in watching
what is charming in the ways of the young. Next, there is the
sense of inescapable responsibility, providing a purpose for
daily activities which scepticism does not easily question. Then
there is an egoistic element, which is very dangerous; the hope
that one's children may succeed when one has failed, that they
may carry on one's work when death or senility puts an end to
one's own efforts, and, in any case, that they will supply a
biological escape from death, making one's own life part of the
whole stream, and not a mere stagnant puddle without any
overflow into the future. All this I experienced, and for some
years it filled my life with happiness and peace.

Is this the Victorian notion of a parental instinct in another guise,
or what Miller called 'the will to parenthood' manifesting itself? Be
that as it may, this is a confession that any African, Hindu, Chinese
and Polynesian men and women would regard as absolutely normal.
Note that there is no mention of property or title. The accent is on
those features to which any ancestor worshipping African or Hindu
would also give pride of place – and which Busfield, like the young
parents Mrs Morgan and I questioned in Cambridge, also stresses –
personal gratification, fulfilment, the promise of immortality. What
is more, here is a definite recognition of the first born as the creator
of parenthood, with its bonds of inescapable responsibility – and,
some of our Cambridge informants would add, of anxiety due to
inexperience.[14]
For some of our informants, both men and women, it is the
burden of first parenthood – the trauma I am inclined to say – that
looms largest in retrospect and might even begin during the wife's
pregnancy and one wonders whether a first pregnancy ritual of
the Tallensi or Trobriand type might not serve as an alleviation of
this.

## IX

What I am labelling the 'traumatic' aspect of first parenthood comes out conspicuously in a Harvard medical and social study by Senn and Hartford (1968). Among the families investigated, the 'neurotic and emotional problems', especially of the mothers, dogged by their feelings of inadequacy, the investigators, comment, loom largest.

In this connection, it would be interesting to know if there is a higher incidence of post-partum depression among primiparae than among multiparae. (I am told there is not.) What does seem to happen, I am informed, is that new mothers sometimes react with dismay to the birth of the first child, even if it is the boy so many of them desire. One exemplary young mother told me that it took the best part of a year for her to learn to love her first-born son. This is an experience Hausa women would regard as customary and normal. And the corresponding reaction of first time fathers, psychiatrists tell me, occasionally takes the form of a psychotic breakdown.

I am not qualified to pursue these issues farther. Their relevance is as a reminder that parenthood is fraught with heavy emotional and moral demands. What is more, they suggest that it is at the very time of becoming a parent, perhaps joyfully, that these burdens raise their head. Becoming a parent is not only a transition – it can be a crisis, our anthropological data suggest, from the parent's point of view. But the tendency of research in our society as I have noted before, is to focus on the relations of parents and children from the situation of that of the latter. The key concern is with the socialization process as the basis of normal development. Studies of the contemporary patterns of adolescent rebellion and youth protest also take this line. So of course do the applied disciplines, such as psychiatry and criminology. But the anthropological data suggest that it might be rewarding to look at filio–parental relationships from the parents' situation, turning the model upside down, so to speak.

Looking again at the customary practices and observances I have reviewed, I am struck by the parallels between them and the filio–parental relationships implied in the classical picture of what Parsons describes as the 'oedipal phase' of development and its sequel (in Parsons and Bales 1955, p. 77). It is as if certain aspects of the drama depicted by Freud as taking its course within the mind and personality of the individual is, in these tribal settings, thrust into the open of custom and social organization. To be sure, one element stressed in the classical picture, the sexual wishes directed towards the mother, is less openly avowed in custom than the rivalry between like sex parent and child. The indications are there, however (cf. the Nuer), and are quite explicit in incest taboos.[15]

But Freud's remark that 'An ambivalent attitude to the father and an object-relation of a purely affectionate kind to the mother make up the content of the simple positive Oedipus complex in the boy' (1927, p. 41), fits very well the customary norms of a people like the Tallensi. He considers father-identification and mother-identification from the same filial direction (*ibid.*, p. 44). In this situation the superego had the 'task of effecting the repression of the Oedipus complex and thus establishing an internal control over the hostile wishes behind the complex'. But, Freud adds, 'the strength to do this was, so to speak, borrowed from the father, and this loan was an extraordinarily momentous act' (p. 45).


## X

Is this the nub of the matter? The tribal and Biblical institutions we have considered suggest an understanding that the 'borrowing' goes on throughout the lifetime of parent and child, and that the 'loan' cannot be repaid in their lifetime. So it is felt to be a continuing drain on the parent's psychological capital. Has not the parent, we might then ask, every incentive to be resentful, suspicious and anxious at the arrival of the offspring which is destined, by moral and legal right, to exact such a price for the fulfilment and immortality he will eventually ensure for the parent? Yet the parent cannot but desire, also, and feel obliged to cherish and rear to maturity the offspring destined by the laws of life and death to replace him.

By this reasoning it could be argued that it is the parent who must initially suppress or at least deflect his filicidal impulses to let devotion to and identification with the child take its place, and who must reconcile himself, from the outset, to the cumulative loss and eventual end of his power and authority (or for the mother, her fecundity and her nurturing and altruistic dominance) and all that is comprised in the notion of mystical potency. To accomplish all this safely, from within oneself so to speak, as Freud's model proposes, must be arduous, to say the least; and I venture to suggest that there is psychopathological evidence of the hazards that beset the task. It is far easier if the necessary controls (Miller's 'moral regulator') are externalized, vested in custom and social organization, decently shrouded in symbolic forms and actions, and fortified by ritual and metaphysical beliefs.

This, in effect, is what the syndrome of the first born as it appears in the ritual and social customs of people like the Tallensi, the Polynesians, the Hindus and the Biblical Hebrews, achieves. And let me emphasize again that it seems to be specially appropriate and useful to pin the whole lot on to the actual first born – the creator of parenthood. I doubt, by the way, if this is influenced by demographic factors, except in the gross sense that every filial generation must have a first born so that first births must at least equal if not out number later births. Whether the chances of a first born's surviving to reproductive age are worse or better than those of the later born, in the type of society I have been dealing with, is a question I have not been able to find an answer to. In any case I doubt if this is a determining factor in the cultural syndrome.[16]

The parent's task, then, is to conquer his ambivalence and identify with his offspring, so as to feel them to be so essentially a part of himself (or herself) as to cast out the destructive impulses. An expression of this is, no doubt, the way parents pin hopes and ambitions they could not realize for themselves on their children – in particular, it seems on their first borns. It is a task that must precede, set the stage for, the filial task of overcoming the oedipal conflict in accepting parental domination. Failure in it is perhaps most grimly shown in such extreme forms of child neglect as the battered baby syndrome, a mode of parent behaviour which no traditional African or Polynesian society – even among those in which neonatal infanticide of economically excessive or anomalous births is customary – would tolerate.

Here again, in tribal societies, customary rules come into play, Freud attributes to the superego the 'precept': 'You ought to be such and such (like your father)', adding 'it also comprises the prohibition: "You must not be such and such (like your father) since many things are his prerogative"' (*ibid*., pp. 44–5). Tribal custom translates this precept into practice backed by the 'categorical imperative,' not of a guilt-ridden conscience, as Freud implies, but of externally effective ritual and moral sanctions. Tribal customs make it unmistakably evident to son and daughter that they are son and daughter, no more and no less. Their social and psychological space is distinctly marked off from that of their parents, sometimes by actual physical separation at vulnerable stages of the offspring's life, sometimes, and perhaps more effectively, by purely symbolical or notional intergenerational barriers of taboo and dogma. The problem facing the society is to ensure that these norms are internalized and obeyed by both sides of the filio–parental nucleus, painful as it often is. Unbridled rejection of either side by the other, whether it results in life-taking or not, could not but destroy society. And it is here, perhaps, that the legal and ritual right of succeeding to and eventually becoming like the parent serves to reconcile the child to his dependent and subordinate place – just as the parent's complementary expectation of immortality through offspring helps to reconcile him or her to eventual physical and social extinction.

## XI

I find myself, at this point, tempted to look again at the Oedipus saga. It seems to me that several important features are overlooked in the received Freudian construct. Oedipus we must note is first and only child. Had he been destroyed in infancy, then, symbolically, the whole human race would have been ended. His fate is to attempt to overturn parenthood's twin pillars of motherhood, protected by the incest taboo, and fatherhood, protected by its sovereign supremacy. But the malign powers of which he is the innocent instrument fail in this, for Oedipus himself survives to become a father. In the Sophoclean version, this is ensured by Jocasta. Hoping to save both her husband's life and her son's – both her wifehood and her motherhood – it is she who gives the babe to the shepherd. Even Laius, according to the version that makes him responsible for exposing his son, might have hoped thus to resolve the agonizing dilemma of how to save his and his wife's marriage and parenthood without sacrificing the child. The Oedipus saga dramatizes the dilemma of how to resolve the parents' conflict between self-preservation and self-sacrifice imposed by Fate – the Greek personification of unconscious urges too monstrous to face – as well as the dilemma of how to reconcile filial dependence and love with the parricidal and incestuous wishes of the offspring.

The same questions are raised from a different point of departure in a short book, *Isaac and Oedipus*, by the late Dr Erich Wellisch.

The argument follows from the classical psychoanalytical theory of the Oedipus complex; but, writes the author, there are in reality three parts to it, the Laius, Jocasta and Oedipus sub-complexes (p. 44). He considers that 'the tragedy of Oedipus was therefore in the last instance actually caused by the defaults of his father Laius', adding however that 'Laius also fought to prevent the impending tragedy' (p. 33). But then he presents a counterpart to the Oedipus story which he claims points to something better than the compromise solution of the Greek tragedy. This is the Biblical story of the 'akedah', the binding of Isaac, in Genesis 22. Here it is not Fate but the Voice of God that is invoked as the source of the command to Abraham to sacrifice his son, and as we know it is only by the miraculous intervention of God at the very last moment, when the father stands with knife poised, that Isaac – and therefore the whole of Abraham's legitimate posterity till the end of time – is saved. Isaac though not his father's actual first born, was the legitimate one,[17] as the opener of the womb for Sarah, his lawful wife.[18] This is not the place to discuss Wellisch's interpretation of this story. As he notes, it has stirred philosophical and theological thought, and has had a magnetic attraction for artists and writers of all three faiths rooted in the Judaeo–Christian scriptures, since before the Christian era. For my part, I do not find that it arouses pity and awe as the Sophoclean saga does; for it is not a tragic story. In contrast to the latter it depicts quite directly the conflict between the urge for offspring to perpetuate oneself and the devotion in cherishing them, on the one side, and the guilty impulse to destroy them, on the other side. But the significant feature is that it shows the voice of conscience, personified in the Angel, to be victorious in the end, though requiring a substitute to be offered, quite as if foreshadowing the later law of the redemption of the first born.

The implication is that the struggle between successive generations can be regulated and indeed overcome by recourse to the authority of right and duty, to Miller's 'moral regulator'. In contrast, the Oedipus story asserts just the opposite. The struggle is inevitable and the outcome is predetermined; for it springs from the

innermost depths of our human nature. Can the tribal customs I
have discussed be interpreted as devices for reconciling the demands
and pressures that come from these opposed poles of our human
make-up?[19]

Here, perhaps, we are presented with a polarity that may be the
key to the whole of the enquiry I have pursued. Is it perhaps the case
that the moral regulation of filio–parental relationships comes
down, in the end to the balance that happens to be achieved, in a
given social and cultural system, between the compulsion that is dramatized in the Oedipus story – and is rooted in human propensities
laid down, some would argue, in the earliest infancy – and the control that is dramatized in the Isaac story – and represents propensities generated by the fact of membership of the larger,
extra-familal social order?

## Summary

I return thus to my starting point in Emanuel Miller's model of the
cycle of the generations. What I have endeavoured to show is that
the first born marks a critical, perhaps the most critical stage in the
cycle. Like him, I take parenthood to be the crucial factor in the
cycle. It is a truism to say that parenthood is a universal human
(some would say primate) institution. What is more to the point is
that how it is created in each case and in general, and how it runs its
course, the relationships and the patterns of custom and of behaviour it generates – these are phenomena where all the human
sciences in which Miller was interested meet on common ground.[20] I
hope that this lecture, deviously as it has wandered and perhaps
tried your patience, will commend itself as a fitting tribute to the
memory of Emanuel Miller.

# 10

## The concept of the person

### I

Since everyone is acquainted with the famous essay by Marcel
Mauss: 'Une catégorie de l'esprit humaine: la notion de personne,
celle de Moi' (*J. Roy. Anth. Inst.,* 1939), I shall not linger over it. I
must, however, remind you that it was given in London, as the
Huxley Memorial Lecture for 1938. I mention this for the personal
reason that I had on this occasion the privilege and the exhilaration
of meeting Mauss, for the first and only time, and also of attending
his lecture. I had just got back from my second expedition to the Tallensi. In the afternoon before the lecture, Evans-Pritchard and I
called on Mauss at his hotel. And I remember particularly sitting
with him on the terrace and discussing his topic. He asked kindly
about my field research and it was then that he made a comment
which has remained engraved on my memory. Ethnology, he said, is
like the ocean. All you need is a net, any kind of net; and then if you
step into the sea and swing your net about, you are sure to catch
some kind of fish. As for field work, he continued, shaking his
head and laughing jovially, you say you have spent two and a half
years with one tribe? Poor man. It will take twenty years to write
it up.

Alas, Mauss' prophecy has been more than borne out. All the
same, it is to the field work of that period in particular that I shall
return in this paper. I shall try to give an account of the Tallensi
notion of the person (in the Maussian sense) and of some of its corre-
lates and implications, as the actors see it. I shall try to show how the
ideas, the beliefs, the linguistic usages, the dogmas and so forth – in

short what the ethnographer represents as a conceptual scheme —
are accessible to discovery primarily by reason of their realization in
the customary or institutionalized activities of people. We have
examples of élites of priests, doctors, men of wisdom and learning,
who have a specialized, in some respects esoteric knowledge of this
subject. There were no such specialists, either on the side of ritual
and religious thought and practices, or on the side of secular matters, among the Tallensi in the nineteen thirties. It was only by
observing and conversing with the common man, so to speak, that
one could see how the ideas and beliefs relating to such abstract
notions as that of the person were channelled through his daily activities. They were more commonly exhibited in action and
utterance than formulated in explicit terms. It was in the way people
carried on their lives from day to day and in the way they died, too,
that the concepts and beliefs I shall try to present here were made
manifest.

I have described the most important features of the social organization and the religious and ritual practices and beliefs of the Tallensi
in earlier publications (Fortes 1945, 1949, 1959) and need only add
here that I have found it necessary before this to try to understand
their notion of the person in order to understand their social organization and system of thought (cf. Fortes 1959, 1961).

Schools and literacy have brought acquaintance with the modern
European-oriented world views and patterns of living to the Tallensi
in the past twenty-five years. Christianity is slowly spreading among
them. Recourse to a hospital and to modern medicine is becoming
an accepted way of dealing with certain kinds of sickness among
them. And yet the traditional concepts and beliefs I shall be discussing are by no means merely of antiquarian interest.

## II

I spent a few days visiting my Tallensi friends in 1971; and right
beside the striking Catholic church that now stands within a stone's
throw of the central *toŋgban* (Earth shrine) at Tongo, I found myself
in the midst of a ritual crisis of the kind I had only heard of in 1934–7.

A tense and anxious divination session was in progress at the
sacred pool of the Zubiung clan. All the elders, still traditionalist, of
course, and quite a few of the younger men, were present, and the

problem was one that Mauss would have been greatly intrigued by. It appeared that spilt blood and other signs had been found showing that one of the crocodiles which have from time immemorial dwelt in the pool, had been wantonly killed in the night. As one elder explained to me, in these days it has been found that crocodile skins and claws are worth a lot of money. So thieves and rascals have been known to come from the neighbouring cosmopolitan town to the sacred pool to trap and kill the crocodiles. He affirmed that no local man, indeed no Tallensi, would commit the crime and sacrilege of injuring these animals. Every Tallensi knows that these crocodiles are the incarnation of important clan ancestors (see Fortes 1945, p. 142). To kill one of these is like killing a person. It is murder of the most heinous kind and it would bring disaster on the whole clan. The divination session was aimed at finding out what sins of omission or commission on the part of the clan had brought down this calamity on them.

A consideration of this crisis points to the heart of my inquiry. It appears that in some contexts and some situations a crocodile from a certain special place is a person (*nit*) to a particular group of Tallensi – as, of course, also happens amongst other Voltaic peoples who share the same broad cultural system. A crocodile in the bush, in the wild (*moog*), however – for instance, in the rivers that are fished in the dry season – is not a person, not sacred. It can be killed and eaten as the home crocodile must not be by those people of Zubiung for whom the whole species is not a totem.

Here, then, we have a peculiar and striking illustration of Mauss' recurrent emphasis on the social derivation of the category of personhood. A decade before the 1938 paper (commenting in 1929, on Lévy-Bruhl's *L'Âme Primitive*) he drew attention to the Roman transformation of the notion of the mask – '*personnalité mythique*' – into the notion of the '*personne morale*', best glossed, in English, as the social person (Mauss, *Œuvres*, 1969, p. 132). Noting the importance of names for placing the individual in society, for defining his personality, and perhaps his destiny, he propounded the generalization that 'la personnalité, l'âme, viennent avec le nom, de la société'. In other words, it is the society that creates, defines, indeed imposes the distinctive signs and indices that characterize, and the moral and jural capacities and qualities that constitute the *personne morale* as we find it in that society.

The concept of the *personne morale* is central to Mauss' analysis; and the significant feature is its social derivation. If personhood is socially generated and culturally defined, how then is it experienced by its bearer, the individual? This is the question of the awareness of the self, *moi* of Mauss' analysis, that is of the connection between the 'inner man' (the 'natural man' some would say) and the 'outer' socially formed person; and it has occupied men of learning from ancient times until today, in the Orient as well as in the West, as Krader has shown (1967). It is worth noting that Durkheim and Mauss were not the only social theorists of modern times who gave precedence to the social sources of person and self. The American sociologist C. H. Cooley had a similar point of view. His country-man, G. H. Mead, in an early paper in 1913 sketched a theory, later elaborated in a famous book (1934), which he summed up in the for-mula 'the "I" of introspection is the self which enters into social re-lations with other selves'.

Ethnologists like Hallowell (1955) and Margaret Mead (1949) and psychologists like E. Goffman (1959) have carried the analysis further. They have brought together observational and field data showing how social organization and culture shape the expression of personhood, and channel the correlative awareness, in contexts as diverse as those of the Ojibway Indians, New Guinea tribes and custodial institutions in urban America; and the same questions are also occupying the attention of various philosophers.

It is evident, therefore, that our theme has wider theoretical impli-cations than merely to add to the ethnographical confirmation of Mauss' main thesis. It concerns the perennial problem of how indi-vidual and society are interconnected in mutual regulation. The African data are, I believe, especially relevant on account of the ex-plicit representation in custom and social organization of some criti-cal features of this inter-connection. The approach I am adopting was introduced into British anthropology by Radcliffe-Brown in 1922 by way of his concept of the social personality which was, I presume, a direct adaptation of the Maussian concept of the '*per-sonne morale*' (Radcliffe-Brown 1922).

## III

So far I have emphasized the actor's situation, seeing him as the recipient and bearer of personhood. But Mauss' concept implies that we could also start from the opposite side. We could start with an inventory of 'masks' available in a given society and inquire into their modes of allocation to individuals or groups. This approach brings the Maussian concept into line with the Weberian concept of 'office'. As I have suggested in Chapter 5, though we usually associate the concept of 'office' with such institutions as kingship or chiefship or priesthood, it can in fact, quite appropriately be extended to include any juridically and socially fixed status.

Thus, from whichever way we approach our enquiry we see how important it is to keep in mind the two aspects of personhood. Looking at it from the objective side, the distinctive qualities, capacities and roles with which society endows a person enable the person to be known to be, and also to show himself to be the person he is supposed to be. Looked at from the subjective side, it is a question of how the individual, as actor, knows himself to be – or not to be – the person he is expected to be in a given situation and status. The individual is not a passive bearer of personhood; he must appropriate the qualities and capacities, and the norms governing its expression to himself. The name is an important cultural device for ensuring this and for fusing together the two aspects; but occupations, rank, and other such office-like attributes also serve this end. Ritual observances such as totemic avoidances are particularly significant foci for the conjunction of the internal awareness and the external expressions of personhood (cf. Chapter 6). Initiation ceremonies bring out another important feature of this conjunction. They dramatize the processes by which an individual is invested with the capacities of personhood specific to defined roles and statuses. A beautiful account of how the change of social personality is experienced and appropriated by the individual is given in Camara Laye's classic *L'enfant noir*. The *chisungu* of the Bemba (Richards 1956) and the Koumen of the Fulbe (Dieterlen & Hampaté Ba 1966) reveal the other side. Initiation ceremonies are aimed as much at legitimizing for the individual his rights to assume and to exercise openly the capacities that pertain to the status acquired by initiation, as at imparting esoteric knowledge. Bemba girls are well acquainted with the facts of sexual life and procreation before their *chisungu* but it is only after the ceremony that they are free to act as sexually mature persons fit for marriage and motherhood.

It is not surprising, perhaps, that what I have been here so laboriously expounding is brought vividly to life by a Parisian novelist of Durkheim's and Mauss' generation. I refer, of course, to Proust who was doubtless responding to the same intellectual climate as they were. In *Du Côté de chez Swann*, there is a gem of a digression on the *fille de cuisine* who is sent up with the coffee. This is what he says:

> La fille de cuisine était une personne morale, une institution permanente à qui des attributions invariables assuraient une sorte de continuité et d'identité, à travers la succession des formes passagères en lesquelles elle s'incarnait, car nous n'eûmes jamais la même deux ans de suite. (Editions Gallimard, Paris, 1954, p. 97)

Mauss himself could hardly have put this more elegantly. And what is specially interesting about this statement is C. K. Scott-Moncrieff's brilliant English translation of it (in *Swann's Way*, The Modern Library edition, New York, 1928, p. 99). This is how it goes:

> The kitchen-maid was an abstract personality, a permanent institution to which an invariable set of attributes assured a sort of fixity and continuity and identity throughout the long series of transitory human shapes in which that personality was incarnate; for we never found the same girl there two years running.

His rendering of Proust's *personne morale* as 'abstract personality' lends point to the institutional character of the kitchen maid's role. We are made to realize that it is a kind of office, distinct from the individual who temporarily fills it – or rather, as Proust more profoundly puts it, incarnates it. And let us note how exquisitely Proust draws out the distinction, one might almost say the contradiction, between the individual and the office by giving the hapless incumbent of that moment exaggerated individuality by reason of her pregnancy and her feeble character.

To sum up, I would maintain that the notion of the person in the

Maussian sense is intrinsic to the very nature and structure of human society and human social behaviour everywhere.

## IV

After this digression, let me return to the slain crocodile. If society is the source of personhood, it follows that society can confer it on any object it chooses, human or non-human, the living or the dead, animate or inanimate, materially tangible or imagined, above all, both on singular and on collective objects. Defining a descent group, or even a political community such as a tribe as a 'person', in the manner that is common throughout West Africa, is perfectly consistent with this mode of thought. And of course there is nothing bizarre from the actor's point of view about defining a particular crocodile as a person. Nevertheless, the elementary model and primary reference of the notion of the person is the human person; and this is convincingly shown in the African data. There is always a terminology of description and reference for the attributes, components and functions of the person and these are also tangibly exhibited in the cognitive categories, in the beliefs and in the juridical and ritual institutions of the society. The now classical studies among the Dogon, the Bambarra, and other Sudanic peoples by Madame Dieterlen and her colleagues amply document this.

The Tallensi also have a distinct vocabulary for these aspects of the person; and the most superficial examination shows that this vocabulary is based on the same lexical roots as appear in the corresponding terminologies of the other Gur-speaking peoples of the Voltaic region and indeed of many other West African peoples, which I take to indicate common underlying beliefs and concepts. But it is, I believe, not unfair to my Tallensi friends and teachers to say that their attitude in matters of this sort is practical and instrumental. They do not have complex myths of the kind that have been reported from other Voltaic groups; and they are relatively uninterested – or so it seemed to me – in the kind of exegetic and conceptual elaborations that have been reported from elsewhere. One has to infer their theories and beliefs, as I have said, from the practices in which they are embedded. Theirs is a schematic variant, with the emphasis on the patterns of action rather than on belief and ideology, of the common underlying Sudanic world view.

The Tallensi term I am translating as '*person*' is (as in all Gur dialects) *nit*, pl. *niriba* (cf. also the Akan *ni-pa*, person; cf. Fortes 1969, p. 167). This term has a very wide range of reference, often meaning 'people' in the most general sense. Questioned about cases such as that of the murdered crocodile, Tallensi say this crocodile (*baŋ*) was a kind of person, *nit*. The most significant indication of this is the fact that the sacred crocodiles of this pool are given burial and a symbolic funeral, if found dead, just as human persons are. Nevertheless, the murdered crocodile *though a person* would not be described as *human*. There is a special term for this, *ni-saal*. The obvious etymology of this word suggests an inference that being human presupposes the possibility of personhood (*nit*). It is difficult to elicit from informants a precise definition of *nisaal*. The synonym *nin-voo* (literally person-alive) often used for it, indicates that it is presumed to imply life and personhood. It also implies certain attributes of normality to which I will presently come.

But the best way of indicating the significance of the concept of *nisaal*, human, is to note how it contrasts with other constituents of the more general category of living things, *bon-vor* (pl. *bon-voya*) (etymologically *bon*, thing, *vor*, alive) on the one hand and with inanimate objects on the other. Among *bonvoya*, living things, contrasted with humans, animals come first. The most general term for an animal is *duu, yini-duus*, home-animals like cattle often being in turn contrasted with *yeog-duus*, animals of the wild, that is, game. However, whereas *nisaal* is a single, universal category, the animal world is split up among a diversity of ecologically-ordered classes or species – earth creatures, water creatures, birds, etc., etc.

Tallensi connect life with the breath, *vo-hem*, hence *bon-vor*. Humans and animals are the possessors of life par excellence and the living humans (*vo-pa*) are contrasted with the dead (*kpeem*) as in the common proverb, *zom kpeem ka di zo vopa* (One must fear the dead (ancestors) and not fear the living). At the same time, as we shall presently see, qualities of livingness, and not merely metaphorically, are attributed to certain quasi-personified religious entities, notably the Earth and ancestral shrines. Furthermore, trees and plants are described as belonging to the living part of the non-animate world as opposed to stones, clay, rivers, etc.[1]

To return to animals, it is accepted that they do not differ from humans in the biological sense. They move of themselves and mate and breed, live and die in the same way. The anatomical and physiological isomorphism is well understood since it is principally from animal husbandry and from sacrificing and butchering animals that the details are learnt. Animals and humans have the same bodily substances of flesh (*numət*), blood (*zeem*), bones (*koba*), etc.

Wherein, then, does the critical difference lie? A good test lies in the attitudes about depriving its bearer of life. If a human is killed, whether in war or in a private quarrel, the killer must be prophylactically treated with a special ritual medication; but so must he be if he kills certain large animals of the bush believed to be by nature capable of aggressive retaliation. These include not only the big carnivores such as lions and leopards, but also large antelopes. The purpose of the prophylaxis in both cases is to prevent the 'soul' (*sii*) of the slain human or animal from becoming magically dangerous. There is, however, a fundamental difference, in that to kill a human, individually, not in war, is sinful, a desecration of the Earth to be atoned for by sacrifice i.e. purificatory ritual, whereas killing an animal is thought of as a justifiable, though possibly dangerous act, a kind of wrong, perhaps, but not a sin.

Not only is there an overlap between animals and humans on the biological side, there is believed to be some connection between them also on the cultural side. In Tallensi folk tales and myths, animals are often presented as speaking, and as acting in a quasi-human manner in other respects too. Dogs and to a lesser extent cats are regarded as quasi-human. They live with humans, eat the same kind of food, and – dogs in particular – respond to human speech. In other ways, too, they behave like humans. Dogs have humanlike traits such as loyalty, courage, intelligence and on the other side greed and thievishness. Cattle, sheep and goats and poultry are domestic animals without qualifications. But some animals of the bush are represented in folktales as living in families and communities like humans.

It is difficult to elicit definite statements as to where the critical difference lies. My inference is that it lies in the facts epitomized by the observation that animals have no genealogies. Though animal species have continuity by reproductive succession, animals do not have descent and kinship credentials. They do not have social organization with the implications of moral and jural rules. They have no ritual practices, no ancestors; they have life and individuality and continuity as species, but not their own forms of society or morality. All the same, animals have attributes and capacities that make them potentially humanizable, if I might coin a word to convey the Tallensi idea. They can be partially incorporated in human society, for example in the totemistic ideology that confers kinship morality on selected species.

And yet, Tallensi are emphatic that animals *as animals* are not humans and definitely not persons (*niriba*). This is true even of those animals that are partially incorporated as a species subject to totemic taboos as the mythologically commemorated saviours of the founding ancestors of lineages and clans to which they count as quasi-kinsfolk (Chaper 6). Crocodiles, as a species, in their animal mode of existence in the wild, are not persons. Only the particular crocodiles abiding in the particular sacred pool and associated with the particular collective person, that is, the clan whose dead elders rise up again (as Tallensi say) in these crocodiles – only these sanctified and in a sense quasi-domesticated crocodiles are invested with personhood. The prohibition on killing them is represented in the same terms as are applied to humans, and the funeral ritual – albeit just symbolical – accorded to a dead crocodile testifies further to this. It is interesting to contrast dogs which, in spite of their quasi-human characteristics, are killed in sacrifice and eaten like any other domestic animal. (But not cats, which are women's mascots.)

The key lies in the belief – more accurately the doctrine – that these crocodiles are the vehicles of ancestral spiritual immortality, the living shrines, as it were, of the ancestors.

## V

Now in the Tallensi cult of the ancestors and the Earth almost any item of the natural or the social environment is capable of becoming a vehicle of ancestral or other mystical presence to those who are under its power. A tree, a stone, an artefact, thus comes to be ritually charged with what appear to be elements of personification. However, this does not amount to personhood, in the specific sense. Tallensi say categorically that the tree, the stone, the old hoe, and so on, which serves as the altar (*bagher*) for the offering of sacrifices to particular named ancestors or the Earth, is not the ancestor but is only his or her sitting place (*zi-ziiga*), his locus of accessibility to prayer and other ritual acts. It is comparable to the homestead where a living elder is accessible. Medicine (*teem*) (which refers both to substances and prescriptions for treating disease and states of pollution, and to purely magical agencies, defensive or aggressive), is also made manifest in material objects and paraphernalia. These are usually of a symbolic kind, similar to the constituents of ancestral shrines. Magical medicines are often said to wander about and to catch or tie up their victims (magically of course) as if they were alive in some way, and Tallensi often speak in the same way of the Earth. Nevertheless, they are quite clear that it is not the material objects as such that are 'alive' but the mystical agencies located in them; and it is equally clear that the livingness attributed to them is only analogous to but not identical with the livingness of physically alive creatures. Ancestors, medicines, and the Earth are personified but not invested with the kind of personhood that accrues primarily to living humans, though it may be conferred in curtailed form and in special circumstances, on a particular animal. Let us look at this a little more closely.

When ancestors and other mystical agencies are credited with forces analogous to life, they may be said to be *bon-voya*, living things, but they are not said to have *ɲo-vor*, the life that is made manifest in breath, that is, biological life. They are not embodied in flesh and blood. To have a body (*neng*) thus constituted is the indispensable foundation for being alive in the way humans have to be to become persons, even though they share this property with other living creatures. A crucial feature of this is that living creatures come into being by birth and what is almost more important, that they are mortal. The significant point here, as I shall have to repeat in different contexts, is the paradox that, according to the Tallensi theory of the person, no one can be certainly known to have been a full human person until he is shown, at the time of his death, to have been slain by his ancestors and therefore to deserve a proper funeral. This carries the implication that the person thus marked is qualified to join his ancestors and become one of them. So one can say that the real test of having achieved personhood is to have had the potentiality, all through life, of becoming a worshipped ancestor – or of incorporating one.

The limiting principle then, for personhood, strictly defined, is to begin or rather to be born with a mortal body. To this I will return again presently. Ancestors and other mystical agencies are not thus endowed. When they are said to be alive, the allusion is to their powers of mystical intervention in human affairs. Tallensi refer to ancestors by kinship terms used for living forbears, such as *banam*, fathers, *yaanam*, grandfathers, *manam*, mothers. Nevertheless, these usages do not reflect the merging or identification of the living with the ancestors. The latter are among men but not of mankind. They belong to the world of the dead, the *kpeem*, and intervene in human affairs in modes of action reserved for those who have mystical not mundane power. The kinship terms by which they are addressed in prayer and sacrifice and the associated ritual usages reflect their genealogical origins and the attributes and powers assigned to them in Tallensi religious doctrine. They are represented as endowed with untrammelled power and authority over human existence, ultimately over life and death. It is as if they were endowed with the quintessence of parental autocracy purged of the elements of affection, solicitude and devotion, and unencumbered by the rational constraints and material sanctions that human parenthood is of necessity subject to.

Ancestors are the dominant supernatural agencies believed to control human existence. In conjunction with the Earth and other mystical agencies they are believed to be instrumental in regulating the course of nature as it affects human existence. But it is not only by reason of the arbitrary, quasi-juridical powers projected on them that they have this aura of personification. It is also because they are believed to respond to men's needs and claims and to take cognizance of human conduct, in ways analogous to those of human parents and elders. But this is where a critical distinction arises. Ancestors and other supernatural agencies have their sitting places in the homes and settlements of living people; to this extent they are incorporated in the social order. But not as humans are. Their place in their dependants' homes and communities is behind an invisible but precisely defined conceptual and dogmatic screen, as it were. This is the screen of religious ideology and ritual prescription, which can only be penetrated at proper times and places by the special instrumentality of prayer and sacrifice and the associated practices and observances which Tallensi call taboo rules (*kihər*). Tallensi identify this domain by generalising the concept of *baghər*, the term primarily signifying the objective vehicle of mystical agencies, as I have mentioned above, in other words, which refers to personified mystical agencies of all kinds as they are fixed in their tangible and material loci of accessibility. It is contrasted with the domain of mundane life with its routines of direct contacts in family and community relations, in work, and in the general affairs of society and its material, rational, framework of order. This is the everyday, normal universe of action for which there is no special label and where ritual is inappropriate. The Tallensi think of the two spheres as mutually complementary, rather than opposed, locked together in the inescapable mutual coercion attempted by the living and the mystical agencies upon one another. But whereas on the human side, future persons are recruited biologically by birth and shed by death, the *baghǝr* entities can only be brought into being by the deliberate social actions of rituals, *'malung'*, establishing them and of the jural allocation of the rights and duties to their custody and service to persons entitled to it.

Considering therefore what I said earlier, namely that full personhood is only finally validated by proper death and qualification for ancesterhood, it emerges that the human persons who make up society remain the ultimate arbiters of personhood. To be sure they are not free to act against the dictates of their religious and metaphysical beliefs and values; but they are the responsible agents; and they fulfil their task by conferring what looks like quasi-personhood on the dead who become ancestors. It is of interest, by the way, that ancestors are, in my experience, never referred to by the term *niriba*, persons. I have heard nonancestral mystical agencies so alluded to but the contexts showed that it was in a metaphorical sense exactly like our use of the pronoun 'she' to refer to a ship.

## VI

The spectrum of personhood is not yet complete, however. For there is another contrast between true, human personhood and the apparent personhood of supernatural agencies that needs to be considered. As we have seen, animals that cannot be redefined as kinds of persons fall into two main categories, those of the home and those of the wild. It is worth nothing that only those of the home may be sacrificed to ancestors and other mystical agencies associated with family and community organization.

In a parallel manner, the wild (bush, *mo'o*) also has what appear at first sight to be its characteristic mystical denizens. These are the *Kolkpaarəs*, the 'bush sprites'. Unlike the ancestral dead on the Earth, however, *Kolkpaarə* cannot be invested with qualities of personhood. They cannot be personified. For one thing, they are *ab initio* bodiless and thus devoid of the fundamental attribute of biological embodiment that is the essential starting point for personhood to be achieved. They are not mystical agencies ritually incorporated in the total system of human social life and therefore having mystical rights to intervene in human affairs. There are no shrines or altars at which they can be approached. In short, they do not complement or even contrast with humanity; they simply negate all that is human, being totally lawless and without any moral capacity, such as is vested in the socially incorporated mystical agencies. Their malice and caprice is typically shown in relation to plural births. It is believed that *Kolkpaares* sometimes quite wantonly enter a woman's womb and are born as twins or triplets, masquerading as incipient humans. Plural births are regarded as anomalous and both the parents and the babies have quickly to be treated with medicine to 'peg them down' (*ba'*) as human. If a twin dies in a very early infancy, this is evidence that it was in reality a *Kolkpaarəg*. But there are circumstances, never foreseeable, in which a bush-sprite can masquerade as human for many years and not be found out until its host dies, as we shall see. Hysterical fugues and even madness are sometimes attributed to persecution by *Kolkpaarəs*.

There is no need to labour the aptness of the symbolism which thus locates lawless and immoral caprice in these faceless creatures of the wild. I cite them here to emphasize that model personhood among the Tallensi postulates biological embodiment on the one hand and legal, moral and ritual status on the other. The concept of *nit*, person, presupposes living humanity contained in a social system.

Incidental evidence for this comes from a belief in ghosts (*kok*). These are said to mimic humans but to be like wraiths, and some people claim to have seen them. However, knowledgeable men and women deride these claims as gross superstition. *Niriba*, human persons, are embodied in tangible, visible, material flesh and blood. The dead, *Kpeem*, who are contrasted with them have their allotted place. The alleged ghosts belong to neither world and must therefore be figments of overheated imagination.

## VII

To return to twins, they exemplify an important rule. To become a person one must be properly and normally born and this, ideally, means singly born, head first, of parents licitly permitted to procreate. A breech presentation is feared, is magically medicated and classed with twins, but anyone successfully born thus is treated as a singlet eventually.

It is characteristic of Tallensi thought and institutions that full personhood is only attained by degrees over the whole course of life. Birth marks only the starting point, the minimum quantum of personhood, as it were. Indeed it is not until an infant is weaned and has a following sibling (*nyeer*) that it can be said to be set on the road to eventual full personhood. It is sometimes not named or placed in the ritual care of its ancestor guardian till then. And, in this connection, even an adult who dies without leaving a following sibling is buried in a way that suggests some lack of full personhood.

To become a person therefore one must begin with normal and legitimate birth into a family, lineage and clan which automatically stamps upon the individual his patrilineal status and binds him in advance to the observances and prescriptions that go with this. He comes equipped with a body, the Tallensi term for which is *neng* (obviously cognate with *nung*, flesh), or *nengbin* (flesh + skin). The skin is a very significant feature of the individual's constitution. Tallensi contrast themselves with Europeans as people of black skin (*ghansableg*) against people of white skin (*gbanpeeleg*). A fresh and glowing (*farr*) skin is the most admired sign of beauty in a maiden. When I was in Taleland in 1971 a young man of my acquaintance complained sadly that it is nowadays impossible to tell what a girl's skin is like because they all wear clothes. Skin diseases, especially leprosy, are particularly abhorred as the spoiling of the body (*neng nsagham*). Ideally, then, a whole body is one with an unblemished skin. It is not only the foundation of personhood but the seat of the self (*meng*) which I shall presently consider more fully.

I have said that birth is the starting point of personhood, but this needs some qualification. Actually the potentiality of birth is sufficient for the ritual and moral recognition of initial personhood. Thus the pregnancy of a child's own mother counts as its next following sibling even if there is a miscarriage; and if the stillbirth is at a stage of foetal development where its sex can be recognized, it counts as a minimal person. It will not be named but will be given normal burial and the parents will have to go through curtailed and symbolic rites of mourning and of the removal of the pollution of bereavement.

Here we have a striking indication of two important structural features. First, as I have previously implied, it is, paradoxically, in the circumstances and the ritual interpretation of an individual's death, and the obsequies accorded to him, that the personhood he attained in life is retrospectively validated. The sacred crocodiles of Zubiung are known to be some kind of persons because they must be buried as, and receive obsequies like those of human persons, as I have already noted. This, too, is a theme I will presently return to.

The second feature is more obvious. From the very outset of life, difference of sex is a significant element of personhood. Though all the terms by which components of the person are distinguished – *nit, ninvoo, vohem, neng, sii,* etc. – are common to both sexes, the difference is constantly brought to notice. Traditionally, it was exhibited in differences of everyday clothing, men always wearing loincloths and women naked till their first pregnancy and being thereafter always girded with a perineal belt. Occupational specialization and the allocation of space for working, eating, sleeping and ritual activities in the homestead also reflect this division (Fortes 1949). One sees it in the normal postures of men and women. Baby girls are admonished to sit properly with their legs tucked under and not sprawl like boys. Women stoop to greet a senior male and kneel when offering food and drink to a visitor. Most striking is the ritual association of the number three with males and four with females. All ritual performances concerned with males are carried out in threes, for females in fours. Clearly, differentiation by sex is a critical factor in a person's whole life cycle from birth and, as we shall see, to death and the attainment of ancestorhood. More than this, it is a basic premiss of Tallensi social structure at all levels. The complementary opposition of patrilineal descent and matrilateral filiation which underlies the whole system of familial, lineage and clan relations is rooted in the opposition between the unity by descent and the distinction by sex of brother and sister. In particular, marriage and parenthood and the complementary patterns of jural and ritual rights and duties that follow for offspring are regulated by this.

It is the more necessary to emphasize that, by contrast, the distinction between males and females is not significant in respect to the ultimate and irreducible determinants of jural and ritual status, those that establish the primary rights to personhood in its various dimensions. I refer to membership of the lineage and clan and such other kinship connections as arise through matrilateral links. These accrue to the individual regardless of sex, by right of birth. To be sure exogamous marriage and lifelong jural minority in relation to father or husband deprive a woman of property and political rights in her natal lineage. But her membership of it never lapses and is even transmitted to her children in a derivative form. It is of interest in this connection, as I have already indicated, that the Tallensi do not have special passage rites for the admission into adulthood of either sex. They would scoff at the Bemba Chisingu ritual, as they do at the female excision rites of some neighbouring tribes. Sexuality is a commonplace matter to Tallensi.

The only form of initiation ritual practised among them is found among the Hill Talis (cf. Fortes 1945, p. 137). There is a ritual of induction into the cult of the External Boghar – that is, the cult of the collective ancestors – which every male must undergo before he is allowed in to the cult centre as a full member. This rite can be undergone at any age from about 6 to adulthood. Except for the fact that he is naked like a new born babe, is bullied mildly by his guards, and is intimidated by the administration of the oath of secrecy required of him, the novice suffers no hardship or pain. Clients coming from other tribes, both male and female, to solicit mystical help from the Boghar, also undergo an induction ceremony. But no wives or daughters of members of this cult have this privilege. From the point of view of the Hill Talis, a man is an incomplete person devoid of critical ritual capacities and elements of jural status, until he has been inducted into the External Boghar Cult. It will make no apparent difference to his everyday life if he is thus incomplete. It will not impede his economic activities or, for instance, prevent him from marrying; but marriage and parenthood would be regarded as somewhat anomalous. For until he is ritually placed under the surveillance of the collective ancestors in the Boghar Cult, he counts as a jural minor without the right to a responsible opinion or autonomous role in lineage affairs and with restrictions on his ritual standing in offering sacrifices to the ancestors on his own behalf. It is only men who have lived away from the home settlement from infancy for many years who are inducted after adolescence. A father who has failed to have his son inducted before adolescence would be laying himself open to punishment by the ancestors.

The position of stranger clients is instructive. They are of course pledged to secrecy, on pain of severe mystical penalties if they default, but they are not considered to be members of the cult on an equal footing with those who are members by right of patrilineal descent. Like the patients of any owner of a medicine, they may benefit from the cult's magical powers, and therefore have to abide by its rules and restrictions, but are never admitted to all its mysteries. Namoos have no truck, as they would put it, with these Hill Talis cults. They have no induction ceremonies corresponding to those of the Hill Talis.

As I have mentioned, women remain all their lives in a status of jural and ritual minority. It would appear, therefore, that they can never attain the complete personhood that a male can attain, especially if he reaches elderhood or becomes the holder of a ritual or political office. Certainly for the Tallensi the ideal of the complete person is an adult male who has reached old age and lineage eldership, who has male descendants in the patrilineal line and who is qualified by a proper death to become their worshipped ancestor. Nevertheless women are not wholly debarred from attaining a degree of personhood corresponding, in their sphere of life, to that of any man. Throughout life they have sanctioned rights, duties, privileges, and capacities. They receive the same kind of mortuary and funeral ceremonies as men and they can also become worshipped ancestresses. It is as mothers and grandmothers, through their children and descendants, that they are elevated to ancestral status in all respects as significant as those of the men. This is characteristic of Tallensi culture, reflecting the complementary relationship of males and females, of paternal and maternal kinship and ancestry in the secular as well as in the religious order of society.

There is one further condition that needs to be noted. It concerns men primarily, since jural and ritual authority and responsibility are vested exclusively in them, but women are also directly affected by it. Favoured by this Destiny, as Tallensi would put it, a man may have reached individual maturity with his children and even grand-children around him. But if his own or proxy father is still alive (and I have known such cases), he is still, strictly speaking, under paternal authority. It is only after his father's death that he gains the unen-cumbered jural and ritual autonomy that marks truly complete per-sonhood. Similar norms apply to women in relation to their own mothers, within the circle of their kinship relations in their natal family and lineage (Fortes 1949, pp. 147–50). One cannot empha-size too much the principle that familial and lineage status is an ines-capable determinant of personhood at every stage. The person emerges through the dialectic interplay of individual and social structure.

## VIII

This brings me back to the apparent paradox that the crucial test of personhood comes at the end of life as we saw with the crocodile. Goody's analysis of the mortuary and funeral ceremonies of the Lo Dagaa (1962) helps to explain why. The basic reason, as he shows, is that it is only when the person is dissolved into his or her constitu-ent parts and statuses that his claims to genuine personhood can be evaluated. He may all his life have been very efficiently masquerad-ing, leading a double life as a non-person concealed under the out-ward trappings of personhood. He might not even have been conscious of this, in his capacity as an individual, for the cause – necessarily a supernatural agency from the Tallensi point of view – would very likely have been undisclosed until revealed by divination at his death.

For the Tallensi, death *kum* (from *ku* = to kill, hence the killed thing) is the end of an individual life (*ŋovor*) in the first place. The word for corpse is also *kum*, though death is often referred to in the abstract, e.g. in proverbs. It is significant that a dying individual must be propped up in the arms of close kin or a spouse. For a person to die unpropped up is a sin that pollutes the whole household and all its goods. This pollution must be immediately removed by a ritual specialist, else more deaths will ensue. Having seen these happenings, I can testify to the anxiety of the deceased's relatives and their relief after the medication. Tallensi describe this as a very serious ancestral taboo which they cannot explain. One can see, however, from the context, and from comparable customs, that if an individual is left to die without such support it would be treating him like an animal which, by definition, has no kin. A dying person's kinsfolk must demonstrate their acknowledgment that he belongs to them and their consequential obligatory concern for him at the moment when he is about to leave them.

Tallensi say that the corpse, *kum*, is like a husk, *foreng*, which they compare to the skin cast by a snake. What, then, has left it that was the source of its life? Firstly, the breath, *vohem*. Death is known to have supervened when the breath stops, but breath is considered to be the expression, not the source, of life. What is essentially lost by death is the soul, *sii*.

It is convenient to translate this notion by the conventional Tylorian term, the soul, but the classical Greek concept of the psyche (as explained for example, by Onians, pp. 93 ff.) seems to me to come nearer to the relatively diffuse and of course much less sophisticated, Tallensi idea. The *sii* is not identified with the breath. As with similar entities that figure in other West African systems of thought, the *sii* is sometimes spoken of as if it were a double of the individual, accompanying him rather than being integral with him. Correspondingly, the *sii* can wander about leaving its embodiment behind in sleep and appear in dreams to someone else. It is definitely not identified with the ghost-like wraith (*kok*) I mentioned earlier; it is part of a living person's constitution having a reality of its own. The *sii* is vulnerable to magical injury. Thus, when a grave is being dug, souls of people attending the mortuary ceremonies are apt to be enticed into the grave without the persons thus affected being aware. It is difficult to get explanations of how this is brought about. The most plausible is that the soul of the deceased, whose body is still lying in his house, has entered the grave which will be his 'home' in due course, and is enticing souls of people the person was attached to in his life to accompany him in death. At all events, it is believed that clairvoyant buriers of the dead (*bayaase*) can detect these souls and rescue them. Medicinal roots and herbs are burnt in the grave to drive out these souls and thus prevent death from over-taking their owners.

These beliefs correspond to an illuminating usage of the notion that can not inappropriately be translated by a term like 'personal identity'. It is put forward to account for special attachments and aversions of individuals, both those that are conventional and those that are idiosyncratic. A person's most intimate belongings are said to be his or her normal clothing, a man's bow and arrows, and such normal tools as a hoe or an axe and for a woman, personal orna-ments such as brass armlets and beadwork. These are all said to be imbued with the owner's *sii*. More particularly, a man's *sii* is said to be specially associated with his granary and a woman's with a selec-tion of her choicest calabashes and storage pots. *Sii*, therefore, in one of its aspects, is the focus, one might almost say the medium, of personal identity which is objectively represented in possessions characteristic of a person's sex and status. In accordance with these representations, when a deceased parent or ancestor reveals himself or herself as an agency claiming service from a particular descend-ant, the chosen vehicle is usually some such intimate and character-istic possession, or its replica, owned by the descendant.

I have described elsewhere (Fortes 1949, Ch. 8) the Namoo taboo on a first-born son's looking into his father's granary or wearing his clothes or using his tools or weapons, during his lifetime, and the parallel taboo on a first-born daughter's opening her mother's stor-age pot or wearing her clothing during her lifetime. These are rep-resented as rules for preventing a hostile confrontation between their respective *siis*. It is in keeping also with these beliefs that a feel-ing of strong affinity with another person is accounted for by the mutual attraction of their *siis*; and, by contrast, a marked aversion is accounted for by the revulsion of the *siis*. *Sii*, in this context, reflects traits of character and disposition.

What seems paradoxical about the notion of the *sii* is that it is credited with a kind of existence in its own right, yet must always remain integrally part of the living person. His very life depends on this until death parts them; yet one could describe the *sii* as a spiri-tual double of the person. Thus when discussing dreams, Tallensi give the impression that they think of them as nocturnal encounters, during sleep, with the *siis* of people seen in a dream. But they are generally vague as to how this comes about. It is not quite certain how they conceive of the *sii* of a sleeper detaching itself temporarily from his body or of a deceased person returning and wandering over to the dreamer. It is more as if they think of dreams as a special mode of communication between *siis*. I have never heard Tallensi associate the *sii* with the shadow (*yilenyilug*) – the behaviour of which in light coming from different directions they are well aware of, but to which they seem to attach no mystical significance. But it is tempting to think of the *sii*, as Tallensi regard it, as having a shadow-like connection with the living person.

It is to be noted that the *sii* is there from the moment of birth, and not only in humans but also, as we have seen, in certain species of big game animals of the bush. It seems to be a rule of cardinal importance that a *sii* must have an abode. That is why a human homicide and a slayer of any of these big, *sii*-endowed animals must be ritually purified. But this is only a necessary preliminary. To avoid being persecuted mystically by his victim's *sii*, the slayer must enshrine the victim – accept him as a mystical presence, as Tallensi might put it – and give him ritual service for the rest of his life.

*Sii* and life are obviously closely interlocked. But they are not coterminous even if sometimes equated in reference. Thus the critical change when life ends for the individual is said to be the severance of the bond between his *sii* and his body. Tallensi have no precise doctrines to explain how the change occurs or to account for the post-mortem immortality which their ancestor cult seems, to the outside observer, to presuppose. But some informants conjecture that it must be the *sii* that, in some way not understood by them, persists after death and is eventually re-incorporated in an ancestor shrine. This gives it an abode parallel to the abode it had in the body of its original possessor. A totally disembodied and anonymous *sii* wandering about wraith-like is not conceivable to Tallensi. It would be so anomalous as to be felt to be mystically very dangerous.

I hesitate to attempt a summary definition of the Tallensi notion of the *sii*. The nearest thing would be to say that it is their representation and objectification of the unity and continuity of the individual as he experiences this waking and sleeping, in his relationships with others, in his feelings about his most personal private possessions, in his image of his connection with his forbears and with his expected posterity. As an individual he is identified to himself and to others most commonly by his names or titles and often also by particular ritual observances relating to food or clothing or permitted and prohibited activities that he does not share with others. I return to this topic presently. For the Tallensi, there is no other way open to them to conceptualize this syndrome than in the concrete and mystically interpreted imagery distinctive of their modes of thought.

Assuming lodgement in an individual body, *sii* is also bound up with notions of the self, *meng*. One's tools, weapons, granary, clothes and so forth, my old friend Naabdiya once declared, *ŋgman ni i.meng*, stand for (resemble) yourself. A polite way of saying that someone is ill to say '*u pu so u meng*' he does not own himself. To enquire of someone politely how he is one asks '*i so i meng?*' do you own yourself? that is, are you well. Truth is *yel mengr* a thing in itself; a personal possession is *u meng bon*, his own thing. It is a notion that embraces the whole person, the way he is at a given time and over time.

The picture that emerges can be summed up as follows:

(1) Breath (*vohem*) plus body (*nengbin*) = a living creature (*bonvor*).

(2) Human living creature (*nisaal*) plus soul (*sii*) = the individual. Though he is normally fused with the person the two are quite clearly distinguished by institutional as well as linguistic and customary indices. Expressions such as '*u a nit pam*' which we can translate as 'he is a fine person' as opposed to '*u ka nit*' ('he is not a person'), that is to say, he has discreditable qualities, reflects the disjunction. It is the individual who is credited with qualities like courage (*suhkpeemer*), truth (*yel mengr*), kindness (*sugeru*) and their opposites. It is the individual for whom a whole, healthy body and a long life is the most desired goal.

## IX

Understandably, it is in funeral rites that the intersection of individual, self and person is most dramatically represented. For example, after the burial of a mature person the rite of secreting his 'dirt' (*daghat*) is carried out. A small strip of the deceased's daily clothing, torn off an old loin cloth or a woman's perineal belt, is tied round a piece of reed and ritually secreted in the thatch roof of his or her room. This is the deceased's 'dirt' in a mystical sense because it is imbued with the sweat of his body. Tallensi say it stands for the deceased. Thus it is brought out by a special ritual act to be placed by the diviner's bag when the ancestral agency responsible for the death is divined for. It represents the dead during the interval between the mortuary and the final funeral ceremonies, while, it is said he is straddling the world of the living and the world of the dead 'one leg on this side and one leg on the other'. It is finally disposed of when a collection of his personal utensils, such as dishes for food and water, is ritually destroyed, to dispatch him finally to the ancestors. This clears the way for him to be brought back into his family and lineage in the character of an ancestor, that is, not a human person, but one endowed with mystical and spiritual powers, and therefore with rights to worship and service (Goody, *op. cit.*, pp. 58–60).

It is significant that only the intimate, private, bodily exudations – sweat, sexual fluids and bodily odour – are regarded as mystical 'dirt' distinctive of the individual. These are all, it will be noted, involuntary exudations through the skin and the reproductive (i.e. 'good') orifices. Other secretions such as saliva, tears, nasal mucus, are not 'dirt' in this sense. The excretory products (urine and faeces) are 'dirt' in a mundane and profane sense only, comparable to the commonplace sense of the English word 'dirt'. There is mystical 'good "dirt"' distinctive of its individual possessor and mundane 'bad "dirt"' to be disposed of outside the home. The head and facial hair and the nail parings of important chiefs are also associated with their mystical dirt and must not be thrown away, as in a commoner's case, in their lifetime. Only chiefs are believed to be vulnerable to sorcery through these items, commoners are not. Mystical 'dirt' is innocuous where there is mutual trust, especially in the procreative relations of husband and wife. It is dangerous where there is enmity as between an adulterer and the woman's husband. Contact with an individual's mystical 'dirt' can be fatal to his enemy, and it is dangerous also if the individual has an incurable disease. Leprosy, for example, is believed to be transmitted contagiously by the sweat of the sufferer.

When we turn from the individual to the person, the critical factor is ancestry operating at the two limits of the life cycle, birth and death. To become a person, the individual human (*nisaal*) must, I repeat, be normally born of a properly married mother in his father's house, as a legitimate member of his father's patrilineage and clan. He must, then, remain alive long enough to achieve personhood and this is believed to be ensured by the benevolence of his ancestral guardian (*segher*). Given life, the individual gradually appropriates to himself, and exhibits in his social relations and activities, the statuses, offices, and positions in society he is born to achieve. Totemistic and other ritual observances such as the specifications of familial position by the avoidances between parent and first born by the same sex are the most important media for this. To achieve full personhood with maximum jural and ritual autonomy, prototypically as realized by the male head of a family, occupying his own house, vested with unencumbered ownership of productive resources, with jural control over female and filial dependants, and with ritual responsibility on behalf of himself and his dependants in relation to the ancestors and other supernatural agencies – to achieve this takes a lifetime. It is indeed not finally proven to have succeeded until it is confirmed in the funeral divination at the time of his death.

Tallensi emphasize that every life history is unique in significant ways, being subject to both unforseeable hazards and unexpected rewards. Therefore what an individual makes of his life depends in the last resort on his inborn *Destiny*, his *Yin* (Fortes 1959).

Given a propitious Destiny, and good relationships with other ancestral and supernatural agencies, a man will have children and grandchildren, well-being and prosperity, and reach old age and eldership before death overtakes him. This marks the acme of personhood. The succession of the parental and filial generations has a crucial role. The Tallensi perceive and experience the succession of the generations as loaded with inevitable ambivalence. As I have already noted, no man can attain jural and ritual autonomy until his father is dead. This is dramatized among Namoos at a father's funeral by the ritual of dressing the eldest son in the tunic of his father, turned inside out, and with mock force compelling him to look into his father's granary (cf. Fortes 1949, Ch. 8). The combination of mutual dependence and rivalry in the relations of parents and children is rationalized in their theory of how Destiny works. Thus it is said that the Destinies of a man and of his firstborn son, who is of course his prospective heir, are antagonistic to one another. As his son advances to maturity under the protection of *his* Destiny, so the father becomes increasingly vulnerable and in need of *his* Destiny's support. The prescribed avoidances between them prevent a mortal clash of their Destinies. Strangely enough, it would be unthinkable, and regarded as equivalent to the sin of parricide for a father's death to be attributed to the power of his son's Destiny. The dilemma resolved in these notions is an obvious and universal one. The individual's time span, as it is lived out in his own life, is an indispensable component of, yet in conflict with, the collective time span of the lineage and the clan. The individual's life cycle is indispensable for the task of social reproduction in lineage and clan; but however he clings to it – chiefly by proper ritual attention to his ancestors – he must accept the inevitability of declining powers and ultimately of death to make place for the next generation. Fortunately for the Tallensi, and consistently with the relative stability sought for and maintained in their traditional social system, there is a way out. The parental authority that must be relinquished and superseded in life is transposed, by the very fact of the death that overturns it, into the transcendant power and authority of the ancestor. The deposed parents get their own back, so to speak, as transposed ancestors (Fortes 1959).

## X

Against this background it is understandable why, paradoxical as it may seem, the conclusive test of genuine personhood is the kind of death a person achieves. Regardless of how one has lived, one must end life in a proper and legitimate way, appropriate to one's status, and one's attainment of genuine personhood must be retrospectively validated by the attainment of ancestorhood.

What, then, are the marks of a proper and normal human death? A Tallensi friend once summed it up pithily in the comment: *Nit pu kpiit wari; bagher nkuut*, a person does not die for nothing (i.e. casually), an ancestral agent (must) kill him. My friend was contrasting the death of a person with that of a mere animal. Likewise, just as a proper birth should take place in the father's house, under the spiritual aegis of the father's ancestors, so a normal death should take place in the deceased's own home under the same spiritual aegis,

thus completing the circle. Nowadays, when it happens not infrequently that people living and working far away from home die in
strange places, a special atonement sacrifice has to be made to the
ancestors.

Catastrophic deaths are, therefore, regarded as abnormal or, as
Tallensi say, bad deaths (*kum biog*). The extreme examples are
death by smallpox, by drowning or by suicide. The victim is not
given a normal burial at home, or a normal funeral. His body is
interred outside the community, as if he were not a person in it. He is
thrust out of clan and community and in theory is debarred from
joining the ancestors. Even if he leaves descendants he cannot, it is
said, achieve ancestorhood. His name is erased from the social
memory by his never being given the spiritual guardianship of any of
his descendants. Retrospectively, someone dying thus must have
fallen short somewhere of genuine personhood. It is significant however that actual cases are extremely difficult to trace and there are indications of inconsistent attitudes among different people. There is
evidence that the actual descendants of a victim may, privately, and
in indirect ways, acknowledge and set up such a forbear as a
worshipped ancestor.

As has already been indicated, a normal death must be attribu-
table to an ancestral or other mystical agency – the very agencies
that are supposed to reward loyal ritual service and good conduct
with blessings and watchful care. Two revealing cases observed in
the field in 1934–7 bring home the point. The first was that of a
childless young man who had been a strapping and vigorous farmer
with what seemed like a bright future ahead of him. During a stay in
Southern Ghana he contracted sleeping sickness. He returned home
sick and slowly wasted away, as Tallensi put it, until death supervened. At the divination session it emerged that the supernatural
agency responsible for his death was his Bad Predestiny (*Noor Yin*).
This signified that before his birth he had declared in Heaven that he
did not want parents or possessions of any kind if or when he would
be born alive. Early in his illness efforts to exorcise the Bad *Yin* had
failed and now it had slain him. He had been human, he had been a
named individual with an admirable character. But having originally, pre-natally, rejected the essential primary attributes of personhood i.e. parentage and its complement, parenthood, as well as
the most significant signs of maturity, i.e. marriage and possessions,

it was inevitable that he should die thus, long before he could have reached full personhood. From the point of view of his bereaved family, deep as was the shock of his death, incidentally looking back over the failure of their efforts to find a cure for his illness, it was a comforting finding.

The second case was that of an old man who died wifeless and childless. The diviner's diagnosis was an unusual one. Heaven (*Nayin*) was revealed to have decided to end his life. In other words, unlike a normal person, he had simply died of natural causes. I was puzzled by this, for he had lived what had seemed to me an ordinary sort of life, until a friend explained it to me privately. He had been a slave (*da'aber*) bought in his very early youth, at least fifty years earlier, by the then Chief. He had lived in the family, ostensibly as a full member of it, but in fact attached to it only by fictitious kinship. Strictly speaking, therefore, he had no ancestors in the community and had therefore never succeeded in acquiring the fundamental credentials of personhood, that is to say, legitimate parentage in a lineage. Had he left a son, especially if the mother was a legitimate member of a Tallensi lineage, this might have been the starting point for an attached lineage (Fortes 1945, Chapter V). But dying thus, without ancestry or progeny, he had proved to be, retrospectively, not a genuine person but a kind of *kolkpaarəg*, who had, as the Tallensi saying goes, 'returned to the hills' (*du zoor*) at his death. Here we see that a human individual can have achieved all the external qualifications of personhood. He might have shown admirable qualities of character such as wisdom, courage, truthfulness and industry. He might well, therefore, have had the reputation of being a 'fine person' (*nit pam*). But he cannot be authentically a person without the basic jural credentials that are conferred only by right of birth as a member of a lineage and clan. There are, to be sure, indirect ways of getting this status through maternal connections, but they are all linked up with the basic patrilineal principle. There is no way to circumvent the limiting condition of kinship credentials for the individual to be a complete person. This is the implication of the phrase *ti nit* (our person), meaning a member of our family or lineage or clan, which one often hears. As I have mentioned, a woman, though exogamously and virilocally married, never loses her membership of her natal lineage. She has what amounts to a dual social personality as wife on the one hand and daughter on the other. This is nicely dramatized at the time of her death. A woman, in effect, receives two funerals, one in her husband's community where she is buried and, later on, a short symbolic one at her father's house. This is why a woman passes on to her descendants the matrilateral connections with her natal lineage that are the basis of the moral claims and sentiments of amity that bind mother's brother and sister's son in a classical patrilineal avunculate.

## XI

Virtuous and admirable traits of character certainly enhance one's standing as a person; they are not, however, as I have noted, critical or even necessary for the attainment of personhood. Similarly, a bad character or vicious habits cannot deprive a person of his lineage status and of the consequential jural and ritual attributes that make him a person. A man may be, as Tallensi put it, *bon wari* (a good for nothing), a thief or an adulterer, incurring censure or even contempt; he cannot upon this account be deprived of his jural status or the citizenship in the community that goes with it.

Here again the final test is whether or not he is transposed after death into an ancestor. To put this the other way round, only a full person is qualified to become an ancestor. And this, too, is regardless of his individual character and disposition. Provided only that he leaves sons, he can join the ancestors (*paa banam*) after death. In other words, as long as there is a successor to perpetuate his status by descent and kinship, he can become an ancestor amongst all the other ancestors. Ancestors and descendants are, as it were, united in complementary continuity, laced with opposition, as if they were mirror images of one another. The structural embodiment of this continuity is the patrilineal lineage. The lineage is conceptualized and represented in its genealogy and in the ancestor cult as the perpetuation of a single founding ancestor, that is to say, of a single person, and this is what makes it logical to accept the lineage as a unitary collective person in jural, political and ritual action. This image is sustained by, and in turn sustains the role of the ancestors as essentially the projections of the jural and moral authority vested in parents in relation to their children (Fortes 1961). Though the lineage emerges as a collective person primarily in its external relations to other like persons, it is important to bear in mind that its members must and do also visualize it as such from within. They are made aware of this in the ritual practices of the ancestor cult and through the medium of the totemistic and similar observances that distinguish lineage from lineage.

It is of interest, in this connection, to recall that a child cannot be a full person. This is sometimes emphasized by pointing out that a child cannot be required or expected to conform to totemistic observances until it becomes capable of the responsibility to herd goats and sheep and to help in other simple economic tasks. According to my observations this would be around the age of seven to eight years. Here the criterion of maturity counts. A pre-adolescent boy, even if he is fatherless, would still be thought of as only incipiently a person. The criterion of responsibility comes out in another context. A madman is not regarded as a person, in the full sense. Like a child, he is said to 'have no sense' (*u ka yam*) which means, in this context, no sense of right and wrong, no capacity for responsibility. The notion of *yam* deserves further comment. According to context it can be glossed as wisdom or good judgment, but it also implies a sense of responsibility and of reality, and an understanding of customary norms. In part, it is supposed to grow with experience of life, but it is also, in part, thought of as an inborn trait. A mature person should have *yam* and the wiser, more responsible he is, the higher the esteem in which he will be held; but though *yam* enhances, deficiency in this respect does not extinguish personhood, as its ostensible absence in a madman does.

I might add that *yam* is located inside the body, *pooni*, in the region of the abdomen. This is where thought and imagination (*poteem*) as well as moral dispositions like goodness and kindness (*popelem*) or its contrary, wickedness (*potoog*), are deemed to reside. The physiological basis of these ideas is indicated by the general term, *poo*, for all abdominal illnesses. Furthermore, *yam* can suffer not only deterioration, as in madness, but acute disturbance, as in terror or despair when it is said *u yam akme*, his *yam* leapt up distraught. (Whether or not this is associated with the bile, as M. Cartry states, is difficult to be certain about. I was unable to find out for certain whether or not the Tallensi word *yam* for the bile is the same morpheme as their word for wisdom, or rather a homonym.) However, while I am on this theme I might note that in contrast with *poo*, the abdominal region, the head, *zug*, is regarded as the seat of luck (*zugsong*, good luck or *zugbiog*, bad luck); illness, if accompanied by headache is 'head illness'. To the best of my knowledge no functions are attributed to the brain, *zopoot*. The heart, *suh* or *sensuh*, is believed to be the seat of fortitude (*suhkpemer*) and courage and their opposites, fear and cowardice as well as of a wide range of emotional states and dispositions, such as mercy (*sugeru*), repose (*sumahem*), chagrin (*suhkpeleg*) anger (*suur*). In all these respects individuals are expected to be as different as they are in appearance, in their habits and in their likes and dislikes.

I have noted that a madman stops being a person. This needs qualification. Life and the soul are at some risk where there is severe emotional disturbance or disruption of personality. But the connection is indirect. Madness does not rob a person of them. What is more important, it does not extinguish credentials of status by kinship and lineage or generation. But above all, a man might well have achieved a high level of personhood before his unpropitious Destiny or offended ancestors permitted madness to overtake him. He (or she) might have had, and might still have, a spouse and children, not to speak of possessions and property appropriate to his or her age. He might thus, at his death, qualify for ancesterhood and so be recognized as having been at one time a full person. In brief, a madman is not a non-person, like an animal or thing, he is human and, as it were, a fragmented and marginal person. That is why he cannot be thrown out but must be cared for by his kinsfolk at home like any ordinary member of a family (Fortes and Mayer 1966). Similar considerations apply to the very old. A person who becomes senile is treated like a child who is not capable of responsibility, but with the respect and motions of compliance that recognize his seniority and the authority this entitles him to.

The rule for the elderly is that once a person has attained a given degree of personhood he cannot be deprived of it during his lifetime. It is not without significance that, whereas mental infirmity diminishes personhood, physical disease does not. For example, his body (*nengbin*) which is the indispensable vessel of his personhood, may deteriorate (*sagham*) and wither away to death owing to a disease like leprosy (*kunkomer*), which is known to be incurable. But he cannot be disowned by his family or deprived of any of his rights and capacities as a person. Modern drugs have enabled leprosy to be successfully controlled in Northern Ghana. Before the war this treatment was not available, but lepers lived at home with their families even though, as I have noted, there was some understanding that it was a contagious disease. Not being catastrophic, like smallpox, death by leprosy was not classified as a bad death. Nevertheless, a leper was buried separately as if to obviate magical contagion. By contrast, a person can endanger his personhood by acts of sacrilege (such as shedding human blood by homicide on the earth) or by mortal sins (such a fratricide) or even lesser wrongdoing such as adultery with a father's wife. Such transgressions destroy kinship amity and the community of worship in the ancestor cult that goes with it. Unless properly atoned for, the outcome is believed to be a childless and forlorn death which means, of course, eventual extinction. Bad deaths carry a worse taint implying as they do transgression on the part of the victim, or of someone responsible for him, that cannot be atoned for. Behind such a death may well be the person's evil Destiny which has prevented his fulfilling his potentialities as a person, or else an irreparable breach of relationship with the ancestral guardian of his life. The supposedly inborn predisposition figured in the notion of Destiny can be the enemy of the long processes of development that lead to personhood.

## XII

So far, I have been concerned principally with the objective features and characteristics of the person, individual or collective, as these are presented to an observer. In the language of Mauss and Proust my concern has been with aspects and dimensions of the *personne morale*. This is evident if we remind ourselves that no man can choose his parents or which lineage he is born into or even, according to Tallensi thought, the kind of Destiny that will direct the course of his life. Conversely, he cannot renounce his lineage membership yet remain in the community as a full citizen. Converts to Christianity nowadays stop taking an active part in ancestor worship; they cannot marry in breach of the laws of lineage exogamy. There are other such similarly imposed limiting factors though Tallensi culture has always been tolerant of deviations from conventional norms and practices that do not threaten other people's conformity and well-being. A man can enrich himself by enterprise and hard work, winning wealth and esteem, but this does not make him a person in the full sense of the concept, if for example he has no children. A man is a person *inter alia* more by reason of the place he is fortunate enough to hold in the succession and alternation of the generations that make up the continuity of lineage and clan, than by reason of his own efforts.

This brings up the question I raised at the outset, as to how the individual knows himself to be the person he is made to be by what amounts, in the last resort, to the combination of the unconscious forces of Destiny and the fiat of society. And likewise, how does he show to others that he is the person he is supposed to be, that he has not simply put on the mask but has taken upon himself the identity it proclaims? For it is surely only by appropriating to himself his socially given personhood that he can exercise the qualities, the rights, the duties and the capacities that are distinctive of it.

These questions are difficult to deal with and in many respects lie outside the range of an ethnographic account. They take us back to the facts of names and titles and other insignia of who and what one is, what is one's due from society and what is due from one to society. Tallensi have no discriminative facial cicatrizations other than the slash on the cheek (*ben*) they share with the tribes adjacent to them. Nor do they have other bodily marks distinguishing clan from clan or person from person. It is primarily through moral, jural and ritual rules and observances and by means of special apparel and other distinctive possessions, corresponding to sex, age, rank, office, etc., that they declare themselves as persons.

I have given some account of Tallensi naming customs elsewhere (Fortes 1955) and will only say here that it is common for a person to have two names. The first is a public name that usually records some state of mind, or some happening, at the time of the person's birth, that seemed significant then to the head of his or her family or marked an important stage of his life cycle. The first child born to a Chief of Tongo after his accession is always named *Soghat*, which signifies 'hidden away', an allusion to the fact that the Chief was formerly hidden in the obscurity of ordinary life but has now come into the open in triumph. My friend *Onmara* was so named because at the time of his birth his father was a poor young man and declared that whether a man has any property (*on mar siel*) at all or none (*on ka siel*) does not matter. As long as he is a man of good character people will hold him in esteem. A man who becomes a Chief or a

Tendaana assumes a new name by which he will thereafter be known. The late Chief of Tongo assumed the name *Na Leeb Salema*, 'will become gold' signifying that as a commoner he had been no better than a stone but had now become like gold.

The second name is a private one often known only to members of the family. It is a name referring to the bearer's *segher*, his ancestor guardian, and it registers his unique and specific dependence on that ancestor for the preservation of his life. It is by this name that a person is exhorted to depart and join his ancestors when the severance offerings are made to him at the end of his funeral, and it is by this name, not her married name, that a dead woman is given a second funeral at her father's house. His public name declares the significance of a person's birth as an event in the life history and career of his parental family, the private name marks him as an individual distinguished from other individuals in his lineage and family by the specific surveillance of the ancestors to whose guardianship he is committed. It is as the bearer of this private name that his Destiny shapes the course of his life and it is in this capacity that he appropriates to himself the roles and the incidents of status that make him a person, though he exhibits his personhood to the outside world as bearer of his public name. The unique individuality implied in this name is often symbolized in the taboos related to dress or occupation or food laid on him by his Destiny or other ancestral agencies to which I refer later.

I have earlier remarked on the differences of clothing that customarily distinguish males from females, and maidens from matrons. However, the significance of names, apparel and other external signs of personhood is most clearly shown in connection with the politico-ritual offices of Chiefship (*Naam*) and of the Custodian of the Earth (*Tendaana*). The rites of installation to these offices show up sharply how society confers and confirms distinctive forms of personhood. On the other side, taking on and exercising the roles of office and the prescribed patterns of behaviour and observance that go with them show up how individuals appropriate to themselves the attributes and capacities of personhood.

When holders of such high offices are selected and installed they become new persons, transformed as it were from ordinary citizens into their new status (Chapter 5). A conspicuous element in these installation ceremonies is the public robing of the new Chief in his tunic of Chiefship and the girding of the new Tendaana with the antelope skins that Tendaanas must wear. It is then that they announce the new names they will take and will subsequently be known by in their lifetime and to their descendants. From now on they must carry themselves with gravity even in the privacy of their home and never appear in public without the garb and other insignia of their office. Most important of all are the new ritual observances in the form of taboos and injunctions that devolve on them by reason of their office. There are new food taboos symbolizing their separation from the mundane life of ordinary people, taboos restricting their movements to keep them from contamination by death and misfortune, new injunctions concerning their duties to offer sacrifice and libation to ancestors and the Earth in order to ensure the well-being of the community, and the prescriptions of moral conduct and social behaviour calculated to emphasize the authority and the ritual responsibilities now vested in them. They are thus constantly reminded of their duties and their responsibilities and thus also are they constantly declaring to society who they are and receiving in return recognition of their office and its significance from society.

Applying this analysis to ordinary people, I believe it is through such institutions as their totemistic observances, as I have previously pointed out, that they are constantly reminded and made aware of who and what they are as persons, of the sources of these attributes in their descent group membership and other kinship connections, of their dependence on their ancestors, of the rights and duties, both secular and ritual that bind them. The representation and the implementation of personhood in all its aspects, in these ways, are carried through with great consistency in Tallensi culture. Every conceptually and institutionally distinguished constituent of the complex whole that is a person is identified to the individual by this means. As I mentioned earlier, a man's Destiny ancestor might impose special obligations on him, for example, to wear only white garments or to give up farming on pain of sickness or even death if he refuses to comply. Particular ritual observances are associated with parenthood and filiation, as we have already seen. Connections with matrilateral kin are similarly marked for each individual. The totemistic observances I have previously referred to play an important part in this connection. Conformity to the taboos on killing and

eating animals of the species respected for having miraculously protected the founding ancestor of a clan or lineage (cf. Fortes 1945,
Ch. 8) is collectively enjoined but must be individually observed.
This holds also for such associated injunctions as the lineage oaths
and forms of funeral ritual. As with the obligations imposed by their
office on a Chief or a Tendaana, so with these rules. Adherence to
them is as much a matter of the individual conscience as of social
pressure. This, at bottom, is the basis of each individual's knowledge of who he is and where he belongs as a person identified by kinship, descent and status. It is the principal medium for appropriating
to himself — for internalizing we might say — the capacity for exercising the rights and duties, the roles and all the proper patterns of
behaviour, that pertain to his status as a person. It is the medium,
also, by which he at the same time exhibits himself as a person to
others (Chapter 6). When young children and madmen are said to be
devoid of sense, this refers primarily to their not being expected to
have the understanding to conform to these prescriptions. It is a con-
cession to their marginal personhood. Thus it devolves upon parents
and other siblings, true and classificatory, to guard them against
inadvertent wrongdoing in these matters.

## XIII

Let me try to recapitulate briefly my discussion of this topic. We can
put it this way: observance of prohibitions and injunctions relating
to the killing and eating of animals, to distinctions of dress, to
speech and etiquette, to a wide range of ritual norms, to the jural
regulations concerning marriage, property, office, inheritance and
succession, play a key part in the identification of persons. Persons
are kept aware of who they are and where they fit into society by criteria of age, sex, and descent, and by other indices of status, through
acting in accordance with these norms. By these actions and forms
of conduct they, at the same time, show to others who they are and
where they fit into society. Self-awareness, or more exactly self discrimination in contraposition to others, must make use of the externally distinctive patterns of conduct and observance that serve for
the public identification of persons and groups. Pride of lineage, reinforced by the parity of status among all Tallensi clans acknowledged by such institutional arrangements as the balanced

distribution of offices and ritual duties in the Great Festivals (Fortes 1945) conduces to this even nowadays.

Individual and collective are not mutually exclusive but are rather two sides of the same structural complex. The scheme of identification employed for individual persons is the same scheme of identification as serves to distinguish lineages and clans. The mechanics of this pattern is obvious if we bear in mind that the individual person is constantly obliged to be aware of himself and to present himself as a member and representative of such a collective unit. The first question a stranger is asked is 'where do you come from and of whose house are you a member?' In ceremonial situations, such as funerals, sacrifices, and the rituals of the Great Festivals, those attending perform their duties and receive their portions of the libations and the sacrificial animals primarily in their representative capacity as members of lineages and clans and politico-ritual groups. Indeed, no matter what kind of transactions an individual or a group is engaged in, be it, for instance, over marriage and bride price, or at the other extreme, over the installation of a matrilateral ancestor shrine, the context of the collective interest is always present. This is patent, of course, whenever the ancestors have to be invoked either in secular terms of genealogical reference or in ritual terms. But the idea that a lineage is a collective person because it is the perpetuation of its founding ancestor in each of his descendants, is seen in other ways too. It is vividly shown in ceremonial and political situations when the head of a lineage or clan is apt to speak and act as if he were the founding ancestor himself, reincarnated or rather immortally present. It is a characteristic expression of the principle that these descent-based collectivities are perpetual corporate bodies, replicating on the collective level the model of the person on the individual level.

To conclude this account I must mention one component, alluded to earlier *en passant* that particularly emphasizes the consistency with which every critical feature of the social structure is reflected in the definition of the person. Side by side with the patrilineal principle, the Tallensi attach special value to the parallel uterine relationship of *soog*, that links descendants in the female line from a common ancestress usually four or five generations back (Fortes 1949, pp. 31ff.). *Soog* kin do not, like patrilineal kin, live together in one clan locality. They tend to be widely scattered. *Soog* kinship does not confer politico-jural or ritual status, nor does it establish membership in corporate descent groups with rights to office and property, in the same way as patrilineal kinship does. *Soog* kinship is based on the extension, outside the framework of the lineage and clan and in complementary opposition to it, of the elementary tie of matrifiliation. It creates purely interpersonal bonds of self-contained, mutual trust and amity, free of jural or ritual constraints. *Soog* ancestresses cannot, by virtue of uterine kinship only, become worshipped ancestresses.

This irreducibly moral relationship is symbolically represented in the belief in the hereditary transmission of the trait of the clairvoyant eye (*nif*). Tallensi say of a *soog* kinsman or kinswoman, 'if he sees, so do I, because we have one mother'. This seeing is a presumed mystical faculty, which is of itself morally neutral. The Tallensi do not have a belief in the 'evil eye' – the comparable belief among them is in the 'evil mouth'. The mystically clairvoyant eyes carries with it, however, a different potentiality for ill-doing. This is the potentiality for witchcraft (*soi*), which therefore is also an inborn trait passing from mother to child by heredity. But witchcraft is almost as marginal to the Tallensi scheme of mystical thought as the belief in ghosts. There is no theory of how it works, and cases have always been extremely rare. The stereotypical case is that of a woman distraught at the death of a young child accusing a co-wife of causing this by her witchcraft, in a manner reminiscent of such accusations in some other African patrilineal family systems. Ordeal by stabbing with a poisoned arrow might formerly have been restored to. The issue is thought of as one of extreme personal rancour and jealousy such as may be expected of rival co-wives in a crisis.

What is most significant is that witchcraft cannot ever be legitimately identified as the cause of death by the due process of divination. This puts it on a par with aggressive medicine, not with the authoritative intervention of ancestors. It is simply the obverse of the prescriptive altruism and love *soog* kin must have for one another, directed away from the soog-by-birth (who cannot injure one another by witchcraft) to the pseudo-soog of co-wives. It is said that the clairvoyant eye can detect witchcraft in non-*soog*, but as the possession of these traits is unknowable to its bearers or others until they become manifest, it is all entirely hypothetical. It is a purely symbolical way of identifying the unique bonds of matri-siblingship regarded as carried on, ideally, forever by uterine descent. It stands for bonds of pure disinterested altruism as opposed to the jurally and ritually sanctioned bonds of patriliny. It stands for the idea taken for granted as absolutely given and beyond any questioning, that motherhood is the source of elementary relationships of unconstrained mutuality between persons. These are assumed to exist and to be binding absolutely, in their own right, by virtue of inborn dispositions that are ultimately inexplicable and would only be flouted by perverted people. Tallensi enjoy and are adepts in discussing their social customs, their religious beliefs and practices and the structure of their society at all levels. But they fight shy of metaphysical exegeses. I have never succeeded in eliciting from a Tallensi friend any exegesis on the subject of *soog* relationships. But there is a special glow on the face and in the eyes of a person introducing a *soog* kinsman, a special tone of pride and pleasure in describing the significance of this relationship that only its prototype, the relations of mother and child, and no other relationship, evokes. For this is the only relationship between persons that is free of all external social constraints, including those that identify persons as persons by their descent and standing. It connects *individual with individual* by a mystical bond which they have to accept as given and which transcends and opposes the diversification of *person from person* by other social and cultural criteria.

I have confined myself to an ethnographical analysis in the foregoing account of the Tallensi notion of the person. I should like to finish off by adding a few general remarks. First, let me emphasize the basic realism of Tallensi culture. By this I mean that for them the external world has a permanence and reality that is not subject to control by the will or the wishes of mankind. This applies not only to the order of nature but in an important sense also to the social order. The centre of gravity of all the constraints, mystical and material, that shape a person's life are felt to lie outside him – in the mystical powers of Earth and ancestors and Fate, in the determinance of descent and kinship and so forth. Personhood comes thus to be in its essence externally oriented. Self awareness means, in the first place, awareness of oneself as a *personne morale* rather than as an idiosyncratic individual. The moral conscience is externally validated, being vested, ultimately, in the ancestors, on the other side of the ritual curtain. The soul, image as it is of the focal element of individuality, is projected on to material objects that will outlast the living person. Person is perceived as a microcosm of the social order, incorporating its distinctive principles of structure and norms of value and implementing a pattern of life that finds satisfaction in its consonance with the constraints and realities (as defined by Tallensi culture) of the social and material world. This is very different, it seems to me, from some other West African societies where the person is conceptualized as incarnating a mythological genesis of culture and humanity and where he is supposed to implement a pattern of life modelled on that mythological design.

# Endpiece: sacrifice among theologians and anthropologists

What is it that anthropologists and theologians have in common, by way of discipline or by way of 'problematic', that makes possible an exchange between them; and, contrariwise, in what ways do their interests and techniques of inquiry diverge? Michael Bourdillon (1980) offers a balanced answer to these questions, one that only someone as equally at home in both camps as he is could provide. Is there anything left for a mere, one-sided social anthropologist to add? I am sometimes impressed by the way in which the theologians and the anthropologists argue from a common ground, and at other times struck by the divergencies, even the contradictions, between their approaches and aims.

No topic in the field of their shared concern with religious institutions and values brings out these alternatives so clearly as does sacrifice. For there is no ritual institution as central to all but a minority of both the scriptural and the non-scriptural religions of mankind. And the alternatives emerge in the ways all the key concepts common to both disciplines are used – concepts such as 'symbol', 'myth', 'belief', 'meaning' etc. Not that there is unanimity of usage or definition in either camp; but granted the grey areas of ambiguity on both sides, the differences are clear enough. They are frankly indicated by Bourdillon, most precisely when he contrasts what he describes as the 'embarrassed silence' of anthropologists on 'the relationship between the effects of rituals and what participants expect to achieve through them', with how theologians regard this relationship. 'Theologians' he continues 'are part of the tradition they study and must be convinced that their rituals have the effects that they want them to have.' In other words, I would suggest, being in part actors in their own religious systems, theologians must *believe*, whereas anthropologists, I would argue, who are primarily observers, cannot but be *agnostic* if they want to achieve objectivity.

To make my point clearer, let me look back thirty years to a celebrated lecture by Evans-Pritchard (1950). Inaugurating in 1948 the annual lecture series at Exeter College, Oxford dedicated to the memory of Rector R. R. Marett, he bluntly accused his fellow anthropologists and even the founding fathers of being incapable of understanding the religions of non-western people. The reason, he claimed, was that they were themselves irreligious or even atheistic. It was a strange shaft to launch in a lecture commemorating the scholar who particularly emphasized the 'sacramental' features of primitive religion – and who, incidentally, was the only British anthropologist cited by the theologian Rudolf Otto in his influential book *Das Heilige* (English translation by J. W. Harvey, 1950); and, let me add that Otto's concept of the numinous as the awe-evoking character of the Holy, appealed in its turn to Marett and indeed met with approval from Evans-Pritchard (1956, p. 8).

With few exceptions the anthropological community rejected Evans-Pritchard's accusation. Had Tylor, Frazer, Marett, Malinowski, Radcliffe-Brown, and Evans-Pritchard himself, in his already famous book on Zande witchcraft, not made fundamental contributions to the study of the religions of mankind? Tylor, indeed, writing at a time when the intellectual climate was still dominated by the bitter Victorian confrontation between the world view of science and the teachings of theology, ends his great book on *Primitive Culture* with a call for co-operation between anthropologists and theologians (1871, Vol. 2, pp. 449ff.).

But there was and there remains a point to Evans-Pritchard's complaint. There is no doubt that most of our illustrious predecessors and we, their successors, were and are, to say the least, agnostic in their and our *professional* attitudes to religion. Moreover, I doubt if any of our famous forebears referred to above, were believing adherents of any theistic, animistic, or other form of cult ordered to doctrines of supernatural powers. And this is certainly the case also with many if not most social anthropologists of Evans-Pritchard's generation. Nor are anthropologists alone in this. The same can be said of sociologists and psychologists engaged in the study of religious systems. It is significant that Durkheim and Mauss, those eloquent lapsed Jewish social philosophers, and their followers, were frankly atheistic; yet it was to their studies of primitive religion that Evans-Pritchard himself turned with admiration for sociological inspiration.

Let me emphasize that what I am here concerned with is not the personal religious beliefs and commitments of anthropologists, but the standpoint that I think is required of them for a professionally correct approach to their task. Nor do I think that this represents a peculiar or sinister value bias. What I am saying is that it is only to the extent to which an anthropologist is able to maintain an agnostic point of view about the beliefs and practices he is examining that he can achieve objectivity in his understanding and presentation of these beliefs and practices. And objectivity, in the sense of analysis and description that are accepted as valid by reason of their compatibility with comparative evidence and the independent observations and analyses of other qualified enquirers in the same field, is, surely, a *sine qua non* for all anthropological scholarship.

This, as I see it, is where the critical distinction lies between anthropologists and theologians – or rather, between an anthropological approach and a theological approach. For, as Bourdillon reminds us, there are theologians who can and do adopt a specifically anthropological approach in their studies even of their own religious beliefs and institutions. (A fine example is that of the late E. O. James.) And more specific, of course, to our interests, are the contributions of such famous 'applied theologians' as Codrington, Junod, Edwin Smith, Westermann, Bryant and many other missionaries whose ethnographic researches have so incomparably enriched our study. Conversely, there are anthropologists, *pace* Evans-Pritchard, who themselves belong to theistic or other supernaturally-directed cults, and who frankly approach their studies from the standpoint of their religious values. And as for the agnostic anthropologists, borrowing concepts and categories from theological scholarship is as common among them as the reverse influence is among theologians.

Evans-Pritchard, as it happens, nicely documents the distinction I have in mind. In his study of Zande witchcraft (1937), the stance which gives this great work its scholarly and scientific authority is that of an agnostic observer judging Zande beliefs and practices by criteria of Western, scientifically-shaped concepts of causality, human nature, and natural laws. In contrast, in *Nuer Religion*, the work which inspired the renewed attention of anthropologists to the institution of sacrifice, his position is almost the reverse. The brilliant ethnography is organized in terms of a model derived from such theoretical sociologists as Hubert and Mauss. But it is also shot through with indirect witness to Evans-Pritchard's personal theistic religious commitment, as Horton and Finnegan suggest (1973, pp.45–6) and with evidence, in his terminology of description and his interpretative scheme, of his borrowings from theological and Biblical scholarship. It is of interest to contrast Monica Wilson's studies of Nyakyusa witchcraft and religion (1951; 1957). The Christian principles and ideals for which she is well known are not obtruded into these studies but are drawn upon in separate, deliberately evaluated contexts (as e.g. 1971).

Let us look more closely at the distinction I am making. Logically speaking, from a theological point of view, there can be no questioning the reality or the actuality of the existence 'out there', independently of the existence of Mankind, of such supernatural power or powers in any religious system. This holds for all religious systems, not only for 'revealed' religions of Judaeo-Christian origin. Such postulates (as an observer would put it) though not always in the form of a conception of a single, omnipotent, omniscient and absolute creator/deity or cosmic force, have been reported for most human societies. Whether or not the Nuer conception of *Kwoth*, or the Dogon *Amma*, or the Akan *Nyame*, and other such African concepts can properly be identified with the Judaeo-Christian concept of God, is not the significant issue. What I am getting at is the assumption, from the actor's point of view, the faith, that the supernatural powers or agencies postulated in his religious system, be they or it deity, divinity, ancestor spirits, nature spirits etc., do really exist, and the corollary is that they can be known and experienced cognitively, affectively, instrumentally, and morally by virtue, *inter alia*, of their (its, his) intervention in human affairs. The Nuer claim to know that *Kwoth* exists because they get ill, among other things, and according to them they are able to show, for instance by divination as well as by the effects of their rituals, that is due to the intervention of *Kwoth* in their life. The Tallensi reason in the same way about their ancestors; and Tikopia, like many other peoples, including some with scriptural religions, claim to have evidence of the reality of their divinities or their ancestors when mediums or seers become possessed.

'If no effect of God can ever be discerned then in effect God is nowhere ...' comments Bowker (1973, p. 84) in the course of his profound and learned study of the very issue I am here considering; and he adds that 'all theistic traditions have at some point suggested discernible (claimed) effects of God ...' A Nuer or Dogon or Akan theologian would agree with reference to the supernatural powers they acknowledge. And they would associate with this the same implications as arise in scriptural religions, namely, that there is an inescapable obligation on the part of mankind to show their sense of their dependence on these supernatural powers by their conduct, and especially in the performance of rituals which, in their eyes, testify to the existence and the powers of these agencies.

It is not relevant to my purpose to go into questions of a general theoretical kind regarding the nature of ritual. I use the term to refer to any customary spoken and/or acted out pattern of behaviour recognized by the actors as directed towards or referring to the supernatural, or as I prefer to say occult powers and agencies (Chapter 1). I see ritual as from the actor's point of view a customary activity of necessity specialized for the task of relating Man's cognizable world of tangible, ponderable, visible and controllable mundane existence – the profane world of Durkheimian sociology – to the intangible, imponderable, invisible, uncontrollable, unrecognizable world of non-material powers and forces assumed and believed by him to exist in a different, not otherwise accessible sphere of reality – the Durkheimian sacred. And sacrifice is such a ritual *par excellence*.

For the believer, and therefore for the theologian, his ritual acts are perceived as being efficacious in relation to the occult in as real a sense for its context as is any technical action in relation to the actor's material world.[1] Sacrifice, from the believer's point of view, is intended and expected *really* to expiate his sin, *really* to propitiate his God or other divinities, *really* to erase mystical pollution, *really* to conduce towards, if not necessarily to succeed in removing his affliction. And the culminating communion of sharing the consumption of the sacrifice with the recipient supernatural agencies marks the transaction as an affirmation of an on-going relationship of mutuality between givers and receivers of the sacrifice.

The common meal as distinct from the communion rite that so often rounds off the sacrificial act may well be, to the observer and in some cases even to the actor, its most significant and most intelligible sociological aspect. Both might see it as sealing or establishing the brotherhood or the fellowship of the actors that is felt to be its most fundamental purpose. But it could also be for the actors no more than the sort of festal addition to the specifically efficacious ritual act that Evans-Pritchard claims to have been the case with the Nuer.

To identify the commensality that accompanies a sacrifice as its true purpose is to draw attention to a context and mode of efficacy which the actor, as believer, might well consider to be incidental and not central to the ritual. But this pragmatic mode and context of efficacy, in which it is the function – as a force in the organization and management of the social and personal relationships of the actors and as a medium for particular cognitive and affective self-realization – is the context of principal significance for the anthropologist. Agnostic as to the physical reality of the gods or ancestors or other supernatural agencies invoked by the actors, the anthropologist looks to the actors themselves, as individuals and as collectivities, not to the cosmos, as the source of the constructions ('the collective representations') they label gods or ancestors or divinities etc. The ritual is not viewed as a theologian might view it as God-seeking, but rather as in reality serving such purposes as the expression or dramatization or catharsis, in customary forms, of human cognitive, affective, moral and instrumental, experiences (cf. Beattie 1966). This is the kind of efficacy with which the anthropologist is primarily concerned; and it is consonant with human nature and man's social existence for this efficacy to be achieved sometimes in ways that appear to the observer, no less than to the actor, as realistic and materially appropriate, and at other times in a manner that is best understood as symbolical or non-materially effective. Curing rituals, such as those described and analysed in Victor Turner's studies of Ndembu medicine, illustrate well the procedure. In other words, what is to the theologian a sacrament and to the actor a mystically binding ritual is to the anthropologist *inter alia* a passage rite or a rite of incorporation, often palpably understandable in terms of its manifest form as a communion meal, or a rite of social control.

Thus, whereas the theologian must in the last resort concede that the supernatural agencies and powers, who are deemed by the actors to be the recipients of their sacrifices, stand for really existent supernatural cosmic, non-terrestrial entities or beings, however dimly cognized, the anthropologist, as Bowker (1973. Ch. 3), demonstrates, must attempt to understand these agencies as conceptualizations or 'objectifications' of otherwise ungraspable and uncontrollable forces of social and individual existence. This is the essence of the Durkheimian hypothesis that society objectifies itself and represents its moral hegemony over individual members in the ceremonies that have their focus in the supernatural agencies towards which devotion and observances are directed. Tylor, earlier, starting from the same premisses of investigation, derived the idea of the supernatural from the doctrine of souls that animate all living things, which he regarded as a logical deduction from such everyday individual experiences as dreaming and from such emotionally-charged dilemmas as how to explain evidence of the apparent continued presence of the dead among the living. In similar vein Malinowski accounted for magic as a symbolic means of coping with anxiety and insecurity in the face of the inevitably uncontrollable and unpredictable factors in every human activity; and Victor Turner sees Ndembu supernatural agencies as projective, symbolical responses to problems of conflict resolution that arise ultimately from a contradiction between a matrilineal kinship structure and the political and jural supremacy of men. And many other examples could be given, the common principle being to look to human social and psychological proclivities, experiences, and relationships for the sources of the actor's ideas and beliefs about supernatural agencies.

But let me emphasize again that these are all observers' judgments and hypotheses. For the actor, I repeat, his gods, divinities, ancestors, witches, and so forth, are real, if not materially tangible, nevertheless not from his point of view merely symbolical. I recollect how often Tallensi impressed on me that their ancestors were there, present, participating in their own inscrutable way in every sacrifice, even when the offering consisted only of a libation of water, and indeed present in some way during the ordinary affairs of their descendants (Chapter 8). And I recollect vividly also a high Akan Christian dignitary, a devout and learned leader in his church and community, explaining earnestly to me, one evening after dinner in his house, how he could 'feel' or 'sense' his ancestors near and around him in that room. Among traditional Japanese there is a shrine dedicated to all the family dead, often going back to scores and even hundreds of recorded generations, in the main house of the dispersed family group; and symbolical – because not more than small token – offerings of food and drink are made every day at this shrine, by the housewife, as if they were present there all the time. Similar practices are found, as is well known, in traditional Chinese lineages (cf. papers by Ooms and Newell in Newell (ed.), 1976).

Thus for peoples like the Tallensi, many other African peoples, the Japanese, the Chinese – and at another level for many pious Christians – the ancestors, gods, saints even the supreme deity are objectively incorporated in the everyday existence of a family or lineage or community at large, in what is to the believer an actually and tangibly accessible form at an altar or shrine. Hayley (1980) gives us a beautifully vivid picture of how the deity is brought down and into the group of worshippers, almost, one might conclude, recreated *ad hoc* each time by his devotees, to receive the offerings made to him. He is then a real presence which the ritual enables the devotees to incorporate, through the food offerings to which he is drawn down, so as to partake with them in the communion of the common meal. It is we, not the devotees, who think that their god is purely imaginary. For them he exists in a way that permits embodiment in comestible offerings and in words and rites that are all materially, tangibly real, efficacious. Regardless of the cultural and geographical distance between them, I am sure that Tallensi, and other West African peoples, would fully understand these rites and relate them to analogous practices in their own religious systems.

As to the symbolic significance of Krishna, this is a complex and many-stranded matter. Hayley (1980) suggests that one strand may be reference in it to the model relationship of mother and child. We could speculate that this corresponds to a 'collective representation' and 'objectification' of the sense of dependence and trust and desire of loving care continually reproduced in this 'initial situation' as Malinowski called it, of individual existence; woven into the texture of their social and cultural life, this could well be the basis of the representation his devotees have of Krishna. Thinking along analogous lines I have interpreted some aspects of Tallensi ancestor worship as providing a cultural defence against the disruptive potentialities of the ambivalence that is intrinsic to the relations of successive generations of fathers and sons in patrilineal family systems such as are found among the Tallensi, the Chinese and other peoples (Chapter 9). Spiro (1971), Turner (1969) and others have applied variants of such Freudian models in their studies of religious institutions among non-western peoples. What concerns me here, however, is not the particular hypotheses that have emerged in these enquiries, but the implication that their common starting point is the premiss that the beliefs and practices they have been concerned with are to be explained in terms of human psychology, social organization, and cultural resources, not by invoking super-human or extra-human agencies or forces.

Hayley (*op. cit.*) brings me back also to the question as to why objectification in the Durkheimian sense, plays so conspicuous and to all intents universal a part in religious institutions. In the form of material objects like altars, shrines, icons, relics, vestments etc. and in the correlative form of the ritual observances, performances, verbal and non-verbal, of prayer, liturgies, taboos and life-styles, it is clearly fundamental to the practice of sacrifice.

Since from the anthropological point of view Krishna is not really brought down amongst his devotees and Tallensi ancestors are not really present on or in the shrine dedicated to them, the beliefs and practices thus deployed could be described as symbolical. To adapt a well-known saying of Clifford Geertz they could be seen (following Devereux, 1979) as 'symbolical of' cultural representations of filial dependence on parental authority or some other psychological or social constituents of existence in particular human societies or in human society in general. On the other side, from a theological point of view, a great deal of religious belief and ritual is 'symbolical for' – that is to say contains guidance, ideals and sanctions for the conduct of life linked to doctrines about the terrestrial world, the cosmos, and usually, forms of continued existence after death. Metaphor, metonym, myths, allegory and the singularity of a religious 'world of meaning' are invoked to deal with this. That cautiously sceptical seventeenth-century physician-philosopher, Sir Thomas Browne, understood the nature of this problem when he wrote 'for unspeakable mysteries in the Scriptures are often delivered in a vulgar and illustrative way; and being written unto man

are delivered, not as they truly are, but as they may be understood
...' (*Religio Medici*, p.52).

Barrington-Ward and Bourdillon (1980) are concerned with this
issue, when, for instance, they say that 'in coming together for a
sacrificial rite, people express acceptance of the principal cosmological symbols and of the moral ideals which the prescribed ritual contains'. The sacrifice of Christ, they say, has for Christians 'universal
application yet remains a concrete symbol', a peculiar reality even
though understood metaphorically. The Mass thus appears as a
symbolic ritual in relation to which a world view and a scheme of
moral conduct are appropriated by each actor.

Granted then, that for the believer, ritual, and in the present
instance specifically the ritual of a sacrificial offering, is deemed to
be efficacious (failure being accountable for within the framework
of the supporting beliefs, as many authorities from Tylor onward
have explained) can general principles – relating, for example, to the
believed efficacy of sacrifice – be discerned? Both Beattie and Bourdillon appear to doubt the possibility of this, considering the great
diversity and flexibility, material, situational, and symbolical of sacrifice in different cultures. The various theories they review – gift
theory, communion theory, abnegation theory, power mobilizing
theory etc. – all appear to have only limited validity. Of more general application is the Maussian formula for what Evans-Pritchard
called the 'grammar' of sacrifice (1964, viii), with its focus on the act
of consecration and its climax in the act of immolation. But this tells
us nothing about the function or the meaning of sacrifice either for
the actor or for the observer.

One feature is clear enough. It is a special ritual procedure for establishing or mobilizing a relationship of mutuality between the
donor (individual or collective) and the recipient; and there is
generally, if not always, an implication of mutual constraint, and
indeed of actual or potential mutual coercion in the act. This is a feature of sacrifice in practice that immediately impresses a participant
ethnographer in the field. Sacrifice is more commonly a response to
a demand or command from supernatural agencies or else a rendering of a standard obligation, than a spontaneous offering; and
whether or not it is thought of as expiation or propitiation or purga-
tion, there is commonly an element of demand, certainly of persuasion, on the donor's side.

Most commonly, as I suggested earlier, the relationship established or mobilized is one of dependence on the donor's side quite palpably modelled on, and a transformation of, the submissive filial dependence ideally expected of offspring in relation to parents. This is a form of dependence in which a sense of impotence and vulnerability is engendered by reason of the inevitable and necessary parental control and care. This sense of impotence and vulnerability is, I believe, deeply ingrained in human consciousness, being continually reinforced by the experience of pain, suffering, and deprivation. And it is a fact of human existence that in all societies receives elaborate customary expression. Founded, as I am suggesting, in the universal infantile experience of helpless dependency, it is continually substantiated and, so to say, objectively validated by experience of environmental hazards, social crises and other such external pressures.

From this angle, sacrifice falls into a wider class of what might be called rituals of defence. It is noteworthy how often the demands for sacrifice on the part of a supernatural agency are signalled by affliction or misfortune, interpreted by the worshippers as punishment for sin or its equivalent, or as warning of troubles to come. Even the joyous sacrifices associated with passage rites, with calendrical (i.e. sowing or harvest) festivals, or in commemoration of historical or mythological events, have an obvious prophylactic intention. Whether the ostensible intention is to get rid of or drive away the supernatural agency believed to be the source of the affliction (as Evans-Pritchard, taking a cue from Old Testament sacrifice, interprets Nuer sacrifice to aim at); or, conversely, to enlist the goodwill of the dangerous supernatural agencies by incorporating them into the communion of the family or the congregation of worshippers, as is the case among peoples like the Tallensi and the Assamese devotees; the common aim is to defend the donors. And it is defence against what I have described as the inescapable vulnerability of humanity, vulnerability to the unexpected, unpredictable and uncontrollable fact of disease or hunger or war or social upheaval that appear to come upon us from the outside, or alternatively the internal vulnerability to the weakness of body or mind which become manifest as lust or anger, jealousy or hate, as sin or mental disorder, and ultimately of course to the totally inescapable vulnerability to death and annihilation.[2] Even sacrifices defined as thanks offerings have a defensive aspect since they purport to be given in gratitude for recovery from affliction or for good fortune or survival, and more often in the spirit of repaying a debt rather than as an expression of spontaneous love.

Although as Rogerson (1980) points out, we have only texts that formulate rules and regulations of sacrifice, and no ethnographic data on the actual conduct of the rites, the Old Testament patterns of sacrifice he discusses are most instructive in this connection. It is interesting to see how many forms of sacrifice are prescribed by divine law to expiate unwitting – that, is, unconsciously motivated rather than intentional – wrong-doing. These are sacrifices for the removal of pollution, whether for such natural occurrences as birth and death, or for leprosy which falls into the same class as pollution, being of course passively, that is not intentionally, incurred. And this is equally true for the calendrically fixed festivals.

The defensive character of Old Testament sacrifice is apparent all through. And likewise, there is generally an implication of sacrifice being obligatory as if in payment of debt, neglect of which could be disastrous. Most of all, the rules of Old Testament sacrifice testify to the mutually coercive relationship of God, on his part insisting on unquestioning obedience to his laws and his unique authority, and the Hebrews, on their part, appealing, often in tones that sound demanding rather than ingratiating, for his fatherly support and protection in spite of their lapses from perfect filial submission; and all this on the strength of the reciprocal commitments implied in the original Covenant. This pattern fits in with the compromise institution of the Temple- and priest-centred cult which, on the one hand, insulates the worshippers from direct contact with and exposure to the dangerous holiness of God, and on the other, purports by means of the sacrifice to bring him into the temple, and thus make him subject to intercession on behalf of the community in the name of the moral norms of kinship amity, as Robertson-Smith conjectured. It is significant that the generic concept for sacrifice in the Old Testament (and in Arabic) is *korban*, as Rogerson notes, from a root meaning to bring near, as if to express a yearning which could never be satisfied. Typically, moreover, as is the case in many other societies, Old Testament sacrifice was never spontaneous, but as Rogerson says 'it was enough that God commanded the sacrifice and Israel should obey the commands'. Hence perhaps the emphasis on sacrifice as expiation of or atonement for unwitting sin or ritual defilement.

In every case – whether the aim of sacrifice as the actor sees it is to thrust away, or, alternatively, to bring near and incorporate – the first step must always be to bring the supernatural power down from his or its sacred world or its hidden existence into the everyday human world where people talk to one another, argue out their disputes and express their emotion in the open. A sacrifice very dramatically brings into the open of an assembly of worshippers entitled and qualified by kinship or descent, or other criteria of membership of the congregation, the circumstances to which it is the proper customary response. This is of necessity a ritual response, since by definition it is impossible for transactions with supernatural powers to be undertaken by secular means. And it makes sense that the ritual of bringing the occult agency 'down to earth' so to speak, to become accessible at an altar for instance, should require the mediation of a material offering. Furthermore an offering that lends itself to presentation in terms of the basic vehicle of kinship mutuality, that is to say the shared meal, would seem to be particularly apt. Its cardinal significance in Old Testament sacrifice was emphasized not only by Robertson-Smith but by other semiticists of his generation, as Rogerson points out. God is thought of as sharing the sacrificial meal in a quite concrete way. The burning of choice parts or even of the whole of the victim is seen as providing 'a sweet savour unto the Lord'.[3]

The theme of blood sacrifice and other offerings being intended by the actor to be in a ritual sense, even to some extent in a material sense, food for the supernatural recipient, is so prominent everywhere that it is surprising to find it overlooked in some theoretical discussions, though Robertson-Smith of course gave it high priority. Starting from the model of sacrifice being normatively an offering from a filial dependant to a parental divinity, the feeding theme can be seen as implying a reversal, in the ritual context, of the food dependency relationship in the context of living reality. It is almost as if the dependent worshipper is by this means enabled to redefine himself as the dominant quasi-parental sustainer of the divinity's existence, and therefore entitled to make demands on him.

Eating and drinking of sanctified offerings is not only the model for, but is seen by the actor as, the efficacious means of incorporating

the divinity into both the commensal group and the consciousness of each of its members. This is what makes it so fundamental a
feature in the ritual of sacrifice (cf. Harris 1978). It signifies the
transformation of what is at first responded to as a punitive or
rejecting, usually remote supernatural agency, into a good, protective, close at hand mystical presence. And to understand better why
incorporation of divinity through the symbolism of the shared meal
is so potent, one must think also of its contrary, namely fasting, and
other forms of abstinence, as sacrificial practices. Whatever else
such forms of self-mortification may signify, their self-defensive
character is patent.

The Hebraic notion, taken over by both theologians and some
anthropologists, that the life is in the blood and that it is this life that
is the essential offering in a blood sacrifice, looks like God's law of
talion in reverse, and this does perhaps make plausible some form of
'ransom' explanation of Hebrew and Nuer types of sacrifice. It is relevant however to bear in mind what Hubert and Mauss particularly
emphasized; the only way living humans can be sure of establishing
reciprocal communication with the supernatural agencies on the
other side of the mystical curtain separating the profane from the
sacred world, is through a mediator that is qualified by sacrificial
death or its equivalent (for e.g. vegetable offerings). This is, from the
actor's point of view, the essential condition for entry into the 'other
world' whether the eventual aim is to ensure that the supernatural
agencies depart and stop intervening in the 'profane' human world,
or whether it is to bring them nearer and into that world.

My aim, here, has not been to propose alternatives to current
anthropological theories of sacrifice. It has been to illustrate ways in
which an anthropological approach is likely to differ from a theological approach to the study of sacrifice. Concluding his discussion
on Old Testament sacrifice, Rogerson sums up the differences neatly
as follows: 'the latter [i.e. the anthropologist] would presumably
concentrate upon the structure and function of the sacrifice. The
theologian would concentrate upon sacrifice as seen in terms of the
story, and the insight into eternal reality which that story might contain.' In the more prosaic language of anthropology that 'eternal reality' might perhaps be glossed as signifying universal moral values
and realization of the ultimate inscrutability of Nature and of the
human situation.

But if the differences between a theological point of view and an anthropological point of view in the study of sacrifice and other religious institutions is obvious, I think it is fair to add that there is also plenty of evidence of common interests and overlapping procedures of enquiry. There is great promise here of the further collaboration which Tylor called for over a century ago

# Notes

## 1 Divination: religious premisses and logical techniques

1  I gave a preliminary account of Tallensi divination at a meeting of the Fellows held at the Center for Advanced Study in the Behavioral Sciences, Stanford, California, in the Spring of 1959. Among many helpful comments made on that occasion, I am particularly indebted to those of Professor Raymond Firth and those of the late Professor A. L. Kroeber.

2  For additional references:

(a) *The Tallensi*. For the ethnographic background of the present paper see Fortes, M. 1949 *The Web of Kinship among the Tallensi*, Oxford University Press; 1959 *Oedipus and Job in West African religion*. Cambridge University Press.

(b) *Divination*. The comprehensive review of the data at that time available in Hasting's *Encyclopaedia of religion and ethics*, 1911; s.v. 'Divination' is still worth consulting.

Among recent studies, my own argument is particularly indebted to Park, G. F. 1963 'Divination and its social contexts', *J. R. Anthrop. Inst.* **93**, no. 2, 195–209; and Turner, V. W. 1961 'Ndembu divination: its symbolism and techniques', *Rhodes–Livingstone Papers*, no. 31.

## 2 Prayer

1  Friedrich Heiler, *Prayer* (originally published 1932), trans. and ed. Samuel McComb, Galaxy Books (O.U.P., New York, 1958), p. xv.

2  I am reminded of Tylor's remark: 'As prayer is a request made to a deity as if he were a man, so sacrifice is a gift made to a deity as if he were a man.' E. B. Tylor, *Primitive Culture*, vol. 2 (1871), p. 375.

3  In the spirit of 1 Cor. 14:9, 'So also ye, unless ye utter by the tongue speech easy to be understood, how shall it to be known what is spoken?'

4  Cf. M. Fortes, *The Dynamics of Clanship among the Tallensi* (1945), pp. 108 ff.

5  Heiler's analysis of 'primitive prayer' remains a useful guide and I have benefited from consulting it. The articles s.v. 'Prayer' in *Hastings Encyclopaedia of Religion and Ethics* are less relevant to my theme but also make a useful introduction to the subject.

6  See M. Fortes, *Oedipus and Job in West African Religion* (1959).

7  Cf. E. E. Evans-Pritchard, *Nuer Religion*, p. 21.

8  E. E. Evans-Pritchard, The morphology and function of magic, *American Anthropologist*, 31, (1929), 619–41. This paper, it should be noted, by the way, does not raise objections to Malinowski's theory of magic; its concern is with the structure of the ritual performance.

9  Evans-Pritchard, *op. cit.*, p. 22.

10  Christian and Muslim prayer and ritual are designated *po'oχ, Nayin* – which, literally translated, means to salute or give thanks to God.

11  Cf. M. Fortes, *The Web of Kinship* (1949), pp. 147 ff.

12  For an account of this notion among the Tallensi cf. Fortes, *op. cit.* (1959).

## 3  Ritual festivals and the ancestors

1  The introduction to the Marett Lecture delivered at Exeter College, Oxford, on November 12, 1974, went:

It is surely in keeping with the characteristic habits and customs of academic communities all over the world for their heroes to be commemorated in lectures dedicated to their names rather than in the marble or the gilded monuments that are more appropriate for poets, princes and statesmen.

We anthropologists have quite a collection of such commemorative lectures in our cultural heritage; and to be chosen to give any of them is an honour much prized. Of course if you live long enough and have done your time adequately in the profession, you will in due course have the privilege of giving one or even some of these named lectures. And I have inevitably been so honoured. But I have actually coveted the honour for only one of them, and that is the Marett lecture. It gives me a chance not only to pay homage to the memory of the true founder of Oxford Anthropology but also to express my gratitude to Oxford for the opportunities, both professional and personal, I was given here. You can understand therefore why I feel particularly grateful for your invitation to deliver the Marett Lecture here today.

To explain more fully I must go back to the year 1937, when I first pitched my anthropological tent in Oxford, and inflict on you a fragment of autobiography. I came here after my second field trip to what was then the Gold Coast primarily to be close to Evans-Pritchard, whom I have elsewhere described as my elder brother in anthropological research, and also to Radcliffe-Brown, who had recently arrived in Oxford. But Marett was an extra and special magnet for somewhat adventitious personal reasons. My choice of the Northern Territories of the Gold Coast for my field research was due to the persuasion of R. S. Rattray and was in fact in continuation of work he had begun; and Rattray became the incomparable ethnographer he turned out to be, because of Marett. I daresay I am not the only one who can remember Rector Marett's jovial yarns about his one and only experience of field research among a primitive people. It was during the famous visit of the British Association for the Advancement of Science to Australia in 1914 when the members of Section H of which he was the Recorder included almost every anthropologist of note or of promise in Great Britain – Malinowski as Marett's secretary (cf. Firth's Introduction to Malinowski's *A Diary in The Strict Sense of the Term* (1967)) and Radcliffe-Brown, among others. Marett 'interviewed' as he modestly puts it in his autobiography some 'black fellows' who were stowed away in reservations and had been, legend relates, transported to Sydney to be exhibited to the visiting scientists, and he also, to quote him again 'got a glimpse of the genuine thing' on a flying visit to the remnants of the Narrinyeri tribe (Marett, 1941, p. 206).

But infinitesimal as his own so-called field experience was, Marett set the greatest store by field research as a basis for his theoretical speculations, and he had a genius for inspiring others to engage in it. As is well known the famous researches among the Australian Aborigines of Spencer and Gillen owe much to Marett, and that, as I have said, is how Rattray was drawn into anthropology as one of a long line of Marett-inspired field ethnographers who opened the way for us of the next generation

My interest in Marett began, however, when I first read the *Threshold of Religion* and was confirmed by his later books. Marett was one of the earliest opponents of Frazer's intellectualist theories of the origins and evolution of magic and religion. In contrast to Frazer Marett argued that magic and religion were not different evolutionary stages but all of one piece, and were based on emotional responses to the world and to the human situation not on intellectual deductions. Magic and religion, he contended, were concerned with the same kinds of fears and hopes and, above all moral dilemmas as the so-called higher religions seek to come to terms with. Furthermore, he insisted again and again on the universality of fundamental religious institutions like the sacrament and sacrifice. Unlike Frazer he emphasized that religion was as he put it 'a product of the corporate life' (*Threshold*, p. 81) and that the critical element was the rite rather than the beliefs. All of this made good sense to me in the light of my own field work.

Marett had a remarkable flair for the telling aphorism. My favourite one is his opening declaration in *Head, Heart and Hands in Human Evolution* (1935) that 'Anthropology is the higher gossipry' and therefore includes 'the sheer intellectual fun of surveying humanity at large' as well as the 'moral gain' of understanding that 'man is of one kind'. 'My own prejudice' he remarks in one place (*ibid.* p. 157) 'is in favour of stretching the word religious to its utmost.' It is in this spirit that I have chosen my topic for this lecture, emphasizing, in particular, its commemorative intention; for, as will become apparent, my theme in the broadest sense is the practice of hoping to ensure the future by invoking the past.

## 4 Ancestor worship in Africa

1 Ashanti often attribute sickness or misfortune to the anger of a ghost (*saman*) and a father's ghost is as frequently cited as that of other kins-folk. But here, as among the Thonga, a ghost is not an ancestor as I define the status.

2 Tallensi enshrine and sacrifice to their deceased mothers and through them to certain maternal kin. This is related to the function of maternal filiation in lineage segmentation.

3 Cf. Kuper's remark (*op. cit.,* p. 188). 'The Ancestors are the ideal not the actual personality.'

4 The foregoing applies, of course, to women (mothers) as well, again in relation to the function of matrifiliation in specifying filial status.

5 Cf. Krige, 1943, p. 232: 'Above all the ancestors complain, a fact which lies at the basis of Lovedu religion...'

6 I stress *inter alia* because in its descriptive totality as I have noted in several places in this essay, ancestor worship also includes mystical notions and metaphysical ideas. I do not want to give the impression that I regard it as being exhaustively specifiable as a purely jural insti-tution. Like all institutions it has what Gluckman has called 'multiplex' meaning; that is, it has a role in every domain of social structure.

## 5 Ritual and office

1 Ralph Linton (1936).

2 Parsons and Nadel, cited later, review some of this literature. See also the thought-provoking paper by A. Southall (1959), pp. 17 ff. An un-usual point of view is expounded with subtlety and wit in Erving Goff-man (1959).

3 A preliminary draft of this paper was written during my tenure of a Fel-lowship at the Center for Advanced Study in the Behavioral Sciences, Stanford, California, and benefited greatly from the comments of several colleagues at the Center.

4 Talcott Parsons (1951), especially Chs. VII and X.

5 S. F. Nadel (1957), p. 35.

6 Van Gennep, *op. cit.*

7 E.g. 'It is apparent that the physiological return from childbirth is not the primary consideration, but that instead there is a *social return from*

*childbirth*, just as there is a social parenthood which is distinct from physical parenthood, and a social marriage which is distinct from sexual union. We will see that there is also a social puberty which does not coincide with physical puberty' (*op. cit.*, trans., p. 46).

8  Van Gennep, *op. cit.*, p. 82.

9  *Op. cit.*, p. 53. But I do not want to minimize the extraordinary insight displayed in Van Gennep's interpretations. An example is his description of initiation rites at adolescence as rites of separation from the asexual world followed by rites of incorporation into the world of sexuality (p. 67).

10  Max Weber (1930), Ch. III, and (1947), Ch. II, sec. 14, 24, *et passim*.

11  Parsons, 'Introduction' to M. Weber (1947), p. 72, and (1937), Chs. 14–15.

12  It is however worth noting that *officium*, the ancestral form of our word, was used by the Romans, e.g. Cicero and Seneca, in much the same sense as Weber's *Beruf*. It is commonly translated as 'moral duty', and 'occupation'. But it was used also to denote ritual and ceremony associated with induction into status, rank and office, e.g. marriage, the assumption of the *toga virilis*, entry upon magisterial office. Cf. Georges (1959), *s.v. cit.*

13  I am indebted to Dr W. D. J. Cargill-Thompson, King's College, Cambridge, for permission to quote him on this subject. 'Luther contrasted the "spiritual, inner, new man" with the "carnal, external, old man" (Luther, *De Libertate Christiana*). Good works could not win salvation because they are performed by the outward natural man, not by spiritual man. Man's two natures involve him in one set of relationships with God and in another with his fellow-men. These Luther called two "callings" (*vocatio, Beruf*), or "persons" (Christ-person and *Welt-person*) or offices (*Ampt*). In his spiritual calling a man is incorporated in Christ through the Word and baptism; in his temporal calling he has offices to serve the needs of mankind, and this may require him to do things that are expressly forbidden to him as a private Christian. Thus as a magistrate, a preacher, a slave or especially as a soldier who is bound to fight or as a parent bound to exercise authority over his children, he is under obligations to his temporal office. As the temporal order is also instituted by God, it is incumbent on a man not to disrupt it by refusing to serve in the office to which he has been called' (Cargill-Thompson, 'The Two Regiments').

14  Gluckman (1955).

15  See R. S. Rattray (1929), Ch. XI.

16  K. A. Busia (1951), Ch. II; Rattray (1929), *op. cit.*, pp. 116–17.

17  It would be interesting to pursue this topic further, especially in relation to Gluckman's previously cited study. But it impinges on an aspect of office which can only be alluded to here. I mean the connection between the concept of office and the juridical concept of the 'corporation sole'. A jurist, I take it, would say that office is none other than the corpor-

ation sole in another guise. There is authority for this in English constitutional history. If we turn to the fountain-head, we find that the question comes up in Pollock and Maitland (1898) in connection with issues that are closely parallel to the conflicts of status illustrated by Ashanti chiefship. Thus (Vol. I, p. 495) they discuss the difficulties of sixteenth-century lawyers over the king's status. Was he to be regarded as 'merely a natural person' or also as an 'ideal person', a 'corporation sole'? They conclude that the 'personification of the kingly office in the guise of a corporation sole was, in the then state of the law, an almost necessary expedient'. And they refer back to a much earlier state of affairs when there was no clear-cut distinction between the king's proprietary rights as king and those he had in his private capacity (*ibid.*, pp. 502–3).

18  Everett C. Hughes (1958), especially pp. 56 ff.

19  Robert Redfield (1953).

20  As Parsons fully explains in *The Social System* (1951).

21  See my introduction to Goody (Ed.), Ch. I (1958).

22  These topics are dealt with at length in my article 'The Political System of the Tallensi', in Fortes and Evans-Pritchard (1940).

23  See Fortes (1945). I use the slightly inexact term 'Earth priest' in the present discussion to save circumlocution and confusing recourse to native words.

24  I have already noted some of the taboos of office that fall upon an Ashanti chief. He is subject to many other constraints of conduct and observance which I have not the space to discuss but which are described in the literature cited. Anthropologists hardly need to be reminded that this is characteristic of chiefship all over Africa and in other parts of the world. To list relevant references would be out of place here.

25  This, again, is a familiar religious (more correctly, cosmological) concomitant of eminent politico-ritual office in Africa. It is most dramatically represented in the well-known institution of Divine Kingship. (Cf. the excellent synopsis in Evans-Pritchard (1948)). The elaborate development of this conception in ancient Egypt is brilliantly expounded by Henri Frankfort (1948).

26  These are the *wirempefo* referred to by Rattray (1927), Ch. XVIII.

27  Gluckman (1954).

28  I infer this from the remarkable ethnographic film of 'The Installation of the Mogho Na'aba' shown by Dr Jean Rouch at the Sixth International Congress of Anthropological Sciences, Paris, 1960.

29  J. D. and E. J. Krige, 'The Lovedu of the Transvaal' in Forde (Ed.), (1954).

30  An idea of course familiar to us from English and European history.

31  In Ashanti the selection and installation of a chief are the jealously guarded prerogatives of the Queen Mother and the councillors. See Rattray (1929), *passim*, and Busia, *op. cit.*

32  Recent references are given in Richards (1960).
33  Details are given in Fortes (1949).
34  Richards (1960).
35  See references in Fortes (1945). Similar annual public ceremonies are widespread in West Africa and play the same part in politico-ritual relations. Cf. the Ashanti *Adae* and *Odwira* ceremonies described by Rattray (1927), Ch. XII, and the first-fruit rites of the Yakö (Forde, (1949)).
36  See Fortes (1949) for further details of such transactions.
37  The sanctity of this rite is enhanced by the belief that an oath which is peculiarly binding is one that is sworn by the Earth. This oath is sworn by touching the Earth with a wet finger and licking the finger.
38  See Forde (1957), p. 11, for an illuminating comment on similar ideas among the Yakö.
39  I here summarize data given the more fully in Fortes (1949), but I failed, there, to appreciate the significance I now see in these facts.
40  See Rattray (1927), Ch. VI. It is worth noting that both Fustel de Coulanges (1864), Ch. VIII, and Van Gennep (*op. cit.*, p. 101) perceived what I am here restating.
41  See Fortes (1959).
42  See Fortes in Goody (ed.), 1958, *No. 1, loc. cit.*

## 6  Totem and taboo

1  Or, in the more disingenuous jargon of today, 'developing' and 'developed' societies.
2  I use the term 'totemistic' in the inclusive sense given to it by Evans-Pritchard (1956).
3  Cf. Rattray, R. S., 1932. 'Totemic' observances are discussed and listed for the 'Nankanse' in Vol. i, Ch. XVIII, p. 232 sqq. and for the other 'tribes' of the area in the relevant chapters in Vol ii. Rattray was apparently not acquainted with the earlier French literature on peoples of the same linguistic and cultural family (the Voltaic peoples) as those he investigated in the then Northern Territories of the Gold Coast.
4  Delafosse's conclusions on the subject of totemism in this area are trenchantly summarized in his paper of 1920. Other French contributions to Voltaic ethnology at this period are referred to in Fortes, 1945.
5  In his 1935 paper 'On the concept of function in social science' there is a revealing footnote which reads (1952: 181) 'Opposition, i.e. organised and regulated antagonism is, of course, an essential feature of every social system.' His theory of the joking relationship presents it as an institutionalized device for resolving a structural opposition, and his whole approach to ritual and to kinship theory was influenced by the same idea. His pupils used it to good effect – e.g. in the brilliant analysis of 'good sacred' and 'bad sacred' by M. N. Srinivas, 1952. As for Malinowski, his classical presentation of the opposition between Trobriand

father and mother's brother is evidence enough of his implicit recognition of the same principle.

6  It is not relevant to my subject to take into account Lévi-Strauss' adaptation, here and elsewhere in his enquiries, of Marxist and other meta-sociological concepts and methods of discourse. See for recent pertinent comment Leach E. R., 1965, Murphy, Robert F., 1963; Heusch, Luc de, 1965.

7  This proviso is of the utmost importance; for it seems that he accepts the 'incontestable primacy of the infrastructures'. Assuming this dichotomy enables him, as I understand it, to posit a 'mediator', in the shape of the conceptual scheme, through whose operations 'matter' and 'form' are fused to constitute 'structure'. Here, too, lie implications outside my scope.

8  E.g. in the 1963 paper cited above.

9  The actor-centred orientation which is more often implicit than explicit in 'functionalist' ethnography and social anthropology, is largely congruent with the social theory developed by Talcott Parsons and his colleagues, against a background of Durkheim, Weber, Malinowski and Freud. See for instance, Parsons, T. and Shils, E., 1951, especially Part II, 1, p. 53 sqq. Firth's presidential addresses of 1954 and 1955 (reprinted in Firth, R., 1962, Chs. II and III) present what I regard (with some reservations) as a basic introduction to an actor-centred theory applicable in the more strictly anthropological context. A tricky problem is how to conceptualize and handle the relation between individual and (social) person in actor-oriented structural theory. A promising approach is outlined in Dorothy Emmett's paper, 1960. An ethnographical study, in which actor-centred theory is expounded and consistently applied, and which is specially relevant to my present theme is Goody, Jack, 1962.

10  As Schneider (1964) points out.

11  As happened with Malinowski and Radcliffe-Brown in the twenties and thirties, in contra-distinction to Boas and Kroeber and the then prevailing tradition of American and Continental ethnology. Lévi-Strauss' predilection for descriptive material drawn from pre-functionalist American ethnology is, perhaps, not without significance.

12  But I must emphasize that it was generally current in British social anthropology in the thirties. I need only mention, in addition to Evans-Pritchard's study of Nuer social structure, first published in *Sudan Notes and Records* between 1933 and 1937, Gregory Bateson's *Naven* (1936) and corresponding parts (e.g. Ch. VI) of Firth's, *We, the Tikopia* (1936).

13  There are many points in the analysis I attempted in 1945 which I should not rephrase, especially in the light of the comments made by Max Gluckman in his paper 'An Advance in African Sociology' (reprinted in his book of 1963, Ch. 1). I was able, however, to satisfy myself, when I revisited the Tallensi in 1963 and consulted a new gener-

ation of informants, that the ethnographical record of their totemistic observances which I presented in 1945 was and remains accurate.

14  Cf. especially Hallowell, 1955, Ch. 4 'The self and its behavioral environment'. Hallowell's thesis is illustrated in these papers and elsewhere by rich material drawn from his studies among the Ojibway and from ethnographic literature in general. These are many points of contact between his model of the 'social self' and those of earlier writers such as G. H. Mead as well as with the Parsons and Shils model (1951: 100–1 and *passim*). Cf. also Gerth, Hans & Mills, C. Wright, 1954, Ch. IV.

15  Mauss, *loc. cit*, points in the same direction as Hallowell but not so explicitly.

16  Cf. Fortes, M., 1953. Gluckman's concept of multiplex relationships, richly documented in his book, *The Judicial Process among the Barotse* (1955), brings out other structural aspects of this fact.

17  Cf. the contrast between a woman's status as daughter and sister, and her status as wife and mother in my *Web of Kinship*, pp. 87 sqq. It is even more prominent in double descent systems, cf. Goody, 1962.

18  Cf. Evans-Pritchard, E. E., 1956, p. 115, 'Given the segmentary political and lineage structure of the Nuer it is understandable that the same complementary tendencies towards fission and fusion and the same relativity that we find in the structure are found also in the action of spirit in the social life.'

19  I use the concept in the structural sense given to it by Gluckman and his colleagues. (Cf. Gluckman & Devons, op. cit. *passim*.) See also Gluckman, M., 1956.

20  Tallensi homesteads are built with the intention that they should stand as long as the agnatic line goes on. In 1963 I found the homesteads of Tongo standing – with only two or three exceptions – on exactly the same sites as in 1934. Many could be shown to have stood on these sites for seven or eight generations. Regular repairs, and if necessary the addition or demolition of rooms to fit changes in the developmental cycle of the family and lineage, serve to preserve them as long as the lineage lasts.

21  The Tallensi are, of course, not unique in thus identifying a person or a family with a dwelling or house site, nor is it rare for the plan of the normal dwelling to mirror in relief, as it were, the structure of the normal family. We, too, project our personalities and biographies into homes that are laid out to reflect our family and other significant relationships. And it is, I am sure, the same in all settled societies. Did not Morgan, long ago, discover this among the Iroquois (Morgan, Lewis H., 1881)? A closer parallel is the Tikopian house and house-site complex described by Firth (1936, pp. 81–7). As for Africa, comparable instances abound. The Dogon, for example, quite explicitly regard the plan of a house as a representation of the male human body and the reproductive process. (Cf. Griaule, M., 1954; cf. for similar notions among the Voltaic Mossi, Zahan, D., 1950.)

22 I have witnessed suits brought for adjudication by chiefs and elders in which the legitimate agnation of a lineage was being disputed. The decisive evidence, then, was invariably the formula of their oath and the loin cover used for their dead; and invariably the principle was cited that it would be sacrilege and unthinkable for anyone to abandon his ancestral taboos, since this would incur the extinction of his descent line. Note that it is the publicly declarative totemistic observances on which most stress is laid.

23 Stories are common of people who succumbed to eating a tabooed animal inadvertently or under pressure of famine and vomiting in revulsion immediately. Cf. Fortes, 1938, pp. 39–40.

24 A slave was in this condition, by definition, but was given assimilated patrilineal status in his owner's lineage. Cf. Mauss, 1938, p. 277, on the Roman concept of persona and the law of persons: 'Seul en est exclu l'esclave ... il n'a pas de personnalité: il n'a pas son corps, il n'a pas d'ancêtres, de nom, de cognomen, de biens propres.' Tallensi and other West African peoples would understand and subscribe to this definition.

25 Which, as I have noted elsewhere, presupposes legitimate incorporation for which the fact of birth is really only the entitlement (cf. Chapter 4).

26 Dr Lienhardt's study is important for my argument, firstly because it concerns an African people of a different ethnic stock and very different way of life from the Tallensi, and secondly because his conclusions appear to have been reached quite independently of mine.

27 Since Dinka clan-divinities receive worship and sacrifice they have mystical and ritual qualities akin to those attributed to their worshipped ancestors by the Tallensi. The 'emblems' appear to represent, much more immediately than do Tallensi totemic objects, personified agencies of mystical power bound to agnatic descent groups. Thus Lienhardt interprets the clan-divinities as reflecting Dinka 'experience of ancestry and agnatic heredity' much on the lines that I suggested for the Tallensi in 1945. Between the Dinka and the Tallensi there appear to be differences in the elaboration of the elements of the configurations rather than in their essential meaning (Lienhardt, 1961: 116–22).

28 As in the passage I have quoted and in a number of other contexts in the book. Here, e.g., is another instance: 'A clan-divinity thus does not face outwards to other clans, so to speak, appearing as a label or sign by which outsiders may know with whom they have to deal, but relates inwards to the clansmen. By knowing from genealogical evidence that they are agnatically related, they know also that they are united in relation to a common divinity, which for them symbolizes their relationship' (Leinhardt, *op. cit.* p. 113).

29 1952, cf., also Lienhardt (1961: 107). He speaks of the 'image' of the totem object.

30  The extreme case is that of Namoos first-borns who are in daily contact
    with domestic fowl and are constantly required to exercise abstention
    from eating it. The same is true of other domestic animals that are
    totems, e.g., the cat or the dog, and of such wild creatures as pythons,
    crocodiles, monitor lizards, etc.

31. To the best of my knowledge species of trees or grasses do not figure
    among Tallensi totemistic objects. But trees are often ancestor shrines
    and some grasses are tabooed in certain circumstances.

32  I have often been present at Talis domestic sacrifices where a Namoo
    sister's son who is known to be a first-born is either not offered the
    portion of a sacrificed chicken due to his kinship status or else politely
    declines it if his hosts do not know that he is a *mokyihib* – one who
    taboos the fowl. It used to remind me of the behaviour of vegetarians
    and teetotalers among my friends at home.

33  Cf. Lienhardt, 1961: 151, Dinka form individual 'respect' relationshps
    with 'emblems' of animals, etc., which have affected them.

34  As both Evans-Pritchard and Lienhardt (1961: 108–18) explain. Since
    insects, tree and grass species, artifacts, parts of animals and a variety of
    other objects serve as 'emblems' of Dinka and to some extent Nuer
    clan-divinities, both Evans-Pritchard and Lienhardt specially empha-
    size the absence of any ascertainable principle, utilitarian or otherwise,
    by which these totemistic objects are selected.

35  Cf. Lienhardt, *op. cit.* p. 155, '... the Dinka themselves often think of
    them [i.e. the clan-divinities] as acquired by chance – a chance associ-
    ation ... between the founding ancestor of a clan and the species....'

36  For example the Hill Talis clans that taboo tortoise (*pakur*) and water
    tortoise (*mieng*) regard them as being akin, that is, as respectively the
    terrestrial and the aquatic representatives of the same animal kind. The
    tree lizard (*uuk*), monitor lizard (*woo*), and crocodile (*bang*) are simi-
    larly regarded as being related kinds, though there is no notion of their
    being of common descent. All of these are regarded as 'earth animals'.
    These associations are obviously governed by perceptual and logical
    connections laid down in Tallensi beliefs and lore. The plural clan-
    divinities of Dinka clans are clustered together by similar culturally
    defined associations. Cf. also the ingenious oppositions utilized by the
    Bemba in coupling together complementary or antagonistic 'joking'
    clans. (See Richards, A. I., 1937.)

37  Where artifacts as well as animal species are amongst the totemic
    objects the relevance of perceived or imputed differences is even less.
    This is much plainer among the Nuer and Dinka whose totem objects
    comprise so miscellaneous an assemblage as to rule out entirely any
    possibility of arranging them by criteria of inter-specific differences.

38  The Tallensi have a considerable vocabulary for distinguishing living
    creatures, humans, persons, animals, things and supernaturals.

39  The Dinka go even further. Lienhardt says of the clan-divinities to
    whom they address prayers and sacrifices – they are 'the very type of

agnatic ancestor; the emblems are the very type of clansmen'. They 'have the status of clansmen when regarded as individual creatures, and as fathers and ancestors when regarded as representatives of the species and thus of divinity itself.' Cf. Lienhardt, 1961: 132, 135. It is of course, not a peculiarity of Africa cultures or of primitive cultures in general to attribute human characteristics to animals. We do this all the time with household pets, horses and dogs. (Cf. Lévi-Strauss' ingenious comparisons between the names popularly given to animals and plants and human proper names, 1962*b*: 266–86). Children identify with their pet rabbits, hamsters, dogs and cats, quite as if they were siblings and can be plunged into profound grief if they die. Adults, especially old people, also identify with their pets and often treat them like children. The story of Androcles nd his lion reminds us that a brotherly relationship with a wild beast is conceivable too. Best of all are the delightful legends of what Helen Waddell calls 'the mutual charities between Saints and beasts' which she has so beautifully translated (Waddell 1934). These legends tell of the mutual beneficence and trust of a variety of wild animals and the hermit saints of the desert. None of those tales, redolent as they are of piety and faith, would astonish Tallensi. Indeed some of them match their own totemic myths. For instance, there is the story of St Puchome who, whenever he had to cross the river was carried over by the crocodiles 'with the utmost subservience'. And, most famous of all, is the story of St Jerome, the lion and the donkey (1934: 30–8). The lion limps into the monastery and offers his injured paw to the Saint, who extracts the thorn. 'And now, all wildness and savagery laid aside, the lion began to go to and fro among them as peaceable and domestic as any animal about the house.' He is put to work to guard the donkey out in the pasture. One day he negligently falls asleep. The donkey is stolen. 'Conscious of guilt,' the tale continues, 'he no longer dared walk in.' After further humiliations a chance encounter – interpreted as a miracle by the pious fathers – enables the lion to retrieve his lapse and all ends happily. This is one of many such stories in which animals are depicted as moral beings symbiotically incorporated in the Saints' world of human and divine relationships. Appropriately enough, as I write this, a news item relating to a familiar sight in the neighbourhood of my own work-place, shows how totemistic identifications of animals with men survive even in sophisticated academic circles and I quote it verbatim from the *Times* of 30 April 1966:

Dr Peter Kapitza, the Russian physicist, walked into the Cavendish Laboratory at Cambridge today for the first time in 32 years.

He looked at a helium liquidiser which he designed in 1932 and is now a museum piece in the laboratory, and with emotion he said: 'This all brings back a lot of memories. It feels very funny to be back again.'

Dr Kapitza, now 71, is director of the Institute of Physical Problems of the Academy of Sciences in Russia. He was assistant director of magnetic research at the Cavendish from 1924 to 1932, and was a member of Lord Rutherford's team of scientists.

Outside the Mond Laboratory, Dr Kapitza gazed up at a carving of a crocodile on the wall, and put an end to years of rumours in Cambridge as to the origin of the crocodile. He said: 'It was my idea that the crocodile should be incorporated in the building to represent Lord Rutherford. In Russia the crocodile represents the father of the family'.

The identification of crocodile with father-figures would strike a Tallensi as perfectly natural and would have gladdened the heart of Freud.

40  These ancestor-incarnating animals can receive offerings in much the same way as Dinka clan-divinities.

41  A curious indication of the same notion is provided by their attitude to domestic cats. These are always owned by women and live in the women's rooms. They are referred to euphemistically as 'head wife'. Every important event – a birth, a marriage, a death, the coming of the harvest and so on – must be reported to the cat. If not it will abandon the house and run off to the bush and this is unlucky. Men speak of this cult of the cat by women with good humoured scorn. They see it as a parallel, for women, in a childish sort of way, to the exclusive control by the men over the domain of serious ritual. Dogs are owned by men. Tallensi say they are 'like humans' because they answer to their names, obey or disobey commands, and behave well or ill as humans do. These attitudes, so like our own, are not explicitly connected with totemistic beliefs but they reflect the feeling Tallensi have of the underlying community of nature between humans and animals.

42  Tallensi do not ordinarily describe or refer to their totem animals as kin. If they are asked why they may not eat or kill a totem animal they are normally content simply to cite the ancestral vow. However, I have had informants who have accounted for the taboos on the grounds that the animals were 'like kin' or even just 'our kin'. The context made it clear that this was not meant literally but 'totemistically'.

43  Some interesting linguistic evidence could be adduced in support of this argument if space permitted. Briefly, *ku*, to kill, *kpi*, to die, *kyih*, to taboo, are cognatically linked concepts. Similarly *gma*, to break, to sever, is applied both to physical objects, to bodily and mental states and to the 'cutting off' of a sinner's descent line.

44  It is obvious that Lévi-Strauss' hypothesis has directed my attention to this important point. In differing thus from his interpretation I foresee one possible objection. It could be argued that the Tallensi system is either a reduced variant or a relic of a fully fledged global system, or else that it is an instance of the kind of shift of structural homology from differences to substance for which Lévi-Strauss makes so persuasive a case (1962b; 152–3). Either argument would be speculative, I submit. The ethnographical facts are as I have described them.

45 The word for 'to eat' is *di*, as in all the Voltaic and many other West African languages. The word has a wide range of meanings. (See Lévi-Strauss' references to the Yoruba concept (1962*b*: 174–7).)

(1) It is the most general term for the act of eating.

(2) It means 'to consume', 'to use up', 'to destroy', as of money or grain.

(3) In the special context of marriage, it is the term for 'to take a wife in marriage' (*di pogha*), the reciprocal term, for the woman, is the word *el* which is a specific term applied to no other context and means to 'go home to the husband's house'.

(4) In the context of office and status it means 'to gain possession of', e.g., *di naam*, to gain chiefship – (cf. our idiom 'to take a degree'), *di faar* – to inherit one's patrimony and paradoxically, *di samr*, to contract a debt.

(5) There are a number of more explicit metaphorical usages, e.g., *di azama*, to have conversation (by analogy with commensality). What is common to all these usages is the notion of 'taking unto or into oneself', 'appropriating'. It is of interest that the causative form, *diix*, to cause to eat, to feed, is used only in the contexts of food giving to a passive recipient (e.g., a young child) and the bestowal of office. As a euphemism for sexual intercourse *di* is never used by Tallensi without the implication of marriage. A synonym for '*di*' 'to eat' is *ɔb* which implies chewing and is used for the eating of anything that must be chewed (e.g., meat). Tallensi often use this term in describing their animal taboos (Fortes, 1949, p. 125). Note the association between the prohibition on eating (*di*) the (lineage) totem-animal and a marrying of (*di*), a lineage sister. This is another line which, obviously important as it is, space does not permit me to explain further.

46 Cf. the absorbing review of the distribution and character of food avoidances in the Old World by Frederick J. Simoons, 1961. The complete irrationality of these avoidances, which often work to the detriment of health and well being, is cogently brought out in this study. That early classic on this theme (Audrey I. Richards, 1932), still provides the best all-round description of the place of food and foodstuffs in the social life of primitive peoples. Among recent ethnographical contributions to this subject, I am specially indebted to the fascinating discussion of the social and symbolic significance of foodstuffs and eating among the Dogon by Madame G. Dieterlen and G. Calame-Griaule, 1960, and to the comprehensive and instructive review of current research relating to this theme, with particular reference to West Africa, by Professor L. V. Thomas, 1965.

47 As Robertson Smith long ago taught us – see the excellent discussion in Richards, 1932, Ch. 7. Recent studies of Indian caste institutions have greatly enriched our understanding of these practices, but as, e.g., Srin-

ivas' penetrating analysis of observances concerned with food in Coorg ritual (op. cit. *passim*) and other ethnographical studies of sacrifice and passage rites have shown, observances of this type have much wider structural incidence and implication. Cf., e.g., among the Tallensi such rules as the prohibition for a Namoo father and first-born son to eat out of the same dish even when they share the same meal (Fortes 1949, Ch. 8) and Goody *op. cit.* pp. 187–8 for description of some of the alimentary rites that set widows and orphans apart.

48  In clans which taboo snakes, varieties known to be poisonous are killed if they appear in the vicinity of a homestead or where there are livestock, but even people who do not taboo snakes do not eat these.

49  Rattray (*op. cit.* Vol. II, 426–7), reports that among the Lobi there are patrilineal clans whose clan taboos are: not to eat porridge out of a basket, not to eat porridge at a cross roads, not to eat porridge if the stirring stick is left in the pot. (See also Goody *op. cit.* p. 101.) This looks like an extension of totemistic taboos to the staple grain foods; but I have some doubts. Similar taboos among the Tallensi are not totemistic but are associated with the opposition between things pertaining to life and things of death (cf. also Goody).

50  E.g. Narcotics – the Tallensi word for 'to smoke (tobacco)' is *nu* to drink.

51  Again, I would draw attention to the perceptive analysis of feeding rituals in funeral ceremonies in Goody. *op. cit. passim.* My argument is greatly indebted to his analysis.

52  Cf. the Christian doctrine of the Eucharist. A distinguished theologian, quotes Rawlinson's translation of 1 Corinthians 10. 17: 'Because there is one loaf we, that are many, are one body for we all partake of the one loaf' and in his commentary concludes: 'In so far then as the Christian community feeds on his body and blood, it becomes the very life and personality of the risen Christ' (Robinson, J. A. T., 1952).

53  Thus even in the thirties young men of Tendaana clans who never wore cloth garments – which would be sacrilegious – at home, usually dressed up in trousers and smocks when visiting outlying markets or settlements. In 1963 I met a Tendaana whom I knew well in a town far from his home. He was wearing an expensive cloth. He would never, as I could confirm from having visited him in his home settlement, even in the privacy of his house have worn anything but a skin cloak. The point of interest, however, is this. He had, he told me, worked as an orderly in a government hospital in Southern Ghana for many years before returning to take up the Tendaanaship; and quite spontaneously he added that during all those years he had never touched the excellent food prepared for the hospital servants because he was afraid it might contain fish or meat of species that were tabooed to him. In the same spirit, orthodox Jews travelling abroad abstain from all meat foods, and often fish as well, lest they *infringe* the dietary taboos. We ourselves habitually put off the uniform, as well as the modes of speech and behaviour,

of occupational life when we are at home with our families in the identity of parent or spouse, child or sibling. However, this does bring out a problem which is fundamental but cannot be dealt with here. It is the problem of the constancy of identity and its dependence upon the structural context. To what extent did my Tendaana friend temporarily lay aside parts of his identity that were a hindrance to him in the Southern environment?

54 A Tallensi does not prevent someone who is allowed to eat his totem animal from killing and eating it.

55 The neuroses, he warned, are 'social formations' trying to achieve 'by private means what arose in society through collective work'. 'In the neuroses', he continued, 'instinctual urges of sexual origin exercise the determining influence whereas the corresponding cultural creations depend upon social drives' (*Totem und Tabu*, Ch. II, p. 91 of the 1925 fourth revised German edition). *Ibid.*, Ch. II, p. 85. (The translation and paraphrase are my own). I regard eating as a 'social drive'.

56 This is not the place to document this statement and I will only instance the Sotho and Venda peoples of Southern Africa (cf. e.g., Schapera, I., 1955, 2nd edn. p. 6) and throughout West Africa (e.g., the Dogon, cf. Dieterlen, G., 1963), the Ashanti, (cf. Rattray, R. S., 1923, pp. 46–50); and numerous other peoples.


## 7 Coping with destiny

1 This distinction is explained at length in *The Dynamics of Clanship among the Tallensi* (Fortes 1945).

2 Among the Sinhalese of Sri Lanka who practise elaborate forms of exorcism of demons supposed to cause sickness and afflictions (cf. Yalman, 1964).

3 As described, for instance, in Field's *Religion and Medicine of the Gā People* (1937) and in the papers of Field and others in *Spirit Mediumship and Society in Africa* (Beattie and Middleton 1969). See also the classical paper by Firth on spirit mediumship (1959).

4 The association of Destiny with the head is common in West Africa. Of particular interest is the rich elaboration of this conception among the Yoruba of Nigeria. The individual's 'fate and his luck', which are derived in part from his ancestral guardian soul, are associated with his head, Bascom tells us in his profound and authoritative study of the Ifa divination system. 'Good things', he says, 'come to a lucky person with little apparent effort, but an unlucky person is not only unfortunate in his own affairs; he also brings bad luck to his relatives and associates. A lucky person is called "one who has a good head" or "one who has a good ancestral guardian soul", whereas an unlucky person is one who has a bad head or ancestral guardian' (Bascom 1969, p. 114). I cite these Yoruba beliefs in particular to show that their obviously very

similar Tallensi counterparts are representative of a wide range of West African cultures.

As to why the head is thus selected as the seat of luck and of fate, Tallensi offer no explanation. They do not regard the head as the organ of thought or of feeling – these are located in the abdomen and heart – but there are linguistic usages which imply that the head is the locus of conduct. What we should, in different contexts, describe as common sense, or wisdom, or sound judgment, or probity, is in Talni comprised in words like *yam*, associated with the head. There is no explicit or implicit association of the head with the phallus, as has been reported for other parts of the world.

5  The shrine of the collective clan ancestors, later referred to as Tongnaab (cf. Fortes 1945, Chapter 6).

6  As a matter of interest, it is worth recording that during 1936–7 I instructed our cook to slaughter our almost daily chicken and throw it to the ground in the proper ritual way and to report whether or not it had 'received'. A hundred birds were thus slaughtered over a period of about four months and the results were forty-eight 'received' and fifty-two 'refused'.

7  Tongnaab is the generic title of all the External Boghars of the Hill Talis, to which cluster both Sii and Kpata'ar belong. It is the altar and sanctuary of all the clan ancestors of each of its adherent groups of clans. The other allusions are to adherent communities outside Taleland. The invocation is a summons to all the clan ancestors.

8  Also known locally as a 'tick-bird' from its habit of following cattle and perching on their backs to pick out the ticks that infest them.

9  He should have done this four times – four being the female ritual number. But such casualness is typical of Tallensi ritual attitudes.

10  My interpretation. This fasting, the elders explained, is obligatory by custom. When the patients fast, they said, the bad Destiny is also deprived of food and drink. For as one is, so is one's Destiny. This is an added spur to it to come and take its 'things' and the offerings and depart.

## 8  Custom and conscience

1  The Ernest Jones Memorial Lecture of the British Psychoanalytical Society, London, 1973, began with the following words: 'I feel uniquely honoured by your invitation to deliver this lecture and thus to be given this chance of paying tribute to Ernest Jones. Social anthropology would not be what it is today without the challenge of psychoanalysis; and next to Freud, Ernest Jones led the way in this, opening up problems of theory and of method that continue to be central to our studies.'

2  Cf. Piaget's (1928, p. 21) remark that 'logic is the morality of thought just as morality is the logic of action'.

3 Rivers (1918), for example, early applied the theory of dream work and of dream symbolism to the interpretation of Melanesian customs and ritual ideas, contrasting himself in this respect with 'anthropologists of the old school'. Seligman was also an early adherent of psychoanalytic theory (see especially Seligman, 1932).

4 The theoretical issues I here allude to, underlie the criticisms that have been made of, for example, the 'culture and personality' movement as represented by Kardiner & Linton (1949) and their successors (cf. LeVine 1973) but the difficulties are not limited to the field of anthropology. They are met with in all studies of the type that produced the so-called 'authoritarian personality'. A recent example is the reconstruction of the character and personality types deemed to be distinctive of Nazi Germany on the basis of interviews with German prisoners of war and with former Nazi party members, attempted by Dicks (1972). Masterly and erudite though they are, Dicks' extrapolations from the level of the individual case history to the social and cultural level of the collectivity, have not convinced critical readers (cf. D. Y. Mayer 1974).

5 A good illustration arises from the work of Berlin and Kay (1969) whose discovery that chromatic colours plus white, black and grey, are recognized in most languages, suggest innate biological determinants of colour perception. Recent anthropological research shows that white, black and red turn up constantly as discriminating features in ritual activities over the world, with black and red being associated with ideas of the dangerous, the threatening and the bad, whereas white and light colours symbolize what is pleasant, good and desirable (cf. Turner 1962). There is, however, nothing to show that these ritual practices arise in response to innate patterns of colour discrimination; it is more plausible to argue that ritual, however it comes into being, makes use of the human capacity to categorize and respond effectively to these colours.

6 The resistance to psychoanalytical ideas among academic anthropologists is due primarily to their theoretical principles and aims. But it is necessary to bear in mind, in partial extenuation, the prevalence of this attitude in the better established, highly respected branches of science and learning to rank with which anthropology has long aspired. Take for instance the following remarks by one of the most eminent of living biologists. Medawar (1969) declares in a characteristically brilliant essay: 'The critical task of science is not complete and never will be, for it is the merest truism that we do not abandon mythologies and superstitions but merely substitute new variants for old. No one of Galton's stature has conducted a statistical enquiry into the efficacy of psychoanalytical treatment. If such a thing were done, might it not show that the therapeutic pretensions of psycho-analysis were not borne out by what it actually achieved? It was perhaps a premonition of what the results of such an enquiry might be that led modern psycho-analysts to dismiss as somewhat vulgar the idea that the chief purpose of psychoanalytical treatment is to effect a cure. Its purpose is rather to give the

patient a new and deeper understanding of himself and of the nature of his relationship to his fellow men. So interpreted, psycho-analysis is best thought of as a secular substitute for prayer. Like prayer, it is conducted in the form of a duologue, and like prayer (if prayer is to bring comfort and refreshment) it requires an act of personal surrender, though in this case to a professional and stipendiary god' (p. 6).

Coming as it does in an essay devoted to applauding the part played by intuition and creative imagination in scientific discovery, this is eloquent testimony to the inveterate physicalism of the life sciences and indeed also of the social sciences (such as economics) that attract most prestige in our academies of learning. The only comment that is fitting is *e pur si muove*!

7  These 'speculations' are based on hypotheses about certain inevitable and universal features in the relationship of successive generations of parents and children which are derived from psychoanalytic theory, ultimately, but which were impressed on me as a result of my field experience among the Tallensi. In discussing Tambiah's work, I purposely chose to look at a social and religious system that is, descriptively speaking, strikingly different from the African systems I am accustomed to, and that is, moreover, depicted in accordance with a current theoretical position which contrasts with my own. Since formulating my speculations, however, I thought it would be interesting to check on their plausibility from an outside point of view. I did have a chance of outlining them to Professor Tambiah himself and was reassured to hear from him that he thought my speculations were not unreasonable, though he did not have the kind of field data that could be used as a direct check. But observations that do have a bearing on the question were brought to my attention by Professor Melford Spiro. In the course of his study of Burmese Buddhism (1971) he investigates in considerable detail the 'recruitment structure' of monkhood (Ch. 14, pp. 320–50). He shows that, despite the obvious economic and status advantages offered by monkhood, 'only a small minority of village boys' choose to enter it (p. 329) which implies that there are selective influences and obstacles of other kinds. He finds that desires to escape from difficulties, responsibilities and personal tragedies are very important. But one of the unconscious factors both of recruitment and of keeping men in the monasteries, one with which the social structure and the customary moral and ritual prescriptions of monkhood seem particularly to fit, is what he describes as the need or wish for dependency and complete security (pp. 338–43). This is tantamount to a desire for, or at least to a readiness to find satisfaction in, being in the 'structural position' of a young child. 'The monk', he writes 'is able to reinstate the (real or fancied) blissful period of infancy, in which all needs are anticipated and satisfied by the all-nurturant mother . . .', the monk's permitted regression being symbolized by his very appearance (shaven head etc.) and his ritually prescribed patterns of conduct. It takes hard self-

discipline, Spiro shows, for the monks to control their sexual desires, celibacy being the crucial moral requirement of monkhood and difficulty to meet this requirement is the main reason why monks revert to lay life (pp. 366–8). These, and other observations I have not the space to cite here, to my mind lend great plausibility to the interpretation I have suggested for Tambiah's data.

8 It is a fact of no little significance that every human death in every human society (and in our society some animal deaths, e.g. of cattle and horses) must be juridically and causally accounted for – that is, in a sense, authorized by society before the life thus physically ended can also be socially and psychologically terminated. That is why we have legal provision for doctors' certificates and, in doubtful cases, coroners' inquests.

9 This needs emphasis because the mystical agencies to which death is ultimately attributed vary widely amongst different peoples. Some peoples (e.g. the Nyakyusa, cf. Wilson 1957; the Azande, cf. Evans-Pritchard 1937; the Trobrianders, cf. Malinowski 1932) blame witchcraft or sorcery. Many New Guinea peoples attribute death, as well as sickness and other affiliations, to the malevolence of vengeful ghosts of both lineal and collateral kin (e.g. the Manus, cf. Fortune 1935; the Mae Enga, cf. Meggit 1965). More complex theories bring in notions of Fate and of outraged divinities as well as of ancestors (e.g. the Fon of Dahomey, cf. Herskovits 1938, vol. 1, Ch. 19). The ancestral dead figure in ways that differ from the Tallensi pattern in theories accounting for death, in other societies. Thus among the Zulu they respond to sin or neglect by withdrawing their protection from their descendants and so permitting sorcery or other noxious powers to attack them (cf. Sibisi 1972). Among the Mandari (cf. Buxton 1973) the dead are believed to act together collectively to slay in association with other malign agencies. An enlightening comment on the common human wish or need to account for death is the quotation from Simone de Beauvoir's book *A Very Easy Death* (1966) alluded to above. The whole passage (quoted by Bowker 1970, p. 25) reads as follows: 'There is no such thing as a natural death: nothing that happens to a man is ever natural, since his presence calls the world into question. All men must die: but for every man his death is an accident and, even if he knows it and consents to it, an unjustifiable violation.'

10 Though I am drawing primarily on my own field observations in this discussion of Ashanti witchcraft beliefs and their social and cultural context, I am indebted also to unpublished field reports of Mr M. D. MacLeod for confirmatory observations and interpretations.

11 'La sorcellerie se situe aux frontières de la société, dans l'opposition entre la brousse et la village' is how Ortigues & Ortigues (1966) formulate their conclusion: and they proceed to develop the hypothesis that 'la sorcellerie-anthropophagie correspondrait au niveau prégénital oral' (pp. 250–1).

### 9  The first born

1  'I feel singularly honoured by your invitation to give the first of these
   lectures dedicated to the memory of Emanuel Miller, and I hope that the
   topic I have chosen will give some indication of this. For I believe that it
   would have greatly interested him. It links up obviously with his life-
   long professional concerns; but I think that it might have appealed to
   him equally as touching upon his wider intellectual and scholarly avo-
   cations. One gets a glimpse of these in the Chairman's address to this
   Association, in January 1959 (cf. Miller 1960). Reading it takes me
   back to those formative years when I was lucky enough to work with
   him.'

2  This is the way the rite is performed among the group of clans known as
   the Namoos (cf. Fortes 1945, *passim*) but parallel rites are carried out
   in all the other clans.

3  I have never, for example, succeeded in eliciting from Tallensi any indications that they are aware of a symbolic association between granary,
   as store of seed and of fertility and paternal (male) potency and authority.

4  In the 1950s, as a result of pressure from missionaries and schools, and
   the influence of contact with southern Ghana, pubescent girls began to
   wear dresses.

5  Which, as is typical of patrilineal systems, is established by the payment
   of a bride price by the groom's paternal kin to the bride's father.

6  As Malinowski (1932) who was one of the first to draw attention to
   such rites believed. Firth shows (1967, Ch. 2) that in Tikopia, too, such
   rites are intended to confer matronhood, not to afford magical protection.

7  I hope to publish this elsewhere.

8  An Englishwoman remarked spontaneously to me that her first child
   made her feel herself to be a parent but it was only with the birth of the
   second (and last) child that she felt 'the family' to have been established.

9  The parallel problem of the daughter is resolved by her removal from
   parental control by marriage when her child-bearing powers mature.

10 Hardly a year passes without one or more major papers concerned with
   the problems of birth order and schizophrenia appearing in such
   periodicals as the *British Journal of Psychiatry*. Both first borns and last
   borns have been found to be peculiarly vulnerable, in different
   countries and different family sizes. Some of the technical complexities,
   demographic as well as psychiatric, that arise in research on this subject
   are indicated by such studies as that of Hare and Price (*British Journal
   of Psychiatry*, 1970, 116, 409–20) in which bias due to changes in birth
   and marriage rates is elucidated, and that of Hinshelwood (*ibid.*, 1970,
   117, 293–301) in which the hypothesis is explored that it is the penulti-
   mate sibling position that is, in all samples, in excess.

11  So we find, for example, Sears, Maccoby and Levin (1957) citing interview evidence that 'only' and first (or oldest) children have a more exacting conscience than younger ones, and attributing this to the combination of stricter discipline and more toleration of aggression on the part of parents, than is accorded to younger children.

12  Rivalry between siblings of successive birth order is assumed to be normal among the Tallensi and other tribal societies. They also believe that it is due to displacement of the older by the younger in parental care. The parallel folk-stereotype I here mention is reinforced by modern psychiatric and psychological research as any textbook of child psychology or psychiatry will show. To take an example at random from one of Emanuel Miller's productions, in *The Foundations of Child Psychiatry* (1968, Pergamon Press) edited by him, there is an authoritative contribution by Dr Portia Holman (pp. 535–53). Writing of the family in relation to personality developments, Dr Holman comments on sibling rivalry and notes that 'the one most likely to suffer is the one who has just been supplanted from his position as the baby. If he is the first born his suffering will be great.' Developing the theme she adds that 'Nevertheless, the first child in the normal family has some compensations in that parents tend to value him more than any other child' (p. 539). One of the most often quoted studies of parental attitudes and practices in relation to first and second children is that of J. K. Lasko, 'Parent Behaviour toward First and Second Children', *Genetic Psychology Monographs* (1954, pp. 49, 96–137). This elaborate and sophisticated longitudinal study of 46 sibling pairs concludes among other things, that parents (of American middle class white children) handle first borns in more restrictive, coercive, and emotionally distant ways than second borns, in early infancy.

13  My own impression is that nulliparous women are just as desirous as their husbands to have a son as their first child, because, they say, this would particularly gratify their husbands. The psychological implications of this need no elaboration. Some American studies suggest, however, that women's preferences are biased towards first girls, men's towards boys (cf. Clare and Kiser 1951). A Swedish study, on the other hand (Uddenberg *et al.* 1971) suggests a tendency for women to prefer boys as first born. The general impression I have formed is that there is a bias in favour of sons rather than daughters for the first born among parents of both sexes in our society. The same preference is found in most non-western societies such as those I have referred to in this paper, usually with direct reference to matters of inheritance, succession and ancestor worship.

14  In her delightful popular book *How to Survive Parenthood* (Penguin Books, 1967) Eda LeShan, writing from an American point of view in a chapter headed 'We all Wanted Babies...' says: 'Parenthood has wonderful attributes which hardly need explanation; it offers a special kind of fulfilment, it brings with it a keener sense of being alive, a renewed

and re-awakened sense of wonder at life and growth, and it is of course an affirmation of love – it makes the meaning of marriage more tangible and real. But even little babies can be big burdens, and why shouldn't we hate and resent them once in a while? Most of us feel overwhelmed with guilt if we are not delighted every second' (p. 32).

15  It would take me far too far afield to discuss the incest taboos of all the tribal groups I have referred to. The Tallensi regard sexual relations with any wife of the father or of a close brother as among the most serious and irremediable of sins. This is symbolically recognized in the taboo prohibiting any man from even sitting on the sleeping mat of any woman so related to him (Fortes 1949, p. 112).

16  Mr Graham Harrison was kind enough to calculate the chances for a sample of sibling groups in the Ashanti community I investigated in 1945 (cf. Fortes 1954) and concluded that first borns in this area had about the same chances of surviving to reproductive age as second and later born siblings. Some Indian data amenable to the same analysis point in the same direction.

17  As we can see from Genesis 25.56, which tells us that Abraham gave all he had to Isaac, clearly in recognition of his rights to his father's property, whereas to his concubine children he gave only gifts before sending them away.

18  That is, married by bride price or its equivalent.

19  This brings us to the brink of a question that has faced anthropologists ever since the publication of Freud's *Totem and Taboo* sixty years ago, but which I can only outline here. Why is it that the opposition, often little short of open enmity, which seems to be an inevitable feature of the relationships of successive generations of parents and children, very rarely leads to killing? Fantasies of parent or child killing are common, not only with individuals in our society but in tribal mythologies, ancient and modern, and in folklore and nursery tales. Yet actual parricide, matricide and filicide – (as opposed to abandoning old people who have become a burden to a nomadic band, as among the Eskimo, to die of exposure – senilicide – or killing newborn infants for economic or magical reasons – infanticide) are extremely rare. Like incest, such acts do, from time to time, occur in our society; but the perpetrators seem generally to be mentally deranged (cf. battered babies). What I am referring to is killing by a person who would be considered as normal in his own culture, and for reasons regarded as at least excusable in the face of provocation. The proverbial French *crime passionel* or the killing of a stepfather caught brutally attacking the stepson's mother, are examples.

Among tribal peoples, even where homicide is an accepted way of reacting to provocation, and fratricide is not unknown, parenticide and filicide are exceptional, the explanation being that they would be irremediably sacrilegeous and criminal. The unusual case of the Bagisu of East Africa proves the rule. Dr LaFontaine (in Bohannan 1959) reports that some fathers, too greedy for wealth or too unwilling to relinquish paternal and political powers, inexcusably delay the initiation ceremonies by which a son is legally emancipated. The son, frustrated beyond endurance, then sometimes, in an outburst of anger, kills his father. Fulani (Stenning, *loc. cit.*) deal with a parallel situation of intergenerational competition, by reducing the father to dependence. Filicide, interestingly, enough, is never resorted to by either Bagisu or Fulani.

I am led to the conclusion that for the majority of mankind, the defences set up by custom, or the outlets provided by fantasy, against intergenerational homicide are so effective as virtually to rule it out. And it is easy to see that if this were not so the whole moral basis of social and cultural continuity would be destroyed.

## 10  The concept of the person

1  I often talked about these matters with Tallensi of all ages. They were unanimous that animals are 'living things' because (a) they move about of their own accord – in contrast to, for instance, an automobile, which can only move about when driven; (b) they grow and change – in contrast to non-living things like stones, which neither move about voluntarily, nor grow and change; (c) they die like humans. Trees and plants were said to be living things, though they do not move about, on the grounds that they grow from seed, undergo changes, shed leaves and regenerate like humans. Some Tallensi insisted also that the sun and the moon must be living things since they move and the moon changes, dies as it were and is reborn every month, but others disagreed.

## Endpiece: sacrifice among theologians and anthropologists

1  From the actor's point of view, as I argue later in this paper, sacrifice must, like any other ritual, be deemed to be efficacious, that is, it must be deemed to fulfil the manifest purpose of the ritual act. This does not mean that it is expected to be successful in every case. For as has long been emphasized, every religious system (like every therapeutic system, scientific no less than magical, and many technical systems) provides rationalizations and loopholes for the explanation of the failure of particular ritual acts. But, as Tylor, Frazer, Durkheim and many later writers have pointed out, failure in an individual case does not destroy the belief in the efficacy of ritual from the actor's point of view. It is around this problem of efficacy that much of the theoretical debate over the meaning and function of ritual revolves. For as I note above, the efficacy of ritual as the anthropologist sees it is of a different order from

that of the actor. Hence we find anthropologists having recourse to Austinian notions about 'performative' or 'illocutionary' utterances. The problem of efficacy as it appears from the opposed interests of actor-believer and observer-anthropologist are cogently analysed in Ahern's paper in *Man* (1979).

2 We may think ourselves exempt from this, but enormously as the threshold of vulnerability has been raised by advances in science, technology, medicine and social organization in our society, the sense of vulnerability still remains with us – in matters of health, economic and social well being, personal and collective existence. Does it not lie behind the whole range of compensating values and practices reflected in our political ideologies and in our moral norms? Does it not play a large part in the proliferation of escapist and salvationist cults, not infrequently of oriental origin, throughout the Western world? Environmental and world-political hazards of an apparently arbitrary kind, unpredictability of the course of personal and social life, and the inevitabilities of disease and death, continue to haunt us and to evoke social and psychological defence reactions which are as apt to take religious or magical forms as among pre-scientific peoples.

3 It is interesting to reflect how widespread is the belief that impulses and motives which are secret or repressed, by cultural definition, are the sources of practices magically or mystically dangerous to others, as in witchcraft and sorcery or the 'anger of the heart' recently described by Grace Harris (1978). In contrast, as she explains, the same impulses and motives openly admitted are likely to be regarded as evidence of human frailty which may cause conflict and trouble, but of an open kind that can be resolved by legal or religious measures or simply in open discussion. It is a principle that has general validity as most psycho-therapists would agree.

# References

Ahern, E. M. 1973. *The Cult of the Dead in a Chinese Village*. Stanford, Cal.: Stanford University Press

1979. The problem of efficacy: strong and weak illocutionary acts. *Man* (n.s.) 14: 1–18

Allen, C. K. 1972. *Law in the Making*. 6th ed. Oxford: Clarendon Press, 1958

Ambrose, J. A. 1966. Ritualization in the human infant-mother bond. In *Philosophical Transactions of the Royal Society*, Series B, vol. 251. London: Royal Society

Barrington-Ward, S. and Bourdillon, M.F.C. 1980. Postscript: a place for sacrifice in modern Christianity? In M.F.C. Bourdillon and M. Fortes (eds.), *Sacrifice*. London

Bascom, W. 1969. *Ifa Divination: Communication between Gods and Men in West Africa*. Bloomington, Indiana: Indiana University Press

Bateson, G. 1936. *Naven*. Cambridge: Cambridge University Press

Beattie, J. 1964. *Other Cultures*. London: Cohen & West

1966. Ritual and social change. *Man* (n.s.) 1: 60–74

Beattie, J. and Middleton, J. 1969. *Spirit Mediumship and Society in Africa*. London: Routledge and Kegan Paul

Beauvoir, S. de. 1966. *A Very Easy Death* (tr. P. O'Brien). Middlesex: Penguin Books

Berlin, B. and Kay, P. 1969. *Basic Color Terms: Their Universality and Evolution*. Berkley, Calif.: University of Calif. Press.

Besmer, F. E. 1977. Initiation into the Bori cult: a case study in Ningi Town. *Africa*, 47: 1–13

Boas, F. 1938. *General Anthropology*. Boston: Heath

Bohannan, L. and P. 1953. *The Tiv of Central Nigeria*. London: International African Institute Ethnographic Survey of Africa, VIII

Bourdillon, M.F.C. 1980. Introduction. In M.F.C. Bourdillon and M. Fortes (eds.), *Sacrifice*. London

Bowdich, T. E. 1819. *Mission to Ashantee*. London: John Murray

Bowker, J. W. 1970. *Problems of Suffering in Religions of the World.*
Cambridge: Cambridge University Press
1973. *The Sense of God.* Oxford: Clarendon Press
Bradbury, R. E. 1957. *The Benin Kingdom and the Edo speaking Peoples of
South West Nigeria.* London: International African Institute
Ethnographic Survey of Africa, XII
1965. Father and senior son in Edo mortuary ritual. In Fortes and
Dieterlen (1965)
Browne, Sir T. 1643. *Religio Medici.* Reprinted in 1968, *Selected Writings,*
ed. Geoffrey Keynes. London: Faber
Busfield, J. 1973. Ideologies of reproduction. In M. P. M. Richards (ed.),
*The Integration of the Child in the Social World.* Cambridge:
Cambridge University Press
Busia, K. A. 1951. *The Position of the Chief in the Modern Political System
of Ashanti.* Oxford University Press for International African Institute
1954. The Ashanti of the Gold Coast. In *African Worlds,* ed. D. Forde,
London
Buxton, J. 1973. *Religion and Healing in Mandari.* Oxford: Clarendon
Press
Cargill-Thompson, W. D. J. 1956. Unpublished dissertation: *The Two
Regiments.* Cambridge: King's College
Carstairs, G. M. 1957. *The Twice Born: A Study of a Community of High-
Caste Hindus.* London: Hogarth Press
Clare, J. E, and Kiser, C. V. 1951. Social and psychological factors affecting
fertility. *Millbank Memorial Fund* Q.29: 440–92
Colson, E. 1954. Ancestoral spirits and social structures among the Plateau
Tonga. *International Archives of Ethnography.* 47: 21–68
Cooper, G. 1961. *Festivals of Europe.* London: Percival Marshall
Coulanges, F. de. 1864. *La Cité Antique.* Paris: Hachette. tr. 1956, *The
Ancient City.* New York: Doubleday Anchor
Davis, K. 1959. The myth of functional analysis as a special method in
sociology and social anthropology. *American Sociol. Rev.* 24: 757–72
De Groot, J. J. M. 1910. *The Religion of the Chinese.* New York:
Macmillan
Delafosse, M. 1912. *Haut-Sénégal-Niger: le pays, les peuples, les langues,
l'histoire, les civilisations.* Paris: Larose
1920. Des soidisants clans totémiques de l'Afrique occidental. *Rev.
Ethnog.* 1: 86–109
Devereux, G. 1979. Fantasy and symbol as dimensions of reality. In
*Fantasy and Symbol: Studies in Anthropological Interpretation,* ed. R.
H. Hook. London: Academic Press
Dicks, H. V. 1972. *Licensed Mass Murder: A Socio-Psychological Study of
some SS. Killers.* (Columbus Centre Series, Studies in the Dynamics of
Persecution and Extermination, gen. ed. N. Cohn.) London: Sussex
Univ. Press–Heinemann Educ. Books
Dieterlen, G. 1963. Notes sur le totémisme dogon. *L'Homme* 3: 106–10

1971. Les ceremonies soixantenaires de Sigui chez les Dogon. *Africa* 41: 1–11

Dieterlen, G. and Calame-Griaule, G. 1960. L'alimentation dogon. *Cahiers d'Etudes Africaines* 3: 49–90

Dieterlen, G. and Hampaté Ba, A. 1966. Koumen. *Cahiers de l'Homme.* Paris: Mouton and Co.

Douglas, J. W. B. 1964. *The Home and the School: A Study of Ability and Attainment in the Primary School.* London: McGibbon and Kee

Douglas, M. (ed.). 1970. *Witchcraft Confessions and Accusations.* (A.S.A. monograph No. 9.) London: Tavistock Publicatons

Dupire, M. 1970 *Organisation Sociale des Peul.* Paris: Plon

Durkheim, E. 1915. *The Elementary Forms of the Religious Life.* English translation, London.

Emmett, D. 1960. How far can structural studies take account of individuals. *J. R. Anthrop. Inst.* 90: 191–200

Erikson, E. E. 1950. *Childhood and Society.* London: Imago
1964. *Insight and Responsibility.* New York: Norton and Co.
1966. Ontogeny of ritualisation in Man. *Philosophical Transactions of the Royal Society*, Series B, Vol. 251, London: Royal Society
1970. *Gandhi's Truth: On the Origins of Militant Non-Violence.* London: Faber and Faber

Evans-Pritchard, E. E. 1929. The morphology and function of magic. *American Anthropologist* 31: 619–41
1933–5. The Nuer tribe and clan. *Sudan Notes and Rec.* 16: 1–53, 17, 1–57; 18: 37–87
1937. *Witchcraft, Oracles and Magic among the Azande.* Oxford: Clarendon Press
1950. Social Anthropology: past and present. The Marett Lecture. *Man* 50
1951. *Kinship and Marriage among the Nuer.* Oxford: Clarendon Press
1956. *Nuer Religion.* Oxford: Clarendon Press
1964. Forward to English translation of Henri Hubert and Marcel Mauss, *Essai sur la nature et la fonction du sacrifice, Ann. Sociologique* vol. II, 1899. London: Cohen and West

Faris, J. C. 1972. *Nuba Personal Art.* London: Duckworth

Field, M. J. 1937. *Religion and Medicine of the Ga People.* London: Oxford University Press
1960. *Search for Security: An Ethno-psychiatric Study of Rural Ghana.* London:Faber and Faber

Firth, R. 1931. Totemism in Polynesia, *Oceania* 1: 291–321, 377–98
1936. *We, the Tikopia.* London: Allen & Unwin
1940. *The Work of the Gods in Tikopia* (2 vols.). L.S.E. Monographs in Sociology, nos. 1 and 2. London: Lund, Humphries
1955. *The Fate of the Soul.* Cambridge
1959. Problem and assumption in an anthropological study of religion. *J. R. Anthrop. Inst.* n.s. 89: 129–48

1960. Succession to chieftainship in Tikopia. *Oceania* 30: 161–80. Reprinted in 1962, *Essays on Social Organisation and Values*, Chap. VI. London: Athlone Press

1962. *Essays on Social Organisation and Values.* (LSE Monographs in Social Anthropology 28) London: Athlone Press

1967. *Tikopia Ritual and Belief.* London: Athlone Press

Flugel, J. C. 1930. *The Psychology of Clothes.* (International Psychoanalytical Library 18). London: Hogarth Press

Forde, D. 1949. Integrative aspects of Yakö first fruits rituals. *J. R. Anthrop. Inst.*, n.s. 75: 1–10

1951. The integration of anthropological studies. *J. R. Anthrop. Inst.* 78: 1–11

1957. *The Context of Belief: a consideration of fetishism among the Yakö.* Liverpool University Press

Fortes, M. 1932. A study of cognitive error. *Brit. J. Educ. Psych.* n.s. 11: 1–22

1933 Influence of position in sibship on juvenile delinquency. *Economica*, August

1936. Ritual festivals and social cohesion in the hinterland of the Gold Coast. *American Anthropologist*, 38, 590–604

1938. Social and psychological aspects of education in Taleland. *Africa* 11(4). Supplement, *International Institute of African Languages and Cultures, Memorandum 7*

1940. The political system of the Tallensi. In *African Political Systems*, M. Fortes and E. E. Evans-Pritchard (eds.). London: Oxford University Press

1945. *The Dynamics of Clanship among the Tallensi, Being the First Part of an Analysis of the Social Structure of a Trans-Volta Tribe.* London: Oxford University Press

1949. *The Web of Kinship among the Tallensi.* London: Oxford University Press

1950. Kinship and Marriage among the Ashanti. In *African Systems of Kinship and Marriage*, eds. A. R. Radcliffe-Brown and D. Forde.

1953. The structure of unilineal descent groups. In Fortes (1970)

1954. A demographic field study in Ashanti. In *Culture and Human Fertility*, ed. F. Lorimer (A study of the relation of cultural conditions to fertility in non-industrial and transitional societies). Paris: UNESCO

1955a. Names among the Tallensi of the Gold Coast. *Afrikanistische Studien*, Deutsche Akad. d. Wissenschaften zu Berlin, Institut f. Orientforschung 26: 337–49

1955b. Radcliffe-Brown's contributions to the study of social organization. In Fortes (1970)

1957. Malinowski and the study of kinship. In R. W. Firth (ed.), *Man and Culture: An Evaluation of the Work of Bronislav Malinowski.* London: Routledge & Kegan Paul

1958. Introduction to Goody, J., ed., *The Developmental Cycle in Domestic Groups*. Cambridge: Cambridge University Press

1959. *Oedipus and Job in West African Religion*. Cambridge: Cambridge University Press

1961. Pietas in ancestor worship. *J. R. Anthrop. Inst.* 91: 166–91

1962a. Ritual and office in tribal society. In *Essays on the Ritual of Social Relations*. ed. M. Gluckman. Manchester University Press

1962b. (ed.), *Marriage in Tribal Society*. (Cambridge Papers in Social Anthropology No. 3). Cambridge: Cambridge University Press

1965. Some reflections on ancestor worship in Africa. In Fortes and Dieterlen (1965)

1966. Totem and taboo. *Proc. R. Anthrop. Inst.* (1966) 5–22

1969. *Kinship and the Social Order*. Chicago: Aldine

1970. *Time and Social Structure and other Essays*. London: Athlone Press

1973. On the concept of the person among the Tallensi. In *La Notion de Personne en Afrique Noire*. No. 544, Paris: Colloques Internationaux du Centre National de la Recherche Scientifique

1974. The first born. *J. Child Psychol. Psychiat.* 15: 81–104

1975. Tallensi prayer. In *Studies in Social Anthropology: Essays in Memory of E. E. Evans-Pritchard*. (eds. J. H. M. Beattie and R. G. Lienhardt). Oxford: Clarendon Press

1977. Custom and conscience in anthropological perspective. *The International Review of Psycho-Analysis* 4: 127–54

Fortes, M. and Dieterlen, G. (eds.). 1965. *African Systems of Thought*. London: Oxford University Press

Fortes, M. and Evans-Pritchard, E. E. (eds.) *African Political Systems*. Oxford University Press for the International African Institute

Fortes, M. and Mayer, D. Y. 1966. Psychosis and social change among the Tallensi of Northern Ghana. *Cahiers d'Etudes Africaines* 6: 5–40. (Also in Psychiatry in a Changing Society 1969, (eds. S. H. Foulkes and G. Stewart Prince.) London: Tavistock)

Fortune, R. F. 1935. *Manus Religion: An Ethnological Study of the Manus Natives of the Admiralty Islands*. Philadelphia: Am. Philos. Soc.

Frankfort, H. 1948. *Kingship and the Gods*. University of Chicago Press

Frazer, Sir J. 1910. *Totemism and Exogamy*. London: Macmillan

Freedman, M. 1958. *Lineage Organisation in South-Eastern China*. London

1967. Ancestor worship: two facets of the Chinese case. In M. Freedman (ed.), *Social Organization: Essays Presented to Raymond Firth*. Chicago: Aldine Press

1970. (ed.) *Family and Kinship in Chinese Society*. Stanford: Stanford University Press

Freeman, J. D. 1960 Review of E. R. Leach: *Rethinking Anthropology*. *Man* 62: 125–6

1968. Thunder, blood, and the nicknaming of God's creatures. *Psychoanal. Q.* 37: 353–99

1927. *The Ego and the Id*. London: Hogarth Press

1933. New introductory lectures on psycho-analysis: *Standard Edition*, vol. 22

Freud, S. 1950. *Totem and Taboo*. (First published 1913, Vienna). London: Routledge and Kegan Paul

Georges, K. E. and H. 1959. *Ausfürhliches Lateinisch-Deutsches Handwörterbuch*. 10th edition. Basel

Gerth, H. and Mills, C. W. 1954. *Character and Social Structure*. London: Routledge and Kegan Paul

Glover, E. 1971. In piam memoriam: Emanuel Miller, 1893–1970. *Brit. J. Criminol.* 11: 4–14

Gluckman, M. 1937. Mortuary customs and the belief in survival after death among the South Eastern Bantu. *Bantu Studies* 2: 117–36

1954. *Rituals of Rebellion in South-East Africa* (the Frazer Lecture, 1952). Manchester University Press. Republished in Gluckman (1963)

1955. *The Judicial Process among the Barotse of Northern Rhodesia*. Manchester: University Press for the Rhodes-Livingstone Institute

1956. *Custom and Conflict in Africa*. Oxford University Press.

1963. *Order and Rebellion in Tribal Africa*. London: Cohen and West.

Gluckman, M. and Devons, E. (eds). 1964. *Closed Systems and Open Minds*. London: Oliver and Boyd

Goffman, E. 1959. *The Presentation of Self in Everyday Life*. New York: Doubleday Anchor

Goody, E. N. 1973. *Contexts of Kinship: An Essay in the Family Sociology of the Gonja of Northern Ghana*. Cambridge: Cambridge University Press

Goody, J. (ed.) 1958. *The Developmental Cycle in Domestic Groups*. Cambridge Papers in Social Anthropology, No 1. Cambridge: Cambridge University Press

1962. *Death, Property and the Ancestors*. Stanford

Gough, E. K. 1958. Cults of the dead among the Nayars. *Journal of American Folklore*, 71

Gough, K. 1955. Female initiation rites on the Malabar coast. *J. R. Anth. Inst.* 85: 45–80

Griaule, M. 1954. The Dogon of the French Sudan. In *African Worlds*, ed. D. Forde. London: Oxford University Press

Guthrie, W. K. C. 1950. *The Greeks and their Gods*. London: Methuen

Hallowell, A. I. 1955. *Culture and Experience*. Philadelphia: University of Pennsylvania Press

Hare, E. H. and Price, J. S. 1970. Birth rank and schizophrenia: with a consideration of the bias due to changes in birth-rate. *Brit. J. Psychiat.* 116: 409–20

Harris, G. G. 1978. *Casting out Anger: Religion among the Taita of Kenya*. Cambridge: Cambridge University Press

Hayley, A. 1980. A commensal relationship with God: the nature of the offering in Assamese Vaishnavism. In M. F. C. Bourdillon and M. Fortes (eds.), *Sacrifice*. London

Herskovits, M. J. 1938. *Dahomey*. 2 vols. New York

Heusch, L. de., 1965. Situation et positions de l'anthropologie structural. *L'Arc* 26:6–16

Heyworth Committee. 1965. Report on the 1965 Heyworth Committee on Social Studies. London: H.M.S.O.

Hindley, C. B. 1970. Obituary: Emanuel Miller 1893–1970. *J. Child Psychol. Psychiat.* 11, 157

Hinshelwood, R. D. 1970. The evidence of a birth order factor in schizophrenia. *Brit. J. Psychiat.* 117: 293–301

Holman, P. 1968. Family vicissitudes in relation to personality development. In *Foundations of Child Psychiatry*, ed. E. Miller. Oxford

Horton, R. 1968. Neo-Tylorianism: sound sense or sinister prejudice? *Man* (n.s.) 3: 625–34

Horton, R. and Finnegan, R. (eds.) 1973. *Modes of Thought: Essays on Thinking in Western and non-Western Societies*. London: Faber

Hughes, E. C. 1958. *Men and their Work* Glencoe, Illinois: The Free Press

Jakobson, R. 1961. Linguistics and communication theory. In *Structure of Language and its Mathematical Aspects*. (Symp. appl. Math. 12). Springfield, Illinois: American Mathematical Society

Jones, E. 1924. Psycho-analysis and anthropology. In *Essays in Applied Psychoanalysis*, vol. 2. London: Hogarth Press, 1951
    1959. *Free Associations: Memoirs of a Psychoanalyst*. New York: Basic Books

Junod, H. A. 1927. *The Life of a South African Tribe*. 2 vols. 2nd. ed. London: Macmillan

Kardiner, A. and Linton, R. 1949. *The Individual and his Society: The Psychodynamics of Primitive Social Organisation*. New York: Columbia University Press

Kluckhohn, C. 1941. *Navaho Witchcraft*. Boston: Beacon Press

Koskinnen, A. A. 1960. *Ariki the First Born: An Analysis of a Polynesian Chieftain Title*. Helsinki: Academia Scientiarum Fennica

Krader, L. 1967. Persona et culture. *Les Etudes Philisophiques* 3: 289–300

Krige, E. J. and J. D. 1943. *The Realm of a Rain Queen*. London
    1954. The Lovedu of the Transvaal. In D. Forde, *African Worlds: Studies in the Cosmological Ideas and Social Values of African Peoples*. Oxford

Kroeber, A. L. and Kluckhohn, C. 1952. Culture: a critical review of concepts. *Museum of American Archaeology and Ethnology, Harvard Univ.* 47, No. 7

Kuper, H. 1947. *An African Aristocracy*. London

LaFontaine, J. 1960. Homicide and suicide among the Gisu. In *African Homicide and Suicide*. (ed. P. Bohannan.) Princeton

1967. Parricide in Bugisu: a study in inter-generational conflict. *Man* (n.s.) 2: 249–59

Lasko, S. K. 1954. Parent behaviour toward first and second children. *Gen. Psychol. Monographs* 49: 97–137

Last, M. 1976. The presentation of sickness in a community of non-Muslim Hausa. In *Social Anthropology and Medicine* (ASA Monograph No. 13), ed. J. L. Loudon. London and New York: Academic Press

Laye, C. 1955. *L'Enfant noir*. Paris: Plon

Leach, E. R. 1958. Magical hair. *J. R. Anth. Inst.* 88: 147–64
    1961. *Rethinking Anthropology* (LSE Monograph Social Anthrop. 22). London: Athlone Press
    1962. On certain unconsidered aspects of double descent. *Man* 62: 130–4
    1965. Claude Lévi-Strauss – anthropologist and philosopher *New Left Review* 34
    1966. Ritualization in man in relation to conceptual and social development. *Philosophical Transactions of the Royal Society*, Series B, vol. 251. London: Royal Society

Lees, J. P. and Newson, L. J. 1954. Family or sibship position and some aspects of juvenile delinquency. *Brit. J. Delinquency* 5

LeShan, E. 1967. *How to Survive Parenthood*. Harmondsworth: Penguin

LeVine, R. A. 1973. *Culture, Behaviour and Personality*. London: Hutchinson

Lévi-Strauss, C. 1953. Social Structure. In *Anthropology Today* (ed.) A. L. Kroeler. Chicago: University Press
    1962a *Le Totémisme aujourd'hui*. Paris: Presses Universitaires de France
    1962b *La Pensée sauvage*. Paris: Plon
    1963. The bear and the barber. *J. R. Anthrop. Inst.* 93: 1–2

Lienhardt, G. 1961. *Divinity and Experience: The Religion of the Dinka*. Oxford: Clarendon Press

Linton, R. 1936. *The Study of Man*. New York: Appleton-Century Co.

Lloyd, B. S. 1972. *Perception and Cognition: A Cross-Cultural Perspective*. Middlesex: Penguin Books

Macfarlane, A. 1970. *Witchcraft in Tudor and Stuart England: A Regional and Comparative Study*. London: Routledge and Kegan Paul

Maine, Sir H. 1864. *Ancient Law*. London

Mair, L. 1969. *Witchcraft*. London: World University Library

Malinowski, B. 1922. *Argonauts of the Western Pacific*. London: Routledge
    1926. *Crime and Custom in Savage Society*. London: Routledge
    1927. *Sex and Repression in Savage Society*. London: Routledge
    1932. *The Sexual Life of Savages in North-Western Melanesia*. (1st ed. 1929). London: Routledge
    1944. *A Scientific Theory of Culture*. Chapel Hill: University of North Carolina
    1954. 'Magic, science and religion'. Reprinted in *Magic, Science and Religion, and Other Essays*, New York: Doubleday

1967. *A Diary in the Strict Sense of the Term*. London: Routledge

Marett, R. R. 1909. (4th ed. 1929). *The Threshold of Religion*. London: Methuen

1935. *Head, Heart and Hands in Human Evolution*. London: Hutchinson

1941. *A Jerseyman at Oxford*. London: Oxford University Press

Marwick, M. 1965. *Sorcery in its Social Setting: A Study of the Northern Rhodesia Cewa*. Manchester: Manchester University Press

Mauss, M. 1929. L'âme, le nom et la personne. In *Oeuvres, 2, Répresentations collectives et diversité des civilisations*, 1969. Paris: Editions de Minuit

1939. Une catégorie de l'esprit humaine: la notion de personne, celle de 'moi'. *J. R. Anthrop. Inst.* 68: 263–82

1969. *Œuvres*.

Mayer, D. Y. 1974. Review of H. V. Dicks, *Licensed Mass Murder* and A. Storr, *Human Destructiveness, Jewish Journal of Sociology* 16: 103–7.

Mayer, P. (ed). 1969. *Socialization: The Approach from Social Anthropology* (ASA monograph No. 8). London: Tavistock

McKnight, J. D. 1967. Extra-descent group ancestor cults in African societies. *Africa* 37: 1–21

Mead, G. H. 1913. The social self. *J. Philosophy, Psychology and Scientific Method* 10: 374–80

1934. *Mind, Self and Society*. Chicago: Chicago University Press

Mead, M. 1930. *Social Organization of Manus (Bishop Museum Bulletin No. 76)*. Honolulu

1949. *Male and Female*. London: Gollancz

Medawar, P. B. 1969. *Induction and Intuition in Scientific Thought*. (The Jayne Lectures for 1968). Philadelphia: Am. Philos. Soc.

Meggitt, M. J. 1965. *The Lineage System of the Mae-Enga of New Guinea*. Edinburgh: Oliver and Boyd

Middleton, J. 1960. *Lugbara Religion*. London

Miller, E. 1938. *The Generations: A Study of the Cycle of Parents and Children*. London

1944. The problem of birth order and delinquency. In *Mental Abnormality and Crime*. (ed. P. H. Winfield et al.) London: Macmillan.

1960. A discourse on method in child psychiatry. *J. Child Psychol. Psychiat.* 10: 3–16

1968 (ed.) *The Foundations of Child Psychiatry*. Oxford: Pergamon Press

Mishnah. 1933. Translated by Herbert Danby, 1933. London: Oxford University Press

Montaigne, M. 1580. *The Essayes*. (Florio's translation, 1928 edn. Dent, London)

Morgan, L. H. 1881. *Houses and Houselife of the American Aborigines*. Washington: Dept. of Interior

Murdock, G. P. 1954. Sociology and Anthropology. In *For a Science of Social Man*, J. Gillin (ed). New York: Macmillan

Murphy, R. F. 1963. On Zen Marxism: filiation and alliance. *Man* 63:17–19

Nadel, S. F. 1947. *The Nuba*. London: Oxford University Press

1951. *The Foundations of Social Anthropology*. London: Cohen and West

1957. *The Theory of Social Structure*. London: Cohen and West

Needham, J. 1951. Natural Law in China and Europe, *J. of the History of Ideas* 12: 3–30, 194–230

Neufeld, E. 1944. *Ancient Hebrew Marriage Law*. London: Longmans Green

Newell, W. H. (ed.). 1976. *Ancestors*. The Hague: Mouton

Ngubane, H. 1977. *Body and Mind in Zulu Medicine: An Ethnography of Health and Disease in Nyuswa-Zulu Thought and Practice*. London and New York: Academic Press

Niangouran-Bouah, G. 1964. 'La division du temps et le calendrier rituel des peuples lagunaires de la Côté d'Ivoire', *Université de Paris. Travaux et mémoires de l'Institute d'Ethnologie*, 68. Paris: Musée de l'Homme

1951. *Notes and Queries in Anthropology* (5th ed.). London: Royal Anthropological Institute

Oliver, D. 1955. *A Solomon Island Society: Kinship and Leadership among the Siuai of Bougainville*. Cambridge Mass: Harvard University Press

Onians, R. B. 1951. *The Origins of European Thought*. Cambridge: Cambridge University Press

Ortigues, M-C. and Ortigues, R. 1966. *Oedipe Africaine*. Paris: Plon, 1973

Otto, R. 1917. *Das Heilige*. English translation by J. W. Harvey, second edition 1950, *The Idea of the Holy*. London: Oxford University Press

Park, G. F. 1963. Divination and its social contexts. *J. R. Anthrop. Inst.* 93: 195–209

Parsons, A. 1964. Is the Oedipus complex universal? The Jones–Malinowski debate revisited. In W. Muensterberg and S. Axelrad (eds.), *The Psychoanalytic Study of Society*, vol. 3. New York: Int. Univ. Press

Parsons, T. 1937. *The Structure of Social Action*. Glencoe, Illinois: The Free Press

1951. *The Social System*. Glencoe, Illinois: The Free Press

1952. The superego and the theory of social systems. *Psychiatry* 15: 15–24

1955. Family structure and the socialization of the child. In T. Parsons and R. F. Bales (eds.), *Family Socialization and Interaction Process*. Glencoe, Ill.: Free Press

Parsons, T. and Shils, E. 1951. *Towards a General Theory of Action*. Cambridge, Mass.: Havard University Press

Peristiany, J. 1951. The age set system of the Pastoral Pokot. *Africa*, 21: 188–206, 279–302

Piaget, J. 1926. *The Language and Thought of the Child*. London: Routledge and Kegan Paul
    1928. *Judgement and Reasoning in the Child*. London: Routledge and Kegan Paul
    1929. *The Child's Conception of the World*. London: Routledge and Kegan Paul
Pollock, Sir F. and Maitland, F. W. 1898. *History of English Law before the Time of Edward I*. Cambridge: Cambridge University Press
Prabhu, P-N. 1954. *Hindu Social Organization*. Bombay: Popular Book Dept.
Proust, M. 1954 edn. *Du Côté de chez Swann*. Paris: Gallimard
    1928. *Swann's Way*, translated by C. K. Scott Moncrieff. New York: Modern Library
Radcliffe-Brown, A. R. 1922. *The Andaman Islanders*. Cambridge
    1929. *The Sociological Theory of Totemism* (cf. 1952)
    1931. The present position of anthropological studies. In *The Advancement of Science*. (*Brit. Ass. Adv. Sci.* Sect. H.)
    1935. On the concept of function in social science (cf. 1952)
    1939. *Taboo* (cf. 1952)
    1945. *Religion and Society* (cf. 1952)
    1952. *Structure and Function in Primitive Society*. London: Cohen & West
Rattray, R. S. 1923. *Ashanti*. Oxford
    1927. *Religion and Art in Ashanti*. Oxford
    1929. *Ashanti Law and Constitution*. Oxford
    1932. *Tribes of the Ashanti Hinterland*. Oxford
Redfield, R. 1953. *The Primitive World and its Transformations*. Cornell: Cornell University Press
Richards, A. I. 1932. *Hunger and Work in a Savage Tribe*. London: Routledge
    1937. Reciprocal clan relationships among the Bemba of North East Rhodesia. *Man* 37: 188–93
    1956. *Chisungu: A Girl's Initiation Ceremony among the Bemba of N. Rhodesia*. London: Faber and Faber
    1960. Social mechanisms for the transfer of political rights in some African tribes'. *J. R. Anthrop. Inst.* 90
Rivers, W. H. R. 1918. Dreams in Primitive Cultures. *Bull. John Ryland's Libr.* (Manchester) 4: 3–4, 4–28
Robinson, J. A. T. 1952. *The Body* (Stud. Bibl. Theol. 5). London: S. C. M.
Robinson, M. S. 1962. Complementary filiation and marriage in the Trobriand Islands: a re-examination of Malinowski's material. In Fortes (1962)
Rogerson, J. W. 1980. Sacrifice in the Old Testament: problems of method and approach. In M. F. C. Bourdillon and M. Fortes (eds.), *Sacrifice*. London

Russell, B. 1968. *Autobiography*. 2 vols. London: Allen and Unwin

Sapir, E. 1932. *Selected Writings on Language, Culture and Personality*, ed. D. G. Mandelbaum. Berkeley: Univ. of Calif. Press, 1949

Schapera, I. 1955. *Handbook of Tswana Law and Custom* (2nd ed). London: Oxford University Press

Schneider, D. 1964. Some muddles in the models, in *The Relevance of Models for Social Anthropology* (Ass. Social Anthrop. Monogr. 1). London: Tavistock

Schneider, D. M. and Gough, K. (eds.). 1961. *Matrilineal Kinship*. Berkeley: Univ. of Calif. Press

Sears, R. R., Maccoby, E. E. and Levin, H. 1957. *Patterns of Child Rearing*. Evanston, Illinois: Row Peterson

Seligman, C. G. 1932. Anthropological perspective and psychological theory. *J. R. Anthrop Inst.* 62: 193–228

Senn, M. J. E. and Hartford, C. 1968. *The First Born*. Cambridge, Mass.: Harvard University Press

Sibisi, H. 1972. Health and disease among the Nyuswa-Zulu (unpublished Phd. thesis, Univ. of Cambridge) (See Ngubane)

Simoons, F. J. 1967. *Eat Not This Flesh*. Madison: University of Wisconsin Press

Skinner, E. P. 1961. Intergenerational conflict among the Mossi – father and son. *J. Conflict Resolution* 5: 55–60

Smith, H. 1831. *Festivals, Games and Amusements*. London: Henry Colburn and Richard Bentley

Smith, E. W. (ed.) 1950. *African Ideas of God*. London

Smith, M. F. 1954. *Baba of Karo: A Woman of the Muslim Hausa*. London: Faber and Faber

Southall, A. W. 1959. An operational theory of role. *Human Relations* 12

Spencer, W. B. and Gillen, F. J. 1914. *Native Tribes of the Northern Territory of Australia*. London: Dover

Spiro, M. 1969. The psychological function of witchcraft belief: the Burmese case. In W. Caudill and T. Lin (eds.), *Mental Health Research in Asia and the Pacific*. Honolulu: East-West Center Press

    1971. *Buddhism and Society: a Great Tradition and its Burmese Vicissitudes*. London: Allen and Unwin

Srinivas, M. N. 1952. *Religion and Society among the Coorgs*. Oxford: Clarendon Press

Stenning, D. J. 1958. Household viability among the pastoral Fulani. In *The Developmental Cycle in Domestic Groups* (ed. Goody, J.), Cambridge Papers in Social Anthropology, No. 1

Sutton-Smith, B. and Rosenberg, B. G. 1970. *The Sibling*. New York: Holt Rinehart

Tambiah, J. S. 1970. *Buddhism and the Spirit Cults in North East Thailand*. Cambridge: Cambridge University Press

Thomas, L. V. 1965. Essai sur la conduite negro-africaine du repas. *Bull. Inst. franç. Afr. noire* 27: 573–635

Turner, V. W. 1957. *Schism and Continuity in an African Society.*
Manchester: Manchester University Press

1961. Ndembu divination: its symbolism and techniques. *Rhodes-Livingstone Papers*, no. 31

1962. Three symbols of passage in Ndembu circumcision ritual: an intepretation. In M. Gluckman (ed.), *Essays on the Ritual of Social Relations*. Manchester: Manchester Univ. Press

1966. The syntax of symbolism in an African religion. *Philosophical Transactions of the Royal Society*, Series B, Vol. 251, London: Royal Society

1969. *The Ritual Process: Structure and Anti-Structure.* Chicago: Aldine

Tylor, Sir E. B. 1871. *Primitive Culture.* 2 vols. London

Uddenberg, N., Almgren, P. E. and Nilsson, A. 1971. Preference for sex of child among pregnant women. *J. Biosocial Sci.* 3: 267–80

Van Gennep, A. 1908. *Les Rites de Passage* (English translation, 1960, The Rites of Passage). London: Routledge.

Waddell, H. 1934. *Saints and Beasts.* London: Constable

Waley, A. 1938. *The Analects of Confucius.* London: Allen & Unwin

Weber, M. 1930. *The Protestant Ethic and the Spirit of Capitalism.*
London: Allen and Unwin

1947. *Theory of Social and Economic Organisation.* London: Hodge and Co.

Weldon, T. D. 1946. *States and Morals.* London

Wellisch, E. 1954. *Isaac and Oedipus: A Study in Biblical Psychology of the Sacrifice of Isaac: The Akedah.* London: Routledge and Kegan Paul

Wilson, M. 1951. *Good Company – A Study of Nyakyusa Age Villages.*
London: Oxford University Press

1957. *Rituals of Kinship among the Nyakyusa.* London: Oxford University Press

1959. *Divine Kings and the 'Breath of Men'.* Cambridge: Cambridge University Press

1971. *Religion and the Transformation of Society.* Cambridge: Cambridge University Press

Yalman, N. 1967. *Under the Bo Tree.* Berkeley: University of California Press

Zahan, D. 1950. L'habitation mossi. *Bull. Inst. franç. Afr. noire* 12: 223–9

# Index